Connecting
Policy
to **Practice**
in the Human
Services

Fourth Edition

Brad McKenzie and Brian Wharf

OXFORD
UNIVERSITY PRESS

OXFORD
UNIVERSITY PRESS

Oxford University Press is a department of the University of Oxford.
It furthers the University's objective of excellence in research, scholarship, and education
by publishing worldwide. Oxford is a registered trade mark of Oxford University Press in
the UK and in certain other countries.

Published in Canada by
Oxford University Press
8 Sampson Mews, Suite 204,
Don Mills, Ontario M3C 0H5 Canada

www.oupcanada.com

First Edition published in 1998
Second Edition published in 2004
Third Edition published in 2010

Library and Archives Canada Cataloguing in Publication

Wharf, Brian, author
Connecting policy to practice in the human services /
Brad McKenzie and Brian Wharf. -- Fourth edition.

Revision of: Wharf, Brian. Connecting policy to practice in
the human services.

Includes bibliographical references and index.
ISBN 978-0-19-901106-3 (paperback)

1. Canada--Social policy. 2. Social planning--Canada.
3. Human services--Canada. I. McKenzie, B. D. (Bradley
Douglas), author II. Title.

HN107.W533 2015   361.6'10971   C2015-903453-1

Cover image: zbruch/Getty Images

Oxford University Press is committed to our environment.
This book is printed on Forest Stewardship Council® certified paper
and comes from responsible sources.

Printed and bound in Canada

1 2 3 4 — 19 18 17 16

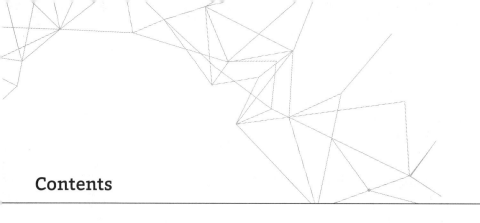

Contents

7 Influencing Policy from Outside the System   180

8 Chalk and Cheese: Feminist Thinking and Policy-Making   198

Marilyn Callahan

9 Policy Resistance: The Rise and Fall of Welfare Time Limits in BC   214

Bruce Wallace and Tim Richards

List of Figures, Tables, and Boxes

Figures

Tables

Boxes

Acknowledgements

Special appreciation is extended to the Oxford team who helped to make the fourth edition of *Connecting Policy to Practice in the Human Services* possible—Stephen Kotowych, acquisitions editor, Phyllis Wilson, managing editor, and Leah-Ann Lymer, developmental editor. Leah-Ann's thoughtful feedback and suggestions were particularly helpful in updating this substantially revised edition. I also thank the copy editor, Richard Tallman, whose careful editing improved the final copy.

This edition also benefited from a number of reviewers who provided suggestions for improvements. These include Jane Arscott (Athabasca University), Robert Case (Renison University College, University of Waterloo), Cynthia Gallop (Mount Royal University), James Mulvale (University of Manitoba), Tina Wu (University of the Fraser Valley), Miu Chung Yan (University of British Columbia), and two additional anonymous reviewers. I was not able to incorporate all suggestions, but I included many, and appreciated the time and effort all took in providing feedback. I hope the changes that have been incorporated help to make this edition a valuable resource for students and instructors who share an interest in developing progressive social policies in ways that engage effectively with practitioners and services users.

I owe a debt to the individuals who revised chapters from previous editions: Marilyn Callahan, Bruce Wallace, and Tim Richards. The contents of these two chapters, one on feminism and social policy and the other on resisting welfare cutbacks, add a great deal to the main theme of the book. Special thanks are also extended to a long-time colleague, Pete Hudson, Senior Scholar, Faculty of Social Work, University of Manitoba, for his section on the voluntary sector, which is included in Chapter 2; to Marlyn Bennett, doctoral candidate in Interdisciplinary Studies at the University of Manitoba, and Cathy Rocke, Assistant Professor of Social Work at the University of Manitoba, for their helpful comments on an earlier version of Chapter 10 on Indigenous policy-making; to Kathleen Kufeldt and Maureen Flaherty for providing some case examples; to Maria Chen, who conducted some early research on changes for the current edition; and to Sasha Kondrashov for his preliminary work on updating websites. Last, but not least, I thank Madeline for her ongoing assistance and support in what at times seemed like another never-ending project that occupied too many weekends.

This book is dedicated to my co-author of the first three editions, Brian Wharf, who died in 2011 and whose many contributions to the theme of connecting policy to practice from a social justice standpoint remain in this edition. His collective works have had an enormous impact on social work policy and practice in Canada, but I remember him most fondly as a compassionate colleague, mentor, and friend whose personal and professional relationships were built on a common theme—caring for others.

Brad McKenzie
Professor Emeritus
University of Manitoba

Introduction

──────────────────── • **In the Introduction you will learn about:** • ────────────────

- the general goals of this book;
- definitions of social policy and social welfare policy;
- definitions of universal and selective social programs;
- the principle of affected interests;
- different levels of policy-making.

General Goals

There are three primary goals of the fourth edition of *Connecting Policy to Practice in the Human Services*. The first two are implied by the book's title: to identify gaps between policy and practice and to argue the case for improving these connections, including an exploration of strategies that may be used to better link these two domains from a social justice standpoint. The third goal is to provide an overview of what social policy is all about and how it is developed. New information on social policy relevant to this third goal not only serves as a platform for discussions on connecting policy to practice but also provides basic information about the place of social policy in dealing with some of the key social issues in Canadian society.

The underlying rationale for these goals is that more inclusive approaches to policy-making will empower front-line practitioners by creating a work environment conducive to effective practice, lead to improved program and service outcomes for service users, and challenge the more restrictive or neo-liberal approaches to policy-making that dominate the political landscapes in Canada and in several other countries. We recognize that inclusive approaches will not always succeed, particularly in heavily bureaucratized work environments that emphasize organizational accountability and compliance with these norms over the needs of service users. Strategies that take up these causes in other ways—both inside and outside the system—will be required. We explore a number of opportunities for policy changes, including resistance to punitive policy measures that move beyond the margins of methods and procedures likely to be supported from inside the system. As this description implies, this is not a value-neutral book on social policy; instead, it adopts a critical stance in its examination of the theory and practice of policy-making within work environments and what can be done to improve the present situation.

In developing the general themes in this book we draw on relevant research and literature; in addition, we incorporate experiential evidence from practice in the form of illustrative examples and case studies. The book is more than just an argument for different approaches to policy-making. If we are to develop progressive policy changes, we must have a good understanding of the policy-making environment, the structures and processes pertaining to policy-making, and the knowledge and skills to use methods of policy-making, including policy analysis, within a more inclusive, value-critical framework.

About the Fourth Edition

Information and tools consistent with this broad purpose have been retained but updated from the third edition. Chapters now open with a list of objectives, and key terms are boldfaced in the text and defined in the Glossary at the back of the book. Feature boxes, many of which are new, continue to provide case examples or further details on particular topics. As before, selected readings and critical thinking questions appear at the end of each chapter.

New and expanded material includes discussion of ideology and neo-liberalism (Chapter 1), poverty and inequality (Chapter 1), the role of the voluntary sector (Chapter 2), diversity issues (Chapter 4), implementation (Chapter 5), and the influence of advocacy and the social media (Chapter 7). More examples of strategies that may influence policy outcomes have been added to several chapters, notably Chapters 1, 6, and 7, and we include a significantly revised chapter on policy-making in Indigenous contexts (Chapter 10). Research and references have been updated throughout, and the Appendix has been expanded to list Canadian and international websites and journals to help students with further research on social policy issues.

Definitions

Definitions of **social policy** vary considerably. For example, Graham, Swift, and Delaney (2012) outline seven different perspectives in their discussion of definitions of social policy. Among these perspectives, they include the identification of different models (Titmuss, 1974), a value-critical perspective (Rein, 1974), a focus on social justice (Gil, 1970), attention to social action (Mishra, 1981), and a focus on different rights or entitlements (Marshall, 1965). Specific definitions in the literature vary from those that are quite broad in scope to those that are somewhat more restrictive.

Among more comprehensive formulations is that proposed by Gil (1990: 523), who views social policies as "guiding principles for ways of life, motivated by basic and perceived human needs." A somewhat more restrictive definition is proposed by Westhues (2012: 6): "Social policy is a course of action or inaction chosen by public authorities to address an issue that deals with human health, safety, or well-being." Public authorities are defined as including "those who work directly with service users, bureaucrats working at international organizations and all levels of government, and elected officials." Although Westhues intends public authorities to include service organizations connected in some way to government, she does not specify, as Yelaja (1987: 2) does, that social policy may be formulated "not only by government, but also by institutions such as voluntary organizations, business, labour, industry, professional groups, public interest groups, and churches." However, Westhues (2012: 6) does recognize that the actions of front-line workers may reinforce or resist the intent of policy decisions. This recognition is consistent with Lipsky's (1980) conclusion that front-line workers make policy because of their ability to exercise discretion about what services are provided to or withheld from individual service users.

Additional characteristics of social policy also merit attention. One is the distinction between grand and ordinary issues (Lindblom, 1979). The grand issues include the distribution of income and wealth, of political power and corporate prerogatives. These are dealt with at the national and, increasingly, the international levels. They represent the major economic and fiscal challenges faced by the state. Although decisions are not immune to the influence of ordinary citizens, it is obviously more difficult for the public to fully engage in policy-making at this level. And while the rhetoric of government often holds that the challenges are dealt with in ways that benefit all citizens, too often the resolution of these grand issues seems to confer more benefits on those with the most power and wealth. The ordinary issues of social policy are concerned with more personal matters, such as the provision of health and social services, income support, housing, and planning for the development of cities and neighbourhoods. Ordinary issues affect the lives of Canadians in very direct and significant ways. Given that one of the primary goals of this book is connecting policy to practice in the human services, we focus more directly on ordinary issues.

The decision-making elements included in the concept "social policy" are a second consideration. Titmuss (1974) has noted that the word "social" reflects a special focus on human well-being and development and their role in society, whereas "policy" implies understanding the implications of choice when one objective must be selected over another. Policy is all about choosing a particular course of action and understanding the values that inform these choices. Indeed, policy-makers at provincial and local levels have considerable scope for determining how health and social services will be provided. For example, provinces provide different levels of support for people on welfare. And although most provinces provide child welfare services through provincial departments or ministries, Ontario and, to a large extent, Manitoba have private, non-profit organizations that deliver services. In addition, First Nations child welfare agencies in all provinces are normally incorporated as non-profit organizations. And whether child welfare services throughout Canada are delivered by provincial departments or voluntary organizations they can, within the limits prescribed by legislation and funding, decide whether to favour a preventive, community-based approach or to focus primarily on crisis-oriented investigation and surveillance services after referrals of abuse or neglect.

Given the special emphasis on "choices" in social policy we focus special attention on a dated, but still useful, definition of social policy:

> Social policy is all about social purposes and the choices between them. These choices and the conflicts between them have continuously to be made at the governmental level, the community level, and the individual level. At each level by acting or not acting, by voting or not voting, by opting in or contracting out we can influence the direction in which choices are made. (Titmuss, 1974: 131)

The relevant parts of this definition are purpose, choice, and level. Policy is all about choosing directions in situations where evidence is, at times, incomplete and contradictory and where values inform the fundamental question of who pays and who benefits. The purpose of the policy and the choices related to this purpose are made at a variety of levels. In Table I.1 these are organized as macro, mezzo, and micro levels.

Policies at the organizational or program levels may sometimes be referred to as **agency-level policies** rather than social policies, and the service provider or practitioner

Table **I.1**	Levels of Policy-Making and Examples of Choices
Level	**Examples of Policy Choices**
Macro • International	• Free trade; financial aid to global crises and countries in need
• Federal	• Fiscal and monetary policy; Old Age Security; Employment Insurance; foreign aid
• Provincial	• Child welfare, welfare rates, health services
Mezzo • Local (i.e., city, municipal, band council)	• Some social services; recreation; neighbourhood development
• Organizational (i.e., agency within government or the voluntary sector)	• Some decisions on access, types of benefits, service focus, and approach within the scope of macro-level policy guidelines; more choice in some voluntary agencies
Micro • Service provider or street level	• Decisions to provide or withhold services; advocacy with or on behalf of service users

level is often omitted as rather unimportant in policy-making. The omission of the practice level reflects the view that policy is what needs to be done "in general" whereas practice is what needs to be done in "a specific situation," implying that the two domains are, by their very nature, quite disconnected. Although this distinction has a ring of truth, we argue that practitioners consistently face difficult "policy choices" in their day-to-day work. For example, physicians, nurses, and others in health care are often faced with the choice of trying to maintain the elderly in their own homes or to place them in a nursing home. Similarly, when confronted with situations of child abuse or neglect, social workers must decide whether to recommend to the family court that a child should be apprehended and placed in the care of the state or remain at home. Such choices are just as complex as those that baffle policy-makers at more senior levels. In addition, practitioners often have to act quickly, while being fully aware that their choices will have significant consequences on people's lives. It is also at this micro level where the connections or lack thereof between policy and practice are most apparent—this is where "the rubber hits the road."

A third consideration in defining social policy involves approaches to analysis. In general, policies are analyzed by the intentions and objectives that lie behind them, the administrative and financial arrangements, including expenditures, used to deliver policies, and the outcomes of policies (i.e., who gains and who loses). Chapter 4 is devoted to this topic.

As earlier noted, it can be argued that social policies can be formulated outside of government, and policies and programs developed by the voluntary sector independent of government support this view. Nevertheless, most social policies are initiated by some level of government; thus, they are **public policies**. The two most important types of government policies are economic and social policies, but public policies also include those pertaining to areas such as immigration and defence. Social policy is concerned with the development and implementation of social programs pertaining to such things as social welfare, health care, education, and housing. This raises another question. How do we distinguish between social policy and **social welfare policy**? Like social policy, social welfare policy is open to several interpretations. Chappell (2014: 4) notes that as a concept, social welfare can be defined as a vision of health, happiness, and well-being. As a system, social welfare may be seen as formalized policies and programs designed to respond to those in need, and this broad focus has tended to produce interpretations of social welfare policy that appear almost synonymous with social policy. As a field of policy, however, social welfare is most often viewed as distinct from other types of social policies related to fields such as health care, education, and housing. From this perspective social welfare policies are a subset of social policies; like all social policies, they represent the deliberate intervention of government and other sectors in society to address human needs that are not adequately provided for by the private market. Social welfare policies focus primarily on two general aspects: income security and the provision of social services, and this focus means that social welfare policies involve some degree of redistribution of resources to disadvantaged citizens.

Although we have drawn a distinction between social welfare policy and social policy, it is important to recognize the various ways that policies in fields such as health, education, and social welfare interact in determining the adequacy of *well-being* or *welfare* in society. It is becoming increasingly important to look at social problems and their solutions from a more integrated social policy perspective that reflects considerations that previously may have been defined as the responsibility of a particular department of government.

One example of this more integrated approach to social policy is the increased attention to the **social determinants of health** not only as a pathway to better health but also as essential to achieving more equality in society and reducing the level of poverty. Raphael (2011) demonstrates how the social determinants of health, which include factors such as income, housing, education, employment, and ethno-racial background, influence both health outcomes and poverty levels. Social policies that directly address these social determinants are essential both to poverty reduction and improvements to health and the quality of life in society. By definition, this perspective calls for a more integrated approach to the development of social policies.

We cannot discuss social policy in Canada without coming across the term **welfare state**. Societies where a substantial part of the production of health and welfare is paid for or provided by government are commonly referred to as welfare states, and Chappell (2014: 24) notes that this term is generally applied to industrial capitalistic societies. Programs such as Employment Insurance (EI), social assistance (welfare), medicare, pensions, home care, and benefits provided through the tax system are examples of welfare state programs. Although Armitage (2003) considers programs such as temporary shelters and food banks as part of this system, many of these are funded through charitable giving and so, in our view, are not welfare state provisions.

The golden age of welfare state development in Canada was between the mid-1940s and the mid-1970s. This era ushered in programs such as the universal family allowance, hospitalization and medicare coverage, major reforms to Unemployment Insurance (now Employment Insurance), the Canada Assistance Plan (CAP), improvements to Old Age Security (OAS), and the Canada Pension Plan (CPP). Most authors (e.g., Graham et al., 2012; Rice and Prince, 2013) regard the 1980s and beyond as a period that has involved significant retrenchment in a number of welfare state provisions. As discussed in Chapter 1, the Canadian welfare state has not yet disappeared, but it has become "frayed" and is in jeopardy.

An important consideration in understanding social policy in Canada is the difference between **universal social programs** and **selective social programs**. Universal programs are comprehensive in that they reach broad segments of the population with limited, qualifying factors for participation. For example, publicly funded health-care services are available to all Canadian citizens and others, such as newcomer immigrants and refugees, with some restrictions (e.g., eligibility for certain social benefits, such as OAS and social assistance, for some newcomers depend on a qualifying period of residency). Education is not only available but an obligation for children from the age of 6 to 16 or 18. At one time the family allowance and the OAS programs were universal in coverage, but these have become more selective over time. A more recent program launched by the federal government in 2006 is the Universal Child Care Benefit (UCCB). Under this program a taxable monthly benefit is paid to parents for each child in their care subject to certain age restrictions (in 2015 the amounts were $160 for each child under the age of 6 and $60 for each child between the ages of 6 and 17). Although intended as a child-care subsidy, parents can use these funds for any purpose.

Selective or targeted programs are limited to more narrowly defined segments of the population considered to be more vulnerable or at greater risk. One example is social assistance or welfare, which targets those without adequate income or assets and no other means of financial support. In selective programs, eligibility is normally determined through some combination of income tests, needs tests, and asset tests. However, selective programs may also target a specific segment of the population who qualify because of other characteristics, such as having a disability.

Universal programs have been traditionally valued over selective programs because they reinforce the notion of a citizen's right to benefits; in addition, they reduce the stigma that often accompanies more selective programs because the service or benefit is available to everyone. Although universal programs may often have lower administrative costs because they avoid costly eligibility tests, benefit costs are higher because they are provided to more recipients, even where some of these benefits may be taxable for those with higher incomes. Selective programs are often regarded as more efficient because they permit the targeting of potentially higher levels of benefits to those most in need. Universality is generally supported in well-entrenched programs like medicare and public education; however, universality in income support programs has fallen out of favour in Canada. For example, clawbacks—where benefits are reduced or eliminated for higher-income earners—were introduced to family allowances and OAS in the late 1980s. Family allowances were eventually eliminated and replaced with the Canada Child Tax Benefit (CCTB) in 1989. The CCTB has become more selective in its application because a larger proportion of benefits are paid to those who need them most. However, it avoids the highly intrusive needs or means testing procedures associated with social assistance; instead, it determines eligibility from family income reported annually on income tax forms, and only those families below a certain level of income receive the benefit. In 1998 the National Child Benefit Supplement was established, and the federal portion of this benefit is added to the CCTB for families who qualify based on their annual income. There is now a Child Disability Benefit provided to families below a certain level of income who are caring for a child who has severe and prolonged disabilities. Programs such as CCTB reflect what is known in Europe as **progressive universalism**, where the emphasis has shifted from providing benefits to all citizens to more targeted poverty reduction strategies.

We conclude our discussion of key definitions by drawing attention to two terms that appear throughout the book. The term "service users" is adopted instead of "clients" in most cases, and this is intended to reflect the fact that these are individuals who receive services or with whom professionals work. We also frequently refer to "practitioners" as "front-line workers" to distinguish these service providers from senior program managers in agencies or organizations. However, at least some of the issues confronting front-line practitioners may also be applicable to those who are their immediate supervisors. Thus the experiences attributed to front-line practitioners may be applied to those in immediate supervisory roles in a number of situations.

The Principle of Affected Interests

While the issue of participation is addressed in later chapters, we clarify our position at the outset, namely that those who are affected by a policy have a right to participate in its formation and in determining its eventual outcome. Dahl (1970: 64) calls this the **principle of affected interests**, and while he acknowledges that it is a broad and ambitious principle that cannot always be acted on, it nevertheless deserves attention whenever possible. For us this is an important principle. As currently organized, policy-making in the human services largely excludes those who are most affected by the outcomes. We are aware of the argument that those most directly affected by social policies are unable or incapable of making a contribution. This argument holds that service users are so overwhelmed with the day-to-day pressures of living that they have no energy left to participate in policy formation. In addition, the view, whether stated or not, is that because service users cannot manage their own lives without assistance from the state or other organizations they do not have the skills or knowledge to contribute in any meaningful way to policy development. These arguments are quite pervasive within policy-making contexts. At the same time, practice methods are often adapted to respond more directly to the aspirations of service users through group methods, self-help, and social action. If these more inclusive approaches to problem-solving work in more direct practice, why would the contributions of service users not be equally useful and valid in the creation of new policies?

Of course, important practical issues need to be considered. First, policy-making initiated from the bottom up may often be a long-term process with indeterminate outcomes; thus, it is often a question of whether an investment in these processes is worth the bother. In the case of service users, they may have other priorities and choose not to participate. These choices need to be respected. However, the participation of service users is likely to be more sustainable on policy issues that matter more directly to them, where their voices will be seriously considered, and where the time horizon for policy change is more predictable. Second, service users may feel unwanted or face challenges around such things as meeting times, transportation, and child care. Special invitations, alternative approaches to enabling input such as special forums for service users, and compensation for time spent or related expenses may help to overcome some of these issues. Third, a more participatory policy-making process involves more time, and in some circumstances there may be an imposed time restriction on making a policy decision. In general, a more inclusive policy-making process may require extending the timelines for decision-making. Although this may not always be possible, it is a small price to pay for policy outcomes that may reflect a better fit with the needs of service users.

Service users are not the only ones excluded from policy-making; indeed, practitioners often have little opportunity to contribute to the policies they are expected to implement. The role of policy-makers has traditionally been reserved for staff with long-standing service records; although there has been a recent shift to somewhat more diversity among those who determine policy, these individuals have been primarily privileged men (i.e., white and middle class or well-off). The consequences are readily apparent: policy-making roles have been dominated by men while the roles of practitioners are filled more often by women and, more recently, Aboriginal people and immigrants. This raises questions of differences based on gender, race, ethnicity, and other forms of diversity. For example, because the values of men and women often differ on gender-related matters, such as caregiving, this gender imbalance has exacerbated the gap between policy and practice. In a similar fashion, how is it possible to derive effective policies to support the adjustment of new immigrants and refugees (often referred to as "newcomers") without engaging them in the process of defining the problems they experience and designing appropriate solutions?

An additional gap between policy and practice is created by the location of policy-makers in head offices, which are too often far removed from the realities of day-to-day practice. Rein (1983: 65) refers to the knowledge of policy-makers in these contexts as "cold and remote." By contrast, the knowledge of practitioners is "hot"—it is directly and intimately connected with particular circumstances of service users. To continue the Rein analogy, mixing these two kinds of knowledge after the policy has been established all too frequently results in "tepid knowledge": too little and too late to significantly improve the lot of either practitioners or service users. What is needed is a way to inject the "hot" knowledge from practice experience directly into the policy process. In our view this can be accomplished by having practitioners and service users as active partners in the development of policies.

Finally, we note that disconnections between policy and practice are exacerbated by how we have organized the delivery of many of our human services. Most services are provided through government or large organizations in the voluntary sector that are best described as "quasi-government" agencies because, although located outside of government, they receive their mandate and almost all of their funding from government. As a result, they are largely responsive to the policy-making decisions that occur at a governmental level. Most of these organizations are structured hierarchically, with the chain of command flowing from the minister, through additional steps to the chief executive officer, and through several additional steps to front-line staff responsible for service provision. This structure, which reflects a corporate style of management, includes what Kouzes and Mico (1979) describe as three somewhat separate organizational domains: policy, management, and practice. The policy domain is legitimized as the primary responsibility of politicians and senior bureaucrats; it is generally preoccupied with policies and programs that must enhance the image of the party in power even while (hopefully) responding to the needs of communities and service users. On the other hand, practitioners are largely confined to their own domain, which involves service delivery in compliance with new policies and standards. Management is caught in the middle, trying to assure policy-makers that the programs they conceived are being run as efficiently and effectively as possible (so policy-makers can assure the public on such issues), and at the same time trying to respond to the demands of practitioners for additional resources or other changes. Although this description oversimplifies policy-making and implementation structures, the differences in these domains can become so large that one of two scenarios is created. One is that the interactions between domains become so discordant that a disproportionate amount of time is spent on asserting conflicting perceptions of policy or practice "realities." A second is that resignation to the status quo and withdrawal from engagement occur, reinforcing the isolation of the policy and practice domains from each other. In either case, opportunities for collaboration and joint problem-solving are squandered.

Policy-Making in the Human Services: Whose Responsibility?

Not everyone in the human services embraces the study of policy-making with enthusiasm. We recall students in social work who were disinterested in the study of social policy, and wanted simply to concentrate on improving their direct practice skills without having to worry about policy issues. This perspective is somewhat understandable if one thinks of the difficulties in exercising influence over the grand issues in social policy. However, making changes in ordinary policy issues can also feel somewhat distant and less rewarding than affecting changes through interaction with a particular individual or family. Despite these understandable biases, we argue that policy is inextricably linked to practice and it needs to be the concern of everyone.

We have already noted that social policies are established at different levels. Policies at the macro level set the context and provide the general mandate and some of the tools from which practice evolves. Policy development at the mezzo level (local and organizational levels) provides more specific guidance for service delivery, and it is at the agency level that the connections between policy and practice take on real meaning. The micro level reflects the transactions that occur between a service provider and service user. Here service providers make choices about the kinds of services to be provided within available policy guidelines and options.

Although this description demonstrates the linkages between policy and practice, it implies that this influence occurs primarily in a top-down, linear fashion. As we argue throughout the book, this should not be the case—practice must also influence policy in meaningful ways to help bridge the gaps between these domains. At the micro level, service providers must be more than just implementers of policies; they must have some discretion to shape the nature of the services they provide. Moreover, professional commitments to social change and social justice obligate them to advocate with or on behalf of service users for entitlements and to bend or challenge certain rules that interfere with the needs and rights of service users. In this role they are using practice knowledge and experience to affect policy; they are becoming engaged in a policy practice role. At the mezzo level, supervisors and front-line staff may both advocate for and participate in the development of new agency policies, along with policy analysts. At the macro level, a policy advocacy role may be a more common form of engagement, as both senior staff and policy analysts may be directly engaged in research and the development of new or revised social policies. In either case one is engaging in policy practice at the macro or mezzo levels.

Jansson (2014) identifies four skills important to policy practice:

- analytical skills to assess social problems, identify policy options, assess their merits, and draft proposals;
- political skills to use power and influence, develop political strategies, and assess feasibility;
- interactional skills to build networks, establish allies, and work collaboratively with groups and organizations;
- value clarification skills to identify and prioritize moral and ethical criteria for decision-making.

Although the skills needed in practice and policy-making overlap, there are also important differences. The nature and scope of policy analysis are different from the situational analysis required in direct practice; in addition, the level of knowledge of the policy-making arena and the strategies that can be used in developing new policies

Box **I.1** | Policy Practice and Direct Practice

The policy practice skills identified by Jansson are also related to responsibilities associated with direct practice. For example, a social worker in direct practice may need to provide assistance in locating independent living accommodation for a young person transitioning from care. S/he will need to be familiar with policies related to landlord and tenant rights; as well, s/he may also need to advocate for an adjustment in agency allowances and guarantees in order to cover current rental rates to overcome landlord resistance in securing a suitable apartment. These actions may include negotiations with landlords and an advocacy role within the agency to ensure independent living allowances are adequate to cover these costs.

As you consider this example, review the policy practice skills identified by Jansson. What different types of skills may be required to meet this service need?

will vary. These and other themes important to the development of social policies that reflect social justice goals are explored in future chapters of the book.

Summary and Conclusion

This chapter has outlined the purpose and objectives of the book, including our general perspective on current approaches to policy-making. We have identified our general commitment to policy-making models that engage both service users and service providers as active participants in shaping the policies that affect their interests. Although we favour more participatory approaches to policy-making, a note of caution is in order. The promotion of public participation is not always associated with progressive policies, as is illustrated by efforts to mobilize public support for harsher penalties for young offenders and for reopening the debate on choice with respect to an abortion.

In making the case that policy development is everyone's business, we have demonstrated that policy-making occurs at different levels. Access to higher levels can be a special challenge for front-line practitioners, who may be overwhelmed by day-to-day caseload and paperwork requirements. However, the importance of linking policy and practice methods and skills to direct service was identified, and human service professionals have a special ethical obligation to include policy-related knowledge and skills in their work. Advocacy efforts by practitioners at the mezzo and macro levels of policy-making can help to bring important front-line knowledge and experience to decisions about the following strategy choices:

- pursuing opportunities for progressive changes through inclusive approaches where these are feasible;
- using participatory approaches and other methods to build alliances and coalitions to effectively resist those policies likely to contribute to further injustices;
- helping to unmask the rhetoric of policy proposals to determine which of the first two pathways ought to be followed.

In Chapter 1 we explore the social and political environment for policy-making in Canada, beginning with a discussion of ideology.

Critical Thinking Questions

1. It might be said that social welfare policies are social policies but that not all social policies are social welfare policies. Using this statement as a guide, distinguish between social policy and social welfare policy as outlined in the Introduction.
2. Define each of the following terms as they apply to social policy and provide an example of each type of provision: universalism; selectivism; progressive universalism.

3. What is the principle of affected interests? What is your view of the strengths and weaknesses of applying this principle to policy-making?
4. What is your opinion of the statement: "Knowledge and skills in policy practice are essential to all who work in the human services"? Defend your opinion.

Recommended Reading

R. Titmuss. *Social Policy*. London: George Allen and Unwin, 1974. This classic on social policy provides insight into the origins of the value criteria model of social policy.

S. Torjman. *What Is Policy?* Ottawa: Caledon Institute of Social Policy, 2005. This brief report identifies different ways to think about public policy in an easily readable format. It also provides an overview of general steps to follow in policy development.

Chapter

1

Ideology and the Social and Political Environment of Policy-Making

----• **In this chapter you will learn about:** •----

- ideology as an important factor in influencing political behaviour and public policy;
- how ideology influences models of social welfare;
- what neo-liberalism is and how it supports a particular approach to economic globalization;
- how neo-liberalism influences social policy;
- poverty and inequality in Canada;
- some of the challenges and opportunities that exist in responding to neo-liberalism, poverty, and inequality.

Introduction

In developing more inclusive approaches to policy-making it is first necessary to understand why and how social policy develops in Canada. Aspects of our political culture, the influence of ideology and how this affects the exercise of power, and social and economic factors, including globalization, poverty, and inequality, are explored in this chapter. Policy-making structures, which include the federal and provincial governments, the voluntary sector, the Charter of Rights and Freedoms, and the Supreme Court, are discussed in the next chapter.

Political culture refers to dominant and relatively durable beliefs and values in a society. These are somewhat difficult to define in the Canadian context because of the recognition of the unique status of Quebec, **First Nations** and other **Aboriginal** or

Indigenous people, and the general Canadian commitment to multiculturalism. The delivery of health and social services was ceded to the provinces in the British North America Act (now the Constitution Act, 1867), but the unique status of Quebec has encouraged the devolution of several national social policies to Quebec, and sometimes to other provinces as well. The Indian Act sets out the special responsibilities of the federal government to First Nations communities and the Inuit, and their aspirations for greater self-determination are shared by other Indigenous groups.

Canadian social and economic policies are also heavily influenced by Canada's proximity to the United States. Canadians generally regard their differences from the US, particularly in relation to social policies such as public health care, as assets. However, the dominance of American media and cultural communication, as well as the extensive economic linkages between the two countries, makes true autonomy difficult to achieve when one lives in the "shadow of the elephant."

Ideology, Politics, and Public Policy

In this section we introduce an ideological framework that helps to demonstrate the links between ideology and political approaches to policy-making. Graham, Swift, and Delaney (2012: 68) define ideology as "a shared way of thinking based on a set of ideas that reflect values, beliefs, attitudes, and experiences of a particular person or group." They go on to discuss how ideologies shape one's perspective about the way the economy should operate, the role of government in economic and social matters, and the nature and causes of social problems and their solutions.

Variations in political ideologies are found in the literature (e.g., George and Wilding, 1985, 1994; Graham et al., 2012; Mishra, 1977; Mullaly, 2007), but we adopt a framework that includes Marxism, social democracy, liberalism, and neo-conservatism or neo-liberalism. Adaptations to these ideal types are also highlighted. Each ideology reflects somewhat different beliefs and values about human nature, the nature of society, the ideal economic system, the role of the state, causes of social problems, and preferred social welfare responses. It is common to plot political ideologies on a continuum from left to right, where those on the left typically hold values that reflect an emphasis on the collective good, equality, and increased state intervention to achieve these ends. In contrast, right-wing views reflect a greater commitment to individualism motivated by self-interests, the importance of freedom defined as the absence of government interference (except to protect individual rights and maintain law and order), and a belief that inequality is an incentive for individuals to improve their own circumstances in life.

As illustrated in Figure 1.1, these ideologies are also linked to political parties in Canada. However, the political ideologies presented in Figure 1.1 are ideal types, whereas the policies emerging from political parties often reflect a combination of ideological positions within the party along with a pragmatic assessment of how these views will be perceived by the public. Thus, some caution should be exercised in equating ideologies with a particular political party.

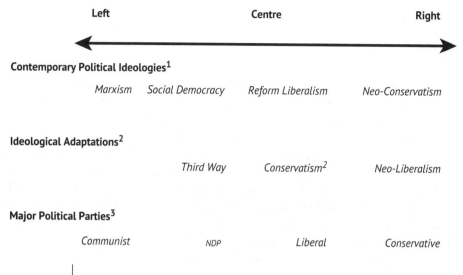

Figure 1.1 | The Ideological Continuum and Political Parties in Canada

Notes
1. Other ideological expressions, such as feminism, anti-racism, and an Indigenous world view, are omitted here because they are more difficult to plot on a left–right continuum. Chapter 8 discusses feminism and social policy and Chapter 10 includes a discussion of Indigenous perspectives on ideology.
2. A more progressive form of conservatism predates the contemporary focus on neo-conservatism; this form of progressive conservatism, sometimes labelled "red Toryism," reflected a greater commitment to government intervention in responding to humanitarian concerns.
3. The location of political parties on this continuum is only approximate as each political party may contain individuals or propose policies that reflect somewhat different ideological positions. As well, certain political parties are difficult to plot on this continuum. For example, the Green Party, which has a strong commitment to environmental protection, may also include members who have more conservative views on the economy.

Marxism

Socialism has a long tradition and is represented by a variety of schools of political thought. The two common schools of thought are Marxism, which is sometimes referred to as "revolutionary socialism," and social democracy, which is sometimes described as "evolutionary socialism" because of its long-standing commitment to democracy as the means to social change.

Marxism is both an ideology and a theory of public policy formation (see Chapter 3). As an ideology, Marxism sees society as divided into two main classes based on their relationship to the economy under capitalism: a dominant or "ruling class" who control the capital and means of production, and a subordinate or "working class" who are exploited for their labour in generating profits for the dominant class. Class conflict leading to the replacement of the ruling class is regarded as necessary to achieve the ideal of a more egalitarian society. The "state"—i.e., the government and all of its institutions and agencies, from the military, the police, and the courts to schools and social welfare agencies—is seen as both part of the ruling class and an instrument that acts primarily in the interests of the capitalist class. Individuals become alienated from society because of their exploitation under capitalism. Poverty and oppression are explained by the structural arrangements in society that locate most power in the hands of a dominant class that favours inequality over equality, and freedom of choice over freedom from want and oppression. Marxists believe that a strong central state role is required in creating a more egalitarian society through public ownership and the provision of social welfare benefits based on need. Developing a state oriented to these goals may be a long-term project that occurs through a "dialectical process" involving a series of advances and retreats before achieving an ideal society oriented to the fundamental value of equality, and with a commitment to the collective good. This dialectical struggle is often confounded by the development of "false consciousness" among many members of the subordinate class, who become convinced, often through advertising and other messaging, that the dominant class can be trusted to act in their interests. Marx saw the pathway to change as one that involved revolutionary socialism leading to dictatorship of the proletariat (the working class), which would govern in the interests of all people in society. Most contemporary Marxists envision a more evolutionary pathway, involving representative and participatory forms of democracy, to such a transformation.

Social Democracy

Social democracy shares most Marxist views on the inherent structural inequalities created by capitalism, and on the importance of fundamental economic and social change leading to equality and social justice for all. Thus, many of the social values associated with Marxism, including the inherent potential for good in all human beings, are at the core of this ideology. However, social democrats are convinced that meaningful social transformation can be achieved through democratic means and reforms to societal institutions, including government structures and welfare state programs. This ideology supports a central role for government in ensuring a planned economy oriented to the fulfillment of human needs instead of relying on the unfettered free market. Although the replacement of capitalism may have been an early goal of social democracy as it evolved in countries like the United Kingdom in the late nineteenth century, many contemporary social democrats now accept an economic system that includes a mix of free-market capitalism with state provision and regulation as important mechanisms in addressing inequalities and oppressions created by free markets. Social indicators in the Scandinavian countries (i.e., Denmark, Norway, Sweden, and Finland), including lower rates of poverty and inequality, are frequently cited as examples of what can be accomplished under social democratic governments.

There is often an intense debate within social democracy about how the values of equality and social justice are to be interpreted, and what measures can be practically adopted by a social democratic party once it is elected as government. Constraints noted are the types of reforms that will be accepted by the public within our liberal capitalist system, and the ability of corporations to impose their will on government by relocating to other jurisdictions if higher taxes and regulatory actions threaten to reduce their profit margins. According to Giddens (1998) these constraints are minimized by social democrats who adhere to more traditional views of "left-wing" social democracy. As well, he argues that class relations have altered significantly over time, the influence of the working class has declined, and people no longer vote according to class lines. These developments have occurred because capitalism has adapted to new realities by creating programs that provide limited but important benefits to citizens, a trend historically underestimated by most socialists. An adaptation of social democracy, labelled the **Third Way**, is advocated by Giddens to combat the excesses of the market-led strategies of neo-conservatives without fundamental changes to the capitalist system. The ideology associated with the Third Way embraces many aspects of globalization, accepts the fact that capitalism is here to stay, and favours relatively conservative approaches to fiscal management at the governmental level. With respect to equality, there is more emphasis on equality of opportunity rather than outcome, and meaningful work is the main focus in ensuring "social inclusion" and lifting people out of poverty. The application of Third Way ideology is often associated with the Labour government of Tony Blair in the UK (1997–2007); however, many of these principles have been adopted by provincial Liberal and New Democratic Party (NDP) governments in Canada.

The political party that best reflects the ideology of social democracy is the former Co-operative Commonwealth Federation (CCF), which transformed itself into the New Democratic Party (NDP) in 1961. Tommy Douglas, who introduced medicare when he was Premier of Saskatchewan (1944–61), is an example of a political leader who held these ideological convictions. More recent NDP provincial governments, as well as the federal NDP, have adopted policy positions more reflective of Third Way principles. This is evident in Manitoba. Although the Manitoba NDP government invested significantly in health care and in child and family welfare, the approach to poverty reduction has focused primarily on training, education, and employment over improvements to income support. The reluctance to adopt significant redistributive measures that would put more income in the hands of the poor and the almost single-minded focus on labour force attachment as the way out of poverty are typical of Third Way policies. As well, the Manitoba NDP approach to the economy suggests it is not a threat to businesses or to capitalism. It remains committed to a modified form of balanced budgets, supports public–private partnerships, and has adopted some modest reductions in corporate taxes. These policies, which are typical of a number of Third Way governments, have led to criticisms that the Third Way has abandoned traditional social democratic approaches to economic policies based on Keynesianism and public ownership. Instead, it is claimed, such policies merely adopt a modified neo-liberal approach, at least in relation to the economy (Frankel, 2013).

Liberalism

At least three types of **liberalism** can be identified. **Classical liberalism** adopts an economic definition of "liberalism" as involving "an absence of government interference" (Stanford, 2008: 48), and this version of liberalism is associated with Adam Smith's ideal that the **invisible hand of the market** is a more effective and efficient method of distributing goods and services to all than either the state or large monopolies (Stanford, 2008: 53). The second type is **reform liberalism**, which supports government intervention to correct for market inadequacies and ensure equal opportunities for all. The third type is **neo-liberalism**, which supports increased reliance on the free market over government programs and regulation, reduced public expenditures, particularly for social programs, and the expansion of free trade agreements with provisions that include disproportionate benefits for multinational corporations. Both classical liberalism and neo-liberalism are associated with neo-conservatism; thus they are discussed in the next section.

Reform liberals have been labelled as "reluctant collectivists" because they believe in a modified form of individualism. There is a common belief in preserving as much individual freedom as possible. At the same time, however, it is often necessary to intervene to curb harmful behaviour or address injustices caused by the failure of the market or more systemic forms of oppression and discrimination. Individuals are generally seen as driven both by personal self-interests and by altruism. It is hypothesized that socialization and opportunities can bring out the best in people and ensure a balance between a concern for self and others. Although serious inequalities in power and privilege need to be addressed, major changes to current structures in society are not advocated. Political beliefs reflect a pluralist view of society where political power is seen as divided between competing interest groups, with government as a somewhat independent arbitrator that makes decisions in the **public interest**. Government intervention to address social problems caused by social disorganization or fundamental inequities caused by capitalism is required.

Even though socialist and conservative perspectives have influenced public policy in Canada, the ideology of liberalism dominated policy development in Canada for most of the second half of the twentieth century. Pierre Trudeau, Canada's fifteenth Prime Minister (1968–79 and 1980–4) is an example of a political leader reflecting this political ideology. Although reform liberalism is best represented by the Liberal Party of Canada, this ideology also reflects some of the policy decisions made historically by the Progressive Conservative Party, both nationally and in provinces like Ontario. At the national level the shift to a more neo-conservative focus began with Brian Mulroney, the Progressive Conservative Prime Minister from 1984 to 1993, and this trend continued with the Liberal government of Jean Chrétien (1993–2003). Neo-conservative or neo-liberal governments were elected in Ontario under Mike Harris in 1995 and in British Columbia under Gordon Campbell in 2001. In 2006, the election of Stephen Harper's neo-conservative government largely completed the transition from liberalism to neo-liberalism as the dominant ideology shaping public policy at the national level in Canada.

Conservatism, Neo-Conservatism, and Neo-Liberalism

Early advocates of conservatism reflected a combination of the classical liberal belief in the free market and the importance of preserving tradition, order, and hierarchy in society. While conservatism endorsed the role of self-interest in accumulating wealth under competitive capitalism and the free market, some government intervention was understood to be important. First, it was essential to preserve order and privilege, including the right to private property and wealth. Thus, measures to control deviant behaviour and punish criminal behaviour were adopted. Over time, a role emerged for the state to take benevolent actions and introduce public services to address major inequalities, including extreme poverty, child neglect, and access to adequate health care. This was an extension, to the public realm, of the long-held conservative value of noblesse oblige, whereby those in society who are privileged—the upper classes—are believed to have a moral obligation to care for those who are less privileged—often considered the "deserving" poor—through various charitable endeavours.

Progressive Conservatives, such as Bill Davis, the Premier of Ontario from 1971 to 1985, reflected a combination of traditional conservative values of individualism and freedom of choice and some reform liberal values supporting equal opportunity and the need for state intervention to ensure a minimum standard of living. Under his leadership a number of social welfare reforms related to health care, income support, and child welfare were introduced in Ontario.

In contrast, **neo-conservatism** sees society as primarily a collection of individuals where individual freedom is fundamental and where the individual is almost entirely responsible for his or her own well-being. Programs such as public welfare and other forms of assistance are defined as part of the problem because they create dependency and discourage people from advancing their own self-interests through hard work, despite any disadvantages they might have experienced in their lives. Underlying this belief is the view that individuals are inherently selfish and lazy, and that behaviour must be shaped by a combination of "carrot" (reward) and "stick" (punishment) approaches. Inequality, then, is embraced because it is viewed as an incentive to "pull oneself up by one's own bootstraps." In social policy, neo-conservatives are preoccupied with dismantling the welfare state through reduced funding and seek to off-load responsibilities to the community, faith groups, non-government organizations, or lower levels of government. This is more than simply a matter of reducing costs; of equal or even more importance is the strong belief that the welfare state has created "welfare bums" and a **nanny state** where people have become too dependent on government programs.

The ideology of neo-conservatism is strongly associated with neo-liberalism. Neo-liberalism needs to be distinguished from classical liberalism and earlier forms of conservatism. In classical liberalism the free play of the market was viewed as the pathway to benefits for all, and in earlier forms of conservatism, beliefs in order and stability dictated a moderately interventionist role for government in addressing social needs. Although neo-liberals champion the concept of a free market, these values are best understood as freedom for corporate capitalism on a scale that could never have been imagined by Adam Smith in the eighteenth century. As noted above, the focus in social policy is on privatization and reduced expenditures on welfare state programs.

Neo-liberal goals are to control or reduce inflation, to restore insecurity as a way of disciplining labour markets so workers will accept lower wages or reduced benefits, to roll back government programs and activities to meet business needs, and to cut taxes. The tools of neo-liberalism include the following:

- the adjustment of interest rates to regulate inflation;
- privatization and deregulation;
- a reduction in social security benefits;
- the use of free trade agreements to expand markets and contain the power of government.

There is one exception to the focus on reducing social expenditures among neo-liberals; they are quite willing to spend more on expanding the scope of penal institutions consistent with a "tough on crime" approach. This commitment is not an accident—it represents their preferred approach of social control for those who commit crimes, even if a significant proportion of such offences have underlying social causes. This approach is reflected in the passage of the omnibus crime bill (known as Bill C-10) in 2012 by the federal government, which increased jail time for more people at higher costs, despite evidence that this approach is ineffective in deterring crime.

The pursuit of neo-liberal policies is not restricted to actors or political parties on the right (i.e., neo-conservatives), although neo-liberalism is most often fully embraced by those adhering to this political philosophy. Governments of all stripes, including the Liberal Party and the NDP, sometimes adopt policies that reflect neo-liberal values. For example, the Liberal government of Canada in the 1990s painted social spending as a major cause of the deficit and pursued policies to reduce such spending, thus reflecting a neo-liberal agenda.

The above discussion demonstrates the connection between ideology and government policy-making; however, any government faces constraints in translating its preferred ideology into new policies. These include such things as the availability of resources, the legal and bureaucratic steps that must be followed in developing policies and programs, and the potential reactions from other levels of government, corporations, and the public, which may oppose new initiatives.

For government, political considerations are always important: how will this policy play out with voters at the next election? And for political parties the most important group of voters are those in the middle of the political spectrum because this group generally determines the outcome of an election.

Ideology and Social Welfare

Ideology is inextricably linked to social welfare. Wilensky and Lebeaux (1965) define two models of social welfare—residual and institutional. The **residual model of welfare**, which is associated with neo-conservative and neo-liberal views, places primary responsibility on the individual, then family, and then voluntary charitable organizations and faith groups for providing help to those in need. Support from government or the "state" is viewed as a last resort. The residual model also suggests that both government and charitable giving should be targeted primarily for the deserving poor or those unable to work because of a disability, age, or family responsibilities. Although government and charitable assistance to the "undeserving" poor is tolerated on a short-term or emergency basis, it is associated with the **principle of less eligibility**, where benefits are set at a level lower than that received by the so-called deserving poor. Those supporting a residual model favour low benefit levels that respond to "absolute needs" (i.e., the minimum required to meet basic survival needs) for the undeserving poor in the belief this will somehow force them to seek employment rather than income support.

The **institutional model of welfare**, which is also included in Titmuss's (1974) list of welfare models, is based on the recognition of ongoing needs in society that result from the existence of an industrial capitalist system. These include such things as income support if unable to work, public health care, protection from injuries, income support in retirement, support for families in raising children, and access to affordable housing. It is argued that individuals cannot be held entirely responsible for meeting these needs; thus, social welfare must be an ongoing institution in society providing a safety net of benefits and services that must be provided to all those in need. This model of welfare recognizes that government has a responsibility to introduce social and economic policies that benefit all citizens, but the focus is on "equality of opportunity" rather than "equality of outcome." The institutional model of welfare is associated with reform liberal ideals, but these may also resonate with many contemporary social democrats and those who identify as "progressive" conservatives.

The **structural model of welfare**, described by Mishra (1981), is adopted by Mullaly (2007) as an ideal model associated with Marxism and social democracy's ideal vision of socialism. In this model the social welfare state promotes equality, redistribution based on need, full employment, and equality of outcome. Although no country fully achieves this model of social welfare, some of the Nordic countries, which have a stronger commitment to social democracy, embrace some of the elements of the structural model.

Neo-Liberalism and Public Policy

Neo-Liberalism and Economic Policy

In economic matters, neo-liberalism relies almost entirely on **monetary policy** to deal with variations in the market cycle. Based on the ideas of Milton Friedman, the monetarist approach pays little attention to the government's direct role in promoting employment. Instead, interest rates are adjusted to control inflation, and low interest rates coupled with low inflation are assumed to be all that is needed to entice the private sector to invest new money in the economy. In turn, "trickle-down" effects are assumed to benefit the general population because of expanding jobs and increased consumer purchasing power. In fact, private-sector investment in the economy is more complex than this, as is demonstrated by the trend observed between 2010 and 2015, which featured a combination of low interest rates, low inflation, high levels of savings by corporations, and limited new investment by these companies in new jobs and economic growth. Strict monetary policy can be contrasted with **Keynesianism**, which stresses a more activist role for government in managing the economy (Stanford, 2008). A Keynesian approach pays more attention to unemployment and the need to stimulate the economy during a recession through government spending, in addition to the adjustment of interest rates. When "good times" return, government can be less interventionist in job creation, emphasize more of a regulatory role, and eliminate any deficits that might have occurred by directly investing in economic growth during the recession.

The neo-liberal agenda of cutbacks, privatization, and deregulation can have disastrous effects on both the economy and the well-being of families. For example, the collapse of the housing market in the US and the related banking crisis that triggered a global recession in 2008 reflected a lack of regulatory oversight of banks and their lending and investment practices. The ensuing economic meltdown resulted in job losses, increased inequality, and hardship for the many families who lost their homes. In the US alone trillions of dollars in government money were required to bail out failing companies and prop up the economy (Monbiot, 2013). The effects of the recession were not limited to the developed world; indeed, Saunders (2008) describes how the economic meltdown resulted in major job losses in the villages of the developing world as well. The recovery from this recession has been very protracted and unemployment remains high, particularly for younger and more vulnerable workers in many countries. Krugman (2012) notes that neo-liberal policies, which rely on spending cuts and low interest rates in recessionary times, make matters worse; and Ivry (2014) indicates that the modest regulatory measures adopted in the US since the recession have not curbed corporate greed and are unlikely to prevent a future crisis similar to that experienced in 2008–9.[1] Meanwhile, the world's 100 richest people became $241 billion richer in 2012 (Pelletier, 2014).

Neo-Liberalism and Free Trade

Neo-liberal governments are generally opposed to measures that might interfere with higher profits for corporations. Thus, they tend to support a form of economic globalization that combines free trade agreements with the transfer of decision-making powers normally reserved for governments to special tribunals focused on protecting the interests of multinational corporations. The three key international bodies that have played major roles in imposing a neo-liberal agenda of free-market, pro-business structures on the world economy in the past few decades are the **International Monetary Fund** (IMF), the **World Bank**, and the **World Trade Organization** (WTO). The IMF focuses on stabilizing and freeing the international flow of money, and the World Bank is intended to assist poor countries with economic development. However, these forms of assistance have often been combined with structural adjustment requirements that impose debt recovery obligations on poorer countries that make it harder for them to achieve self-sufficiency. The WTO encourages the development of free trade agreements throughout the world. But how does globalization affect social policy and the well-being of citizens living in specific nation-states?

Globalization is not really new in the sense that it can refer to the strengthening of international economic linkages for the purposes of trade through free trade agreements, improved communications, and better transportation systems. Obviously, there are some benefits to globalization through increased opportunities for trade, and it is neither desirable nor feasible to eliminate such exchanges. However, the structure of free trade agreements often produces adverse effects on one or more of the participating partners.

The new era of globalization is led by transnational corporations (TNCs), and these parent companies and their affiliates produce 25 per cent of the world's economic output (Silver, 2002: 30). TNCs differ from the older version of nationally based companies in that they are motivated almost exclusively by profit, with limited regard for workers or the interests of countries. Thus, they move their operations at will to countries where labour is cheapest and environmental laws are the most lax. Governments are increasingly unable to regulate the activities and tax the surplus of globalized capital because of the fear that these corporations will relocate to other countries. As well, neo-liberal governments frequently collude with these corporations in actions to further the aims of globalized capital. This trend is illustrated in the Trans-Pacific Partnership (TPP), a proposed free trade agreement between countries in the Pacific Rim and North America, which was nearing final approval in the summer of 2014. The lack of transparency in negotiations related to the TPP is particularly problematic in that leaked documents suggest that the agreement is about much more than tariff reduction and trade promotion. For example, corporations will be able to demand compensation from TPP governments related to domestic, financial, health, and environmental policies that they claim undermine their corporate rights to profit. As a result the ability of governments to introduce their own policies pertaining to such policies will be restricted.

Of concern to many in regard to trade agreements is the loss of national forms of democracy because elected governments become increasingly subservient to the interests of transnational corporations. The ability of large TNCs to relocate operations is also a constraint on both governments and organized labour in establishing fair wages and benefits. This occurs because TNCs and other corporations often pressure governments to reduce the level of benefits in income support programs to help ensure a ready supply of cheap labour or to relax protective legislation, such as minimum-wage laws or environmental protection legislation.

In developed countries, neo-liberal forms of economic globalization often place working people at risk of losing employment through plant closings or the transfer of production to non-union, low-wage sites. In addition, technological advances reduce the need for labour and workers are transferred from permanent jobs to short-term employment in order to reduce wage and benefit packages. But globalization can also have adverse effects in the developing world, as is illustrated in Box 1.1.

Perhaps one of the most important effects of neo-liberal forms of globalization is its influence on civil society. **Civil society** is a concept frequently associated with community capacity-building and the development of local democracy. In our view, one of the essential attributes of a civil society is the ability to hold others, including institutions, accountable for both their actions and their inactions. This may occur informally or through formal complaints, the influence of public opinion, redress through the legal system, and elections to replace those in power. Some of these activities may occur under the umbrella of voluntary organizations, advocacy groups and networks, membership groups (e.g., professional and union), faith groups, or self-help groups. Although accountability mechanisms are often imperfect, they do exist, even in the case of elected officials who are subject to the preferences of voters at election time.

Neo-liberalism reinforces the prominence of the free-market economy, although in truth the ideal market advanced by this ideology is anything but free. Whereas government has been seen in a welfare state economy as playing an important role in reducing the adverse effects of capitalism, neo-liberalism advances the goal of corporate control with limited regard for local communities or those who are marginalized. And when some of the powers normally vested in government and local institutions are transferred to TNCs, which are accountable to international shareholders primarily concerned with profits rather than to the citizens of the country where they are located, the equation is altered. Although globalization is not the only reason people feel unable to

Box **1.1** | Economic Globalization and the Exploitation of Workers in the Developing World

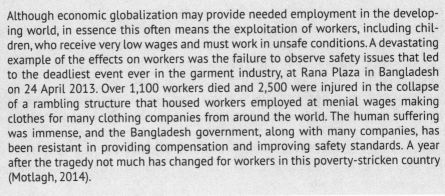

Although economic globalization may provide needed employment in the developing world, in essence this often means the exploitation of workers, including children, who receive very low wages and must work in unsafe conditions. A devastating example of the effects on workers was the failure to observe safety issues that led to the deadliest event ever in the garment industry, at Rana Plaza in Bangladesh on 24 April 2013. Over 1,100 workers died and 2,500 were injured in the collapse of a rambling structure that housed workers employed at menial wages making clothes for many clothing companies from around the world. The human suffering was immense, and the Bangladesh government, along with many companies, has been resistant in providing compensation and improving safety standards. A year after the tragedy not much has changed for workers in this poverty-stricken country (Motlagh, 2014).

influence the policies affecting their lives, it contributes to the weakening of civil society, particularly in relation to social policy, by placing the authority for these decisions out of the reach of local citizens.

The future remains unclear. For example, opposition to the negative effects of globalization may result in important changes to these policies. Alternatively, social policy may be forced to adapt to a diminished state role in determining the future of the health and social programs we have come to rely on.

Neo-Liberalism and Social Policy

Retrenching Social Welfare

Rice and Prince (2013) suggest that neo-liberal governments respond to corporate pressure and follow their own ideological commitments in restricting social investment through a series of retrenchment strategies aimed at limiting or dismantling components of the welfare state. Two of the most important are **programmatic retrenchment** and **systemic retrenchment**.

Programmatic retrenchment is designed to reduce the size and cost of social programs by reducing benefits, cutting entire programs, or introducing provisions to restrict eligibility. Chapter 9 describes an attempt by the BC government to limit eligibility for income assistance (i.e., welfare) and the mobilization of communities to fight these cuts. Other examples include the decision of the federal government led by Stephen Harper to increase the age of eligibility for Old Age Security from 65 to 67 beginning in 2023, and changes made over time by successive governments to Unemployment Insurance (see Box 1.2). There have also been a wide variety of federal funding cuts to such things as sex offender intervention programs and rehabilitation programs for drug-related offenders. As discussed in Chapter 4, the federal government in 2012 also cut supplemental health benefits for certain groups of refugees, limiting their access to needed health-care services and hampering their ability to become self-sufficient in their new country.

Rice and Prince (2013) describe systemic retrenchment as efforts, primarily by the federal government, to weaken policy-making processes by restricting the power of labour unions, eliminating funding for interest groups that advocate for improved social policies, and limiting funding for cost-shared social programs. Legislating workers back to work in cases of a strike and new onerous financial reporting requirements for unions are designed to restrict their influence. The elimination of funding in 2012 to Rights and Democracy, a respected international human rights agency established by the Mulroney government in 1988, and the severe cuts imposed on the Canadian HIV/AIDS Legal Network in 2012 reflect systemic retrenchment in action.

Although several examples noted above involve the Harper federal government, systemic retrenchment is not limited to the actions of this government to reduce the effectiveness of advocacy groups or organizations that take on issues out of favour with government. In 1996 the Liberals under Jean Chrétien eliminated the Canada

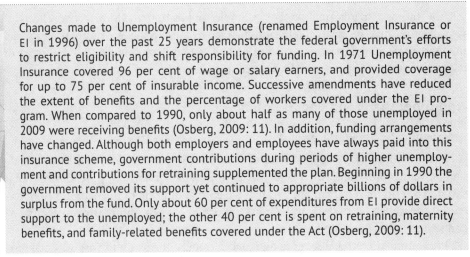

Assistance Plan (CAP), a cost-shared program for social programs with the provinces, and replaced this with a block funding transfer arrangement. Under CAP, program initiatives developed by the provinces received 50 per cent of their costs from the federal government, and this arrangement helped encourage innovation in programs such as child welfare and income assistance. The block funding arrangement adopted by the federal government was followed by cuts in the amounts of money provided to the provinces; in addition, it allowed the federal government to determine how much funding would be provided for social programs on an annual basis, opening the door to ongoing cuts as determined by the federal government and the downloading of more responsibilities to the provinces.

Systemic retrenchment also includes efforts to prioritize and off-load service responsibilities to non-profit charitable organizations and the for-profit sector. Non-profit social service agencies often become the last resort for people as publicly provided services adopt more restrictive eligibility requirements in the face of funding constraints. The continued reliance of all governments on food banks as an alternative to providing adequate income support benefits is an example of the growing reliance on the non-profit sector.

Challenges and Opportunities in Addressing Neo-Liberalism

The Challenges

Neo-liberalism presents some daunting challenges for progressive policy-making. First, neo-liberal arguments do resonate with the concerns of many people because many less-advantaged citizens are faced with declining incomes, difficulties accessing services, past failures with health and social programs, and increased costs, either in relation to taxes or increased fees for goods and services. Although the media play an important role in providing information that promotes public accountability and civil society, their disproportionate focus on "things gone wrong" influences the views of the public on matters such as taxes and social spending. Driven in part by their own ideology and in part by pro-business lobby groups, neo-liberal governments have been quite successful in promoting an anti-tax agenda with the Canadian public. Thus, successive federal and provincial governments have reduced tax revenues by hundreds of billions of dollars over the past several years (CCPA, 2014).

Second, the influence of the union movement has diminished, and unions have long advocated for adequate salaries and benefits for their members as well as for broader social programs like pensions and publicly sponsored child care. In spite of the growth in public-sector unions, in 2012 only 31.5 per cent of all workers in Canada were union members. Contributing causes to the gradual decline in union membership include the relocation of jobs to other countries by TNCs, increased technology, and a growth in the outsourcing of production and service responsibilities to smaller, independent contractors. This has given rise to a dual economy: multinational corporations with growing power but fewer Canadians employed, and a growth in the number of private contractors and small enterprises dependent on subcontracts from government or companies (Rice and Prince, 2013).

Third, neo-liberal governments continue to focus on reducing public expenditures. Although the 2008 global recession caused many governments, including those of the US and Canada, to rethink their aversion to Keynesian economic policy and to stimulate the economy, this approach was largely abandoned in Canada by 2011. Since then the preoccupation has been on reducing public spending in an effort to achieve a balanced budget, despite an unemployment rate in 2013–14 in excess of 7 per cent. This focus on reduced public spending is accompanied by a social policy discourse that emphasizes the costs of social programs without adequate attention to their offsetting benefits, including reduced social costs in the future.

Reducing the costs of social programs is a complex issue. For example, social spending in 2006 as a percentage of GDP was virtually the same as in 1978 but down significantly from the high in 1992 (Graham et al., 2012: 40). However, total social spending in constant dollars more than doubled between 1978 and 2007 (Graham et al., 2012: 39). Even at the national level in a neo-liberal era, federal transfers to the provinces and territories for health, social programs, and post-secondary education increased modestly between 2012–13 and 2014–15, although future increases are less certain (Torjman, 2014).

Why, then, are we falling behind? Two related factors that help to explain this are rising costs and expanding needs. Increased costs relate to factors such as inflation and cost drivers that exceed the rate of inflation in service delivery. Factors related to need include growing numbers of those in need and new or expanded definitions of need.

Some examples help to illustrate these patterns. In health-care spending the growing number of older Canadians and the expense of treatment, including diagnostic tests, pharmaceuticals, and salaries, have contributed to costs that exceed the rate of inflation. With regard to income support, higher unemployment rates and growth in the number of low-income single-parent households create new demands for income support. In child welfare, an expanded definition of child maltreatment to include exposure to domestic violence and emotional maltreatment has a direct impact on increased service delivery expenditures in child welfare. Finally, health and social programs in general are subject to demands by the public for qualitative improvements in services independent of the actual numbers of those needing services. For example, improvements to accessibility and accommodation services for persons with disabilities are influenced by advocacy efforts by and on behalf of disability groups and organizations, and by a growing public awareness of the barriers affecting people with disabilities.

Higher costs and increased needs help to explain why neo-liberalism has been, at best, only partially successful in dismantling the welfare state. This ideological push towards retrenchment also raises important questions that need to be further considered. First, can cost savings be achieved without reducing the quantity and quality of welfare state benefits and services? Second, if needs are expanding and these require attention to maintain or improve the quality of life, is this not an argument for higher rather than lower expenditures on social programs? Finally, if additional revenue is required, why are we reducing taxes rather than seeking additional contributions from those who can afford to pay?

Part of the answer to these questions relates to one of the objectives of this book. We must enhance our capacity to analyze and evaluate policy so that we can better answer questions about adequacy and effectiveness, and then we need to use this knowledge to contribute to new and existing strategies to better respond to needs. In taking up this challenge we need to recognize that neo-liberalism is not the only way forward. Indeed, opposition to the solutions proposed by neo-liberals in areas such as health care and the promotion of anti-poverty strategies demonstrates the power of advocacy and community mobilization in responding to these trends. We identified the role that social workers can play in their day-to-day work in our discussion of policy practice in the Introduction, and more specific examples of alternatives to the neo-liberal agenda are outlined in Chapters 6 through 10.

The Opportunities

At a global level, there have been modest successes in the struggle against undemocratic forms of economic globalization, and across the world social movements are actively campaigning for an agenda oriented more towards ecological and social justice issues. Some governments and political parties are more likely than others to critically examine the effects of globalization; moreover, even in cases where the state chooses to support a neo-liberal model of globalization, it can be held accountable for its actions through interest group pressure and the ballot box.

Neo-liberal approaches to domestic social policies can also be successfully challenged, and governments can and do make choices—influenced by the public—about their social policies. A number of European countries spend considerably more per capita on social welfare, and these expenditures reflect both different policy objectives and different results. For example, the Nordic countries and the Netherlands embrace a stronger commitment to full employment and social equality and in 2009 had the lowest rate of child poverty among industrialized countries, at about 7 per cent, using the After-Tax Low-Income Measure (UNICEF, 2012). The comparative rate for Canada in 2009 was double this, at 14 per cent (UNICEF Canada, n.d.). An example such as this helps to inform alternative visions for progressive policy changes. It is also helpful to recognize that there are competing social policy orientations to neo-liberalism, which Rice and Prince (2013: 13) describe as **social protection** and **cultural recognition**. In the social protection orientation, advocates advance an agenda that includes redistribution through state intervention, a national system of social security, and social investment based on needs. In the cultural recognition orientation, more marginalized groups, including persons with disabilities, Indigenous people, immigrants and refugees, and lesbian, gay, bisexual, transgendered, two-spirited, and queer (LGBTTQ) people, advocate for social and legal rights that can redress past wrongs, gain acceptance of identities, and achieve self-determination. At the local level, social workers and many others are engaged in community-based strategies that tackle issues related to poverty, community safety, and social support in ways that challenge the neo-liberal policy agenda.

The anti-tax movement promoted by neo-liberals can be challenged by greater focus on the benefits associated with tax revenues. For example, various goods and services are more effectively and efficiently provided by the public sector. These include regulatory functions such as environmental protection and food and drug safety, income support programs, public health care, and infrastructure, such as roads, sewers, and water distribution systems. As well, the tax system is an important instrument of redistribution. Tax-supported programs like public health care support the principle of equity, and a more progressive tax system provides the means to redistribute income and services to low-income Canadians through programs such as the Canada Child Tax Benefit, shelter subsidies, and the Guaranteed Income Supplement (GIS) for low-income seniors on OAS.

The anti-tax movement also fails to consider who bears the heaviest burden in paying taxes. While an increasing proportion of tax revenues are extracted from the middle class, income inequality has grown. A contributing factor has been reduced taxes for Canadians with the highest incomes (Russell, 2012: A10). Cuts to corporate taxes have also occurred, and these cuts have been based on the argument that Canada's high tax rate discouraged business investment. In fact, Canada's corporate tax rate in 2011 was lower than that of many other countries (Rosenblum and Frankel, 2011). Shifting the dialogue on taxes to recognize related benefits both now and in the future—and to identify who can afford to pay more to preserve and enhance welfare state programs—is an important priority.

Neo-liberal governments strive to centralize power because it permits policies that override the **public interest** and the rights of minorities. However, power is not only exercised in a top-down manner; it can be acted upon by individual and collective action through structures, such as advocacy groups and social movements, that mediate the rights and claims of citizens and the state. As well, policy-makers within government can play an important role in facilitating new and potentially beneficial policies even in times characterized by neo-liberalism. In concert with government actions or when there is resistance at the state level, voluntary organizations and grassroots community groups also play important roles in building civil society by providing mechanisms for citizens, including social workers, to participate in influencing social policies. Progressive policy-making is all about influencing and shaping more of these kinds of policies at the local, provincial, and federal levels.

Poverty and Inequality

We have reviewed different ideological perspectives in this chapter and how these influence social policy, and special attention has been given to the growth of neo-liberalism and its influence on economic and social policy. But what are the effects of neo-liberalism on poverty, Canada's most persistent social problem? Anti-poverty strategies, including those implemented and those proposed, contrast sharply with the approaches associated with neo-liberalism; indeed, Marxism, social democracy, and reform liberalism all support more progressive measures to address poverty, although it is important to consider how policy responses vary among these ideological perspectives and their political advocates. Presently, the evidence is conflicting about whether poverty has increased or decreased during the neo-liberal era; however, policies based on this ideology certainly have restricted the adoption of more comprehensive anti-poverty measures.

Poverty Rates

From a social justice standpoint, more attention to poverty is required, particularly in view of the fact that Canada has the capacity to dramatically reduce the rate and depth of poverty for its citizens. Using the After-Tax Low-Income Measure (AT-LIM), the 2013 *Report Card on Child and Family Poverty in Canada* (Campaign 2000, 2013) indicates that nearly one in seven children still live in poverty. Many of these children lose opportunities to experience success through their developmental years and into adulthood. But poverty extends beyond childhood and is a major challenge for significant proportions of single parents, those experiencing homelessness or a disability, those working in low-wage jobs, the elderly, recent immigrants and refugees, and Indigenous people. There is also an economic case for increased attention to poverty reduction. Poverty is associated with higher health-care costs, higher crime rates, higher rates of child maltreatment, lower rates of educational achievement, and lower employment rates. The economic costs of poverty can be calculated (see National Council of Welfare, 2011), and Canada Without Poverty (2014) estimates these costs at between $72 billion and $86 billion annually. Estimates for British Columbia (Ivanova, 2011) pegged the cost for a comprehensive poverty reduction plan for this province at $3 billion to $4 billion per year. In BC the direct cost to government of doing nothing was between $2.2 billion and $2.3 billion annually in such areas as increased health-care costs and criminal justice expenditures. The cost to society, which includes costs associated with lost productivity and direct costs to government, drives up the annual costs to between $8.1 billion and $9.2 billion. And this is for BC alone.

Poverty, particularly child poverty, has been a focal point for social policy for some time, and in 1989 members of Parliament voted unanimously to end poverty by the year 2000. Although some measures of poverty indicate that progress has been made, and advocacy organizations like Campaign 2000 (named after the 1989 commitment in Parliament) and Canada Without Poverty have kept poverty on the social policy agenda, many gaps remain.

One of the difficulties in responding to poverty is the absence of an official poverty line; the debates that arise from different estimates of how many are "really poor" can be a distraction from focusing on solutions. Several measures of low income in Canada are used to estimate poverty rates. Table 1.1 outlines the most commonly used measures.[2]

Table **1.1**	Measures of Low Income in Canada

Type of Measure	Approach	Assessment
Sarlo Basic Needs (Fraser Institute)	Costs determined for a minimal basket of basic needs required for survival.	Omits many needed items such as school and recreation costs. Often used by neo-liberals to minimize poverty rates.
Before- and After-Tax Low-Income Cut-Off (BT-LICO and AT-LICO) (Statistics Canada)	Based on a calculation that would normally require a family to pay at least 20 per cent more of its income on food, clothing, and shelter than the average family.	Relative measure of low income that adjusts amounts for families and communities of different sizes.
Market Basket Measure (MBM) (Statistics Canada)	Based on a calculation for a basket of goods and services for a modest basic standard of living, which is then compared to disposable income.	Adjustments can be made for different provinces and living circumstances; definition of necessities is higher than Sarlo Basic Needs.
Before- and After-Tax Low-Income Measure (BT-LIM and AT-LIM) (Statistics Canada)	Threshold determined by calculating one-half of the median income for Canadian families.	Easier to calculate and can be more readily used for international comparisons.

Absolute measures of poverty, such as the Sarlo Basic Needs measure, define minimum requirements for survival in determining poverty rates whereas relative measures, such as the LIM, consider poverty relative to general standards in society. Before- and after-tax calculations of the LICO and LIM are available, and these make a difference in calculating poverty rates. After-tax measures factor in the effects of taxes and transfer payments to individuals; thus, they have the effect of reducing poverty rates somewhat. LIMs, LICOs, and MBMs are all used to calculate poverty in Canada, but the most commonly used measure has been the After-Tax Low-Income Cut-Off (AT-LICO). Because each measure will produce somewhat different results and each has advantages and disadvantages, it is important to outline the approach being used to estimate poverty and the rationale for this choice.

Between 2000 and 2006 Canada experienced a decrease in child poverty from 13.9 per cent to 11.1 per cent using the AT-LICO (Statistics Canada, 2013a). Using this measure, the 2011 Canadian child poverty rate declined further to 8.5 per cent. When the After-Tax Low-Income Measure (AT-LIM) is used, the child poverty rate was 14.3 per cent in 2011, somewhat higher than 1989 when the pledge to end poverty was passed unanimously in the House of Commons. The 2011 poverty rate for all Canadians was 8.8 per cent using the AT-LICO and 12.6 per cent using the AT-LIM. These comparisons indicate that different measures of poverty make a significant difference in the proportion of people defined as living in poverty; however, all figures demonstrate the widespread persistence of poverty in Canada.

Canada does not fare well in international comparisons. For example, UNICEF's (2012) Report Card 10 on child poverty ranks Canada 24th of the 35 richest industrialized countries. Social spending does make a difference in that the rate of poverty declined from 25.8 per cent in Canada to about 14 per cent using the LIM after transfers and taxes were taken into account (see UNICEF Canada, n.d.).

Rates of poverty are only part of the story in that the depth of poverty or poverty "gap," which is the amount of money required to bring people up to the poverty line, is important to consider. An additional factor is duration. It is much easier to cope with a temporary period of low income than a period of poverty that lasts years.

Welfare incomes can be used to illustrate the poverty gap. Comparisons made by Tweedle, Battle, and Torjman (2013) illustrate both the size of some of these gaps and the variations among provinces. For example, welfare incomes for single-parent households with a two-year-old child ranged from a low of $15,018 or 63 per cent of the AT-LICO in Manitoba to a high of $20,811 or 103 per cent of the AT-LICO in Newfoundland and Labrador.

Food insecurity is a major problem and the use of food banks is a reflection of inadequate social benefits, including welfare rates. More than 833,000 Canadians used food banks in March 2013, down somewhat from the previous year but up significantly from numbers reported just prior to the 2008 recession (*Winnipeg Free Press*, 2013).

Of course, poverty is about more than numbers. Stories about poverty vary a great deal and living in poverty is not only about hardship and despair but also about resilience, strength, and success. But too often the struggles against steep odds make it hard to get ahead, or even to remain at the same level of impoverishment, as the following excerpts from Fayant and Kerr (2007) demonstrate.

- You feel hungry all the time, depressed and tired like a car that ran out of gas. I don't feel good enough because I can't build energy. Your self-esteem is so low and my self-confidence because I can't provide food for my kids.
- My son was embarrassed that we used the food bank. He doesn't always understand there is little or no money. It affects my mood and my ability to sleep.
- I have worked all my life, 35 years and right now I'm injured and I can't work. . . . I am so disappointed at how life is here. I have lost my dignity having to get stuff from others.
- Once bills and rent were paid I think I had $30 for the month for groceries.

Inequality and Social Exclusion

An important factor to consider is the extent to which poverty leads to social exclusion, that is, the opportunities to participate in activities commonly available to citizens in an industrialized country like Canada. The effects of social exclusion include greater exposure to stressful environments and the inability to access adequate supports and services (Raphael, 2011). This understanding of poverty supports a relative approach to the definition and measurement of poverty, rather than a minimalist or absolute approach. In turn, a relative approach to poverty directs attention to income inequality and the underlying factors, including discrimination, that lead to social exclusion. The Conference Board of Canada (2013) notes that income inequality in Canada has grown over the past 20 years and that Canada now ranks 12th of 17 in income inequality among the wealthiest countries in the world with populations of more than one million and a land area of more than 10,000 square kilometres. Macdonald (2014), in a report completed for the Canadian Centre for Policy Alternatives (CCPA), reports that the richest 20 per cent of Canadian families capture about 50 per cent of all income and hold almost 70 per cent of all net worth. Increasingly, younger and middle-income earners are being held back, and all gains in income are being made by those at the top. Income disparity in Canada has not escaped the attention of the Organisation for Economic Co-operation and Development (OECD), which noted in a 2011 report that the average income for the highest 10 per cent of Canadians in 2008 was 10 times higher than that for the bottom 10 per cent, up from a ratio of 8 to 1 in the 1990s. The OECD also noted that the growth in income inequality was exacerbated by the fact that Canada spent less on cash benefits, such as unemployment and family benefits, than many other OECD countries. Although social spending helps to reduce extreme poverty and income inequality, the reduced effectiveness of social transfers and tax breaks for corporations and higher-income earners make matters worse. Unemployment and low-wage jobs are also contributing causes. As earlier noted, Canada's official unemployment rate was around 7 per cent in 2013–14.

However, this fails to capture the full extent of the problem in that unemployment rates for certain groups, including Aboriginal Canadians, those who are disabled, and youth, are much higher. In addition, these rates do not consider those working part-time who would prefer full-time work, nor do they consider those who have given up trying to find a job.

Although CEO compensation for Canada's largest companies does not tell the full story of inequality in Canada, it does serve to highlight the growing disparity between those at the top and the average wage earner (see Box 1.3).

As noted earlier, increased investment in poverty reduction has long-term benefits in reducing social costs associated with services, such as health care, crime control, and child maltreatment, directed towards those who are poor. More investment to reduce poverty is needed, and evidence of income and wealth inequality demonstrates that the more equitable distribution of resources could provide the means to support such investment.

Different perspectives on how to reduce poverty are summarized by Levitas (2005) as MUD, RED, and SID:

- The **moral underclass discourse** (MUD), advanced by groups such as the Fraser Institute in Canada, sees poverty as the responsibility of the individual who is poor because of a lack of motivation and moral fibre. This view of poverty suggests that what the poor need most is more hardship and more stigmatization— not improved opportunities or resources—to rise out of poverty.
- The **redistribution discourse** (RED) sees poverty as causing the exclusion of individuals from the economic and social resources required for meaningful participation in society. In this discourse, problems of poverty are not caused

---

Box **1.3** | Inequality and CEO Salaries

By 11:41 a.m. on 2 January 2014 the average top-paid Canadian CEO had earned as much as the average full-time worker's annual income for 2014. In 2013, the average compensation for Canada's top 100 CEOs was $9.21 million as compared with the average worker's salary of $47,358. Comparisons become even more outrageous if one compares CEO salaries to those of a minimum-wage worker, who earned an average of $21,216 a year in 2013. Between 2008 and 2013, salaries for the top-paid CEOs of companies trading on the Toronto Stock Exchange increased by 25 per cent (98 per cent if adjusted for inflation), yet over the same period an average worker's full-time salary increased by only 12 per cent (7 per cent if adjusted for inflation). The average compensation among the top 100 CEOs was a staggering 195 times the earnings of an average worker in 2013, up from 105 times in 1998. Topping the list was Gerald Schwartz, the CEO of Onex Corporation, at $87.9 million in 2013, including salary, stock options, and bonuses (Mackenzie, 2015).

by individual failings but by the failure of society to meet the needs of citizens. Proposed solutions include increased benefits, the reduction of inequality, and more opportunities for the excluded to be active participants in defining and realizing their rights.

- The **social integrationist discourse** (SID) recognizes the exclusion of individuals by virtue of living in poverty, but focuses solutions on integrating the non-working poor into the labour force. Although this strategy has some merit (e.g., provision of employment training opportunities), its policy manifestations in Canada have also included programs, such as workfare, where punitive provisions for non-participation have more in common with a MUD discourse on poverty. This discourse also pays less attention to the need to enhance income support benefits for the poor.

Poverty Reduction: Are We Making Any Progress?

As of 2013, poverty reduction plans were in place in nine provinces and territories, and two more were in the process of developing plans. Only Saskatchewan and BC lacked a plan. Social workers have been directly involved in developing poverty reduction strategies. Some specialized approaches to poverty reduction also show promise. One example is new investment in dealing with homelessness, where providing housing and a more co-ordinated approach to services demonstrate some early positive results (Paul, 2013; Turner, 2014).

Poverty reduction requires a comprehensive strategy that integrates a number of program responses. This reflects a social determinants of health approach (see Raphael, 2011) that recognizes factors supporting social inclusion, including education, employment, housing, income support, and special efforts to address barriers related to inequalities must be addressed to significantly reduce poverty. Although some of these factors, such as education, training, and employment supports, are included within the SID approach, these are inadequate as the only approach to poverty reduction. Quite simply, these strategies fail to account for the circumstances faced by those who cannot work or who work in jobs with poverty-level wages. Significant attention to providing increased benefits associated with the RED approach is required.

Reports on poverty reduction plans for Newfoundland and Labrador, New Brunswick, and Ontario show reductions in child poverty based on the LIM and MBM between 2006 and 2011, and all three of these provinces have poverty reduction plans (Statistics Canada, 2013a). Saskatchewan, which recorded a significant drop in child poverty between 2006 and 2011, and Alberta, which had the lowest poverty rate in the country in 2011, are anomalies in that poverty rates appear to have been influenced primarily by employment growth in the resource sectors rather than through a co-ordinated poverty reduction plan.

Provincial poverty reduction plans typically include some efforts to co-ordinate approaches across sectors as well as some combination of subsidies to low-income families and new programs or services. Ideally, a poverty reduction plan includes measurable targets and timelines, an accountability structure within government, and a public consultation and reporting protocol. For example, the 2008 target in Ontario was to reduce poverty by 25 per cent in five years. In some cases, clear targets and timelines have not been identified, and the absence of these weakens the accountability framework. In addition, because poverty reduction strategies typically roll together a number of government initiatives, it is sometimes hard to distinguish between programs that would have been implemented in the absence of an official poverty reduction strategy and the amount of new investment being allocated to poverty reduction.

Provincial efforts at poverty reduction are important, but only so much can be done without a more co-ordinated strategy between the federal and provincial/territorial governments. The federal government provides a number of benefit programs through the tax system, and enriching these would make a difference. One of the most important is the Canada Child Tax Benefit (CCTB). Improvements to this income-tested program were made in 1998, and incremental increases were phased in between 1998 and 2007. These were quite beneficial to low-income Canadians; however, the federal government turned its back on needed improvements to the program between 2007 and 2014. Instead, it opted for measures that are much less effective in addressing poverty, such as the non-refundable Child Tax Credit and the taxable Universal Child Care Benefit (UCCB). A number of organizations have called for improvements to the CCTB, and the Caledon Institute for Social Policy (Torjman and Battle, 2013) recommends that the base for the CCTB be raised so the combined payment for the basic allowance and the federal portion of the National Child Benefit Supplement is $5,400 per child.

Poverty reduction has also been adversely affected by federal changes to Employment Insurance and the inadequacy of the Guaranteed Income Supplement (GIS) for low-income seniors. Improvements to these programs are good social policies.

Summary and Conclusion

In this chapter foundational knowledge important to social policy analysis in Canada has been reviewed. An ideological framework that helps to identify different perspectives on social problems and their solutions was introduced. The connection between ideology and political action allows us to better understand the actions not only of government in enacting social policies but also of those who advocate for particular types of policies.

Neo-liberalism was defined and its connection to economic globalization described. Although the current realities imposed by globalization and the ascendancy of neo-liberalism pose challenges, important efforts are being made to respond to these developments, and these represent continuing opportunities for progressive changes.

Social policy reforms in Canada will remain modest unless the problem of poverty and inequality receives serious attention. Despite the growth of neo-liberalism, advocacy efforts have forced more attention on measures to address social problems, such as poverty and homelessness, and some promising directions in poverty reduction have been highlighted. Although it remains a challenge to convince governments to make new social investments in a political and social environment characterized by neo-liberalism, the long-term benefits in reduced social costs make this investment worthwhile. We could make a good start at new social investment if we were to forgo future tax cuts, impose even modest tax increases on those at the top, and redirect some funding from programs less effective in addressing poverty to those that are more effective.

Chapter 2 discusses policy-making structures within the federal and provincial levels of government and the role of the voluntary sector.

Critical Thinking Questions

1. Locate some recent policy-related statements made by your provincial government that may be available online or in newspapers. Based on the ideological perspectives identified in the first part of this chapter, what ideological perspective(s) are represented in these statements?
2. What are the main features of neo-liberalism outlined in this chapter? What is your critique of neo-liberalism?
3. What are the benefits and costs of globalization for Canada? Can you identify any strategies that might help reduce the adverse effects from the neo-liberal model of globalization?
4. Determine whether your province or territory has a poverty reduction plan. If so, does the plan include specific targets for poverty reduction and timelines? What approach does it use for reporting results? If your province or territory does not have a poverty reduction plan, select one that does and answer the above questions for that jurisdiction.

Recommended Reading

Canadian Centre for Policy Alternatives website, at www.policyalternatives.ca. The Canadian Centre for Policy Alternatives offers useful reports and information on poverty, inequality, and other social policy issues from a progressive standpoint.

P. Krugman. *End This Depression Now*. New York: W.W. Norton, 2012. Although focused on the US, this book provides a very readable account of why the neo-liberal return to austerity is the wrong path to take in responding to the global recession triggered in 2008.

J.J. Rice and M.J. Prince. *Changing Politics in Canadian Social Policy*, 2nd edn. Toronto: University of Toronto Press, 2013. Rice and Prince provide an advanced discussion of competing policy orientations in Canada with special attention to the influence of neo-liberalism.

J. Stanford. *Economics for Everyone: A Short Guide to the Economics of Capitalism.* Halifax: Fernwood and the Canadian Centre for Policy Alternatives, 2008. This primer on the Canadian economic system in an era of globalization is both pragmatic and idealistic.

Notes

1. A variety of Internet sources provide a more detailed description of the causes and consequences of the 2008 economic recession. Although you may begin with information provided in Wikipedia, other sources, such as Krugman (2012) and Ivry (2014), provide useful insight. For a brief summary, see *The Economist*, "Crash Course: The Origins of the Financial Crisis," 7 Sept. 2013, at: www.economist.com/news/schoolsbrief/21584534-effects-financial-crisis-are-still-being-felt-five-years-article.

2. More details on the calculation of the Statistics Canada low-income measures can be obtained by searching Statistics Canada using the title for each measure. Information on the Sarlo Basic Needs measure can be obtained from the Fraser Institute: www.fraserinstitute.org.

2

Making Social Policy in Canada: Structures and Processes

Brad McKenzie and Pete Hudson*

─────────────── • **In this chapter you will learn about:** • ───────────────

- the general policy-making structures of the Canadian federal government;
- common policy-making processes at the provincial government level;
- the role of the voluntary sector in policy-making in the human services.

···

Introduction

This chapter identifies major policy-making structures and processes at the federal and provincial levels of government. These two levels of government are particularly important to the development of social policies; however, the role of third-level governance structures such as cities, towns, municipalities, and First Nations band councils should not be entirely dismissed. Third-level structures can often develop or influence policies related to recreation, housing and urban renewal, responses to policing and crime, and bylaws related to such issues as smoking. As well, local and regional governance structures in First Nations communities have significant influence in the development of human service programs in their communities. As we move down the policy-making ladder we see how policies and programs designed and implemented at the local and regional level have a significant impact on service users. We can operationally define the organizational level to include private and non-profit organizations in the non-government sector, faith communities, and government organizations at the service delivery level. Although the latter group of organizations is a part of government, they are some distance from the central policy-making apparatus and maintain some degree of control over elements of the policy-making agenda. Within the

───────────────
* Pete Hudson is Senior Scholar, Faculty of Social Work, University of Manitoba.

non-government sector, non-profit organizations (often referred to in the human services as the voluntary sector or non-government organizations [NGOs]) provide a wide range of services, including those mandated by legislation and funded primarily by government. The degree of autonomy within this sector varies considerably depending on the type of service, whether or not the mandate for service is delegated from government, and the nature of accountability mechanisms that exist between the agency and government. In general, the voluntary sector plays a more prominent role in the human services than third-level government structures. This sector and its potential to connect policy to practice are examined in the third section of this chapter.

Social Policy and the Federal Government

Constitutional Issues and the Division of Powers

The federal government's role in social policy is somewhat overshadowed by the role of provincial governments. This is a function of arrangements established in the Constitution Act, 1867 (formerly the British North America Act), which ceded most responsibility for local affairs, including the delivery of health and social services, to the provinces. The Canadian Constitution comprises a number of documents and Acts but the primary sections dealing with the division of powers are sections 91, 92, and 93 of the Constitution Act, 1867. Section 91 sets out the major responsibilities of the federal government, including primary responsibility for taxation and laws related to peace, order, and good government, trade and commerce, banking, and defence. The federal government also has primary responsibility for funding for First Nations people (the term "Indians" is used in the Constitution Act, 1867), particularly those living on reserves, the Inuit, and others who qualify for services under the Indian Act. Section 92 outlines areas of provincial jurisdiction, including local works and undertakings, property and civil rights, the administration of justice, hospitals and health care, municipal affairs, and direct taxation within provinces. Section 93 gives jurisdiction over education to the provinces. Although 29 enumerated federal powers are listed in the Constitution Act, 1867, residual powers were left to the federal government. Coupled with primary control over taxation and laws that permitted the federal government to overrule the provinces on matters deemed to be of national interest, a strong central government was assured at the time of Confederation. Although the delivery of health and social services remained a provincial area of responsibility, state involvement in social welfare was relatively minor at the nation-building stage. Thus, these powers were regarded as relatively inconsequential in 1867.

Over time the involvement of both levels of government in social policy has increased. First, the nature and scope of services provided for health, education, and social welfare have grown, and the costs of these services have increased accordingly. Regional differences and the federal government's central role in revenue generation have required the federal government to play a significant role in funding these services. Although the federal government directly funds several national income support programs, it also provides resources to the provinces through three major fiscal transfer programs. One is the transfer of funds to provinces for health care (the Canada Health Transfer); the second is for social services and post-secondary education (the Canada Social Transfer); and the third is equalization payments that can be used for a broader range of public services. There are also other smaller but not insignificant transfers. Fiscal transfers are a significant source of revenue for many provinces—in 2009–10, transfers amounted to about 19 per cent of all provincial spending (Graham et al., 2012: 51). Amounts vary by province and are especially significant for less wealthy provinces. The principle of cost-shared services for health, social services, and post-secondary education, as well as for a broader range of public services, is a central feature of Canada's federated structure. Federal funding for the human services accelerated after the provinces' inability to respond adequately to the needs of its citizens during the Great Depression, and the recognition that federal government involvement was required to implement the welfare state reforms that emerged after World War II.

The federal government's role in social policy has been established through several methods. In some situations, as in the case of Employment Insurance (EI), this responsibility has been added to the list of federal powers; in other circumstances (e.g., Old Age pensions), the concurrent power of both levels of government has been recognized. Shared-cost programs, where the federal government provides some funding but leaves service delivery to the provinces, were established for post-secondary education in 1952, hospital insurance in 1957, and medical insurance in 1968. Within the social services the most significant shared-cost program was the 1966 Canada Assistance Plan (CAP), described in Chapter 1, which provided federal funding for certain social services, such as child welfare and income assistance (welfare) on a 50–50 cost-shared basis until 1996. Over time the federal government has expanded the use of the tax system to provide a number of benefits to both low-income Canadians (e.g., Canada Child Tax Benefit) and those with higher levels of income (e.g., Registered Retirement Savings and investment tax credit programs). There has also been an increase in the use of the tax system to distribute benefits by provincial governments.

Despite the growth in the federal government's role in social policy, countervailing forces have promoted greater provincial autonomy. Jurisdictional challenges have been raised by many provinces, but Quebec has been the most vocal in asserting provincial rights. The assertion of provincial jurisdiction led to the Established Programs Act in 1965, which allowed provinces to opt out of conditional grant programs and continue to receive federal funding as long as they offered equivalent programs (Dyck, 2004). In addition, the ideological orientations of some federal governments, particularly in the neo-liberal era since the 1980s, at times have favoured the transfer of more responsibility to the provinces, often with some concurrent responsibilities for funding.

Cost-sharing arrangements have been a constant source of conflict between the provinces and the federal government. For example, when health insurance payments were transferred from a conditional grant to a block grant under the Established

Programs Financing Act in 1977, the federal government's contribution levels were no longer guaranteed at 50 per cent. Further federal cuts occurred during the deficit-cutting era of the 1990s as social spending became a convenient, but unwarranted, target for cost-cutting. When CAP was phased out in 1996, all funding for post-secondary education, health, and the social services was combined under one block grant, known as the Canada Health and Social Transfer (CHST). The 1995 budget also included reductions in transfers to the provinces of $7 billion over three years for these programs (Finkel, 2006: 292). Although the provision of a block grant for health, post-secondary education, and social services provided the provinces with greater flexibility in how the money could be used, the reduced proportion of costs covered by the federal government meant that health care often emerged as the priority for expenditures. Concerns about the allocation of federal funding between sectors led to the division of the CHST into the Canada Health Transfer and the Canada Social Transfer in 2004.

Although some of the federal cuts to transfers for the human services were restored after 1996–7, the replacement of CAP with a block grant arrangement enabled the federal government to gain more control over its own spending on the social services. For example, it was no longer obligated to meet half the costs of programs established by the provinces; instead, it could unilaterally cap its transfers for such programs to the provinces. This change gave it more flexibility to reduce these expenditures and target some of the savings to new initiatives for the increased political capital that comes from newly announced expenditures. Cost-sharing arrangements between the federal and provincial governments are a frequent source of tension, and ongoing efforts to develop a more collaborative approach to resolving these issues have had mixed success.

The Federal Policy-Making Apparatus

All organizations create formal mechanisms—referred to here as "structures"—for developing policies. Here we examine the general structures at the federal level. Although many of these structures, including the role of Parliament, remain somewhat impervious to change, the governing party may alter the approach to governing, including the number and role of committee structures inside government, in ways that can have significant effects on how policy-making processes are carried out. In addition, the roles of the Prime Minister and cabinet are influenced by those occupying these positions. For example, the degree of centralized control exercised by the Prime Minister (PM) over policy-making increased during the Chrétien years and this control, even over the role of ministers in dealing with the media, was extended even further after Prime Minister Harper and the Conservatives came to power in 2006.

Canada's governmental model can be described as a constitutional monarchy with operating principles based on the **Westminster model**, as established in Great Britain. Based on this model, immense power is placed in the hands of the executive branch (i.e., the Prime Minister and cabinet). The two other branches of government are the legislative branch (i.e., Parliament consisting of the House of Commons and the Senate at the federal level, and legislative assemblies at the provincial level) and the judiciary. The Prime Minister and cabinet have considerable freedom to govern, and party discipline, which is the expectation that all members of a party caucus will vote as a bloc, particularly on matters of confidence, normally ensures the passage of legislation when the government holds the majority of seats in the House of Commons. When there is a minority government, this outcome is less certain and the defeat of the government on matters of confidence such as the Throne Speech, the budget, legislative changes, or motions of non-confidence will bring down the government. The command-and-control nature of party discipline, which pressures members to vote with their party regardless of their views or those of their constituents, is more evident in Canada than in many other countries (Loat and MacMillan, 2014). The result is a decline in parliamentary democracy, which extends beyond voting along party lines to include restrictions on members, imposed by party leaders, that all public comments conform to party policy.

There are a number of independent officers of the House of Commons, including the Speaker, the Clerk, and the Chief Electoral Officer, but the most important of these is the Auditor General (the provincial counterpart is the Provincial Auditor). The Auditor General plays an important role in reviewing public spending and management, but the office also undertakes special investigations of funding relative to such things as policy compliance, value for money, and adequacy of funding.

Although the Senate is part of the legislative branch because it must approve new legislation, it plays a relatively minor role in government. It was originally designed to reflect regional interests by including 24 seats each for Ontario, Quebec, and the three Maritime provinces of Nova Scotia, Prince Edward Island, and New Brunswick (and 24 seats were later added for the four western provinces, then six seats for Newfoundland, and one for each territory). Despite repeated calls for reform, it has become largely a location for patronage appointments by the Prime Minister. Occasionally the Senate exercises its power to obstruct or delay the government's legislation, and it has sponsored useful inquiries into a variety of policy issues, including studies of poverty, public health-care provision, and children affected by separation and divorce.

The Queen's representative in Canada is the Governor General, and this role is exercised by lieutenant-governors at the provincial level. Even though these individuals represent the Queen, appointments are made by the federal government. These representatives formally assent to laws passed by the legislative branch, dissolve Parliament or provincial legislatures to call elections, and perform tasks such as reading the annual Speech from the Throne, the government's statement on the state of the nation and its policy and legislative intentions for the coming year.

The judicial branch, which includes both provincial and federal courts, is the third branch of government. At the federal level, the courts making up this branch include the Federal Court of Canada, with two branches, the Federal Court (Trial Division) and the Federal Court of Appeal; the Tax Court of Canada, which deals with tax disputes involving the federal government; and the Supreme Court of Canada. The most important of these is the Supreme Court. Federal courts deal with two general types of disputes. First are those related to constitutional law, and these may include matters related to the Constitution or appeals by citizens under the Charter of Rights and Freedoms, which is part of the Constitution Act, 1982. Such issues are dealt with primarily by the Supreme Court at the federal level, and decisions at the provincial level may be appealed to the Supreme Court. Second, the judicial branch is also concerned with administrative law, that is, whether federal policy regulations are being followed and whether these have been applied in a fair and consistent manner.

The Charter of Rights and Freedoms and the Human Rights Act

The Canadian Charter of Rights and Freedoms has social policy implications because of the nature and scope of rights it enumerates. These include fundamental freedoms, democratic rights, mobility rights, legal rights, equality rights, and language rights.

The equality and mobility rights in the Charter are particularly important to social policy, and the Supreme Court is the ultimate body that interprets Charter challenges. Decisions based on challenges to the Charter have clarified a number of rights for Canadians, including increased rights pertaining to sexual orientation, the decriminalization of abortion, and certain economic rights for women. The Supreme Court's rulings can clarify how rights are to be interpreted, but the Court may often do so in a manner that defers responsibility for corrective legislation to government. One example of this occurred in 2004. By conveying a message that the failure to pass legislation legalizing marriages between same-sex couples could contravene the Charter and that the federal government had jurisdiction to deal with this matter, Parliament was encouraged to pass the Civil Marriage Act in 2005 permitting legal marriages between same-sex partners. A second example concerns the 2013 decision by the Supreme Court to strike down current prostitution laws prohibiting street soliciting, brothels, and people living off the avails of prostitution because such laws increase dangers to vulnerable women and therefore violate basic Canadian values (Fine, 2013). This ruling did not legalize prostitution in Canada; instead, the Supreme Court gave Parliament a year to respond with new laws to ensure the safety of those involved in sex work. Although new legislation was passed in November 2014, the new law has been criticized because it is unlikely to protect those engaged in prostitution who are most vulnerable.

Although the Charter is a major social policy instrument in Canadian society, it is not without its critics. For example, a number of Charter challenges, including one to prohibit the corporal punishment of children, have failed, and some regard the Supreme Court as too conservative in its thinking about certain issues. Others have voiced criticism of the Charter's provisions because they focus too much on individual rights to the exclusion of social and group rights, such as the right of unions to strike and the right to health care. Finally, there are criticisms that Charter challenges are too easily used as a way of circumventing the power of government to set policy on certain issues. The latter criticism reflects a view that justices of the Supreme Court are not accountable to the public for their decisions, and therefore should not be permitted to use their interpretive powers to broaden the scope of certain provisions that may effectively create new policies.

Individuals or groups may also file complaints of discrimination based on prohibited grounds such as sex, disability, or religion under the Human Rights Act. Although the Act is applicable throughout Canada, it applies only to federally regulated activities; provinces have their own human rights legislation for matters related to provincial jurisdiction. At the federal level, the Human Rights Act established a Human Rights Commission that investigates claims of discrimination and tribunals to judge cases. Before a case is brought to a tribunal it must go through several stages of investigation and attempted resolution. Failing resolution at these stages, it may be referred to a tribunal.

Power within Government

The Prime Minister's influence over government is significant because of the powers attached to this office. For example, the PM makes all appointments to cabinet, the Senate, and other senior-level posts in government, including the Bank of Canada. There are between 20 and 30 ministers in a typical cabinet, and about 10 junior ministers or secretaries of state whose responsibilities lie within the portfolio of another minister.

The committee structure within the executive branch is of particular importance to the exercise of power. Government committee structures can vary but several core committees play key roles. In the 2015 Harper government, a central committee, identified as the Priorities and Planning Committee and chaired by the Prime Minister, provide strategic direction on government priorities. Ministers who were members of this committee operated somewhat like an inner cabinet in determining overall government priorities. The Treasury Board in all governments has a great deal of influence over expenditures and is supported by a highly specialized bureaucracy known as the Treasury Board Secretariat.

Other key committees in the Harper government in 2015 included Operations, Foreign Affairs and Security, Economic Prosperity and Sustainable Growth, and Social Affairs. Executive support to cabinet is provided by the Privy Council Office (PCO), and the Clerk of the Privy Council is the top civil servant. This individual acts as the secretary to cabinet and occupies a role somewhat like a deputy minister to the Prime Minister. The Prime Minister's Office (PMO) is a very important centre of power. Unlike the PCO, which is composed of civil servants, the PMO is made up of appointees selected because of their loyalty to the PM. They provide ongoing advice to the PM, and manage communications and media relations. Central agencies like the PCO, the PMO, the Treasury Board, and the Department of Finance overshadow the role of cabinet in policy-making and exert significant influence over the general direction of government policy at the federal level. Although cabinet used to have a central role in setting policy directions, strategic decision-making more often occurs now within committees of cabinet or through direct control by the Prime Minister. The centralization of control extends to the management of government communications, a pattern that became particularly apparent with the Harper Conservative government.

The centralization of power within the PMO, where the Chief of Staff plays a key decision-making role, has been a trend that has expanded over several decades, and it has been accompanied by a hollowing out of policy-making autonomy within ministries. This more closed decision-making model is also affected by the personality of the Prime Minister, and Prime Minister Stephen Harper has always exercised a high degree of control over government actions. Some observers defend greater centralization as important in managing the complex nature of policy responses in a world characterized by increased corporate power and the realities of globalization. Even if there is some truth to such arguments, there are related costs. Centralization is often accompanied by lower levels of transparency and limited participation by other members in government, those in the bureaucracy, and the general public. Meaningful inputs from this broader range of potential actors are often denied or marginalized, leading to questionable policy outcomes and growing public alienation regarding the political process. When these patterns occur, the centralization of power becomes more about gaining and maintaining control than achieving increased effectiveness and efficiency.

The Bureaucracy and Influences External to Government

There are two other important influences on policy-making. First, significant policy-making still occurs at the departmental level or across departments. Thus, the bureaucracy, as discussed later in this chapter, remains a very important aspect of the policy-making apparatus. Second, groups external to government seek to exert influence on policy. These include interest groups, such as social movements, policy communities, and think-tanks (see Box 2.1). As noted, there is some overlap between these types of groups. The most powerful interest group is the Canadian Council of Chief Executives (CCCE). Composed of CEOs of about 150 of Canada's major corporations, this group lobbies government to adopt business-friendly policies, and often participates directly with government in shaping national and international policy responses. The importance of these structures to policy-making is discussed in more depth in Chapter 7.

Social Policy and the Provincial Government

Key Policy-Making Structures at the Provincial and Territorial Level

The dominant role of provincial and territorial governments in the development of social policy requires us to pay particular attention to this level of government. These

Box **2.1** | Common Types of Interest Groups and Their Definitions

1. An **interest or advocacy group** is broadly defined as any group that seeks to influence policy development, primarily with government, without contesting an election.

2. **Social movements** are informal networks or coalitions of organizations and/or interest groups that, on the basis of a collective identity and shared values on a policy issue, engage in political or social action to bring about some change within society or government.

3. **Policy communities or networks** are loosely knit groups of individuals knowledgeable about a particular public policy topic or area. Their goal is similar to that of social movements, but their structure often includes representatives from government agencies as well as interest groups and other organizations with a particular interest in the policy topic. Policy communities attempt to gain recognition of a particular policy problem and seek to co-ordinate advocacy efforts for solutions (e.g., Campaign 2000 and efforts to address poverty).

4. **Think-tanks** are policy research and advocacy organizations, normally incorporated as non-profit organizations that focus on a broad range of public policy issues. Some think-tanks claim to offer objective research evidence whereas others incorporate a specific advocacy stance in disseminating information. Examples include the Conference Board of Canada, the Canadian Council on Social Development, the Caledon Institute of Social Policy, the Fraser Institute, and the Canadian Centre for Policy Alternatives.

governments are unicameral in that there is no additional branch of the legislature, such as a Senate, as is the case at the federal level. As earlier noted, a Lieutenant-Governor is appointed as the Queen's representative at the provincial level, and this individual performs functions similar to those of the Governor General at the national level.

Although the provinces and Yukon Territory form governments based on the political party system, Nunavut and the Northwest Territories (NWT) have adopted a more consensus style of government intended to be more consistent with the culture of Indigenous peoples, which make up the majority of the population in these territories. In these two territories, members of the Legislative Assembly (MLAs) are elected by those living in their constituencies as independent representatives without any political party affiliation. Once elected, MLAs meet to select a Speaker, Premier, and ministers. Although a ministerial portfolio can be removed by the Premier, a vote in the Legislative Assembly is required to remove an individual from cabinet. Decisions can be made by a majority vote; however, efforts are made to achieve unanimity in passing bills and other matters before the Legislative Assembly in Nunavut and the NWT.

Although structures such as cabinet committees vary somewhat from province to province, the process of policy-making within different provincial and territorial governments is quite similar. We draw on examples from Manitoba and Ontario to illustrate these structures, but readers from other jurisdictions are encouraged to familiarize themselves with the government policy-making structures in their province or territory. Generally, the term "provincial" is used in the following discussion to include territorial governments.

The Premier and cabinet comprise the executive branch at the provincial level. At the federal level, the importance of the PMO was noted, and provincial premiers will have a staff complement headed by someone who occupies the role of Chief of Staff. The Premier and his or her Chief of Staff exert significant control over policy issues that are politically sensitive.

As is the case with the federal government, a key standing committee in provincial governments is the Treasury Board. Once initiatives have been approved by cabinet or a committee of cabinet, this committee reviews and makes recommendations on all new initiatives, particularly those involving new expenditures. Treasury Board's role in decision-making focuses primarily on the implications for expenditures, and analysts with Treasury Board play a key role in reviewing all submissions, and referring these back for revisions, if required. The process of approving a new initiative by Treasury Board can often take considerable time, and this is exacerbated if Treasury Board tries to micromanage the development of new policies. If this posture is assumed, proposals may be repeatedly referred back to departments or committees for more information.

Most provincial governments use committees of cabinet to co-ordinate the government policy-making process across ministries or departments. For example, in Ontario in 2011, besides the Priorities and Planning Board, there were two major policy committees—Health, Education and Social Policy, and Jobs and Economic Policy. These two policy committees reflect the general distinction between social and economic policy, a pattern common to many provincial governments. The Priorities and Planning Board, composed of the most influential ministers in cabinet, was directly accountable to the Premier. It functioned like an executive committee in determining major government policy directions.

An increasingly important function to all governments is a mechanism to manage information and communication flow with the public. This may be led by the staff within the Premier's office, and departments will also have their own information officers. Communications staff work directly with ministers to put a positive spin on government initiatives in a manner designed to connect with the public. Government is an important source of policy information, but announcements of new initiatives and government publicity on programs must be critically assessed to ascertain the true significance of new announcements.

Governments are often slow in adopting major innovations in social policy, and new policies are prompted by initiatives that originate in the non-governmental social service sector or through the advocacy efforts of policy networks and lobby groups. There are several reasons for this. First, government is risk-averse; it always has one eye on how the public will react and how this might "play out" in the next election. Because

new social policies generally require new public spending, there may often be significant resistance to new expenditures, particularly from those favouring a more residual
response to social problems. Second, government operates like a bureaucratic machine
with layers of decision-making structures, each with its own set of requirements that
serve to slow down the policy-making process. Finally, the financial resources available
to government are often more restricted than it might appear. For example, the ongoing
operations of government departments leave relatively small amounts for new initiatives
unless there are new sources of revenue. While internal reallocation or expenditure cuts
can increase the amount of resources available for new investments somewhat, there is
always intense competition among departments for new money. Despite restrictions in
resources and the competing demands for these resources, provincial governments play
a very important role in policy-making in the human services.

Within government, individual ministers may have significant influence over matters in their own departments; however, their influence over general government policy
is much more circumscribed. General government policy is more likely to be heavily
influenced by the Premier, senior staff, and a few key ministers. And although other
elected members from the government party may be appointed to provide some support to cabinet ministers with larger portfolios, similar to the pattern of junior ministers within the federal government, elected members who are not members of cabinet
have limited influence.

The drift to centralization in provincial policy-making may be more nuanced than
at the federal level but it is apparent here as well. Some of this shift is defended as
necessary to co-ordinate policy analysis and strategic planning. Nonetheless, this shift
in power to the Premier, an inner circle of ministers, and non-elected political aides
involves a reduced role for cabinet, which becomes more of a vehicle to implement the
main objectives of government than a source of new policy-making. This trend makes
inclusive policy-making, one of the themes of this book, more difficult to implement.

In a study of centralization in the Ontario government, Desimini (2011) examined
the styles of different governments in the province through key informant interviews.
She reported variations in the number of cabinet committees and degree of centralized
power exercised by the Premier, but there was a continuing trend to centralization during a period of time that featured Liberal, NDP, and Conservative governments. Several
findings from this study are of interest. First, centralization was associated with the
under-utilization of talents of less powerful ministers and members of caucus. Second,
centralization appeared to reduce the level of debate and opportunities to express more
critical views on more centrally orchestrated policy proposals within the government.
Third, the degree of autonomy reported by ministers varied. Some, who enjoyed a more
personal, trusting relationship with the Premier, felt less constrained whereas others
felt more disengaged and somewhat marginalized. Finally, a commonly voiced concern
was raised about party discipline, which requires all government MLAs to support government policy. This, and the ability of the Premier to confer or withhold favourable
appointments, tended to reduce dissent and debate, even within meetings of the caucus,

cabinet, or committees, thus constraining the ability of members to represent the needs and views of their constituents.

How New Policies Are Developed Inside Government

New policies are developed in response to at least some of the problems that land on the government agenda. This agenda is shaped by issues that arise from the cycle of government planning or the influence of interest groups. Issues that appear on the government's agenda may be foreshadowed in items such as departmental priorities, the Throne Speech, or the budget. In these circumstances, policy windows or opportunities for new initiatives may exist. Policy windows can also be triggered by unexpected events such as a crisis or the exposure of an issue by the media or pressure groups.

Developing policies in response to policy windows has become increasingly complex as governments engage in efforts to co-ordinate policies across departments or with other levels of government. Policy specialists with knowledge of and experience with the policy environment play an important role in determining the success of these endeavours. Some of these specialists are located in policy and planning branches of departments, and they are instrumental in generating planning options and advising the departmental minister; however, other specialists may be located within interdepartmental or cabinet committees. Three different types of policy-making within government are identified here. Although these general types may oversimplify the policy-making process somewhat, they illustrate the different pathways that may cause a policy issue to become a priority for government action.

One type of policy-making is confined to the bureaucratic structures of the department, and emerges as a result of information generated by the normal operating phases of a department. Many activities carried out at the departmental level will receive only limited attention from the minister. For example, new policy directives, regulations, policy manuals, and protocols for service delivery may be established within departments without any significant discussion at the ministerial level and without ever entering the radar screen of cabinet. In other cases, such as significant over-expenditures in a program area, matters will be referred to the minister and, if required, to more senior levels within government.

A second type of policy-making involves issues that require political attention. An issue may come to the attention of the department because of external pressure or because it has been referred to the department by another level of government. Departments of government are usually composed of divisions (program areas) that might be headed by assistant deputy ministers. These individuals are accountable to a deputy minister, who is the chief staff member to the minister. Detailed policy changes may be developed by staff within program divisions. For example, an income assistance division might draft policies related to a change in eligibility requirements for social assistance. These might then be forwarded to a senior departmental level, such

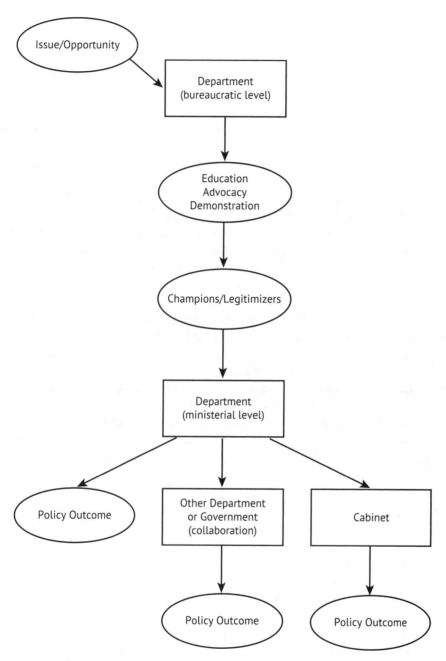

Figure **2.1** Government Policy Process in Response to an Issue Beginning at the Department Level

as a policy and planning branch, which undertakes further development and reports directly to the deputy minister and minister.

If a new issue or opportunity emerges and becomes a policy priority for government, a process like that depicted in Figure 2.1 may unfold. At an early stage, there may be efforts to educate others about the need for a policy response or to advocate for a particular solution. In some cases, research may be undertaken or a demonstration project may be launched. If the need for a particular policy response is substantiated, it will be brought forward to the political level of the department (i.e., the minister) by champions and/or legitimizers who try to establish the credibility of a recommended policy response. Policy champions and legitimizers may be from inside government, from outside government, or a combination of insiders and outsiders. If the minister is convinced that a policy response is required, three possible actions may be taken. First, where the minister has the required authority s/he will initiate the policy response leading to an outcome. Second, if approval for a policy response must come from central government, then the matter will be referred to cabinet. Third, in some cases collaboration with other departments or governments may be required. While collaboration with another department may be initiated by the minister directly, cabinet may also demand this. Collaborative efforts with other levels of government are usually sanctioned by cabinet or the Premier's office, and will often involve activities by one of the standing committees of cabinet.

The third type of policy-making within government unfolds more directly at the political level (i.e., cabinet). In this case an issue or opportunity is viewed as important enough to require the immediate attention of cabinet, a number of departments, and staff from the central government secretariat. Policy issues here may have originated from party policy, electoral commitments, special commissions, or interest group pressure. In such instances policy is led by central government (cabinet, the Premier's office, and related staff), which assumes the role of the policy-making authority even though matters may be referred back to various departments for action. As indicated in Figure 2.2, policy is co-ordinated from the centre in these circumstances. One example was the development of the Aboriginal Justice Inquiry–Child Welfare Initiative in Manitoba. This initiative, which was pursued from 2003 to 2005, involved the transfer of responsibility for all child welfare services provided to Aboriginal people in the province to newly created Aboriginal authorities. Because the implications of such a shift in policy transcended several departments and the issue was politically sensitive, the government's general response was developed centrally with more specific actions assigned primarily to the department responsible for child welfare services.

Policies that require only cabinet approval are referred to as Orders-in-Council, whereas the budget and changes in legislation require the approval of the Legislative Assembly. Quite often, governments try to shift the authority for making decisions from the legislature to cabinet to avoid public and opposition scrutiny of controversial issues. Although this may enable government to manage sensitive issues more effectively, it

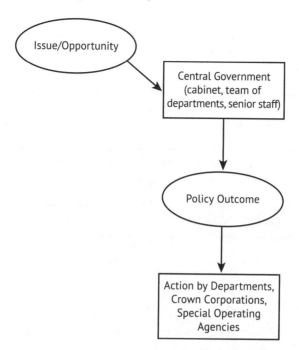

Figure **2.2** | Government Policy Process in Response to an Issue Beginning with Central Government

often contributes to a policy-making process that contradicts the essential principles of transparency and accountability.

The Canadian parliamentary system has a well-entrenched protocol that must be followed when changes in legislation are required, and these processes are similar at both the federal and provincial levels of government. Although bills may be introduced by any member of the legislature, private member bills require unanimous approval if they are to be further considered. Because this occurs only on rare occasions, most changes to existing legislation or new bills are introduced by government through the respective ministers responsible for the policy issue being considered.

Legislation is normally introduced into the legislature in the form of public bills. These bills result from a process that includes policy review and development, the minister's approval, cabinet approval, the drafting of the bill, and detailed approval of the bill for introduction to the legislature by cabinet or a committee of government (see Figure 2.3). Once a government bill is introduced to the legislature, government members are expected to support the bill, thus ensuring its passage if the governing party holds a majority of seats.

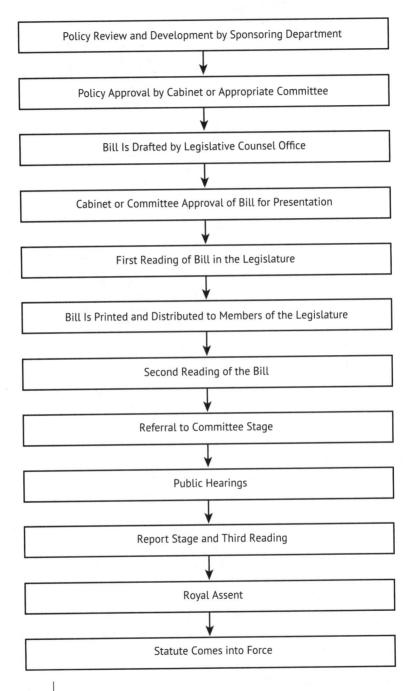

Figure **2.3**   How a Government Bill Becomes Law

The minister's first introduction of a new bill is known as "first reading." Although the minister may give a brief explanation of the purpose of the bill at first reading and provide background information, no detailed statement is given and debate is not permitted at this stage. The vote that takes place on first reading simply signifies the approval of the House to consider the bill and to approve printing. The bill is then printed and distributed to all members of the legislature.

"Second reading" normally cannot occur until at least two days after the bill has been distributed. Second reading begins with the sponsoring minister making a motion that the bill be given second reading, making a speech to explain the bill, and opening debate. Any member of the legislature may speak on the bill during debate, which at second reading is generally confined to the basic principles of the bill rather than specific provisions, and amendments are not introduced at this stage.

After second reading the bill is normally referred to a standing or special committee for review. This review stage may be avoided if there is unanimous consent that it may be referred for third reading. On rare occasions, such as when emergency legislation is being considered, the bill may be simply referred to the Committee of the Whole (i.e., the legislature). In addition, supply bills and taxation bills are also considered in Committee of the Whole rather than by a standing or special committee. Both government and opposition members sit on standing and special committees. The sponsoring minister of a bill is normally a member of the committee and departmental officials may sit with the minister to provide advice. The purpose of the committee stage is to consider details of the bill and to propose any amendments to its various sections. This stage also allows members of the committee to receive representation from the public. Following public presentations, the bill is considered "clause by clause" by the committee. Each clause is voted on, and it is at this stage that amendments can be moved by the minister and by opposition members.

On completion of the committee review, the chairperson of the committee reports to the legislature on the committee's deliberations, including any proposed amendments. Following adoption of the committee report the bill is presented for third reading. At this stage further debate may occur. The normal rules of debate prevail and motions to amend legislation may occur at this stage. On particularly controversial legislation, the opposition may choose to continue debating the matter for some time. In some cases this reflects a strategy to mobilize public opinion against the legislation, but it also slows down the government's ability to move forward on other legislative matters. When debate concludes, a motion to approve the bill occurs. If the motion passes, it is presented to the Lieutenant-Governor for royal assent. The bill has the force of law once it is given royal assent unless it contains a provision that indicates it comes into force on a specified date or on a date fixed by proclamation. In some cases, certain sections of the bill may come into force at different dates. Implementation is commonly delayed for the development of new regulations, forms, and procedures that may be required.

Proposals for major changes to draft legislation or policies of government are often difficult to change. However, the combined efforts of opposition parties and public campaigns can sometimes lead to changes, even when the government holds the majority of seats. A federal example helps to illustrate such a shift, although in this case the government did not hold the majority of seats in Parliament. In December 2008, the minority government led by Stephen Harper presented an economic update to Parliament that promised a balanced budget and failed to include an adequate economic stimulus plan to counter the recessionary trends apparent in the economy at that time. This neo-liberal stance was roundly condemned by economists, industry, labour, and the opposition parties, and it almost led to the government's defeat. Within two weeks the government had changed its tune, and the Minister of Finance said he would do everything necessary to stimulate the economy and that this would lead to a significant operating deficit in fiscal year 2009–10.

On occasion, a government with a cause may pursue a particular policy agenda even if there may be significant political costs to bear. This approach reflects political will, defined here as the willingness of a government to take significant risks with public opinion by developing a policy response in conditions of uncertainty or where there is a strong ideological commitment to action. Political will can lead one government to follow a social justice agenda and restore welfare benefits to recipients who are unable to live with dignity on existing allowances. Conversely, a neo-liberal government may impose severe cutbacks despite the likelihood of widespread public resistance.

Social Policy and the Voluntary Sector

In this section we consider the characteristics of the voluntary sector, some of the challenges affecting policy-making in this sector, and the potential to connect policy to practice in this sector in ways that support innovation and social change.

Defining the Voluntary Sector

The terms **not-for-profit (NFP) sector**, non-profit sector, and **voluntary sector** are frequently used interchangeably. However, the term "voluntary sector" is defined here as a subset of the NFP sector that is primarily concerned with social policy and the delivery of social welfare services. Because the larger NFP sector rarely separates out the voluntary sector, the characteristics of the voluntary sector must often be estimated from what is known about the NFP sector as a whole.

The defining characteristic of all registered NFP organizations is that they are governed by citizen boards of directors. Within NFP organizations there are also prescribed forms of annual reporting (e.g., audits).

A number of NFP organizations are informal in that they are just a loosely knit group of citizens who have come together for some common purpose, but who have not bothered to register with their province of residence. Although many NFP organizations begin in this way, most move quickly to formally incorporate as NFP organizations in accordance with the provisions of the relevant province. Many take a second step, which is to apply for, and achieve, the status of a registered charity. This is a federal government matter administered by a branch within the Canada Revenue Agency. All charities are NFP organizations but not all NFP organizations are charities.

The NFP sector in Canada has not been well researched, an omission that is just beginning to be addressed. Recent estimates, which exclude hospitals, universities, colleges, and religious organizations, identify nearly 60,000 NFP organizations in Canada with a workforce of 1.2 million (Human Resources Council on the Nonprofit Sector, 2012). One of the difficulties in studying the sector is its diversity. It includes organizations concerned about sports, the environment, culture, international aid, health, education, and social welfare. Although hospitals, religious organizations, and universities and colleges are part of the sector, they are often treated as a separate group due to their size and the specialized roles they play in Canadian society.

The voluntary sector is a large portion of the NFP sector, especially if we exclude the "big three"—hospitals, post-secondary education, and religious institutions. Advocacy organizations range from those concerned with collective advocacy, such as Canada Without Poverty, which does research, public education, and lobbying on behalf of those who are poor, to those advocating on behalf of individuals, such as Manitoba's Community Unemployed Help Centre, which assists those who have been denied social benefits, such as EI and social assistance. Direct service organizations cover just about any conceivable aspect of social welfare. Services are provided to the mentally ill, the disabled, the homeless, those experiencing a particular health difficulty, the elderly, and youth, to name a few. In Ontario, and to a lesser extent in Manitoba, unlike the other provinces and territories, child protection services are delivered by voluntary agencies, mandated by provincial legislation and operating in accordance with these provisions. Recreation services and a variety of non-profit housing initiatives attempting to provide decent affordable housing also are part of the voluntary sector, as are organizations such as the Canadian Centre for Policy Alternatives, which conducts research and disseminates findings on social justice and equity issues. The complexity of the voluntary sector is illustrated in Table 2.1, which outlines the characteristics of four general types of voluntary organization. This typology is arranged by relationship proximity to government.

Although the voluntary sector as a whole enjoys a significant complement of paid staff, it takes its name from the use of volunteer labour in its operations. In this regard, it is somewhat similar to organizations in the larger NFP sector, where one-half of such organizations are run entirely by volunteers (Imagine Canada, 2013). In 2010, an estimated 13.3 million people volunteered in the non-profit sector as a whole—the equivalent of 1.1 million full-time jobs and a participation rate of 47 per cent of the population over 15 (Statistics Canada, 2012). The single largest group of volunteers is comprised of those on governing boards.

The voluntary sector is also indistinguishable from the larger group of NFP organizations in that, while very large in number, individual organizations are generally small in size. What usually follows is a much flatter decision-making structure than is customarily

Table **2.1**	Typology of Voluntary Organizations in the Human Services

Type[1]	General Characteristics	Examples
Quasi-autonomous government organizations	• Typically larger organizations receiving mandate and most funding from government • More bureaucratic in structure • Focused primarily on service provision • Highly dependent on government for policy direction, with major accountability responsibilities to government	Non-government agencies providing delegated child welfare services, hospitals, and health services
Semi-independent from government	• Multiple revenue sources are common: charitable giving, membership fees, fees for service, service contracts and/or grants from government, foundations, corporations, and United Ways • Political advocacy not forbidden but limited; direct service is primary • Some may devote a small portion of resources and activities to research, public education, and non-partisan advocacy and policy-making • Required to maintain a formal governance structure in the form of a community board of directors and must file an annual report to Revenue Canada to retain registered charity status • Vary greatly in size from very small organizations with relatively flat organizational structures to larger agencies with a formal departmental structure and more hierarchy • A tendency for smaller agencies to be more community-based and rely more heavily on volunteers	Includes the largest number of agencies within the voluntary sector: national charity organizations, organizations that combine service and advocacy (e.g., mental health organizations, disability organizations, immigrant and settlement services), and agencies that are primarily service focused (e.g., family service agencies, Meals on Wheels, Big Brothers and Big Sisters, Boys and Girls Club). If recreation services are included, community clubs and special programs targeting specific groups of children and youth belong in this type
Primarily independent of government	• Typically small organizations established to generate social policy research, provide public education, advocate on behalf of particular policy issues, or advocate on behalf of a particular constituency • Normally receive most funding through fees, membership dues, or donations; may receive some government or foundation grants or service contracts • Some may be registered as charities with the ability to issue charitable tax receipts for donations to non-advocacy functions (e.g., research, education); others prohibited from registering as a charity because of proportion of activities considered to be "political advocacy"; and others choose to avoid contributions from government or corporations	Canadian Doctors for Medicare, Council of Canadians, Canada Without Poverty, think-tanks, such as the Canadian Centre for Policy Alternatives and the Fraser Institute. The Centre for Social Justice has separated its advocacy role from its public education and research roles, thus facilitating charitable tax receipts for activities related to the latter two roles

Continued ▶

▶ *Continued*

| Informal[2] | • Loosely formed organizations with limited formal structure
 • Funding primarily dependent on member fees and in-kind contributions, such as space from other organizations
 • Not usually incorporated as a non-profit organization or registered as a charity
 • Heavily reliant on volunteer labour for decision-making and service | Various self-help organizations such as Alcoholics Anonymous, depression support groups, mood disorder associations, and cancer support groups |

1. This typology is based on the proximity of the relationship between the voluntary organization and government. Religious and educational organizations are excluded.
2. This type is often excluded in discussions about the voluntary sector because of its informal nature and the related difficulties in identifying its characteristics. However, it is important to include because it is often the embryo of the more formal types of organizations; in addition, it makes important contributions to individual and community well-being.

found in the public sector. This, in turn, is thought to lead to greater job satisfaction. Although there are exceptions, remuneration for paid staff is generally lower than in the public sector. Unionization rates are also much lower than in the public sector, and this, along with limited resources in many agencies, likely contributes to somewhat lower wages. In some cases there may also be a culture and expectation of unpaid overtime because of pressing need or the importance of "the cause."

Challenges to Policy-Making in the Voluntary Sector

Historically, the voluntary sector has played an important role in responding quickly to social problems, addressing gaps in service coverage, and developing more innovative service responses. Yet there are significant challenges, particularly in the face of increased government reliance on this sector to backstop the holes in the social safety net. Two of the most important are funding and the shifting relationship between the voluntary and public sectors in a neo-liberal policy environment.

Financing the Voluntary Sector

Funding for the voluntary sector comes from a variety of sources, and a significant proportion of revenues, particularly for agencies providing social welfare services, is provided by government. Other sources include charitable or non-charitable donations from individuals or corporations, membership fees, service fees, and grants. For core NFP organizations (excluding hospitals, post-secondary education, and religious organizations), it has been estimated that 20 per cent of revenues come from government (Statistics Canada, 2009). This likely underestimates the percentage of support received by the voluntary social welfare sector since a larger proportion of NFP organizations, such as environmental organizations, receive little or no state funding. Individual donations are the second most important source of revenues, and in 2010 nearly 78 million charitable contributions, including to the "big three," were made by Canadians, totalling $10.6 billion (Statistics Canada, 2012). However, the voluntary sector receives only a relatively small proportion of that total. Turcotte (2012) notes that religious organizations receive roughly 40 per cent of annual donations, followed by the health sector, including hospitals (21 per cent), and then social service agencies (11 per cent). Among corporations, education was the most funded program category at 29 per cent of the average company's giving (CECP, 2013). User fees and research or development grants from foundations are a relatively small proportion of funding for the voluntary sector. If user fees are assessed, many voluntary organizations adjust or waive these for low-income service users in order to honour the principle of accessibility.

A key funding issue for this sector is the uncertainty of revenues from year to year, which makes long-term planning extremely difficult. This is a result of the sector's dependency on annual government grants and contracts as well as the success of other fundraising efforts that may vary from year to year. Smaller organizations that provide services regarded as less important or those that have initiated special projects are particularly vulnerable. An additional complication is that government and quasi-autonomous government organizations can often have any deficits absorbed through intra-government transfers. In most social service organizations in the voluntary sector this is not the case.

Almost all social service organizations in the voluntary sector are registered charities under provisions in the Income Tax Act. This enables receipts for charitable donations, which allow donors to deduct a proportion of these amounts from taxes payable to government; this is believed to encourage charitable giving. Of course, the often neglected consequences are that this reduces government revenues for the portion of contributions that are tax deductible, and tax deductions provide greater benefits to more affluent donors. While charitable donations open up opportunities to receive new revenues for services or program maintenance for some agencies, it is also difficult to predict ongoing annual revenues from this source. For example, charitable giving to the NFP sector declined following the 2008 recession, although comparisons between 2007 and 2010 indicate that charitable giving was slightly higher in 2010 when compared with 2007 figures (Turcotte, 2012). Of perhaps more concern is that the long-term trend reflects a decline in the percentage of Canadians donating to charities (i.e., 23 per cent of those who filed tax returns in 2011, down from 29.5 per cent in 1990 (*Toronto Star*, 2013). An additional complication is the prohibition against political activity contained in section 149.1 of the Income Tax Act. This gives the Canada Revenue Agency and the federal government the ability to use the threat of withdrawing registered charitable status from voluntary organizations who engage in advocacy activities that may be construed as politically partisan in nature.

The Changing Relationships between Government and the Voluntary Sector

In Chapter 1 it was noted that the policy objectives of neo-liberalism include reduced public services, greater reliance on the private sector, and a lower tax regime. These objectives have had dramatic implications for the voluntary sector. For example, service needs have increased because of the tendency on the part of the state to off-load responsibilities, eliminate certain programs, and discontinue subsidies that might have been previously available to support certain initiatives. At the same time, new revenues have not expanded sufficiently to enable the voluntary sector to meet these funding gaps.

However, the relationship between the public and voluntary sectors is more complex than this. In a neo-liberal policy environment, the state often strives to discredit those organizations engaged in policy advocacy by de-funding such agencies or imposing new requirements for financial accountability, a trend that has become more common in the past few years. One example is the government-initiated audit of Canada Without Poverty to determine whether charitable donations are being used to advocate for poverty prevention in ways that might be interpreted as critical of government policies. In addition, government has sought to contract out previously provided public services to voluntary or for-profit agencies. Although service contracts with the voluntary sector can provide opportunities for community-based agencies to establish more responsive services, there are potential pitfalls. One is that opportunities for service collaboration and innovation may be limited by the amount of funding provided. Second, neo-liberal governments favour reduced taxes and a balanced budget, even in a low-growth economy, yet during these times service demand is most likely to expand as more and more families find themselves in need. Voluntary services such as shelters for the homeless, food banks, and soup kitchens are particularly vulnerable. In turn, poverty and unemployment are often associated with a rise in problems such as mental health issues and family violence, which are often addressed, at least in part, by the voluntary sector.

Governments expect the voluntary sector to pick up the slack, but it has neither adequate resources nor the infrastructure to respond in a comprehensive fashion. In Canada a recent survey of nearly 2,000 charity leaders found that one-half reported an increased demand they were having difficulty meeting (Lasby and Barr, 2013). Even where there was an increase in revenues from government, these frequently covered only the direct costs of service delivery, leaving the agency to seek other sources of funding for overhead and core administrative functions. This discussion underscores a misconception about the voluntary sector promoted by neo-liberals—that the state has assumed too much responsibility for social welfare and that this has undermined the role of communities, voluntary agencies, and faith communities in providing services. By extension, critics of the "nanny state" suggest that government reductions in social welfare support will result in an expansion of the voluntary sector to meet these gaps. In an analysis of this assumption, Finlayson (1994) demonstrated that the opposite was true—increased state support and partnership with the voluntary sector enhanced the ability of this sector to provide effective services.

Neo-liberalism promotes a return to the charity model where voluntary social welfare agencies and faith-based organizations are expected to meet essential social welfare needs. These types of organizations play an important role, but the growing gap between available funding and community needs is not the only problem. Other limitations of over-reliance on the voluntary sector include the following:

- Increased expectations that the voluntary sector should respond to basic social welfare needs and services, such as food, emergency shelter, and crisis counselling, undermine the ability of these organizations to target unmet community needs that fall outside the normal mandates of services that should be provided, or at least fully funded, by the government.
- Voluntary agencies providing essential services are less well developed in smaller communities and almost non-existent in remote Aboriginal communities, resulting in significant gaps in service coverage.
- Policy and service co-ordination challenges are increased in a system where a large number of independent agencies providing services must be closely linked to maximize effectiveness and efficiency.

The voluntary sector, which plays an increasingly important role in the delivery of social welfare services in the twenty-first century, struggles to respond to these challenges. What, then, is the potential of this sector to connect policy to practice in ways that promote social justice?

Realizing the Potential of the Voluntary Sector

We consider here, first, the voluntary sector's role in establishing new services and paradigm shifts in policy and practice, and then conclude with a brief discussion of directions that could help to manage some of the funding and service challenges faced by more established voluntary sector agencies.

The voluntary sector has played a pioneering role in developing Canada's social welfare system, often as the initiator of what are now regarded as essential services funded either directly or indirectly by government. For example, child welfare services were first developed by voluntary agencies, including religious organizations; women's shelters as a refuge from male violence followed a similar trajectory. The continuing role of the voluntary sector in identifying unmet needs and devising and promoting policy and program responses is unquestionable, and researchers are just beginning to gather information to help understand its role and impact on Canadian society.

The activities of the voluntary sector as an initiator and innovator often occur on two levels. One relates to a self-help service model that begins small but often expands

Box **2.2** | Wood's Homes: From Charity to a Major Multi-Service Agency

In 1914 George Wood, a Presbyterian minister, moved to Innisfail, Alberta, with his young son after the death of his wife in a tragic house fire. Despite his own care-giving responsibilities he was soon asked by a soldier, whose wife had also died, to care for his two children while he went to fight in World War I. The soldier died a few years later and Reverend Wood became their guardian. He later remarried and the Woods' home became known as a place that would care for troubled and destitute children. The family was dependent for many years on informal charity, but in 1927 fundraising by the Calgary Order of Odd Fellows, a charitable organization, provided the orphanage with a steady source of financial support.

Over time, Wood's Homes expanded its operations by responding in innovative ways to emerging community needs for children and families. The range of services offered by the agency now includes specialized residential care for youth, crisis counselling, foster family care, child and adolescent mental health services, counselling and support services to families, and services to homeless youth. The agency's initial involvement with homeless youth began with a response to a needs study commissioned by the Boys and Girls Club, another voluntary sector agency (Kufeldt and Nimmo, 1987). Based on this research, the agency partnered with the Calgary Board of Education to establish a storefront school for homeless youth and EXIT, a drop-in service centre. The agency, which operates in several Alberta communities, is now funded by both government and charitable donations, and has more than 400 staff. More than 450 children and their families are served daily from this highly respected agency, which was named one of Canada's top 100 workplaces in 2011 and 2012 (see www.woodshomes.ca).

as it secures significant funding. An example is Wood's Homes, which celebrated its hundredth anniversary in 2014 (see Box 2.2).

A second level of innovation involves the voluntary sector as an agent of transformative change. An example is the role disability organizations have played in shifting the focus of services to the disabled by adopting a human rights orientation to an understanding of disability issues.

The more traditional approach to services for the disabled has been based primarily on the rehabilitative paradigm common to the medical model. Here the problem is defined as the disability and its symptoms, with a need to treat the condition and help the person adapt to his or her surroundings. Similarly, past fundraising efforts had emphasized the vulnerability of those with a disability in an effort to appeal to sympathetic donors. By the late 1960s and early 1970s the single-minded focus on the rehabilitative paradigm began to be challenged, led by disability organizations in the voluntary sector that were either established directly by people with disabilities or incorporated the voices of those with a disability within existing agencies. Influenced by the Independent Living Movement (see Chapter 7), these organizations promoted the strengths of people with a disability rather than the weaknesses. Beginning first with those with physical challenges (e.g., requiring wheelchairs for mobility) and expanding later to other types of disability, the problem was redefined primarily as a lack of accessibility within the community and its related institutions, rather than an impairment in the individual that focused only on adaptation to the existing physical and social environment.

Existing legislative provisions since the 1970s, encouraged by supportive human rights legislation and the United Nations Convention on the Rights of Persons with Disabilities (2006), have led to better access to buildings, more accessible public transportation, and accommodation for education and employment. However, much remains to be done to achieve equality. Box 2.3 illustrates the proactive role of the voluntary sector in influencing government policy towards this end.

The examples of Wood's Homes in Alberta and Barrier-Free Manitoba illustrate the role of the voluntary sector in new service developments and in contributing to paradigm shifts in the definition of social problems and related policy responses. It is also important to consider some of the assets in voluntary sector agencies that continue to provide important community services and some of the changes that could enhance the capacity of these organizations.

Box 2.3 | Barrier-Free Manitoba

Based on precedents established in passing accessibility rights legislation in the US, Australia, the UK, and especially Ontario in 2005, Barrier-Free Manitoba was formed as a non-partisan, cross-disability initiative in 2008 to promote disability rights legislation. This organization was led by a steering committee representing Manitoba's disability community. It identified principles to guide the legislation, including the importance of overcoming barriers for people with all types of disabilities (i.e., architectural, physical, communication, attitudinal, technological, and organizational), a leadership role for the disability community, and the development of standards and target dates for addressing major factors that impede accessibility. The group hired a consultant to help draft the new legislative requirements and lobby the provincial government and other potential allies, including the opposition and the business community.

In 2013, the Accessibility for Manitobans Act was passed by the provincial legislature. Although the legislation did not achieve every objective set by the coalition, Barrier-Free Manitoba was able to influence what is regarded as a progressive law that should help to enforce the human rights of all citizens with a disability in the province. The coalition continues to be actively involved in monitoring the current situation and lobbying government for improvements to the standards, which will guide implementation of the legislation. The provincial government, for its part, is receptive to such input in that it is developing standards by first producing discussion documents and soliciting responses to these proposals.

Smaller community-based voluntary agencies, because of their flatter, less hierarchical organizational structure, often can more easily engage in and respond to inputs from both service providers and service users. Although public-sector organizations can also adopt more inclusive strategies, many voluntary organizations have incorporated the voices of service users on their boards and employ other strategies to ensure ongoing input and feedback to policy and program development. Not only is this expertise relevant to the services provided by a specific organization, but it can be expanded and used to influence decision-makers on broader policy issues through coalition-building among similar organizations (e.g., disability organizations, organizations concerned with Aboriginal issues). Although voluntary organizations dependent on government revenues are somewhat constrained in their advocacy efforts with government because of the potential repercussions from such criticism, coalitions and public campaigns can help to mitigate the likelihood of retaliatory measures.

Funding is an important challenge to the voluntary sector, and this often is difficult to address. One aspect pertains to project-related funding and contracts, which often fail to adequately fund core operations. Ideally, contracting with the voluntary sector should be built on a partnership where the goals of funding to the agency permit increased flexibility for agencies, increased predictability, reduced administrative burden, and strengthened relationships between the funder and the recipient agency (Struthers, 2013). In building relationships based on trust it is important to recognize the different levels of risk associated with funding different programs. For example, an agency launching a more innovative project that contains higher levels of risk should not necessarily be denied funding even if outcomes are somewhat less predictable than they are for other programs. By extension, these agencies should not be penalized if outcomes are less than anticipated. After all, the knowledge gained is often worth the investment. Indeed, pilot project funding and demonstration grants are primarily intended to explore the potential of new innovations and to learn from these experiences.

Even in the absence of a more collaborative approach to funding from the public sector, voluntary agencies that have been more successful in coping with shifts to project and contract funding have built personal relationships with funding officers, planned effectively with diverse groups, communicated stories about their work to both government and the public, and built successful models for sustainability (Hudson, 1998; Struthers, 2004).

Program coverage and co-ordination are service challenges. Finding solutions to the problems of service coverage, particularly for voluntary agencies that provide more specialized services, is an important priority. Some foundations, such as the Ontario Trillium Foundation, have taken a leadership role in adapting their approaches for funding projects in more remote First Nations communities, and the Circle of Philanthropy and Aboriginal Peoples in Canada has been created to learn how to be effective funders of Indigenous peoples' projects (Struthers, 2013).

The solution to service co-ordination is a shared responsibility between the public and voluntary sectors. Although voluntary sector agencies can be quite successful in

building community partnerships, a leadership role in service co-ordination by government is important, particularly in circumstances where government locates essential
services like child welfare in the voluntary sector. Where services are contracted to a
variety of agencies, funding a lead agency to facilitate service co-ordination might assist
in developing improved service delivery partnerships.

Organizational Policy-Making

Agencies, particularly those in the voluntary sector, will have their own policy-
making structures. These are much simpler than those found in government. For
example, the board of directors may approve particular policies but policy development
may occur through a subcommittee of the board, a joint staff–board committee, or a
senior management committee of staff. When major programs or policy changes are
contemplated, an agency may establish a committee composed of a cross-section of direct service staff, senior staff, and board members, and, depending on the relative commitment of the agency to inclusiveness, service user representatives to develop or frame
the new policy. Such "vertical slices" represent a greater commitment to a participatory
approach in the development of new policies. Forms of strategic planning are also used
in government and small-scale community policy-making initiatives, and in Chapter 6
we discuss small-scale policy-making.

Although it is easier to incorporate an inclusive approach to policy-making within
voluntary organizations than in governments, there is no guarantee that this will be
the case. Smaller organizations characterized by an elitist, centralized approach to
management can ignore the voices of front-line staff and service users in ways that
are characteristic of some government policy-making bodies. This raises the issue of
governance models in organizations, whether located in the government or voluntary
agencies. **Governance** is not simply about structures for decision-making; as outlined
by Graham, Amos, and Plumptre (2003: 1), it is the "agreements, procedures, conven-
tions or policies that define who gets power, how decisions are taken and how accountability is rendered." As noted in Chapter 6, some relatively large organizations with
dispersed local offices can create a governance model that renders a significant degree
of autonomy to these offices under certain conditions.

If organizations have boards of directors or advisory committees, it is important to
consider how staff and service users play a role in decision-making. Is staff represented
on the board? Are there representatives of service users? Are committee structures in
place to permit input? Is there a practice of consultation and open discussion prior to
decision-making? These questions are related to the organization's culture pertaining
to legitimacy and voice, that is, who should be involved in decision-making. It will be
apparent that a more inclusive governance model will provide greater opportunities
for input from front-line staff, community members, and service users. Organizational
policy-making is also heavily influenced by the values and style of the person in the pri-

mary leadership position. The approach of this individual will have a major impact on whether planning becomes more inclusive or whether a more traditional, centralized model will be adopted.

Particular attention should be given to the decentralization of various service functions to diversity-related communities and Indigenous organizations. This trend in ethnocultural communities provides important opportunities to adapt service models to local community and cultural norms; however, models of governance adopted by these organizations will influence the extent to which goals related to inclusiveness and improved service are achieved.

As earlier noted, Indigenous organizations continue to acquire greater policy-making authority in the areas of health, education, and social services, and structures developed to implement these programs are usually community-based if authority is assumed at the community level or regionally based if authority is vested in a regional structure that serves several communities. Because approaches to policy-making are less complex than those at a provincial or federal government level, the structures and policy-making processes are more like those that exist within organizations.

Summary and Conclusion

At the time Canada was created in 1867 by the British North America Act (now called the Constitution Act, 1867), most responsibility for social policy and the delivery of human services was deemed to fall within the authority of the provinces. State involvement in the delivery of health and social services was quite limited but welfare state programs grew dramatically over the course of the twentieth century, especially following World War II, and the roles of both the federal and provincial governments have increased. Constitutional provisions have limited the federal government's direct role in service delivery in many areas, including the delivery of services pertaining to health, justice, education, and social services. However, the federal government does provide funding for these services and is directly involved in the delivery of human services to First Nations people living on reserves. In addition, the growth in the nature and scope of health and social policies has led to more direct involvement by the federal government in areas such as pensions, employment insurance, child care, and the provision of benefits through the taxation system to low-income families.

Two general trends in policy-making have been identified in more recent years at the federal government level. One is the tendency to decentralize (and in some cases off-load) related policies and funding responsibilities to the provinces; the other is the tendency to centralize power and control in the PMO and one or two key committees of cabinet.

A similar trend is also apparent in many provincial governments. In these circumstances, the Premier's office exercises enormous influence over policy development, with limited attention being paid to a review of alternatives or how the implementation process can be managed.

Phillips and Orsini (2002) focus on possible reforms to enhance the role of citizens in political and public-sector institutions. Although they are somewhat pessimistic about the possibility of reversing the centralizing trend at the top of the policy-making pyramid at the federal government level, they recommend changes to promote more citizen involvement in policy-making. One involves reforms to the political party system and to Parliament to promote increased policy-oriented discussions between elected political officials and citizens. They also recommend greater investment in promoting civil society, including relaxing the rules on charitable organizations so they can speak out on issues without fear of losing their funding, and promoting the responsibility of public and community institutions to build approaches that involve service users and community members in policy design. We suggest an additional reform that might reverse the widespread apathy in electoral politics. Our current electoral system rewards individuals and political parties based on who is "first past the post"—even if the percentage of the popular vote for the winning candidate and party is quite low. This could be reformed to introduce some kind of proportional representation. Such a change might encourage more citizen engagement with our political process, and in turn could make the policy-making process more participatory. It is also important to note the contradiction between the centralizing trend among some governments and the demand for more input and participation that emerges from increased recognition of diversity and minority rights. Perhaps this contradiction can be exposed in building more active advocacy efforts to promote social justice.

In this chapter we also examined the role of the voluntary sector. Despite the challenges facing voluntary sector agencies, there is somewhat more potential for engaging in inclusive policy-making. Although some of these policies may be limited in scope, the programs and services that emerge at the ordinary policy level can make a profound difference to the lives of service users.

Chapter 3 focuses on common frameworks used for policy-making and the opportunities these present for connecting policy to practice.

Critical Thinking Questions

1. What are the three branches of government in Canada and the structures within each branch?
2. Do you favour a stronger federal role or a stronger provincial role in the field of social policy? What are the advantages and disadvantages of each option?
3. Policy-making power in Canada, particularly at the federal level, has become more centralized in the PMO and one or two cabinet committees. What are the advantages and disadvantages of this trend, and for whom?
4. Select a recent social policy issue that has been addressed either by the provincial government or an organization with which you are familiar. Try to map out the

process and the steps or activities that occurred as the policy moved through the various decision-making structures. What did you learn about policy-making by trying to map out the process in this way?

5.   Several challenges to the role of the voluntary sector in developing progressive social policies were identified in this chapter. What are the strengths and weaknesses of the public and voluntary sectors in developing programs and services that are more responsive to communities?

6.   Identify a voluntary sector organization in your community or area within one of the types identified in Table 2.1. Locate information about this agency or organization through personal knowledge, a brief interview, and/or online research. What are its purposes and how are these carried out? How important is its role in your community?

Recommended Reading

R. Dyck. *Canadian Politics: Critical Approaches*, 6th edn. Scarborough, Ont.: Nelson, 2011. Dyck offers a critical perspective on politics and policy-making at the federal level.

A. Finkel. *Social Policy and Practice in Canada: A History*. Waterloo, Ont.: Wilfrid Laurier University Press, 2006. This is a general history of social policy in Canada and covers several social policy topics in more depth.

E.A. Forsey. *How Canadians Govern Themselves*, 6th edn. Ottawa: Her Majesty the Queen in Right of Canada, 2005. This handbook provides a brief summary of federal government structures and is available online at: www.parl.gc.ca/Content/LOP/researchpublications/styles/tsfwbtrds/how.pdf.

3

Policy-Making and Policy-Makers

────────────● **In this chapter you will learn about:** ●────────────

- three common theories that provide explanations of how public policies are established;
- who wields the most power at the macro level of policy-making;
- five common models or frameworks for policy-making;
- how models of policy-making are applied in developing new policies and programs.

Introduction

In Chapter 1 we discussed how the ideology of the government in power, within certain limits, influences the nature and scope of social policies that will be introduced. Ideologies are also influential in shaping theories of public policy. These theories of public policy are important because they can help us understand the factors that may contribute to the success or failure of efforts to establish new policies. In this chapter we first describe three theories of public policy-making, and this is followed by a discussion of five general frameworks commonly used in policy development.

Theories of Public Policy

Several theories focus on Canadian public policy (see Brooks, 1998; Howlett and Ramesh, 2003; Miljan, 2012), and we briefly summarize three here. Although some precision is lost by selecting only three, these are common to all of the authors identified above. These are also the most common prototypes used to explain the relationship between political processes and policy-making in Canada. The three theories are

Marxism, **pluralism**, and **public choice**. However, we do make an important adaptation in describing Marxism under the more general label of **structural theories**.

Structural Theories

The Marxist theory of policy formation is the most influential structural theory. As discussed in Chapter 1 there are different adaptations of Marxism, but the inherent conflict between the interests of the dominant and subordinate classes is central to understanding this view of public policy-making.

Marxist theory has modified its understanding of the role of the state since Karl Marx first proposed his theory of the state over 150 years ago. According to this view, although the state operates primarily in the interests of the dominant class, it does respond to pressures from the working class and its advocates in enacting policies favourable to this class. However, government also risks a loss of business confidence and related impacts on economic growth if it imposes too many restrictions on business, particularly during times of economic downturn when there may be increased pressure to respond to the needs of the subordinate class rather than the needs of capital. Thus, policy development is seen by Marxists to evolve from contradictions between two policy pressures at the state level. One is to introduce **accumulation policies**, which largely support businesses through grants, reduced taxes and subsidies, state expenditures on public works required by business (e.g., roads and other infrastructure), and bailout loans or guarantees to corporations. A second is the pressure to introduce **legitimation policies** to reduce class conflict. These consist of benefits to the subordinate class that also serve to reduce their dissatisfaction with the inequalities associated with the market. These policies, which include health care and economic benefits such as EI, promote social harmony by legitimizing the capitalist system in the eyes of those who benefit least from its operation. At the same time these policies provide important benefits to service users.

Other structural theories, including feminism, environmental determinism, and post-colonialism, are based on somewhat similar descriptions of the politics of policy-making. For example, a central premise in feminism is the structural imperative flowing from patriarchy. In this view, patriarchy acts as the dominant force in the adoption of policies affecting women. Similarly, post-colonialism, which has characterized Canadian public policies towards First Nations and other Indigenous peoples, is based on a structural model that defines differences in terms of a fundamental conflict between the dominant mainstream society (i.e., the colonizer) and the subordinate group (i.e., the colonized). In each case, the structure of society and its institutions create an unequal distribution of power between dominant and subordinate groups. That is, dominant control in society rests with individuals and groups that are not representative of women or Aboriginal people, and the dominant group ensures that policies evolve in a manner that largely preserves the status quo for the dominant group. Without minimizing important differences, the similarity in these theories about the central cause of economic and social inequalities (i.e., the structure of society into more and less privileged groups) provides a basis for adopting the more general label of *structural theories* for this perspective.

There are, of course, criticisms of structural theories. For example, it is argued, particularly in the case of Marxism, that intra-class differences in interests and preferences are minimized by a dichotomous division into dominant and subordinate classes. A somewhat related criticism is that policy changes to provide increased benefits to those in need cannot be fully explained by class conflict or the influence of the subordinate class on decision-makers, and that most changes have a more complex causal chain.

Pluralism

Pluralism reflects the observation that interest groups influence the outcomes of governmental decisions. Although society is a collection of individuals, these individuals recognize the value of organizing as groups to advance their collective interests. Policies are shaped primarily by the outcomes of competition between groups, not unlike a sports tournament where teams compete for the top prize. Although some pluralists suggest that there are relatively equal competitions among interest groups, with the state acting as an independent arbiter of conflict, many pluralists have come to recognize significant divisions in society related to inequality, gender, ethnicity, disability, and other forms of diversity. These factors influence the capacity of groups to compete on an equal footing, even though this is not indicative of divisions into dominant and subordinate classes as defined by structural theorists. Miljan (2012) notes how the recognition of more privileged or elite groups in society is incorporated within the theory of pluralism. First, it is argued that competition for political office is a contest among political elites (e.g., political parties); however, voters do get to choose between the policies of different political parties, thus preserving the democratic nature of how these elites are selected. Second, once in power, governments have to be somewhat responsive to popular demands because of the risk they may be replaced at the next election, and because shifting coalitions among interest groups can place political pressure on governments to take certain actions.

Some pluralists have recognized that certain groups, such as pro-business lobby groups, possess greater power and resources than others. In addition, large corporations also carry a "big stick" in that they can exercise significant influence by deferring new investment or perhaps relocating their businesses to other countries or regions. Because pluralism is based on the principle of competition between groups with more or less equal power, there is some support for the provision of additional resources or preferences for disadvantaged groups so they are more able to represent their own interests. An example of this was the Court Challenges Program in Canada, which was ended by the Conservative government when it came to power in 2006. For nearly 25 years this program provided funding to disadvantaged groups and official-language minorities so they could pursue court cases. Although pluralism may recognize a preference for a "level playing field," and efforts to promote more equitable competition have achieved some successes, notably through Charter and human rights challenges, these have largely failed to make much of a difference in preventing growing inequality. In part, critics argue that this reflects the pluralists' failure to recognize or address the disproportionate power exercised by elites in the policy-making process.

Public Choice Theory

We draw on Brooks (1998), Miljan (2012), and Trebilock, Hartle, Pritchard, and Dewees (1982) in describing the main features of public choice theory. Public choice is based on the classical theory of microeconomics where the only political actor that really matters is the individual. Although it is similar to pluralism in some respects, analysis focuses on individuals rather than groups. These individuals are assumed to make rational political choices based on their own self-interest, just as they would in purchasing goods or services in a free market context. Thus, they will seek to maximize their self-interest or personal gain and minimize losses in any transaction.

Within government, politicians, bureaucrats, and interest group advocates attempt to maximize their self-interest, and policy outcomes are the result of what is described as a series of "games" characterized by competition, bargaining, and negotiation. Exchange theory is used to explain the nature of behaviours that occur between actors involved in these games, and policy outcomes are the result of these transactions. Four distinct games are hypothesized: the political game, the bureaucratic game, the interest group game, and the media group game. Each game has its own set of rules and relationships among players, and teams can involve coalitions and conflicts. However, the rules place some limits on the nature of conflicts and how each game is played. The general relationship between these four groups is shown in Figure 3.1. The electorate confers power on politicians, but the perceived capacity of the media to influence the views held by voters on issues or political parties gives the media significant influence. The influence of special interest groups is affected by their ability to mobilize supporters and allies for collective action, which may offer credible support to a particular interest or, in some cases, a significant threat to politicians. For their part, bureaucrats exercise control over the flow of vital information and the delivery of programs. The capacity of politicians within governments to manage the public agenda and to confer benefits on voters or special interest groups whose support is up for grabs, or alternatively to soften the adverse effects of policies on their supporters, will determine the nature of policies that are developed and the ability of governments to maintain power.

In the political game certain kinds of benefits and costs are accepted. For example, politicians gain personal prestige and knowledge of the system once elected, which is enhanced by the effective use of power and influence. They also acquire the right to favours from participants in the system in exchange for favours provided to them.

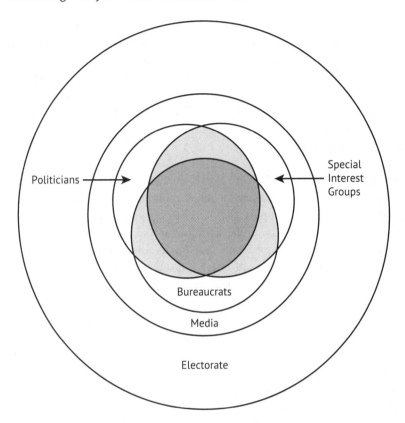

Figure 3.1 | The Policy Process According to the Public Choice Perspective: Four Interrelated Games

Notes
1. The darkest area in the centre is the heart of the decision-making process and the lighter shaded areas show the interplay between each pair of policy participants.
2. The media interact with each set of policy participants and are the channel through which the electorate perceives participants.
3. The voters are treated as non-participants in decision-making but choose the players in the political game.

However, there are related costs such as time, money, loss of privacy, and loss of time with family. To maximize benefits relative to costs it is in the interests of the politician to be elected, to be a part of the governing party, and to be a minister in an important portfolio. There are generally accepted rules in the political game, including trading favours (e.g., supporting another's position in return for a future favour from that individual) and putting the party's interests ahead of personal interests after extracting the best possible price (i.e., a future benefit or position of some kind). These rules also apply to the Senate where patronage appointments by the Prime Minister have become the normal approach to filling vacancies. On occasion, the rules of the game are violated, as was the case with the Senate spending scandal of 2013, and there are often consequences, both for the individuals who break the rules and for the political party that is involved (see Box 3.1).

Most senior bureaucrats are friendly adversaries with other bureaucrats, competing for funding, ministerial time, and appointments to other offices of greater prestige. They also attempt to enlarge the span of control and budget of their own departments as a means to achieve greater recognition both for themselves and for their minister.

There is some similarity between the media and interest group games. Both interest group leaders and media professionals need access to decision-makers, yet the nature of their roles often places them in positions where they become public critics of government policy or expose issues that can be embarrassing to government or a particular individual. For example, the special interest group leader frequently needs to develop strong, and often critical, positions of current policies and actions to mobilize interest

---

Box **3.1**   Public Choice and the 2013 Senate Scandal

In late 2012, the Senate began investigating the housing expense claims of Senator Mike Duffy, a former television reporter, and Senator Patrick Brazeau, formerly the head of the Congress of Aboriginal Peoples, on the basis that they were ineligible to receive these. In February 2013 Senator Pamela Wallin, also a former reporter, was added to the list because of money received for housing and travel that was deemed ineligible for expense claims. All three were appointed by Prime Minister Harper and had championed the Conservative cause in earlier federal elections. Mike Duffy received a cheque for over $90,000 from Nigel Wright, Prime Minister Harper's Chief of Staff, to cover Duffy's alleged invalid expense claims, action that led to Wright's resignation in May 2013. Prime Minister Harper denied any knowledge of the cheque and later claimed to have dismissed his Chief of Staff for making the payment. The three senators were eventually suspended from the Senate without pay for two years but not without objecting to their dismissal in a very public manner. In an explosive speech within the Senate, Senator Duffy claimed that he had been pressured to pay back the $90,000, which he said was a legitimate expense, but also he had been issued a second cheque of $13,000 to pay legal expenses, a move designed to buy his silence and save further embarrassment to the party. He alleged that the Prime Minister's Office, including Prime Minister Harper, knew about the payoffs and demanded he lie about the money he had accepted. An RCMP investigation resulted in 31 charges of fraud, breach of trust, and bribery in July 2014 against Senator Duffy, who has vowed to fight the charges in court (Bronskill and Ward, 2014). Although the scandal has damaged the Senate and its culture of entitlement, it has also raised questions about the amount of control exercised by the PMO and the credibility of the Prime Minister in his handling of the affair. How can the public choice perspective be used to explain elements of the political game in this example? Who are the winners and losers?

group membership. At the same time, the leader's influence often depends on access to ministers or senior bureaucrats and one's perceived ability either to deliver something of value to them (e.g., support or votes) or to impose negative sanctions that might impede policy adoption. On the other hand, the successful media professional is one who uncovers "hot information" that can make the major headlines, and access to key decision-makers is essential in securing such information. Although some of this information may lead to positive coverage and enhance the image of the political party or government with the public, too much negative publicity can lead government officials to impose restrictions on access to information or limit the access of particular individuals to key sources of information.

Public choice theorists argue that the nature of these games leads to inefficiencies within government in both policy formation and expenditure allocation. For example, the short time horizons of government often lead senior bureaucrats to favour short-term solutions to long-term problems. On the expenditure management side, departments are discouraged from running surpluses because these are generally clawed back by the central financial authority at the end of the year; as well, surpluses may lead to a reduction in allocations in the following year because future budget allocations are often based, in large part, on expenditure patterns from the previous year rather than on evidence-based data.

At a macro policy level, many public choice theorists identify a growing trend among voters to seek more and better programs from government, subject to certain limits in taxes they are prepared to pay, because it is in their interests to do so. In turn, this leads to an increase in the level of state intervention, which interferes with the natural operation of the market. Many public programs, but particularly welfare state programs, are seen as encouraging "free riders" who do not require such programs. Public policy, it is argued, should focus on supplementing the free market only when necessary, providing social programs as a last resort, and reinforcing individual responsibility as much as possible in policies and programs.

The underlying orientation of public choice, which is based on the ideology of a free market and a more residual orientation to social policy, has many critics both at home and in an international development context (see Klein, 2007). Some similarities clearly exist between this theory and the ideology of neo-liberalism.

Public choice explanations of governmental policy-making also share certain characteristics with the pluralist model. For example, both uphold the same competitive world view, and the role of the state is largely seen as responsible for mediating conflicts over scarce resources. In public choice theory some evidence supports the nature of relationships among the various political actors in the political and bureaucratic arenas, but there are also significant limitations. Similar to pluralism, public choice theory ignores the fact that the deck is stacked so that too often a small minority wins approval for what they want. This is largely a result of the ability of those with more power to influence the nature of choices that are made either inside government or by the public in elections. In the latter case, considerable influence is exercised over public opinion through advertising and the media, and major control over these institutions remains in the hands of those with the most power.

Another criticism of the public choice explanation for policy-making is its assumption that all actions are based on rational economic choices motivated by self-interest. In fact, engagement in interest group activity and personal advocacy, particularly in the social policy area, is at least partially motivated by altruism and idealism. This is true in politics as well, in that some advance policy goals that are unlikely to get them elected; and, if elected, they are unlikely to form the government (e.g., the Green Party). Although Olson (1965) in his critique of public choice concluded that politically active people may not be motivated by self-interests but by altruistic or idealistic goals, we draw a more cautious conclusion; that is, policy actors in political and bureaucratic arenas include both those driven more by self-interest and those espousing more altruistic goals. Public choice theory may be correct in reminding us of the role of rational self-interest in policy-making, but it is clear that other motives are also present.

Making Sense of Theories of Public Policy

The theoretical perspectives summarized—structural theories, pluralism, and public choice—vary in their interpretations of the focus of analysis, the constraints on the policy process, and the role of the state.

The focus of analysis in Marxism and other structural theories is on classes or major divisions in society, pluralism focuses more on organized groups, and public choice identifies the individual as the unit of analysis. Second, structural theorists define the dominant ideology of capitalism or the prevailing power of other forms of domination as major constraints to policy reform, and this is largely absent from the other perspectives. Third, each perspective contains very different views of the state. For the pluralist, the state is essentially democratic but able to pursue some of its own interests. For the public choice theorist, the state is seen as heavily bureaucratic and often inefficient in trying to cope with the never-ending demands for more and better services. Structural theorists see the state as primarily identified and acting on behalf of the dominant class but with a margin of independence that enables it to respond to the demands of a subordinate class when pressured to do so.

If we observe political behaviour leading to public policies, we can identify patterns that seem to support each of these theories, yet no single theory appears to fully explain the policy-making process. One is tempted to suggest that a combination of theories might be the best solution, yet this is difficult because the same events are likely to be interpreted differently by each theory. For example, evidence of different groups and interests may be seen as supporting a pluralist perspective or as a result of actions by the state to divide and conquer the subordinate class within the structural perspective.

An important question relates to whether one's position on these theories matters. The answer is "yes" because this will have some influence on how one approaches policy change. More specifically, the extent to which both individual and structural conditions are considered reflects different political stances regarding the role of the state and how individual and social responsibilities and obligations are allocated. Although we identify more strongly with the critique offered by the structural perspective and the extent to which structural factors contribute to policy-making by elites, it is important for readers to develop their own perspectives on these theories and to recognize how their perspectives shape their interpretation of the policy-making process. It is also important to consider how the three theories we have just summarized are related to the models of policy-making outlined later in this chapter (i.e., the rational model, incrementalism, mixed scanning, the value criteria model, and the garbage can model). These models illustrate different approaches to planning, but with the possible exception of the garbage can model they do not refer to the political processes that influence policy-making. Theories of public policy, on the other hand, provide us with models for understanding the relationship between the political process and social policy in ways that can help us apply these results to the policy-making process.

Who Makes Social Policy?

In our view too much power over the grand issues of social policy rests in the hands of a relatively small number of individuals holding key positions in business and government. In some cases these people may change positions, serving for a time as a senior bureaucrat or politician and then assuming responsibilities in the business world. Our conclusion about the dominance of elites in decision-making at the macro policy level is based on two arguments. We first examine the theories of public policy that have just been summarized to identify their explanations about who influences the major policy decisions at a senior governmental level. We then consider the evidence from the Canadian context on this question.

Each of the theoretical perspectives draws different conclusions about the policy-making process and the level of importance attached to the influence of elites. Nevertheless, each theory is remarkably similar in highlighting the disproportionate influence of those with privilege. Structural theorists are the clearest about the role of elites. For Marxists, the elite includes representatives of the capitalist class who exercise primary control over the economy and, by extension, the state; for feminists, the elite is composed of a dominant class of primarily males in positions of power who are in opposition to or ambivalent about gender equality; for Aboriginal Canadians, those in control hold mainstream values and perspectives that fail to adequately recognize the different aspirations of Aboriginal people. Although pluralists initially viewed the state as a somewhat independent arbiter of shifting coalitions of interest groups, many have recognized the dominant position of business in the political marketplace (Lindblom, 1982; Lowi, 1979) and the ability of business leaders to maintain privileged access to decision-makers. This view has been extended to the role of policy communities. For example, Coleman and Skogstad (1990) found that groups enjoying political advantages were able to exclude other groups from the policy-making process, and policy communities within the business and financial sectors had the most success in advancing their interests with government. Public choice explanations of government policy-making focus on the roles of two key groups of individuals—politicians and bureaucrats—and how their self-interested actions affect policy outcomes. Based on this analysis and the preferred solution of public choice theorists to devolve more authority to a private market dominated by corporations, it is clear that policy directions in the public choice tradition will be dominated by elites, even if this is not a major foundation of the theory. And although many pluralists and public choice advocates might argue that elections at least provide the public with a choice over which elite is to govern, the declining percentage of eligible voters who actually vote in elections raises additional questions about the effectiveness of representative democracy as it is currently practised in Canada.

The evidence of who makes the major policy decisions in Canada is based on a number of studies dating back to the groundbreaking research of Porter (1965), and then the continuing work of Clement (1975, 1983), Panitch (1977), and Newman (1975, 1981, 1998). These studies found that a relatively few individuals, mostly male of Euro-Canadian descent, prospered greatly under existing policies and structures, enjoyed a disproportionate amount of influence, and exercised this power to ensure that these conditions remained in place.

Compelling accounts of who rules in Canada and the influence of elites are also provided in a series of books by Linda McQuaig. These include an examination of the tax system (*Behind Closed Doors*, 1987), an inquiry into free trade and the GST (*The Quick and the Dead*, 1991), an investigation into the reductions in funding for social and health programs (*The Wealthy Banker's Wife*, 1993), an examination of the reasons for the national debt (*Shooting the Hippo*, 1995), and a study of privilege and the super-rich, with Neil Brooks (*Billionaires' Ball: Gluttony and Hubris in an Age of Epic Inequality*, 2012). All of these books reveal consistent themes: the growing influence of elites, including the growth of multinational corporations and their independence from control by the state, the unequal distribution of wealth and income, the decline in the tax system's ability to redistribute income, and the declining support for the health and social service sector. Another study, by Brownlee (2005), demonstrates how the corporate elite in Canada, aided by conservative think-tanks such as the Fraser Institute, were able to promote the neo-liberal agenda. Indicators of who exercise major decision-making roles in Canada often focus on the CEOs for major companies and Crown corporations, government leaders, and the directors of major companies and Crown corporations. In Canada there has been some progress in the number of women who have become premiers and ministers of important cabinet portfolios. At the same time, women held less than 25 per cent of the seats in Parliament in 2014, well behind many other countries, and only three of the top 100 publicly traded companies were headed by female CEOs. As well, most boards are still heavily dominated by white males; for example, the boards of Manitoba's 12 largest companies have an average of less than 10 per cent women.

The research summarized above pertains to who rules on the grand issues of policy. It might be argued that a more balanced picture of participation would be seen with respect to decisions on ordinary policy issues. These include the decisions made by municipal governments, health facilities, school boards, social service organizations, and special commissions. Such decisions affect people directly in their day-to-day lives and the opportunities for public participation, including participation by services users and providers, would seem to be easier to facilitate.

Indeed, some recent experiences in Canada with respect to participation on ordinary issues tend to confirm that opportunities are available and that people do take advantage of these opportunities. For example:

- "Tens of thousands of Canadians" provided input to the Romanow Commission established to chart the future of health care in Canada (Romanow, 2002).
- In British Columbia, the Citizens' Assembly on Electoral Reform held 50 public meetings across the province, attended by 3,000 people, before issuing its report in 2004. In Ontario, the Citizens' Assembly on Electoral Reform incorporated a wide range of participatory processes, including a website that led more than 50,000 different visitors to download at least 10,000 key documents pertaining to electoral reform in that province (Institute on Governance, 2007).
- The Truth and Reconciliation Commission, which investigated the legacy of residential schools between 2010 and 2014, visited more than 300 communities and received more than 6,500 statements from those affected by residential schools. Thousands of people, both survivors and those welcomed as witnesses, attended the final four-day event held in Edmonton in March 2014 (Canadian Press, 2014).

Yet, closer examination of participation in the ordinary affairs of policy-making is required to determine the scope of public participation in decision-making. In the field of health care, citizen participation has been championed for some time, and the importance of redefining the citizen's role from passive consumer to active participant in the governance of health care was given special attention in the 2002 Romanow Report on health-care reforms. Despite some attempt to act on these recommendations, a recent review of current commitments at both the national and provincial levels suggests a significant shift from citizen involvement in decision-making to governments' merely seeking input on an advisory basis (Rodriques, 2013). This change from "public participation" to "public engagement," which is evident in the terminology currently used in Manitoba's regional health-care system, appears largely oriented to developing public support for priorities determined by health-care authorities. Another consideration is whether those who are engaged are representative of service users. In a study of citizen governance boards in 134 regional health authorities across Canada, Chessie (2009) found that the majority of board members were male, middle-aged, and university-educated, and there was little evidence of participation from more marginalized groups in society.

In general, those who are most often affected by decisions around health care, welfare reform, or housing availability are the least able and least likely to participate. In order to facilitate service user participation, the sites, times, and formality of the meetings must be adapted to respond to their needs and schedules. In the absence of meaningful opportunities to participate proactively in creating new policies or reforming existing ones, these citizens will have no choice but to exercise their democratic rights through protests, demonstrations, and movements such as Idle No More and the Occupy movement.

Policy-Making Models and Their Connection to Practice

The policy-making process outlined in this chapter introduces five different models. Three commonly identified approaches are the *rational* or *synoptic approach, incrementalism*, and *mixed scanning*. These models have stood the test of time, although each has its limitations. A fourth, the *value criteria model*, incorporates values as an explicit component of the policy-making process. This model is an adaptation of the rational model and was developed by the Institute for the Study of Child and Family Policy at North Carolina (Dobelstein, 1990; Moroney, 1991). Rein (1970) and Titmuss (1968) were early advocates of the need to explicitly examine values in the policy-making process.

The final model summarized in this chapter is the *garbage can model*, originally developed by Cohen, March, and Olsen (1972) for universities and related organizations, and later adapted by Kingdon (1995) to explain how policies are developed at the governmental level. This model identifies the importance of both problems and solutions as major ingredients in the policy-making process; however, it also explicitly recognizes the central role of politics, a somewhat neglected attribute of other models. We have selected these models for inclusion because they can be applied to planning and policy-making at both the organizational and governmental levels. The characteristics of each of these models are identified below.

The rational, value criteria, and mixed scanning approaches focus more on the prescribed steps to be followed to develop a set of policy recommendations, while the incremental and garbage can models focus somewhat more on the interactive processes that appear to result in new policies. Although evidence supports the application of each of these models, the incremental and garbage can models were developed more directly by observing the behaviours of policy actors that led to new policies.

There are a number of factors to consider in selecting an appropriate policy-making model. For example, the scope of the issue, its complexity, the resources available for planning, and requirements related to timing will influence which model or combination of models is selected.

In presenting these models we include a number of case examples. Although most of our examples are drawn from the field of child and family services, similar examples are to be found in other policy fields. If you have experience in another field of practice, try to identify examples from that field that might correspond to some of the models identified below.

The Rational Model

The rational or synoptic approach is based almost entirely on the analysis of objective data in an orderly sequence. This approach to policy-making is anchored in systems theory and the analysis of factual or observable data using the scientific method. While the irrationality of the policy process may be acknowledged, proponents of this model are more likely to attribute this irrationality to the unwarranted interference of politics, politicians, and political agendas. The preferred role for the planner is that of the expert technician who co-ordinates the complex tasks associated with policy-making.

The **rational model** is a goal-oriented approach to policy development in which goals and measurable objectives are clearly identified and options are evaluated, often including a calculation of benefits and costs. The rational model features five general steps (Carley, 1980):

1. Define the problem in objective (behavioural) terms.
2. Develop a list of all feasible alternatives that would resolve the problem under prescribed circumstances.
3. Project the general consequences likely to flow from each strategy and the probability of those consequences occurring.
4. Collect and examine data appropriate to each alternative strategy; then assess the relationship between predicted outcomes and policy objectives and the relative benefit–cost ratio of each alternative strategy.
5. Select the strategy that best approximates identified goals and objectives and achieves the best benefit–cost ratio.

Several problems have been identified with the rational model. One is the difficulty of identifying and analyzing all feasible alternatives in determining the single best solution. In the field of social policy, this can be characterized as an information- or a knowledge-related problem in that most policy decisions involve situations or circumstances that are somewhat unique, where the consequences cannot be adequately predicted, and where only a limited number of variables can be considered (Moroney, 1991). A second issue is that of values. Value assumptions are often not clarified, and if these are identified, it is assumed they can be ranked and dealt with in the same way as other types of information. In effect, the policy-maker is assumed to play a neutral or value-free role. Thus, policy-making within the rational model stresses technical rationality where the focus is on examining the most efficient means to achieve a predetermined end. However, the focus on means often results in inadequate attention to goals and related outcomes. The result may be that we are left with policies that may work on technical grounds but are inadequate in responding to the fundamental needs of service users. Finally, the rational model often assumes that implementation follows logically from policy initiation and formulation; thus, it pays inadequate attention to the complexity of implementation.

Although the comprehensive version of the rational model calls for an analysis of all possible alternatives, a later modification of the model limited the number of alternatives to be examined. Although this helps to restrict the scope of analysis to locating a "good enough" solution, limitations pertaining to the lack of transparency about values and the neglect of implementation issues remain.

In applying the rational model, policy development will typically begin with a data collection phase. The complexity of problems facing policy-makers is such that they often feel overwhelmed. Sometimes task forces, Royal Commissions, or special inquiries will be mandated to outline a policy direction after gathering information, hearing from stakeholders, and initiating special studies. These strategies reflect a rational approach to policy development, and such groups can perform a useful role in policy-making in some circumstances. However, the appointment of such bodies by governments or other decision-makers can also be used as a method to avoid taking action on controversial, complex, or costly issues while appearing to give these matters serious attention.

Certain aspects of the rational model are widely used by human service practitioners. The medical model, which begins with diagnosis, then follows with the identification of optional treatment approaches, and finally selects the most appropriate intervention, is based on the rational model. Similarly, the planned change model found in many frameworks for social work practice stresses an orderly, systematic approach to change. In either case, professionals most often take on the role of the expert or change agent working on, rather than with, a patient or client, who is considered to be a largely passive recipient of services.

Incrementalism

If the rational model of policy-making is seen as too isolated from the real world of politics and policy-making, a second model—incrementalism—has been criticized for being too closely associated with the status quo. **Incrementalism** is commonly associated with Charles Lindblom (1959, 1968, 1979), who referred to the process as "the science of muddling through." Lindblom argued that the consequences of alternatives remote from existing reality are more difficult to predict and that the best pathway to needed changes is found by calculating the marginal benefits of small adaptations from current approaches. Thus, analysis in incrementalism is limited to alternatives that are only slightly different from the status quo. Because different actors prepare policies for different problems quite independently, the term "disjointed incrementalism" is often applied to this approach.

Advocates of incrementalism suggest several benefits:

- Small-scale changes avoid major disruptions and the possibility of avoiding unanticipated negative outcomes that often result from large-scale changes. If a small change results in positive effects, it can be accelerated; if it leads to adverse effects, it can be halted and reversed without causing major problems.
- Incremental changes can usually be incorporated within existing organizational arrangements.
- The approach accounts for political and normative realities by incorporating these considerations into discussions of alternatives during the change process. Furthermore, such discussions can include the views of those who make policy, those who implement it, and those who are affected by it.

Incrementalism generally accepts that existing service mandates, program delivery, and power structures within service organizations are legitimate and appropriate. Because it relies primarily on small reforms to the status quo, it has been described as a conservative approach to change that tends to limit more innovative approaches. Although incrementalism may be appropriate if the existing system or program requires only limited changes (see Box 3.2), even Lindblom (1979) recognizes that it may not be appropriate when existing responses are clearly inadequate and more significant departures from the status quo are needed.

Box **3.2** | Incrementalism in Juvenile Justice

The following is a constructed case study created to illustrate incrementalism.

The juvenile justice program in Newtown had a long history of working with juvenile offenders using a supervision model that required young people to report to their probation officers on an individualized basis. Over a two-year period a commonly identified problem was the lack of job readiness skills for youth between the ages of 16 and 18. Despite the awareness of this problem, there were no resources to develop or implement a program that might be beneficial to this group of young people. In an effort to address the issue a management team examined the possibility of implementing a group supervision model for some young people on the agency's caseload as well as a model for implementing job readiness training. This process led to a six-month trial of a group supervision model for selected youth. During this period, some staff resources were diverted to planning a job readiness training program and mapping out a possible implementation plan. The six-month trial of the group supervision model demonstrated efficiencies in staff time that could be used to deliver job readiness training. The group supervision model for selected youth was adopted as an ongoing program and the new training program was launched.

Mixed Scanning

Mixed scanning was advanced by Etzioni (1967, 1976) in an attempt to integrate the best aspects of the rational and incremental models. Mixed scanning suggests that situational factors will determine when each approach should be emphasized. It advocates an approach to policy development that begins with a comprehensive analysis of the existing policy, including problems and possible alternatives, and then adopts an incremental approach to the implementation of new policies.

"Mixed scanning" is a cumbersome term for a model that captures what happens on many occasions, and a successful example of using mixed scanning is summarized in Box 3.3. Policy implementation often takes place in an incremental fashion, yet the use of more comprehensive approaches, including working groups, task forces, and commissions, to examine the broad policy environment attests to the influence of the rational model.

There are a number of similarities between mixed scanning at a macro level and strategic planning, which has been widely adopted within government departments and human service organizations over the past two decades. Although strategic planning

---

| Box **3.3** | Assessment of Risk in Child Welfare: Mixed Scanning in Action |

"Differential response" (DR) systems in child welfare involve the development of at least one alternative stream of services that focuses on family support services as a first response rather than the more intrusive investigation of child abuse and neglect. In Manitoba, a new initiative in DR announced in 2007 was accompanied by a commitment for new resources, but there was an important caveat: the service delivery system needed to develop and implement an improved model for assessing future risk of abuse and neglect, as well as family strengths and needs, in order to ensure that child safety was protected in the new service model.

A working group representative of the four main child welfare authorities in the province was formed, and two consultants were hired to help complete research tasks and co-ordinate activities of the working group. An initial literature review of approaches to risk assessment used in a wide range of jurisdictions in Canada, the US, and New Zealand was conducted. Information on the instruments (i.e., the assessment forms and protocols) and experiences in applying the models was then obtained. From this more extensive list, three different risk assessment instruments were selected for detailed analysis. Interviews were conducted with key informants who had used these instruments, and relevant research studies were examined in more detail. This led to the selection of a preferred option for implementation by authorities and approval by government. Once approved, a detailed and more incremental implementation plan was designed. This included engagement with practitioners to obtain recommendations for modifying the tools, a contract with trainers from the organization with copyright control of the tools, revisions to the tools, pretesting of the tools, and an implementation plan for ongoing roll-out of the new assessment model and protocols.

has been a popular approach to policy-making at the organizational level, it requires continued organizational investment to realize potential benefits. It is also plagued by three of the difficulties associated with many forms of policy-making. (1) It remains difficult to predict consequences, particularly in a policy environment where so much lies outside the effective control of organizations. (2) Too often, the failure to follow through in implementing the plan undermines the benefits associated with the new policy. (3) Most importantly, service users and front-line staff are frequently excluded from or under-represented in the planning process.

The Value Criteria Model

There are different versions of the **value criteria model**, sometimes referred to as the value-analytic model (Gallagher and Haskins, 1984), but they are similar in their over- all approach to policy-making. First, the problem is defined and available alternatives for dealing with it are identified. Although responses to a problem may represent only a limited range of alternatives, problem analysis can direct attention to important normative elements of the problem, including causality. For example, the conventional child welfare system has too often separated First Nations children from their fam- ilies, communities, and culture. Identifying and analyzing the negative consequences of this approach can spur a consideration of alternatives such as First Nations control over child and family services, the development of more community-based foster care resources, and the development of more culturally appropriate services.

A second step is the development of value criteria for evaluating alternatives. These value criteria should include both universal and selective criteria. Universal criteria may represent general value considerations such as effectiveness, efficiency, and feas- ibility, whereas selective criteria represent those values that are more specific to the problem or issue being considered. In the example above concerning First Nations child and family services, selective criteria may include self-determination, community responsibility, and cultural appropriateness.

The third step involves the gathering of data required to assess each alternative, and the analysis of each alternative according to value criteria.

In the final step, the alternative that maximizes the greatest number of values, including efficiency, is recommended, or various alternatives with identified strengths and weaknesses are presented to decision-makers.

The value criteria model, which includes steps similar to those in the rational model, can be infused with a participatory element that brings it closer to an inclusive model of planning. For example, in January 2013 Ontario announced its intention to work closely with First Nations, Métis, Inuit, and urban Aboriginal people to develop an Aboriginal Children and Youth Strategy that would transform the way services are designed and delivered, and improve outcomes for First Nations, Métis, Inuit, and urban Aboriginal children and youth. A Strategy Planning Unit within the Ministry of Children and Youth Services was established to co-ordinate the planning process. The strategy included steps to work in partnership with Aboriginal people based on a joint vision, with principles and actions that stress putting the needs of children and youth first. Representatives from Aboriginal groups, youth, and government participated in a joint planning process that included an examination of different service models and related action plans. The planning process was designed to lead to a strategic plan for implementation, beginning in 2015. As the strategy unfolds it will be important to assess whether this planning process leads to new innovations in service delivery and improved outcomes for Aboriginal children and youth.

Although the value criteria model has considerable appeal to policy development in the human services because of its explicit consideration of values, conflicts can arise over the criteria that ought to guide final policy selection. For example, if a particular policy choice maximizes more of the selected values but also requires higher costs, how is this conflict to be resolved? And who sets the primary values to be used in policy selection—the decision-maker, the policy researcher, the service user, or others?

The selection of value criteria, particularly those specific to the problem or issue, is the most controversial stage of this policy model, but it should be recognized that other policy-making models incorporate values even if this is done implicitly. In the value criteria model, values are explicitly identified and, at the very least, they become more visible and open to debate. While the selection of value criteria depends on the nature of the policy being considered, this step is the point at which an ethical framework for policy-making can be proposed. Therefore, it is important to identify guidelines, especially for the development of selective value criteria. Saleebey (1990) has identified some broad philosophical cornerstones relevant to policy-making in the human services:

- Begin with an ethic of indignation about the denial of human dignity and opportunities.
- Incorporate humane inquiry and understanding based on dialogue.
- Focus on compassion and caring.
- Incorporate a quest for social justice.

These four cornerstones foster empowerment and social change to promote equity. In a discussion of criteria for theory evaluation in social work research, Witkin and Gottschalk (1988) arrive at similar conclusions. As adapted to our purposes, the steps in developing value criteria for policy-making include the following:

1. The approach should be explicitly critical in considering historical, cultural, political, and economic factors.
2. People must be recognized as active agents in shaping as well as reacting to their environment.
3. The life experiences of service users must be considered.
4. Solutions should promote social justice.

The term **social justice** is frequently evoked, yet it is open to various interpretations. We adopt the position advanced by Rawls (1971), who argued persuasively that social and economic inequalities created in society should be adjusted to provide the greatest benefit to the least advantaged. Social justice, then, is about redressing problems of inequality.

The Garbage Can Model

The **garbage can model** was first developed by Cohen et al. (1972) in an effort to explain how organizations make decisions under conditions of uncertainty. Although universities were the original focus of analysis, application was generalized to other similar organizations. These organizations were described as "organized anarchies," characterized by problematic preferences, unclear technology, and fluid participation. Four streams or processes were originally conceptualized—problems, solutions, participation, and choice opportunities—although Kingdon (1995), who revised the model for widespread use, reduced the number of streams to three. The "choice opportunity" in the original model was likened to a "garbage can" into which various kinds of problems and solutions were dumped by participants as they were generated, and outcomes were a function of the mix in the can and how it was processed.

The modified garbage can model of policy-making developed by Kingdon (1995: 86–8) builds on the earlier work and is an attempt to describe policy-making as it unfolds in the day-to-day life of governments and organizations. Three "families" of processes are observed to exist in setting organizational or governmental agendas: problems, policies, and politics. These are likened to separate streams that often operate quite independently of each other. First, a "stream of problems" captures the attention of policy-makers in a government or an organization. Second, a policy community of specialists, which may include people inside or outside the organization, concentrates on generating policy proposals. These individuals or groups advance a "stream of solutions." Some of these ideas and solutions are taken seriously, while others are not. The third ingredient, the "political stream," is composed of elements such as public opinion, election results, administration changes, ideological shifts, and interest group campaigns. Participants in the policy-making process may be active in all three process streams at the same time, or they may be active in only one or two of these streams.

Each of the actors and processes associated with these streams can function as either an impetus or a constraint to change. There may be some overlap and some connection between the streams (e.g., groups may propose both their understanding of a problem and their preferred solution), but they are often separate from each other, governed by different considerations and styles. For example, significant problems with feasible solutions may not make it to the policy agenda because the problem lacks political support or the solution is inconsistent with the ideology of the government in power. In addition, feasible solutions may not gain acceptance if governments anticipate strong public resistance.

Although these streams usually operate independently, they do connect at times. This opens a **policy window** (see Figure 3.2) that can lead to problem recognition, agenda-setting, and the creation of new policies or programs. However, if these opportunities are missed (e.g., if no action is taken or if the political mood shifts), then the policy window will close and the opportunity will be lost, at least for the time being.

A key stage in the process is problem recognition and definition. Recognition, according to Kingdon, generally occurs through three mechanisms. The first is a change in indicators such as unemployment rates, economic growth, interest rates, or the rate of children in care. A second mechanism is a focusing event that directs attention and sometimes action in response to an issue. For example, the murder of a child in child welfare care or following the child's return to his/her parents can sometimes trigger significant policy changes in the delivery of child welfare services. The third mechanism is normal feedback from the operations of programs, including the role of evaluation in influencing policy development. Actuarial information on future requirements for

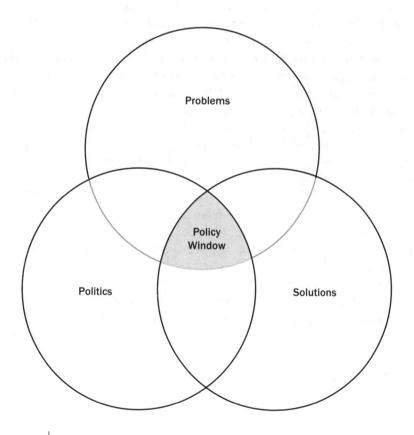

Figure **3.2** | Policy Window in the Garbage Can Model

pension payments, for instance, can lead to important policy questions about whether these obligations can be met through the current plan or whether there is a need to either reduce future benefits or increase contributions.

Pal (1992: 135) elaborates on Kingdon's list of mechanisms leading to problem recognition by identifying criteria that can be used to determine when a problem becomes a public problem. In order to define something as a public problem, he suggests that it must affect a substantial proportion of the public, offend or affront widely held public views or mores, or be the direct result of previous public policies.

It is often difficult to predict which issue will be defined as a public problem in that recognition depends on a combination of objective data and subjective perceptions that change is required. Indeed, in some cases, subjective perceptions become more important than objective data. For example, youth crime in Canada has been a major focus of the federal government in recent years despite the fact that the actual rate of youth crime has declined. This has not prevented a growing perception among the public that youth crime is increasing, a perception driven by government and fuelled by media attention on the operation of organized street gangs. Needless to say, "being tough on crime" is politically expedient, and sensational stories of organized gangs sell newspapers and attract television viewers.

Issues can remain on the policy agenda for some time, although the level of priority attached to certain issues may vary at different times depending on how the three streams interact. Furthermore, items can fall off the policy agenda because they cannot be sustained or because the problem may appear to be solved.

The garbage can model provides useful insights into the policy-making process, and it directs attention to the political environment that plays such a significant role both in determining how the process unfolds and, ultimately, in the outcomes that emerge.

A summary of the policy-making steps in each of the models is provided in Table 3.1, although we stress that these steps rarely follow each other in a linear fashion. We have also presented the models as discrete approaches, but in the real world of policy-making, this oversimplifies the policy development process. First, policy-making often combines elements from more than one approach, and this combination of approaches often provides a more accurate description of the policy-making process in a given context (see Box 3.4). Second, policy-making is a process of trying to decide what to do in situations in which values and opinions are often in conflict and where the final choice is heavily shaped by differing ideologies.

Summary and Conclusion

In this summary we consider how the policy-making models connect to the work of practitioners in the human services and to the lived experience of service users. At the outset we acknowledge the difference in purpose between policy and practice, a difference that often creates a gap between the two that is difficult to bridge. Policies

| Table **3.1** | Models of Policy-Making: A Summary |

A. The Rational Model

1. Define the problem in objective terms and classify goals.

2. Develop a comprehensive list of alternatives to address the problem.

3. Project possible consequences and the probability of occurrence for each set of alternatives.

4. Examine data for each strategy in relation to goals and benefit–cost calculations.

5. Select a strategy to maximize goals and to achieve the best benefit–cost ratio.

B. Incrementalism

1. Calculate the marginal benefits of a limited number of alternatives for addressing the problem.

2. Initiate small choices towards a solution that would achieve intended results on a trial-and-error basis.

3. Increase the emphasis on choices that produce positive results; reduce the emphasis on choices leading to negative results.

4. Allow new policies to emerge from a combination of choices that work.

C. Mixed Scanning

1. Define the problem and classify goals.

2. Conduct a comprehensive scan of alternatives.

3. Select alternatives for detailed analysis based on potential for goal achievement and feasibility.

4. Collect data and select the alternative best able to maximize goals and feasibility considerations.

5. Project incremental incorporation of policy choices.

D. The Value Criteria Model

1. Define the problem and identify policy alternatives available to deal with the problem.

2. Establish universal and selective criteria (values) for evaluating alternatives.

Continued ▶

▶ *Continued*

3. Gather data related to each alternative, and assess each alternative relative to value criteria.

4. Recommend the alternative that maximizes the value criteria, or offer a range of alternatives that maximize different criteria in different ways.

E. The Garbage Can Model

1. Three types of processes exist in agenda-setting for policy-making. These are characterized as streams of problems, solutions, and politics.

2. These streams exist somewhat independently of each other, and each actor and process can act as an impetus or a constraint to change. The streams are conceptualized as floating around in a garbage can, where on occasion the streams may come together and a window of opportunity opens. A key stage is public recognition of a problem and three mechanisms can contribute to this stage. These are a change in economic or social indicators, an unpredictable event, or feedback from program operations.

3. Once a policy window opens, the combination of problems, solutions, and political opportunity can lead to a new policy with the outcome dependent on characteristics associated with the problems, alternatives, and participants included in this mix.

4. If the opportunity is missed or if no action is taken, the policy window closes, and one must wait for the next opportunity. Issues can also sit on the policy agenda although they may be weighted differently at different times. In addition, items can fall off the policy agenda because interest cannot be sustained or because the problem appears to be resolved.

Sources: Rational model: adapted from Carley (1980: 11); incrementalism: adapted from Lindblom (1959); mixed scanning: adapted from Etzioni (1976); value criteria model: adapted from Dobelstein (1990: 71); garbage can model: adapted from Kingdon (1995: 86–8).

represent a general course of action to deal with a need or problem that affects a large number of individuals, whereas practice is concerned about what should be done for one or more service users in a particular context. Too often policies, when rigidly adopted, fail to consider the specific circumstances or needs of individuals or communities, which are, in fact, the primary concerns of both service users and practitioners. As noted in the Introduction, one way of closing the gap between policy and practice is to include service users and practitioners in the development of policy. Moreover, if policies in the human services retain some elements of flexibility, practitioners will be able to adapt these to the particular needs of individuals, families, and communities. We give special attention to inclusive models of policy development in Chapter 6.

Do any of the policy-making models ensure that the wisdom of practitioners and service users will be combined with that of policy-makers? The rational approach is primarily a top-down process that clearly assigns a primary role to policy analysts, who are responsible for drafting new policies or legislation. As the name suggests, incrementalism is a more informal process that may well facilitate partnerships

Box 3.4 | Policy-Making Often Involves a Combination of Planning Models

The transfer of jurisdictional control for the delivery of Aboriginal child welfare services to Aboriginal organizations in Manitoba, which occurred between 2001 and 2005, is described in more detail in Chapter 10. Early in the process, the highly publicized death of Phoenix Sinclair, a child who had been returned to the care of her parents, led to several reviews of the child welfare system in 2006. These reviews identified a wide range of recommendations to improve the system. Government's willingness to fund a broad range of these recommendations resulted in a co-ordinated implementation planning initiative called Changes for Children to implement these changes.

In describing the policy-making models used by government in response to these reviews, we conclude that none of the policy models provides a complete explanation for how policies emerged from the Changes for Children initiative. However, when several models are combined the development process is more accurately depicted. The initial recognition of a problem that required a policy response was precipitated by the murder of Phoenix Sinclair, who had received services from the child welfare system. This unpredictable event led the government to recognize issues in the child welfare system as a public problem requiring action, and a policy window, consistent with steps outlined in the *garbage can model*, was suddenly opened. At an early stage, framing of the problems occurred, and as options were generated there was often a reframing of the issues to be addressed. Of importance was a political commitment to maintain the newly created administrative structure but also to invest in options to improve the system.

The government's action to appoint committees to conduct comprehensive reviews (one of the service delivery system, one of children in institutions, and another of child deaths) and bring forward recommendations reflects steps associated with the *rational model*. At the same time, shifting the understanding of problems from recognition of the high number of children in care to the inadequate front-end response to this reality reflects processes outlined in the *garbage can model* because different interpretations of the problem were combined with several possible solutions (e.g., more training, more front-line staff, and a model of service that focused on better risk assessment and enhanced family support).

In its response to the reviews, the government committed $130 million to system improvements over a three-year period, embraced a differential response model of services (i.e., better front-end assessment and two streams of service: child protection and earlier intervention and support), and set up a special committee to co-ordinate planning and implementation. This committee first identified principles (i.e., value criteria) to guide its work, against which any new measures to be implemented would be assessed. This step draws on the *value criteria model* of planning. Finally, planning proceeded by outlining strategic directions based on recommendations from the reviews but quickly proceeded to a series of tasks, such as defining better assessment instruments and identifying pilot projects to test the new differential response system. This approach is consistent with a *mixed scanning model* of policy-making, including its incremental approach to implementation.

(With acknowledgement to Jay Rodgers, CEO, General Child and Family Services Authority, Winnipeg, Manitoba.)

between policy-makers and practitioners. Although a series of small steps can eventually lead to substantial changes, it is more likely that these steps will continue in a well-established direction and will not significantly challenge accepted ways of doing things, whether in policy or practice. Thus, incrementalism is unlikely to lead to major reforms; instead, incrementalism is more likely to promote an environment in which policy becomes routinized and practitioners become its caretakers. Although incrementalism allows for some limited contributions from practitioners, opportunities are not usually extended to service users. Like the rational approach, it is not seen here as the approach of choice. Although there are some advantages to mixed scanning because it represents a combination of both the rational and the incremental approaches, this combination means it cannot escape some of the limitations associated with these approaches. The value criteria model is an adaptation of the rational model; however, it incorporates the explicit treatment of values. This is its most important strength, but its ability to serve as a useful tool in connecting policy and practice is highly dependent on what values are selected for consideration and on how the process of value analysis is conducted. The garbage can model of policy-making incorporates political processes as a consideration in policy adoption. This model also recognizes a role for policy communities that contribute to the stream of solutions by recommending particular policies. Although practitioners and service users may be involved in these policy communities, their involvement is often quite limited. One of the reasons is that policy communities must usually sustain their efforts over a relatively long period of time to obtain relatively modest gains. Such long-term commitments are often difficult for both practitioners and service users.

Each of these approaches may be adapted to be more inclusive in ways that increase the potential of connecting policy and practice; however, none of them insist on inclusiveness. The value criteria model comes closest to realizing this potential in that it allows for the specification of values that can include consultation and/or decision-making input from practitioners and service users. Clearly, this policy-making model must adopt the central principle of inclusiveness if it is to succeed in connecting policy and practice concerns. But to achieve this principle, policy-making must be transformed from a process in which decisions are made in isolation at the highest level of the organization, and then packaged within this arena for marketing to a largely uninformed group of practitioners and service users.

Chapter 4 examines the policy-making process in more detail, including the steps involved in conducting policy analysis.

Critical Thinking Questions

1. Three theories were outlined to explain political behaviour and policy-making. How might each theory approach policies to reduce the rate of poverty in Canada?

2. Front-line staff often seem reluctant to engage in activities designed to influence policies, both within their immediate workplace and in the larger political environment. What are some of the possible reasons for this reluctance? What could be done to promote more active engagement?

3. Select a recently developed policy or program with which you are familiar. Using the policy-making models described in this chapter as options, what model or combination of models best explains the process of developing this policy? What is your critique of the process that was used?

4. What are the differences between the value criteria model of policy-making and the rational model? What is your critique of each model?

5. The public recognition stage of a problem is defined as central in the garbage can model of policy-making. What are the three mechanisms that can contribute to this stage? Illustrate two of these stages with examples.

Recommended Reading

J. Graham, K. Swift, and R. Delaney. *Canadian Social Policy: An Introduction*, 4th edn. Toronto: Pearson, 2012. The book provides an overview of social policy in Canada, including a chapter on diversity and social policy.

L. Miljan. *Public Policy in Canada: An Introduction*, 6th edn. Toronto: Oxford University Press, 2012. This book focuses both on the public policy-making process and on the policy developments in six fields of practice in Canada, including the social services.

A. Westhues and B. Wharf, eds. *Canadian Social Policy: Issues and Perspectives*, 5th edn. Waterloo, Ont.: Wilfrid Laurier University Press, 2012. This edited volume reviews some of the key factors affecting policy-making and includes separate chapters by leading scholars on a number of important social policy issues.

Chapter **4**

The Policy-Making Process

──────────────● **In this chapter you will learn about:** ●──────────────

- the common stages of the policy-making process and the related tasks within each of these stages;
- different perspectives and approaches to assessing needs;
- the importance of policy analysis and some of the frameworks used in policy analysis;
- a recommended framework to use in policy analysis that incorporates value considerations in decision-making.

Introduction

There are five stages in the policy-making process: initiation, formulation, adoption, implementation, and evaluation. As indicated in Figure 4.1, these stages can be compared to five commonly recognized stages in direct practice: problem identification, assessment, contracting, intervention, and evaluation. As in direct practice, careful attention to assessment or analysis is required. Analysis should occur throughout the policy-making process; however, it is useful to identify the different ways we apply this during each policy-making process. Analysis in the initiation stage can be conceptualized as **problem analysis**, and general application of what we refer to as **policy analysis** occurs at this stage and at the formulation stage. In our preferred model of policy analysis, discussed later in this chapter, we make it clear that one must clearly understand the nature and scope of the problem before identifying policy options and a preferred strategy. Many authors extend the nature and scope of policy analysis to include the evaluation stage; however, we prefer to define this stage as **policy evaluation**. A discussion of this stage is included later in the chapter. The adoption or execution stage is where options and implications from analytical activities are weighed and the policy decision

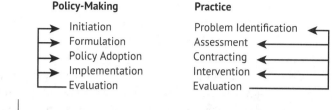

Figure **4.1**   Corresponding Stages of Policy and Practice Process

is made. Given the close connection between policy and practice in implementation, detailed discussion of this stage is included in the next chapter.

Policy-Making Stages

The Initiation Stage

In both policy-making and practice, action or change begins at a discernible point. In practice, the beginning point might take the form of a request by a service user for assistance, a referral from another agency, or a complaint by a neighbour or another professional. Initiation, or "issue identification and agenda-building" as it is sometimes called in policy-making, may result from interest group pressure, changes in economic or social indicators (e.g., unemployment, poverty), a crisis of some kind, or government response to a campaign promise.

In most scenarios, a **convergence of interest** (Sower, Holland, Tiedke, and Freeman, 1957) must occur before action to develop a new policy can happen. As conceptualized by Sower and his colleagues, a convergence of interest reflects the notion of an idea whose time has come: the perception that something simply has to be done about a particular condition. In the garbage can model of policy development, a convergence of interest is defined as a "window of opportunity" that occurs when the political stream, the stream of problems, and the stream of policy solutions come together. A convergence of interest is generally influenced by the amount of authority, legitimacy, and commitment demonstrated by the person, group, or organization advocating for change. Those in leadership positions within organizations or government have obvious advantages, but that does not mean either that a "policy window" will open or that those in non-leadership positions have no influence. For example, a change proposed by those in key leadership roles may encounter resistance from the public, staff within the organization, or those in more senior positions. As well, a staff person or an interest group with credibility or the power to impose sanctions may exert significant influence at this stage. Causes pursued by dedicated champions inside or outside the system can succeed despite the absence of other factors usually considered essential in bringing about change.

Factors that help in assessing the likelihood of policy initiation are evidence of need for the change, availability of resources, the complexity of the change being contemplated, organizational readiness, environmental readiness, and the commitment of key actors (see Table 4.1). The answers to the questions posed in Table 4.1 will help to determine whether this is the right time for policy initiation. Thus, a relatively simple change proposed by a minister in government and backed by resources has a high likelihood of being initiated. However, the scenario may shift if the minister's proposal involves a complex issue about which there is widespread disagreement. The prospect of a successful launch is more remote if the proposal for change comes from a community or a professional organization lacking close connections with the minister and the party in power.

The explanatory power of convergence of interest takes a different form in the event of a crisis such as the death of a child who has been receiving child welfare services. A crisis often provokes more immediate, previously unanticipated actions. For example, in Manitoba the 2006 discovery of the body of Phoenix Sinclair, a four-year-old child who had been killed by her parents after contact with the child welfare system, received so much media attention that it triggered a number of government-appointed reviews. Although these reviews resulted in a number of changes to the system, continuing concerns about the failures of the child welfare system led the government to appoint a commission to inquire into the circumstances surrounding the death and to recommend actions in its 2013 report (Hughes, 2013) to improve child welfare services in the province.

Table **4.1**	Factors to Consider in Assessing the Likelihood of Policy Initiation
Factors	**Key Questions**
Need for change	Is the change a political priority or do results from a formal needs assessment support change?
Complexity of issue	How complex is the issue and is action required by several sectors?
Commitment of key actors	Do key decision-makers and those with influence over the decision support the change?
Organizational readiness	Do organizations that must plan and implement the change have the motivation and capacity to do so?
Environmental readiness	Do important stakeholders in the policy environment, including the public, support the change?
Availability of resources	Are sufficient resources available to implement the change?

The most complex aspect of the initiation stage involves defining the problem to be addressed. Social problems are difficult to pin down and yet the definition sets the stage for the rest of the policy-making process. Although it is commonly used, the term "definition" is problematic because it connotes clarity and precision. In many respects, the term "framing," which outlines the general parameters of the issue being addressed, is a more accurate description of this process. Framing provides a sense of direction. It sets out preferences and prescribes limits based on ideologies and experiences, but refrains from the explicitness expected of a definition. Although Rittel and Webber (1973) use "definition" rather than "framing," the essence of the latter notion is captured by their description of social problems as "**wicked problems**."

Wicked problems have a number of distinguishing properties.

- There is no definitive formulation of a wicked problem.
- Wicked problems have a "no stopping rule": they are resolved over and over again.
- Solutions to wicked problems are not true or false but are good or bad, depending on one's values and experience.
- Every solution to a wicked problem is a "one-shot operation"; because there is no opportunity to learn by trial and error every attempt counts significantly.
- Every wicked problem is essentially unique.
- Every wicked problem is a symptom of another problem (Rittel and Webber, 1973: 167–8).

Framing the problem is the most important aspect of the initiation stage because it involves consideration of underlying causes. Thus, if the problem of poverty is framed as the unwillingness of people to work, then the solution would be to force people to work or to provide incentives so that more individuals will find and keep employment. However, if poverty is framed as the consequence of a lack of employment opportunities, faulty public policies such as gaps in educational preparation and job readiness training, and inequality, then, besides determining if there are sufficient opportunities for employment, the task becomes one of examining the very concept of work, who receives compensation, and the adequacy of compensation to lower-income individuals and families. Framing the problem of poverty in this way implies the need for a more comprehensive examination of issues and options.

The framing of wicked problems is heavily influenced by the ideologies outlined in Chapter 1. Many of those who have had influence in framing problems and developing social policies in the past three decades have reflected responses to crises which have been limited to searches for short-term solutions. Thus, health-care funding was restricted and directed primarily to hospitals and doctors at the expense of health promotion and early intervention, in turn contributing to a crisis in medicare. Similarly, child welfare programs have focused on child protection rather than early intervention and prevention. Paradoxically, this focus has led to higher numbers of children in care and increased costs. These frames have set the context for practice, and a deep and continuing fault line has been created by the gap between the needs of service users and the policies ostensibly designed to serve them. As a result, practitioners have been forced to focus their energy on crisis-oriented responses or on trying to address the gap with too few resources or supports to make a real difference.

Assessing Problems, Needs, and Resources

The problem analysis phase of the initiation stage involves careful consideration of both objective and subjective aspects of the problem. Central issues include how many people are affected by the condition and how they feel about and react to the issue. In policy analysis, analyzing problems differs from the way problems are defined in traditional research. While both are concerned with who, what, and where issues, in policy analysis it is particularly important to understand the history and causality of the problem, previous attempts to address the problem, and the community's readiness to deal with the problem.

Once problems have been framed and defined, they have to be translated into needs. Problems are closely related to needs, but needs reflect the gap between what the situation is and what it should be. If there is insufficient information available on these needs, it will be necessary to conduct a needs assessment. "Need" can be a difficult concept to define and measure. One can distinguish between needs and wants; where wants are what people are willing to pay for, needs are closer to what people are willing to march for. In this context, needs take on attributes more closely related to rights, or what all people should have available to them.

Needs also differ in terms of importance, and this depends on circumstances. This is illustrated by Maslow's (1954) approach to the definition of needs for individuals. He argued that needs can be conceptualized in a hierarchical fashion. Therefore, a person is primarily concerned with meeting physiological needs first (i.e., food and shelter), safety and security needs later, and then higher-level needs such as love and self-actualization. As a person's needs at a more basic level are met, more attention can be paid to higher-level needs. This approach is demonstrated by the provision of services to abused women and their children in cases of domestic violence. For example, if the abuse is serious the first response will be to refer the woman and her children to a shelter. Only after this basic need is met will consideration be given to such things as restraining orders (security and safety), counselling services (to help restore self-esteem), and longer-term employment (to achieve autonomy and self-sufficiency).

Need is a relative concept that is affected by both values and context. As well, standards and public attitudes change over time. Accessible transportation for the disabled, which is clearly identified as a need in most urban centres in Canada today, would have likely been defined as a want or luxury a generation or two ago. Because of our interest in relating needs to the development of programs, there must also be some expectation that resources can be identified to respond to these needs and that the technology is available to solve the problem.

Four different types of need commonly recognized are normative, perceived, expressed, and relative (Kettner, Moroney, and Martin, 2013). As outlined in Table 4.2, each perspective has both advantages and disadvantages. A **normative perspective on need** suggests that one can measure the existence of need through the use of a commonly accepted standard. The Statistics Canada LICO, described in Chapter 1 as one measure to estimate the number of people living in poverty, is one such standard. Other standards have been developed to define the adequacy of housing, nutrition, and the ratio of hospital beds to population in a community or region. Although standards are helpful in defining needs, they are not always available.

Perceived needs are what people think or feel they need. Perceived needs are measured by asking people what they need through survey methods or interviews. But perceived needs are not always a good reflection of who would actually use services. For example, estimates of those who are sexually abused are commonly provided to demonstrate the prevalence of sexual abuse, yet not all of these victims would use services that might be developed to respond to this need.

Expressed needs can sometimes be confused with perceived needs; however, they are not the same thing. If a need is expressed, there must be some attempt to obtain a service. Wait lists or the number of referrals for service are common methods of measuring expressed needs. Although this approach to needs assessment brings us closer to understanding the demand for a service, it also has its flaws. If people know there are long wait lists for family counselling at a family service agency, they may not bother to register because they are not prepared to wait six months for a service they require now. Instead, they may seek out a private practitioner or go without this service. As well, people cannot be expected to express a need by registering for a service that does not yet exist!

The final perspective is **relative need**. Relative need does not begin with the assumption that a standard or criterion exists. Instead, the level of need in one area or community is compared with the level in another community to identify differences that may require attention. Comparisons of the unemployment rate in a First Nations community with another community or with the national or provincial average reflect a relative perspective on need. Although a relative approach to needs assessment provides for a wider range of comparisons than might exist if one used a normative perspective, this perspective also has limitations. Comparative studies of child poverty may lead to preoccupation with differences between provinces, and these differences may then divert attention from the substantive issue of child poverty. To summarize, it is most often appropriate to include data that reflect more than one perspective on needs because this will provide a more complete understanding of the issue.

A number of different methods can be used to measure needs within the four perspectives identified above. The first step is to examine what information already exists. This might involve a review of such things as social indicators, including data available through Statistics Canada, local and national research studies, and records on service utilization. New information may be collected through surveys or interviews

Table 4.2	Four Types of Need		
Type	**Definition**	**Example**	**Strengths and Limitations**
Normative need	Need defined as falling below an accepted standard	The number of Canadians in poverty as defined by those falling below the Statistics Canada LICO (after tax)	• Gap between documented level and standard provides evidence-based support for action (strength) • Standards often not available or accepted (weakness)
Perceived need	Need determined by what people think or feel	The number of people in a community survey who define their neighbourhood as lacking in recreation services	• Provides representative views of a potential target group (strength) • Perceptions can change quite quickly (weakness) • May not reflect demand or potential use of a new service (weakness)
Expressed need	Need defined as number of people who have actually tried to obtain a service	The number of people who have requested family counselling and been placed on a wait list	• Provides a good predictor of the number of people likely to use a service (strength) • May omit people who have given up trying to obtain the service (weakness) • Is not a useful measure when no service exists for a newly identified problem (weakness)
Relative need	Need determined by a comparison of data from one area or community with another or with a provincial or national average	The rate of First Nations children in care compared to the rate of non-First Nations children in care	• Allows one to measure gaps where standards do not exist (strength) • May focus on differences in need to the exclusion of other factors such as available services or factors amenable to intervention (weakness)

with service users and providers. Wait lists, trends in the number of referrals, and rates under treatment are examples of information on need that may be able to be obtained from service providers. More interactive techniques, employing primarily qualitative methods, can also be used (see Witkin and Altshuld, 1995). These include community forums, focus groups, and nominal group methods. Public hearings, sometimes organized as a component of special commissions, are an expanded version of a community forum in which an individual or group may present a brief on the issue being examined.

Needs studies also make use of evaluation research methods, particularly in cases where studies can demonstrate a cause-and-effect relationship. For example, the development of needle exchange programs in Canadian cities was based on evidence linking the multiple uses of needles by users to the spread of HIV.

While needs assessment studies are useful in policy-making, they should be combined with an assessment of assets and capacities. Here again, a parallel between policy and practice can be drawn. In the human services, there is a growing awareness of the need to build on strengths at the individual, family, and community levels in order to promote change, and this process begins with an identification of existing strengths and resources as an important aspect of the assessment stage. McKnight and Kretzmann (1996) apply a similar approach to policy-making at the community level in suggesting that needs-oriented assessments give us only half the picture. What is required to complete the picture is an identification of strengths and resources—a process described as mapping community capacity or **asset mapping**.

Using the community as an example, three types or levels of strengths and resources should be considered. First, there are the resources and strengths of individuals and organizations within the community that are largely subject to community control. Next are the assets located within the community that are largely controlled by outsiders. These assets may include both private and public institutions such as hospitals, schools, and social service agencies. Finally, potential building blocks include those resources located outside the community that are controlled by outsiders. These may include actual or potential social transfer payments and capital improvement expenditures. With this kind of information, a policy analyst is in a better position to match existing needs to options that build both on identified strengths and potential resources. While the principle of assessing strengths and resources is perhaps easier to apply in the case of a geographic community, it can also be applied to groups linked through affiliation or interest. In order to make a helpful contribution to the policy-making process, conventional approaches to needs assessment must be modified to incorporate procedures that develop an inventory of resources and capacities. Developing a resource inventory is not always a complicated process. For example, a matrix that lists potential resources and then assesses whether these are available and adequate, available but inadequate, or not available, can be quite helpful to the analysis of needs and resources. A key issue in project development is localized capacity development, that is, does the project use local assets and help them to grow?

Policy Formulation Stage

The second stage of the policy-making process—formulation—involves developing and analyzing alternatives. The methods used in policy analysis are particularly relevant to this stage of the planning process, and a model for policy analysis is outlined later in this chapter. Policy analysis, as it is applied in the formulation stage, is concerned with predicting the future consequences of different policy options. This requires a focus on both empirical data and the political aspects of decision-making. Because policy analysis tries to predict the anticipated outcomes of policy alternatives, it often considers outcome evaluation studies conducted on similar policies that have been implemented elsewhere. Even though the major thrust or direction for change may have been set by how the problem has been framed, a number of different potential responses still need to be considered. Thus, in formulating a response to youth crime, policy-makers may want to consider whether expanding the number of police and probation officers is preferable to an increase in the number of juvenile detention facilities, or whether more community-based responses are preferred over either of these options.

Formulating alternatives may begin in brainstorming sessions in which no suggestion, however improbable, is rejected (see Box 4.1). Once all possible alternatives have been identified, research should be conducted to identify potential outcomes from selected alternatives. Criteria may be identified to assist in the selection process and considerations may include the anticipated cost, the feasibility of implementation, and potential outcomes for beneficiaries. The ranking of preferred options will normally reflect some mix of value considerations and available evidence. Often, certain trade-offs will be required. For example, do benefits to those at greatest risk outweigh increased financial costs? And does the accessibility of a new service take precedence over a more centralized service system that would be easier to administer?

Box **4.1** | Learning Activity: Formulating Alternatives for Poverty Reduction

Select a special target group affected by poverty in your community that requires new or increased efforts aimed at poverty reduction. Examples are recent immigrants or refugees, children, single parents, and Indigenous Canadians.

- Identify the main causes of poverty among this group. What are some of the needs to be addressed?
- Select one priority need and brainstorm possible solutions (i.e., policy alternatives or options) to this need.
- Now prioritize the alternatives to be explored in more detail. Why have you selected these alternatives for further research and examination?

This process can be used again to examine other needs for your target group.

Special commissions and task forces are favourite vehicles for dealing with complex issues at the formulation stage. Although these structures can be important in addressing complex issues, they also can have a particular advantage to government in dealing with controversial issues: they give the appearance of action while buying time before a decision is required, thus permitting government to assure everyone that the problem is being studied in depth by experts! While special commissions can be a means of postponing a policy response, they can also draw attention to the need for a significant policy response. One example is the Romanow Commission on the Future of Health Care, which released its report in November 2002. This raised expectations for both reform of medicare and new investment in health care by the federal government. Another example is the Commission on the Reform of Ontario's Public Services (2012), whose report includes recommendations to improve the province's public finances as well as reform health, education, and social programs.

The Royal Commission on Aboriginal Peoples (RCAP) (1996) is perhaps the most comprehensive study of any policy field ever conducted in Canada. Although it formulated a variety of recommendations to address the rights of Aboriginal peoples in Canada, there has been only limited progress in responding to these findings. Nevertheless, the Commission's findings have provided evidence that has been used to frame the "problem" of underdevelopment and colonization in Aboriginal communities.

An integral part of government consultations, special commissions, and task forces is inviting the public to attend hearings and to submit briefs. However, in government-controlled consultations there is no way to be sure that all views will be represented in an equal and fair fashion. For example, a government may select those views more consistent with its own perspective or exercise control at the input stage by selecting who is allowed to present briefs. Commissions that are independent or at arm's length from government have greater autonomy in presenting recommendations, but even here government has the option of selecting those recommendations it chooses to consider.

One useful way of analyzing the extent of the influence of citizens in the policy-making process is provided by a framework called "a ladder of citizen participation." The ladder has eight rungs (see Figure 4.2). The top three rungs—citizen control, delegated power, and partnerships—represent differing degrees of citizen power. The next three, which include placation, consultation, and informing, symbolize degrees of tokenism. Consultation, the middle rung of this group, allows "the have-nots to hear and have a voice, but ... they lack the power to ensure that their views will be heeded by the powerful" (Arnstein, 1969: 217). The two bottom rungs—therapy and manipulation—refer to processes that do not enable participation. We refer again to this useful conceptualization in the discussion of community governance in Chapter 6.

Policy Adoption

At the policy adoption or execution stage, policy options are reviewed and a decision is made. As noted in Chapter 3, in federal and provincial policy matters, recommendations

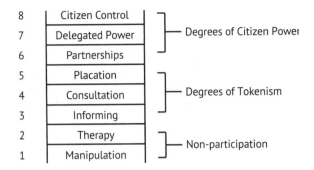

Source: Reproduced from Arnstein (1969: 217).

involving major changes and/or a substantial increase in resources will be reviewed by analysts from a standing committee of the cabinet and/or Treasury Board before a final decision is made. When the policy takes the form of new legislation or changes to existing laws, the cabinet will review and approve these plans prior to sending the draft bill to Parliament or the legislature for a decision.

At the organizational level, new policy proposals will generally be reviewed by senior staff, and by the board of directors in the case of a voluntary agency. In a voluntary agency, the board, acting most often on advice from the executive director, will decide whether to proceed with the plans.

Implementation

Implementation is the fourth stage of the policy-making process, and in practice there are some similarities between this stage and the intervention stage. For example, resistance to intervention in practice is not uncommon in non-voluntary service contexts such as corrections and child welfare; in policy implementation, resistance may emerge from service users and providers if new policies are assessed as imposing additional obligations on front-line staff and/or as failing to match the particular needs of service users. At the same time, one should not underestimate the differences. Intervention in front-line practice is shaped by the nature and scope of policies and the ways these have been implemented. Because policy implementation is generally mediated by a larger number of political and bureaucratic decision-makers and is designed to meet the general needs of a target population, there is a greater likelihood that policies may fail to match the specific needs of an individual service user. In these circumstances the ability of the practitioner to modify and adapt policies often will determine the extent to which service users' needs are met. We return to the topic of policy implementation in the next chapter.

Evaluation

Policy Research and Evaluation

Evaluation is the final stage of the policy-making process, but all stages should be subjected to evaluation in order to improve the process as it unfolds. Evaluation results from policy implementation are particularly important, and this information may cause us to alter our understanding of the problem, to modify goals, or to include new activities in the implementation stage.

It is not always easy to distinguish between program and policy evaluation because there is considerable overlap. First, a new policy often leads to one or more programs that may be established to carry out the policy. For example, changes to child welfare legislation that incorporate both mediation and family group conferencing as alternative methods of dealing with child protection concerns can lead to the development of programs to promote these approaches. And even if family group conferencing is identified as a separate policy under a new legislative framework that includes several new policy initiatives, there may be a variety of family group conferencing programs set up across the province. Second, many of the methods used to evaluate programs can be used to evaluate the impact of more general policies. However, program evaluation generally refers to measuring the effects from a specific program, whereas policy evaluation is concerned with the broader assessment of a general course of action, framework, or piece of legislation.

A policy study may involve a large-scale study of multiple sites, or a review of program evaluation results from separate studies of individual programs. In addition, a policy study often involves a review of research or evaluation studies on the topic from other jurisdictions. Policy evaluation studies, then, often combine direct research with secondary analysis of research that has been conducted on the issue. In the family group conferencing example, a specific program evaluation might be conducted on the family conferencing initiative launched by a particular agency. However, government may be interested in whether family conferencing, in general, is an important policy initiative and whether it should be expanded to new sites. Thus, a more general policy evaluation of all sites might be commissioned with specific guidelines to examine effectiveness and efficiency on a province-wide basis; as well, the study may involve a review of family group conferencing models and outcomes from other jurisdictions.

An important consideration is the extent to which policy is shaped by research and evaluation information about what works. Too often we have contradictory knowledge about what works in the social services or our evidence is limited to results from small studies that are unable to accurately predict the long-term effects of new initiatives. The uncertainty of social service knowledge has produced an increased interest in outcome-based research and **evidence-based practice**.

Evidence-based research has been influential in health policy for some time, but there has been increased attention to this in the social services over the past 15 years. Although focused policy evaluation studies can influence the adoption of specific policies, major shifts in policy seldom occur from a single study. Rather, the accumulation of evidence from a variety of research studies influences significant changes in policy direction. Such studies often draw on quantitative research that can provide evidence of sustainable, positive outcomes. One of the best examples of this in the Canadian context is the research demonstrating a need to focus on the early years in improving outcomes for Canadian children, particularly those who are identified as vulnerable (see Box 4.2).

Policy research units, such as the Manitoba Centre for Health Policy, have been instrumental in demonstrating the links between risk factors, such as poverty and child maltreatment, and health and educational outcomes by analyzing datasets compiled by different government departments (Brownell et al., 2010). Research studies such as this and the *Canadian Incidence Study of Reported Child Abuse and Neglect* (Trocmé et al., 2010) (see Box 4.3) provide important data on trends that can be used to counter more residual views on social policies. At the same time, there is no guarantee that empirical evidence alone will be used to transform social policies or trump strongly

---

Box **4.2** | Linking Research to Policy Development

Research on the early years by McCain and Mustard (1999) using data collected by the National Longitudinal Study of Children and Youth in Canada and research results from other jurisdictions, such as the US, drew particular attention to the importance of the early years of life in setting a firm base for competence and coping in later life. This study was followed by further research and the examination of studies from other countries that linked early brain development to future learning, mental health and behaviour, and physical health. The evidence identifying pathways to poor outcomes was used to recommend programs promoting resilience and to calculate the cost-effectiveness of early childhood development programs. Although the benefits to individuals directly involved with these programs cannot be measured simply in dollars, this is important to government and other funders. Using this criterion the evidence is persuasive.

The Perry Pre-School Project was an influential American study that has helped to support increased attention to the early years. This project demonstrated that for every $1 spent in the program, $17 in public expenditures was saved by the time the child reached age 40. As well, research on publicly funded child care in Canada has demonstrated that initial investments are more than repaid in additional tax revenues from working parents while providing benefits associated with quality child care for children. The accumulation of evidence on the importance of early years programming has led to new policies and programs focused on screening and support services for vulnerable children from birth and in pre-school and child-care programs that target young children at risk. In addition, this evidence has brought about the expansion of kindergarten programs across Canada and elsewhere. Despite these positive developments, much is yet to be done as Canada's spending on early childhood education remains well below the average for OECD countries (Alexander and Ignjatovic, 2012).

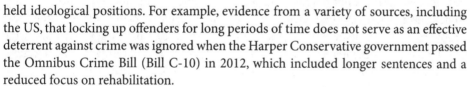

Box **4.3** | Using Policy Research to Provide Information for Policy Analysis

The lack of national information on the incidence of child abuse and neglect in Canada led the federal government to provide funding for a first national study on this issue that was completed in 1998 (see Trocmé et al., 2001). This study was replicated in 2003 (Trocmé et al., 2005) and 2008 (Trocmé et al., 2010) by using a cluster sampling design that reported on child maltreatment investigations in child welfare sites across the country. A common classification for types of maltreatment was used to avoid definitional and tracking differences within the provinces and territories. By applying weights, a national picture of the nature of child maltreatment, worker characteristics, placement patterns, and factors associated with maltreatment and placement was obtained. Comparative data provide policy-relevant information on a number of issues. Of particular significance are the following findings: in 48 per cent of 2008 investigations the child had been previously referred for suspected maltreatment; in only 27 per cent of 2008 investigations was the case to remain open for ongoing services; and the higher proportion of Aboriginal children who were investigated and placed in alternative care resources was associated with poverty and related parenting difficulties that require policies aimed at poverty reduction and an increase in family support services. These findings have been used to shape policy responses within the child welfare field, including support for more emphasis on early intervention and family support as a first response to families referred to the child welfare system.

held ideological positions. For example, evidence from a variety of sources, including the US, that locking up offenders for long periods of time does not serve as an effective deterrent against crime was ignored when the Harper Conservative government passed the Omnibus Crime Bill (Bill C-10) in 2012, which included longer sentences and a reduced focus on rehabilitation.

The adoption of new initiatives is encouraged when evaluation is able to influence a shift in public opinion; in these circumstances government is more likely to respond. Obviously, the use of policy-relevant research will be enhanced if the research provides credible evidence and is based on sound methodology. And while the application of research results is shaped by a number of other factors, such as political context, timing, and the presence of leaders or champions who promote the use of findings, Nutley, Walter, and Davies (2007) suggest a number of strategies that can help:

- Tailor dissemination to potential users and provide support for the discussion of findings.
- Include interactive approaches wherever possible, such as partnerships between researchers and practitioners, and promote the testing of findings within the local context.
- Offer technical, financial, organizational, and emotional support for the implementation of research-based protocols, tools, and programs.

At a general level, program or policy evaluation involves the systematic collection, analysis, and reporting of information about a program, service, or intervention for use in decision-making. While this identifies evaluation as a technical process, contextual, resource, and political factors also affect use. These issues mean that policy and program evaluation involves activities that are partly social, partly political, and only partly technical.

Types of Evaluation

Program or policy studies make use of methods associated with different approaches to evaluation (Patton, 2008), and we can distinguish between formative and summative approaches. A formative evaluation examines program or policy processes in an effort to improve or enhance a program, while a summative evaluation examines the outcomes, impact, and efficiency of a program or policy (i.e., its overall effectiveness).

Formative evaluations—sometimes referred to as process evaluations—are concerned with the components of a policy or program, what services are being provided, and whether the policy or program is reaching those for whom it was intended. Implementation studies involving an assessment of policy processes are particularly relevant to new policies because they attempt to describe the details of the policy in order to ascertain what is causing certain effects or whether the policy is being implemented as planned. Two major sets of issues are considered: (1) coverage or actual participation in the program by the intended target population; and (2) service delivery, including the sequence of activities undertaken to achieve policy objectives. If a policy or program is not operating effectively, an implementation evaluation can help to determine what has gone wrong and what improvements can be made. Often these problems exist in one or more of the following areas: (a) a policy approach or design that fails to meet the needs of service users; (b) a lack of program acceptance caused by the attitudes of staff or administrative policies that create barriers to access; (c) program management; and (d) program costs (Love, 1992).

Summative evaluations concentrate on policy or program outcomes and efficiency. An outcome study is concerned with the extent to which a policy meets its objectives, and, where those objectives involve changes for service users, how long those changes last. Efficiency evaluation is concerned with the ratio of benefits to costs; various forms of cost–utility analysis may be performed, including benefit–cost and cost-effectiveness studies.

Formative and summative approaches to policy evaluation have been discussed as separate strategies; however, many studies combine these approaches. For example, an evaluation may be concerned both with whether the policy is being implemented as intended and what the effects of the policy are on service users. However, we stress that the evaluation of new policies requires a special focus on formative issues, that is, the activities and the organizational processes associated with implementation. While both quantitative and qualitative methods are relevant to such studies, the collection of data often includes a special focus on qualitative interviews with key informants, service user feedback, and a review of documents. **Triangulation**, which involves collecting data from more than one source, using different data collection methods or different investigators, is recommended in such studies.

There is considerable overlap between policy and program evaluation studies and functions associated with performance measures and monitoring. Performance measurement can be defined as the ongoing reporting of program outputs (i.e., services provided and individuals served) and outcomes (i.e., indicators of results and related costs). Performance measurement systems provide feedback on program performance to funders and program sponsors as well as management. Monitoring can be defined as the assessment of the extent to which a program is implemented as designed and reaches its intended target group. Although program monitoring focuses more on questions of who is being served than on what is being accomplished, its functions overlap with those of performance measurement. For example, both functions may make use of management information systems and standard ongoing reporting protocols. Information from performance measurement and monitoring is relevant to program and policy evaluation; however, it may lack the comprehensive details on services provided and outcomes that can be obtained through more targeted program and policy evaluation studies.

A primary focus on outcomes may become the purpose of evaluation in mature programs, and in such studies the use of control or comparison groups can provide additional evidence of whether the policy or program is responsible for observed changes in behaviour or outcomes. Computer-based monitoring systems that incorporate outcome measures have become more popular in the human services, and such systems can meet some of the purposes associated with performance measurement systems and program evaluation. While these systems can be helpful, certain disadvantages exist. They are less likely to include feedback from service users, and they focus largely on recording and retrieving quantitative information. In addition, they often fail to promote community and service user empowerment because the organization controls both the technology and the information.

The evaluation dilemma posed here is not easy to resolve. Information on needs and resources, program design, activities, effectiveness, and costs are essential requirements for good policy-making. Methods for program and policy monitoring, as well as carefully designed outcome studies, can help to provide this information. But these approaches are not sufficient. In many situations these approaches must be accompanied by more **participatory evaluation methods** if we are to generate information needed to respond to the differing cultural and social needs of service users.

A wide range of literature focuses on the use of participatory research and empowerment-oriented evaluations (see, e.g., Community Tool Box, 2013; Fetterman and Wandersman, 2007). The principles and methods discussed in these approaches should be carefully considered because they promote greater community and service user control over both the evaluation process and results.

Our understanding of effectiveness in many human service programs also needs to be broadened to capture some of the building blocks of front-line work. For example, human services work requires the development of positive relationships with service users, and intervention needs to be focused on efforts to promote empowerment and link people with other services in responding to their needs. These efforts and the inherent changes in self-efficacy that may occur as a result are often missed in assessing more commonly measured program outcomes, such as whether independent living goals were achieved or whether a child was admitted to care. As Benjamin and Campbell (2014) suggest, the focus of evaluation needs to be extended beyond the more concrete, measurable aspects of program objectives to capture such things as the relational aspects of service because the results from these types of interactions may lead to sustainable changes over time.

To this point we have described policy analysis and evaluation as if all activities were carried out in relation to a single policy. In fact, policy-making often involves the development of several policies embedded within a more general policy direction. This requires the co-ordinated assessment and development of several policies at different levels, often simultaneously. Thus, a new policy in health care designed to integrate community and institutional-based services is likely to require a new role for hospitals, as well as several new policies that might affect training, use, and expenditures within hospitals. For community-based health-care services there will also be a number of new policies, such as an increased emphasis on home care, that may emerge from this more general policy change. In circumstances such as these, policy analysis and evaluation must be concerned with both the actual and the anticipated effects of several different policies. Different methods and sources of data as well as different approaches to analysis will be required, and policy recommendations reflecting a more co-ordinated approach to policy development in a particular field of practice are the desired goal. Unfortunately, this more integrated approach to policy evaluation and reform is all too rare in the human services.

Policy Analysis

At the beginning of this chapter we drew a distinction between policy analysis, which occurs at the planning stage, and policy evaluation, which examines actual rather than predicted outcomes from a specified policy. Although this distinction has merit, some authors use the term "policy analysis" to cover both sets of activities, and while models for policy analysis are commonly used in planning new programs, with some shift in focus they can also be used to evaluate an existing policy. There are various frameworks for policy analysis and it is sometimes difficult to select a particular model for use. To some extent this decision depends on the type of policy you are examining, the particular context, and the focus of your analysis.

General Models of Policy Analysis

Policy analysis is not without certain limitations. Five of these are outlined by Westhues (2012):

- The policy analysis process can be exceedingly slow.
- Efforts to make changes in policies can be resource-intensive and involve a considerable commitment of time, money, and energy. These limitations can make it harder to sustain engagement in the process.
- Even with the investment of resources it may not be possible to produce changes consistent with social justice principles.
- The policy analyst in government or an organization often faces a dilemma about how political factors will influence the presentation of proposals.
- Approaches to policy analysis often fail to adequately consider issues of difference, such as gender and diversity, in the development of policy proposals. Although increased attention to the use of policy lenses, as discussed later, is helpful in responding to this limitation, there is often no requirement to incorporate such considerations in analyzing social policies.

Despite these limitations, developing knowledge and skills in policy analysis is essential for promoting progressive policy changes.

Westhues outlines four general models of policy analysis. One is the *evidence-based model* where data is systematically gathered from existing or new research, and the analyst as the expert determines the implications for change. This positivist approach to policy analysis was dominant in Canada from 1960 to 1980, and it has become more popular again recently with increased use of **meta-analysis and synthesis reviews** that can help to improve our collective understanding of the evidence about a particular phenomenon. Pawson (2006), who advocates the evidence-based model, suggests it adopts a post-positivist stance in favouring neither quantitative nor qualitative research. While he believes that evidence-based knowledge can influence policy direction, he also acknowledges that politics will play a major role in any policy choice.

Westhues's second model is described as a *values-based model* where the policy stance is determined by guiding principles and values. In this model the analyst is more an advocate for a particular policy position than a neutral expert. This approach to policy analysis is not unlike advocacy evaluation or planning, and a user's guide to this approach to planning is available from Harvard Family Research Project at www.hfrp.org.

The third model is a *participatory model* where the analyst plays more of a facilitative role in engaging with those who have a vested interest in the policy. This model incorporates the principle of affected interests we outlined in the Introduction.

The fourth model is the *strengths-based, integrated model*, which draws heavily on the framework we present later in this chapter. A mix of empirical and experiential knowledge is used in this model, and steps to engage with those most affected by the policy are also included.

Although the above are labelled as models by Westhues (2012: 44), they reflect general approaches, and more precise frameworks for use in policy analysis can be found within each of the models. It is also important to note that a framework used in analyzing any particular policy may employ methods of generating information from more than one model or approach.

An important distinction in policy analysis is the relative emphasis placed on "content" or "process" issues. A **content approach to policy analysis** stresses the actual ingredients of a policy, that is, the substance of the policy, its goals and value preferences, and the types of benefits it provides. Chapin (2014) outlines the following general elements for analysis in this type of approach:

- policy goals;
- benefits and services;
- eligibility rules;
- service delivery systems;
- financing.

The contents of policies are important because these are related to actual or anticipated results. However, content approaches do not focus on how policies emerge and why they are developed in a particular fashion. For example, content approaches pay little attention to the political processes that shape policy-making and the trade-offs and compromises that may characterize the policy development stage. As noted in Chapter 3, this is one of the appealing attributes of the garbage can model of policy-making. A pure content approach to policy analysis may also tend to reinforce an elitist approach in that the policy expert, as an "armchair critic," gathers data on the policy issue, subjects these data to critical scrutiny, and draws conclusions about the potential effects of the policy.

Without minimizing the importance of analyses of policy contents, we argue that process considerations must also be included as components in a preferred model for policy analysis. A **process approach to policy analysis** pays more attention to who influences the development of policies, how action is generated, and who makes decisions (Flynn, 1992). Additional considerations include questions of feasibility and how the implementation stage will affect the intent of a new policy on the ground. These considerations demand that policy analysts get out of their offices and discuss some of these issues with service users and staff responsible for delivering new programs. From a process perspective, policy analysis and policy-making become an ongoing set of activities that involves creating and adapting policies and programs, and this emphasis is consistent with efforts to encourage ongoing inclusiveness and connections between practice and policy. For example, process questions, such as who influences policy development and how policy provisions are implemented, enable the use of this information in trying to influence changes to particular policies or programs. Such changes may involve information-sharing, negotiation, and partisan-based advocacy. At the end of the day, policy analysis must be designed to make a contribution to a new or revised policy. If it is not undertaken with this goal in mind, it will remain aloof from practice and disconnected from the change process.

Diversity and Policy Analysis

Systemic injustices related to factors such as class, gender, race, culture, (dis)ability, and sexual orientation must be carefully considered in policy-making. Class differences and conflict in the more traditional Marxist framework (i.e., between the ruling and working classes) are often minimized in Canadian society because of the number of people who identify as "middle class." However, as noted in Chapter 1, growing inequality is making it more difficult for many, including the middle class, to improve their income levels. Consequently, many of these individuals have unequal access to income and power in ways that are somewhat similar to those more likely to identify as members of the working class.

Class differences based on income also intersect with other forms of oppression, and separate chapters are devoted to feminism (Chapter 8) and Indigenous policy-making (Chapter 10). Here, we include a brief summary of some of the challenges faced by new immigrants and refugees, persons with disabilities, and those facing discrimination because of sexual orientation or identity. These challenges, along with special consideration to gender and Indigenous issues, require special attention in analyzing policies relevant to these populations.

In discussing diversity, the terms "minority" and "subordinate group status" are sometimes used. However, they are not intended to reflect the size of the group but their relationship to dominant society in regard to power and access to equal rights. Graham et al. (2012: 123) point out that diversity reflects the reality that different people occupy different statuses and social locations relative to the state and its policies. The cultural recognition orientation to social policy introduced in Chapter 1 reflects the efforts of particular groups to advocate for social and legal rights based on these differences. A significant challenge for diversity groups, who are understandably focused primarily on their concerns, is to work across differences in collaborating with other groups on issues of shared concern.

Immigrants and Refugees

The 2011 National Household Survey (Statistics Canada, 2013b) indicated there were more than 200 ethnic groups in Canada; 20.6 per cent of the population were foreign-born; and approximately 19 per cent of all people in Canada were members of a visible minority group.

Early immigration policies in Canada were extremely discriminatory against non-whites, but the introduction in 1967 of a points system and more liberalized policy towards family-class immigrants began to influence immigration patterns. Two general pathways for immigrants entering Canada are outlined in the Immigration and Refugee Protection Act (2002). One is the family class, whereby immigrants are sponsored by family members already living in Canada. Although these immigrants are eligible for Canadian health coverage, sponsoring families must provide other forms of support, if these are required, for a period of time. Eligibility for certain programs is a particular problem if a sponsoring family reneges on their commitment or is unable to meet these costs. The second general pathway is the economic class, whereby immigrants are admitted based on available employment opportunities relative to skills, education, and work history. More recently, there has been a decrease in skilled workers admitted within the economic class and an increase in temporary foreign workers. Although some temporary workers may apply for permanent resident status, no federal settlement funding is available until they become permanent residents. Fear of deportation and exploitation are common complaints among those admitted as temporary workers. Immigrants may also apply to live in a particular province under the Provincial Nominee Program. This program, which was earlier operated by provinces, is now administered by the federal government.

There are also two pathways of entry for refugees. Most are admitted as "Convention" refugees consistent with the definition outlined by the United Nations. This definition applies to a person who has experienced or faces persecution because of race, religion, membership in a particular social group, or political opinion and who lives outside the country of his or her nationality. Convention refugees have full access to Canadian services and programs. A range of services are provided for government-sponsored refugees; however, refugees can also be sponsored by organizations in the voluntary sector, including churches, and these organizations will then assume some of these responsibilities. Other refugees enter Canada "in need of protection." These individuals must establish a claim to "refugee status" in order to be eligible for work permits and certain services.

Although multiculturalism has been a specific and often celebrated policy in Canada since 1971, and today is reflected in goals set out in the Act for the Preservation and Enhancement of Multiculturalism in Canada (1988), these ideals are not easy to achieve. Settlement issues, including language and cultural barriers, are major challenges, and discrimination related to employment, wage rates, and housing are not uncommon.

Several issues can face newcomers to Canada. First is the problem in gaining recognition for foreign credentials. This forces new immigrants, who may enter Canada based on the availability of employment in their field, to take alternative work at a fraction of the pay rate associated with their occupation. Although programs are in place to try to address this (e.g., Federal Skilled Worker Program), this problem persists for many. Second is the difficulty in resolving acts of discrimination and institutional racism. In many cases, it is difficult to establish the evidence to support such claims, and efforts to seek redress have been exceedingly problematic. For example, Mullings (2012) reports on the disturbing trend to dismiss claims of discrimination brought before employment standards and human rights bodies at the federal level. Third, it is particularly unhelpful when government adopts policies that are counterproductive to equity and resettlement goals, as was the case in 2012 when the federal government eliminated supplemental health coverage for certain groups of refugees. This example is described in more detail later in this chapter. Finally, the evidence of higher rates of poverty among immigrant and racialized children cannot be ignored. In this regard, Macdonald and Wilson (2013) describe three tiers of poverty using 2006 census data. Based on the AT-LIM, the poverty rate in Canada for racialized and immigrant children was 33 per cent, below that of First Nations children on reserves (50 per cent) but much higher than other Canadian children (excluding Indigenous, racialized, and immigrant children), 12 per cent of whom live in poverty. Targeted social policies to address this and other disparities faced by immigrants and refugees require much more attention.

Persons with Disabilities

A number of changes to policies and legislation have helped to extend disability rights, but arguably the most significant was the inclusion of disability rights in the Charter of Rights and Freedoms in 1982. Activists from disability communities were instrumental in ensuring this inclusion. Both human rights legislation and international covenants such as the United Nations Convention on the Rights of Persons with Disabilities have been helpful in advancing policies pertaining to disability issues in Canada.

Persons with disabilities often face a number of physical, attitudinal, economic, and legal barriers that prevent full and equal participation in society. The results are lower than average employment rates and poverty rates that are much higher than average. Overcoming persistent barriers to employment, housing, and other services requires a comprehensive strategy by all governments, the private sector, and voluntary sector organizations. Examples of policies developed to further the rights of those with disabilities are included in Chapters 2 and 6.

Three developments have been particularly significant in improving the circumstances of those with one or more disabilities. One is the evolution of a consumer-led philosophy that has shifted attention away from a medical model of service to one focusing on removing barriers and replacing these with measures that help to accommodate people with disabilities to achieve goals related to **equity**. Dunn (2012) describes this as a shift from a medical/rehabilitation paradigm to a critical disability paradigm. The critical disability paradigm, which is associated with the Independent Living Movement, has focused attention on the rights of the disabled. Second and somewhat related is the deinstitutionalization of those with certain types of disabilities, based on the principle of normalization. Third is the attention to cross-disability issues and the importance of building connections between different disability communities through policy and programs. Legislation in provinces such as Ontario and Manitoba that focuses on eliminating barriers across disabilities reflects this focus.

Sexual Orientation and Identity

O'Neill (2012: 315) describes the increased acceptance of lesbian, gay, and bisexual people as "one of the most striking social changes in Canada and much of the world." The recognition of certain rights in the Charter and in provincial human rights legislation has challenged the dominance of heterosexism in society. Nevertheless, we need to be reminded of the ongoing struggles for equality, and in 77 countries around the world in 2014 it was still a crime to be gay. It is also important to recognize that some of these changes have been quite recent. For example, until 2002 Canadian residents were unable to sponsor a same-sex partner as an immigrant, and it was not until 2005 that same-sex marriages were legalized in this country. Stigmatization, in Canada and elsewhere, is a continuing issue.

The use of an acronym to define diversity in sexual orientation and identity is common but these vary. We adopt the acronym LGBTTQ to include people who are lesbian, gay, bisexual, transgender, two-spirited, and queer. The term "two-spirited" is generally used in an Aboriginal context to refer to gay or lesbian individuals, and transgender (including transsexual) is used here to refer to people whose identity differs from that typically associated with the sex assigned at birth. The term "queer" is more of an umbrella term that rejects the binary identities associated with being man or woman; thus it may include people who move between these identities or who do not place a name on their identity. Queer theory, which is related to the use of the term "queer," focuses on the limitations of identity categories, how these are socially constructed, and how these can vary over time. This brief description suggests the acronym used here (i.e., LGBTTQ) reflects a mix of terms, some of which identify sexual orientation and some of which refer more to sexual identity (e.g., transgender).

While recognizing some of the policy benefits achieved with respect to lesbian and gay rights, recognition of the rights and services for those who are transgender have been less apparent. Transgender people are more likely to live in poverty; they face more significant health and discrimination issues, particularly in transitioning, and support services are limited. Although challenges remain, policies pertaining to some services, including health and medical services for those who are transitioning, have expanded. Nonetheless, it is often cumbersome to change gender markers on such things as birth certificates, passports, and drivers' licences. Several families have filed human rights complaints indicating that the failure to permit changes in sex designation unless one is 18 years of age and has undergone sex-reassignment surgery is discriminatory (Purdy, 2014).

Using Special Lenses in Policy Analysis

Special lenses have become quite popular in policy analysis. This approach attempts to integrate content and process concerns in identifying a special lens or focus, often framed as a series of questions, to assess the particular impact of a policy on diversity or other special groups in the population.

The identification of special effects can help to focus policy attention on traditionally neglected aspects of the policy-making process. For example, questions regarding health and social service policy that focus on impacts related to women, minority groups, disability groups, and front-line service providers can be routinely incorporated as components of policy analysis if this approach is adapted to reflect such considerations. Three illustrative examples of special lenses are identified below.

Anti-racist and anti-colonial approaches are identified in the literature (see Chapter 10), and an Aboriginal framework for social work practice that includes five core elements has been proposed by McKenzie and Morrissette (2003). These are:

1. recognition of a distinct Aboriginal world view;
2. recognition of the effects of colonialism;
3. recognition of the importance of Aboriginal identity or consciousness;
4. appreciation of the value of cultural knowledge and traditions in promoting healing and empowerment;
5. an understanding of the diversity of Aboriginal cultural expression.

These elements do not constitute a fully developed Indigenous lens for policy analysis, but they do highlight some considerations that can be used for this purpose. For example, a policy affecting Indigenous people needs to be designed to respect the distinct world view of Indigenous people as well as their cultural diversity.

Because policy analysis is also about process considerations, methods of analysis in an Aboriginal context should include a commitment to collaborative, community-based strategies for data collection; the promotion of Indigenous knowledge and methods, as appropriate; and culturally appropriate responses as determined by Indigenous people (see Chapter 10 for a more extensive discussion of Aboriginal policy-making).

A framework for assessing the impact of a policy on women's equality was developed by the British Columbia Ministry of Women's Equality in 1997. This framework was based on the use of two different lenses. One was an analytical lens, which included questions about whether knowledge, ways of working, and consultation processes were inclusive of women and women's perspectives. A second lens focused attention on outcomes and their impact on equality for women.

A gender-inclusive framework incorporating eight phases or stages of analysis was later developed. This framework, summarized in Table 4.3, outlines a more comprehensive approach to analysis (British Columbia Ministry of Community, Aboriginal and Women's Services, 2003). The stages indicated in Table 4.3 are generally consistent with those outlined in the gender-based guide for policy-making developed by the Status of Women Canada (1996), and this framework has been used for policy analysis at both the provincial and federal levels. However, despite the existence of special lenses and requirements to consider issues such as gender in policy development, these considerations are too often neglected.

The disability lens is a third example. One model is that developed by the government of British Columbia (n.d.). In this model a checklist includes questions relevant to the following considerations in the design of services for people with disabilities:

Table **4.3**	Steps in Integrating Gender-Inclusive Analysis within the Policy and Program Development Cycle

Phase 1   Identify and Define the Issue

- Consider the key factors affecting men and women (e.g., income levels, family responsibility, diversity).

Phase 2   Define Goals and Outcomes

- Determine the gender composition of people to be affected by the policy and anticipated outcomes for women and men.

- Consider gender-specific factors that could affect outcomes and whether goals of the policy need to be modified to address barriers.

- Review any evaluations or data that exist on policies or programs with similar goals and target populations.

Phase 3   Define Inputs

- Determine whether relevant information is available by gender, and when consultations occur include women and men.

Phase 4   Conduct Research

- Consult women and men in the design of research and ensure gender-specific data can be collected.

- Collect both quantitative and qualitative information.

Phase 5   Develop and Analyze Options

- Consider how each option will affect women and men as a key element in analysis.

- Consider how each option can be monitored and evaluated to determine the impact on women and men.

Phase 6   Recommendations

- Review recommended options in light of legal, economic, social, or cultural constraints to the full participation of women and men in society and identify these impacts in any decision-making documents.

- Outline methods to ensure the recommended policy or program is implemented in a manner that considers gender.

Continued ▶

Phase 7 Communication

- Use communication strategies that will reach women and men from diverse communities.

Phase 8 Assess Quality

- Design, implement, and interpret evaluations that assess the impacts on both women and men.

Source: Adapted from British Columbia Ministry of Community, Aboriginal and Women's Services, *Guide to Best Practices in Gender Analysis* (2003).

- consultation and data collection;
- accessibility and appropriate accommodation;
- discrimination and legal implications;
- economic status, education, training, and development;
- communication;
- safety and protection from victimization;
- health and well-being.

Special lenses may be used as a supplementary policy analysis tool, although some, such as the gender-inclusive lens outlined in Table 4.3, include many of the elements of a full model for policy analysis. The use of special lenses may not always be appropriate or necessary and, if used, guidelines and questions need to be adapted to the particular policy context or issue being considered.

Some recent attention has been directed to intersectionality-based policy analysis (Hankivsky et al., 2012), which focuses on the combined effects of inequalities related to different forms of diversity and social location (e.g., class, gender, race, ethnicity, sexual orientation, disability). A set of eight principles related to such things as power differences and social justice are included in the framework. The framework also includes 12 general questions and a series of sub-questions to guide analysis in helping to ensure that special attention is paid to equity considerations.

The Integrated Model for Policy Analysis

The Integrated Model for Policy Analysis incorporates both content and process factors, as earlier discussed. Our focus on content directs attention to policy outcomes— who benefits and who loses and to what extent—whereas process considerations help us to understand the factors that will influence policy change and direct attention to how these must be managed to influence policy-related outcomes. The integrated, value-critical model of policy analysis that follows also permits the inclusion of special criteria to assess the effects on diverse populations.

Our proposed model is accompanied by the following qualifications. First, policy analysis, like policy-making, is not a linear process, and related tasks must be approached with this recognition. Second, the tasks in policy analysis are affected by the scope of the problem or issue being considered. However, despite differences in the complexity of policies, the general process is similar. Third, additional questions or considerations should be incorporated whenever necessary, but this is particularly true when assessing small-scale policies at the organizational level.

The Integrated Model has five stages: (1) problem analysis and goal specification; (2) identification of value criteria; (3) assessment of alternatives; (4) feasibility assessment; and (5) recommendations. As earlier noted, the model can be used to analyze policies in the developmental stage or evaluate existing policies in order to recommend improvements.

1. Problem Analysis and Goal Specification

Policy analysis begins with an examination of the problem or need, and several key questions are important to consider:

1. What is the nature of the problem; that is, how is the problem framed?
2. Who are the people experiencing the problem, and what are their characteristics?
3. How does the problem affect individuals, the community, and society?
4. What are the barriers to services at this time for the particular group of people most affected by the problem?
5. Who recognizes that the problem exists?
6. What are the causes of the problem, including relevant theoretical considerations and historical factors?
7. Are there special equity issues related to class, race, gender, ethnicity, sexual orientation, and other types of inequalities related to social location that need to be considered? In answering this question it may be important to consider whether more specific questions from a special policy lens could be helpful. For example, policies likely to have a particular impact on women might be assessed through some of the steps or questions identified in the gender lens perspective.
8. What previous strategies have been tried and what has been their level of success?

There is some overlap between these questions and results that might be obtained from a needs assessment study. However, information on needs can often extend our understanding of problems in beginning to focus on what might be required to respond to the problem. Relevant actors and interest groups—and the extent of their power and influence—should also be identified at this stage. Recognition of a problem as a public problem requiring a policy response is necessary before decision-makers will introduce a new policy, and interest groups are important when a policy response is being introduced from outside the power structure (see Box 4.4). In this first stage one must identify those likely to be affected by the policy change as well as desired outcomes.

A related consideration is the salience of the issue. Salience refers to the ability of the issue to give rise to group action either in support of or opposition to a policy, and anticipating this will help to determine whether interest group influence will be an asset or a deterrent in mobilizing support. Another task relevant to both problem analysis and assessing alternatives involves reviewing data on policies or programs where the goals and target populations are similar to those outlined in the policy issue being considered.

In examining an existing policy at the agency or program level, there are some additional questions to consider:

1. Is the policy established by legislation, regulation, or a directive, and where does this authority or responsibility lie?
2. Does the desired outcome require system change or system maintenance?
3. What is the level of agreement regarding the policy?

Box **4.4** | Campaigning for Welfare Rate Increases

Poverty advocacy groups in Winnipeg had been pressuring the provincial NDP government for welfare rate increases for several years with limited success, but in 2012 Make Poverty History Manitoba, a coalition of interest groups formed to champion poverty reduction strategies, focused attention on the inadequacy of the welfare housing allowance, which was less than half the median market rent for basic accommodation in the city. A proposal to increase the rental allowance to 75 per cent of the median market rental rate was adopted. A public awareness campaign followed, accompanied by lobbying efforts directed towards the provincial government, but these efforts were unsuccessful in elevating the issue to the top of the government's priority list in the 2013 budget. Interest group pressure persisted on several fronts: internally within the NDP party and with the minister; advocacy with the opposition Conservatives who pledged support for the issue; and attention-grabbing events such as depositing shoes on the steps of the legislative building to draw attention to the fact that welfare recipients were having to use money allocated for food and clothing to meet the high cost of rent. An additional strategy was to engage with faith groups around this issue; this led to the display of large billboards at many of the city's churches supporting the campaign.

The campaign was successful in convincing the Manitoba government to recognize this issue as a priority in its 2014 budget. Despite significant pressures on expenditures, the government promised increases to meet the recommended rent target over the next four years, provided an immediate increase for 2014, and extended the subsidy to include low-income workers who were not receiving welfare.

4. What is the nature of linkages between the agency and other relevant systems in the policy environment?

When one is evaluating a policy that has already been implemented (e.g., a new housing initiative for the homeless), a frequent question is whether to focus on the problem that existed prior to the initiative or the problem with the new initiative in place. We recommend focusing on the problem currently being experienced with the new initiative in place, which will also include some assessment about whether the new policy is an adequate response to the original problem or need.

2. Identifying Value Criteria

The second stage in this model is the identification of relevant value criteria. Like the value criteria model for policy-making, we include the identification of both general criteria and selective criteria that are specific to the policy issue under consideration. Effectiveness and efficiency are essential criteria, and efficiency assessment may include strategies such as **cost-effectiveness** or **benefit–cost analysis**. Another consideration is adequacy. Adequacy and effectiveness are related concepts, yet it is often important to distinguish between the two. Adequacy can be defined as the extent to which the provision of benefits or services meets the identified need for particular target group members or the group in general. In other words, do the benefits provided meet the identified need? Effectiveness, on the other hand, is directly related to the outcome goals and objectives of the policy. For example, a poverty reduction strategy may meet its defined goal of reducing the percentage of children in poverty by 5 per cent, thereby achieving some level of effectiveness. However, the strategy may be regarded as far from adequate if 20 per cent of the province's children are still living in poverty.

Two other general value criteria we include are (1) the policy's impact on rights and social justice (equity) for groups experiencing inequalities; and (2) the ability of the policy to promote self-determination among service users.

Special or selected value criteria may be identified based on the policy issue under consideration. One example of special criteria that may need to be considered is whether service users and front-line staff have had opportunities to participate in shaping the policy response under consideration. This participatory element is often omitted from general policy-making models, although efforts are sometimes made to elicit selected input from these constituencies through a consultative process. If a policy to strengthen community capacity is being developed, elements from Arnstein's ladder of citizen participation (Figure 4.2) may be important to consider.

Another important consideration is whether special value criteria are required to address equity issues related to the policy for a specific group or population. Although equity issues may be addressed under general value criteria related to rights and social justice, policies targeted for particular groups, such as Indigenous people, women, temporary foreign workers, and persons with disabilities, may require additional criteria that specifically examine the policy and its intended target group (e.g., the different dimensions of accessibility for people with disabilities). This is also where one may consider adopting principles derived from a special policy lens or the framework for intersectionality-based policy analysis.

The specification of value criteria is included at an early stage in policy analysis, although it should be noted that values can also be examined later, particularly in assessing an existing agency policy or in completing an evaluation study of a policy. It is worth repeating that any approach to policy analysis that gives limited attention to values will be incomplete.

Three issues are particularly relevant to the value criteria stage in policy analysis. First, the model of policy analysis outlined here requires the explicit identification of criteria to be used in assessing alternatives and identifying your preferred policy choice. There is an advantage to being explicit about value criteria because these will have a major impact on the policy decision, and their identification supports the goals of transparency and accountability in policy analysis.

Second, value criteria are often used to assess both the existing policy response and alternatives generated to respond to the problem. This may be required if policy analysis involves the assessment of different policy options where a policy response already exists. Two approaches need to be considered in completing policy analysis where a policy already exists. One is to assess the existing policy response (i.e., the status quo) as one of the policy options and apply value criteria when assessing alternatives in Stage 3. A second option is to use value criteria to assess the existing policy response at the problem analysis stage prior to applying value criteria to the assessment of new policy options. It is difficult to provide advice on which approach is preferred because this somewhat depends on context. If the status quo can be considered a viable option, we prefer applying value criteria at the stage of assessing alternatives with the status quo as one of the options. On the other hand, if the existing policy response is recognized as so inadequate that a significant change from what exists is required, a preliminary review of this response may be considered in the problem analysis stage or prior to the specification of new alternatives.

Finally, it is important to recognize that the identification of value criteria is not intended to be an arbitrary exercise that allows analysts to simply impose their particular values on the policy under consideration. Like the conclusions emerging from other types of data, most value criteria should be logically defended as relevant to the policy issue being considered. Part of this justification may emerge from the problem analysis stage in that these results may foreshadow values to be considered in the assessment stage. Some value criteria, such as effectiveness and efficiency, are likely to be considered in most policy reviews and it is not necessary to defend these. Others need to be identified based on the issue being considered, and a rationale for these becomes more important. This can become more difficult if a policy analyst works for government. In this case, value criteria set by government may differ from those that would be viewed as important by the analyst; alternatively, they may be missing or implied only in a very general sense. In some cases it may be possible to identify principles that can act as a guide to values or identify alternatives that challenge or stretch the boundaries of pre-set criteria in conducting the policy analysis study. It is much easier when an analyst is working with affected groups from outside government, as was the case with Barrier-Free Manitoba (see Chapter 2). In developing its proposals for new legislation on accessibility, one of the first steps was to identify principles (a form of value criteria) to guide the development process. Examples of value criteria are illustrated in Table 4.4, but these are only examples. After all, value criteria should be selected based on their relevance to the particular policy issue being considered.

We have argued earlier that policy-making in the human services imposes a professional responsibility to address issues pertaining to social justice, that is, a focus on achieving more equality in outcomes between more and less-advantaged groups. In spite of this ethical obligation, differing interpretations of value criteria can arise. However, explicit attention to values will, at least, permit more open dialogue and debate about the normative aspects of the policy issue being considered. While we stipulate this as an obligation in an ethical approach to policy analysis, we are also aware that this is often not done. In fact, new policy proposals often contain language designed to obscure rather than clarify underlying values. For example, the language of community partnerships and decentralization is often used to disguise a government's intent to off-load service responsibility to community groups and organizations. Another job in analyzing public policies, then, is distinguishing between rhetoric and reality in specifying principles or values!

3. Assessing Alternatives

The third stage in policy analysis involves collecting data on alternatives to be considered to meet specified goals that respond to the problem. Here one is estimating both the anticipated and unanticipated effects of policy alternatives. Both quantitative and qualitative data collection approaches are relevant, and techniques such as cost–benefit analysis, cost-effectiveness analysis, forecasting, survey research, and other types of evaluation research may be used. On smaller issues, alternatives may be assessed by discussing the relative strengths and weaknesses of each alternative. Consultation with representatives of the target populations affected by the policy is a very important step in this stage, and this is useful in assessing the extent to which more subjective value criteria will be met.

New policies often emerge without adequate attention to the lessons that can be learned from research studies of various aspects of the policy or similar policies adopted elsewhere. This may be a result of strongly held political or ideological beliefs, which lead either to the selective use of research that reinforces the particular ideology of decision-makers or to the complete disregard for research evidence. In these circumstances, policy-makers may omit the policy analysis stage of policy development entirely, or use it narrowly to justify a policy decision that has already been made. For example, in 2012 the federal government cut supplemental health benefits for certain groups of refugees without any real consultation process or consideration of research evidence. The cost-cutting measure, rationalized on the basis of equity with other

Canadian taxpayers, gave no consideration to the vulnerability of affected refugees or to the fact that denying them early access to needed health services would make it more difficult for them to become self-sufficient and increase future social costs when medical problems became more severe.

In cases such as these, arguments for more consultation or attention to research studies may fall on deaf ears. However, it may be possible to engage external groups or think-tanks to analyze such policies. These analyses at least can provide other viewpoints on possible effects. In this particular case, a coalition of organizations, led by Doctors for Refugee Care, documented potential effects and mounted a legal challenge to the government decision. In July 2014 the Federal Court overturned the policy, agreeing that it violated Section 12 of the Charter of Rights and Freedoms, which prohibits "cruel and unusual treatment or punishment" (Meili, 2014). Although the federal government initially indicated it would appeal the decision, it reinstated partial benefits to selected groups of refugees by November 2014, as required in the court order. However, the reinstatement of these benefits was accompanied by a list of exclusions, including the denial of benefits to refugees from certain countries. This example illustrates the importance of combining research informed policy advocacy with legal action to address a social justice issue that emerges when information from policy analysis is ignored.

At a general level, the assessment of alternatives may conclude with a clear specification of anticipated consequences. If policies pertain to agency-level issues or require a careful consideration of service delivery questions, this will be insufficient, however. In such cases, an additional concern will be the effects of policy change on organizational functioning. This may require an assessment of the nature of authority, influence, and leadership; patterns of communication; and constraints on policy adoption, including any anticipated resistance to change.

4. Feasibility Assessment

Feasibility assessment is identified here as a fourth stage in policy analysis. It is included as a separate stage because of its particular relevance in agency or program-level policies and its importance to implementation issues. But it is not a substitute for the detailed planning and preparation that must occur at the implementation stage of policy-making, discussed in more detail in Chapter 5. In assessing feasibility, it is important to consider the type of policy instrument to be used. For example, is legal compliance required? Will change be accomplished by the provision of information and increased public awareness, or are new regulations, services, or benefits required? An early step in this process should involve consultation with key implementing officials and, wherever possible, with service users. Resource requirements and their availability are also central considerations.

Three other questions may be important. First, does the policy give rise to newly perceived self-interests that might mobilize opposition to the policy? Second, is there a logical link between policy options and the original problem as defined, including research or theoretical support showing that the intervention is likely to achieve intended results? This question involves examining the extent to which each option is likely to address the problem. Finally, are there political implications that need to be considered?

5. Recommendations

The final stage in policy analysis involves recommendations. These may include support for or criticism of a particular strategy and the specification of anticipated or realized effects of a particular policy. The strengths and weaknesses of a limited number of policy options may also be summarized at this point if the intent is to present a range of options to senior policy-makers for final selection. If this approach is taken, selected alternatives should be considered in relation to value criteria and their ability to address the policy problem.

Table 4.4 summarizes the integrated model for policy analysis. It includes elements that encourage connections between the realities of practice and the more general policy questions confronting policy-makers. The addition of a feasibility assessment stage directs attention to the implementation stage in the policy process, and it is at this stage that the interests of policy-makers and practitioners are most likely to either collide or to coalesce in rolling out the new policy.

| Table **4.4** | The Integrated Model for Social Policy Analysis |

Stage One: Problem Analysis and Goal Specification

1. Describe the nature and scope of the problem.

2. Identify needs and strengths.

3. Identify causal factors, including assumptions, theories for explanation, and key historical factors.

4. Identify targets for change and expected outcomes (goals).

5. Identify important actors and interest groups that shape problem recognition and definition, including their power and influence.

6. Review data on the policy issue and responses where program and goals are similar, and consider diversity and equity dimensions of the issue.

7. Consult with significant stakeholders, including service users, wherever possible.

Continued ▶

Stage Two: Identifying Value Criteria

1. General criteria to be considered may include:

   a) effectiveness;

   b) efficiency;

   c) adequacy;

   d) impact on rights and social justice (e.g., equity);

   e) impact on service user self-determination.

1. Special criteria specific to the policy under consideration should be identified along with a rationale for their inclusion. Special criteria may include such things as:

   a) level of staff and consumer involvement;

   b) principles from a special policy lens or criteria that relate directly to the policy problem being experienced by a particular equity-seeking group.

Stage Three: Assessing Alternatives

1. Consult with populations affected by the policy and ensure assessment considers these perspectives.

2. Identify alternatives to be considered.

3. Collect quantitative and qualitative data on alternatives to be assessed relative to problem analysis, goal selection, and relevant value criteria, and summarize the strengths and weaknesses of each alternative.

Stage Four: Feasibility Assessment (especially for agency- or program-level policies)

1. Identify the type of policy instrument to be used (e.g., education and awareness campaign, voluntary service option, new benefit or incentive, or regulation requiring compliance).

2. Consult with implementing officials and service users on implementation.

3. Identify the resource requirements and availability.

4. Consider whether the policy gives rise to newly perceived self-interests that need to be considered.

5. Examine whether there is a logical link (theoretical or otherwise) between the policy and the problem or goals initially identified.

Continued ▶

Stage Five: Recommendations

1. Specify the policy choice and its relationship to intended goals and the identified means for goal achievement (i.e., rationale for choice), and/or specify anticipated or actual effects flowing from a particular policy.

2. If requested, summarize the strengths and weaknesses of optional policy choices in relation to value criteria and the extent to which each option addresses the nature and scope of the problem.

Summary and Conclusion

In this chapter the five stages of the policy-making process were outlined in some detail. Particular attention was given to how a convergence of interest can open a "policy window" or an opportunity to launch a new policy or program. Problem definition or framing and needs assessment are important activities at the initiation stage, either in advocating for policy change or in developing a particular policy proposal to respond to a public problem. A policy analysis model that considers activities important to both problem definition and the formulation stage in policy-making was presented. Approaches to evaluation were also explored. Although we briefly reviewed the implementation stage, a more detailed discussion of this stage is taken up in the next chapter.

Some of the focus in this chapter has been on factors that lead to policy change at the macro level, and these are important because the results can make a major difference to service users. However, small-scale policy changes also make a difference. Many of these changes, such as the launch of a new independent living preparation program for youth in care, can be led by social workers who might apply some of the steps of the policy analysis model identified in this chapter. Launching new policies, even on a small scale, can be difficult to do. But individuals, including students, can make a significant contribution through participation in advocacy groups concerned with poverty, human rights, refugees and immigrants, and Aboriginal peoples.

Students can also participate more directly in contributing to helpful policy responses. In one instance, an instructor and his class of social work students became involved in launching a community event to raise funds for the development of an inner-city child-care centre. When combined with other efforts, this helped to open a policy window with government that led to the development of the new, sustainable child-care centre. In another case, graduates from a social work program in Ukraine concerned about the plight of the homeless developed a small agency, initially staffed by volunteers, to provide support, referral, and advocacy-related services. Over time this small agency received core funding to provide services to the homeless. Policy analysis for progressive policy change is a value-informed process that should give attention to empirical evidence and the need to actively engage both service providers and service users. The activities and skills associated with this role are important to policy-making at the governmental and organizational levels, but they are also relevant at the community level. At this level, skills and activities may be used to shape small-scale policy changes or inform strategies to be used in policy advocacy.

Critical Thinking Questions

1. Poverty reduction strategies have been adopted in several provinces, including Ontario, Quebec, Manitoba, and Newfoundland and Labrador. Review the Integrated Model for Social Policy Analysis. What value criteria would you propose for strategies that might be designed to reduce poverty? Consider both general and special criteria in your answer and provide a rationale for your choices.
2. Framing a problem is different from simply identifying a problem. What are these differences?
3. Four different types of needs were identified in this chapter. Select a policy issue and review how these different perspectives on need might be applied to your policy issue.
4. Think of a policy issue that affects Indigenous people or another group of special interest to you. Design some questions or guidelines that you might use to create a special policy lens that could assist you in conducting a policy analysis of this issue.

Recommended Reading

P.M. Kettner, R.M. Moroney, and L.L. Martin. *Designing and Managing Programs: An Effectiveness-Based Approach*, 4th edn. Thousand Oaks, Calif.: Sage, 2013. This book provides a step-by-step approach to program design. It includes particularly useful coverage of needs assessment, setting goals and objectives, and budgeting systems.

Status of Women Canada. *Gender-Based Analysis: A Guide for Policy-Making*. 1996. This guide offers a comprehensive outline of gender-based considerations in policy-making. At: www.pacificwater.org/userfiles/file/IWRM/Toolboxes/gender/gender_based_analysis.pdf.

A. Westhues. "Approaches to Policy Analysis," in A. Westhues and B. Wharf, eds. *Canadian Social Policy: Issues and Perspectives*, 5th edn, pp. 43–59. Waterloo, Ont.: Wilfrid Laurier University Press, 2012. Westhues provides more information on the four general approaches to policy analysis summarized in this chapter.

B.R. Witkin and J.W. Altschuld. *Planning and Conducting Needs Assessments: A Practical Guide*. Thousand Oaks, Calif.: Sage, 1995. This book presents a three-phased approach to needs assessment—pre-assessment, assessment, and post-assessment—and summarizes a wide variety of methods for conducting needs assessment. It is particularly helpful in outlining interactive methods that can be used to estimate needs and establish priorities for action.

5

The Implementation Stage

─────────────── • **In this chapter you will learn about:** • ───────────────

- the importance of the implementation stage in connecting policy to practice and achieving policy goals;
- the major theoretical perspectives used in examining implementation;
- factors that can help to promote successful policy implementation;
- the ways discretion may be used by front-line practitioners.

Introduction

Policy implementation can be defined as "the carrying out of a basic policy decision" (Mazmanian and Sabatier, 1983: 20), or what happens between policy expectations and policy results (Ferman, 1990). In small-scale changes, implementation can be described as action plans and activities that are usually relatively short in duration. In complex policies this process can be quite extensive, including phases that may be described as **implementation planning** and **field implementation**. This distinction is important in that implementation planning is more about operational planning or design, whereas field implementation is concerned about translating guidelines and regulations into practice. Although the implementation stage is somewhat fluid in time duration, it is in the field implementation phase that front-line practitioners are particularly influential in determining how the policy affects the lives of service users.

There is a compelling reason for devoting a chapter to implementation: it is the stage of the policy-making process where the connections between policy and practice—for better or worse—are most apparent. It is at this point that practitioners become responsible for translating program objectives and guidelines into services. They may implement new policies and programs as intended by head office, make improvements to certain provisions within their span of control to enhance benefits to service users, or resist new policies through non-compliance or other means. In some cases planning for implementation may occur without major engagement of field staff; in other more complex cases, there may have been an implementation planning stage and preparation stage that might have included advanced training and the development of new forms and protocols. Too often there is insufficient time to prepare for implementation, and even with such time it is often difficult to anticipate all of the challenges that may arise in a major policy change. The lack of attention to implementation is complicated by two factors. First, senior policy-makers often move quickly to other issues once a new policy is adopted, partly because developing new policies is more interesting than dealing with the "nuts and bolts" of implementation. Second, other issues in government or the organization may demand their attention. Historically, this neglect of implementation was based on the rather naive assumption that once a new policy was developed it was up to field offices to figure out the steps to ensure the policy was implemented as intended. Past failures to translate policy goals into meaningful practice objectives and activities contributed to the labelling of implementation as "the missing link" in transforming good intentions into policy outcomes.

We begin with a review of some of the key literature on implementation, then examine some experiences in implementation, and conclude with considerations that may help to improve implementation in the human services. Although we devote a separate chapter to implementation, we stress that policy implementation is inextricably linked to the other policy-making stages; this connection is most often not linear but interactive as experiences in implementation can lead to new adjustments at the formulation stage and vice versa. That said, we note the special relationship of evaluation to implementation. The evaluation stage was discussed in the previous chapter and we drew special attention to implementation evaluation in describing the differences between formative and summative evaluation. As identified in Chapter 4, formative approaches to evaluating the early stages of implementation are most appropriate, whereas longer-term assessment of policy outcomes will place greater emphasis on a summative approach.

Perspectives on Implementation

The majority of implementation literature has emerged from the US, and special attention to this topic can be traced to the early 1970s with the publication of *Implementation: How Great Hopes in Washington Are Dashed in Oakland* (Pressman and Wildavsky, 1973). This seminal study described the implementation of an economic development program funded by the US federal government and implemented in Oakland, California. As the subtitle indicates, the story is one of disappointment not because of any wrongdoing or incompetence, but mainly because of the many and largely unanticipated difficulties encountered between the ideas identified in Washington and the realities experienced in Oakland. This study triggered a focus that has been referred to as first-generation research on implementation.

A notable contribution of this book was the concept of "clearance points." Like a barge passing through a number of locks where the water has to be raised in order to allow it to continue, policies encounter crucial junctures where opportunities exist to alter direction. The longer the chain from head to field offices, the vaguer the statement of policy objectives, the more clearance points in place, the less likely the policy will be implemented as intended. These authors argued that in order to improve implementation the number of clearance points should be kept to a minimum, objectives should be stated clearly and precisely, and the head office should take charge of the process. This triggered a focus on factors that must be set in place by central authorities to facilitate successful implementation. The conditions needed in what has come to be known as the **top-down approach to implementation** are:

1. clear and consistent objectives;
2. an adequate causal theory;
3. a structured implementation process to ensure compliance by implementing officials;
4. committed and skilful implementers;
5. the support of interest groups and the legislature;
6. a relatively stable environment (Sabatier, 1986).

Although theoretically appealing, these conditions are rarely evident in practice. For example, these conditions ignore the roles of front-line practitioners responsible for implementation and the fact that many policies change as they are being implemented.

Difficulties associated with the top-down model, which has been characterized as a simplistic extension of the rational, bureaucratic model, focused attention on the importance of front-line practitioners as the most important people in determining whether a policy was implemented as intended (Williams,1980). Elmore extended this argument in suggesting that implementation planning should be turned on its head. Rather than emanating from the top (i.e., the head office), policy should be made in a "backwards mapping fashion": "The closer one is to the source of the problem, the greater is one's ability to influence it; and the problem solving ability of complex systems depends not on hierarchical control but on maximizing discretion at the point where the problem is most immediate" (Elmore, 1982: 21). This perspective came to be known as the **bottom-up** or **backwards mapping approach to implementation**. The bottom-up approach defines implementation as more of an interactive process; it also incorporates the distinct possibility that policy may change or be adapted during the implementation stage. Although this more inclusive approach to implementation is appealing, it may underestimate the influence of senior management and others on the implementation process; as well, it makes the evaluation of effects more difficult. Chapter 6 explores the backwards mapping approach in more detail.

By the 1980s several scholars concluded that neither approach was satisfactory. This launched a search for a synthesis during a phase sometimes referred to as second-generation research on implementation. Elmore combined his notion of backwards mapping with forward mapping in recognizing that leadership in policy-making usually emanated from politicians and senior bureaucrats. Nevertheless, these policy-makers neglect field offices at their peril, and meshing the interests and commitment of those at the top and the bottom of the organization is essential for effective implementation. Another attempt to synthesize the approaches came from Sabatier (1986), who proposed drawing on elements of the top-down model in the initial stages of implementation planning, and then approaching field implementation in a more adaptive fashion by engaging with a whole variety of public and private actors responsible for service delivery. Champions within an organization and influential supporters in the policy environment were viewed as important in supporting successful implementation.

To many, the synthesis approach seemed to be little more than a combination of selected variables from the top-down and bottom-up approaches. However, the focus on relationships in a more recent variation, known as **principal-agent theory** (PHAST, 2011), may be more helpful. In this approach importance is placed on the relationship between actors who define the policy and agents that implement the policy. The amount of discretion provided to front-line implementers and the characteristics of the relationship between policy designers and implementers are determined by three factors: the nature of the policy problem, including scale of change and complexity of intervention; the context or circumstances surrounding the problem, such as political and economic climate and degree of technological change required; and organizational factors, such as number of agencies and resources required.

An adaptation of the synthesis model of implementation was Berman's (1980) contingency theory of implementation. He argued that some policies prescribe benefits or responses that leave little room for discretion (e.g., OAS benefits and EI benefits), and in these circumstances a more programmed (top-down) approach to implementation is justified. In other cases policies require a more bottom-up or adaptive approach because they outline benefits and services that must be adapted to the needs of communities and service users. He suggested that the choice between a programmed or adaptive approach to implementation should be made by assessing the following factors:

1. scope of the change (incremental versus major);
2. certainty of the theory or technology underlying the change (certain within risk versus uncertain);
3. conflict over policy goals and means (low conflict versus high conflict);
4. degree of control over clearance points (tightly coupled versus loosely coupled);
5. stability of the environment (stable versus unstable).

Analyzing a policy by using these criteria determines whether it can be implemented in a rather mechanistic, rule-bound fashion or whether a considerable amount of discretion must be left to the implementers. According to Berman, policies that must be implemented in an adaptive fashion are characterized by one or more of the following characteristics: major change; a weak or uncertain theory underlying the change; disagreement regarding goals and objectives; limited control over clearance points; and an unstable environment. The presence of one or more of these factors in human service policies and programs is common, and this suggests an approach to implementation that relies heavily on an adaptive or bottom-up approach.

Conteh (2011) describes a third generation of researchers who attempted to establish more integrated implementation theories that might lend themselves to broader generalization (see Goggin, 1990). There is debate about the value of this focus. Those who support the need for a more integrated model with the potential to facilitate more effective implementation cite the continuing efforts of policies that fail to live up to expectations at the implementation stage (see Box 5.1). Conteh acknowledges the evidence of failures, although he argues that this general conclusion is somewhat overstated. He points to the many organizational and government programs that work pretty well, and even where failures are evident some of the fault lies at the design stage (i.e., formulation stage and implementation planning phase) rather than in the field implementation stage, where policies are translated into services and benefits by front-line staff. In any event, third-generation research in the 1990s largely failed to yield much in the way of new

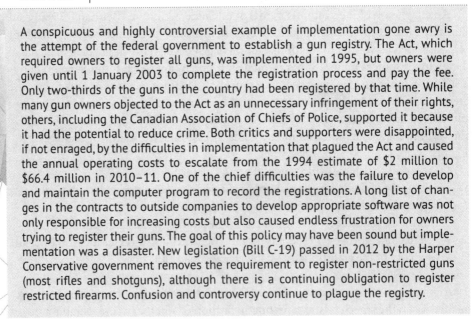

Box **5.1** | An Implementation Disaster

A conspicuous and highly controversial example of implementation gone awry is the attempt of the federal government to establish a gun registry. The Act, which required owners to register all guns, was implemented in 1995, but owners were given until 1 January 2003 to complete the registration process and pay the fee. Only two-thirds of the guns in the country had been registered by that time. While many gun owners objected to the Act as an unnecessary infringement of their rights, others, including the Canadian Association of Chiefs of Police, supported it because it had the potential to reduce crime. Both critics and supporters were disappointed, if not enraged, by the difficulties in implementation that plagued the Act and caused the annual operating costs to escalate from the 1994 estimate of $2 million to $66.4 million in 2010–11. One of the chief difficulties was the failure to develop and maintain the computer program to record the registrations. A long list of changes in the contracts to outside companies to develop appropriate software was not only responsible for increasing costs but also caused endless frustration for owners trying to register their guns. The goal of this policy may have been sound but implementation was a disaster. New legislation (Bill C-19) passed in 2012 by the Harper Conservative government removes the requirement to register non-restricted guns (most rifles and shotguns), although there is a continuing obligation to register restricted firearms. Confusion and controversy continue to plague the registry.

insights, in part because it was overtaken by a focus on organizational changes favouring decentralization and partnership with non-government organizations. Attention shifted to issues of governance and organizational change, and the specific focus on implementation declined. Nevertheless, the link between organizational change and implementation in an environment where there are often a variety of agencies and actors remains a major challenge, and we return to an example that attempts to link these two processes later in this chapter.

Despite some proposed models intended to improve implementation, the primary debate has continued to focus on the relative merits of a top-down or bottom-up approach and whether some integration of these two approaches is possible. Proponents of a more centralized command-and-control model of governance stand with the top-downers. We see evidence of this model whenever something goes wrong at the service delivery level—whether it involves the death of a child in the child welfare system or a crisis in emergency room health-care services. The immediate response is to impose new rules and develop measures to ensure increased compliance with these new requirements. Others (e.g., deLeon and deLeon, 2002) make a strong argument for refinement to the bottom-up approach because of its ability to link democratic principles, including increased public participation, with effectiveness in policy implementation. In their view, improvements in implementation require efforts to clarify differing interpretations of new policies, resolve any conflicts that might exist through negotiation, and adapt policies to realities in the field. In this context, ongoing evaluation of implementation makes a particularly important contribution.

Implementing Complex Policies: Lessons to Be Learned

Major changes in child welfare and health service delivery are particularly challenging to implement because, as identified in the previous section, these systems are characterized by several of the factors Berman (1980) identified as requiring a more adaptive approach to implementation. The following examples are drawn from the child welfare field; these were selected because of the complexity of the change process and the inclusion of a clearly defined implementation stage.

Example 1: Implementation of New Child Welfare Legislation in British Columbia

Legislative changes to the Child, Family and Community Service Act and the Child, Youth and Family Advocacy Act in British Columbia were passed by the provincial legislature in June 1994 but were not proclaimed by the lieutenant-governor until January 1996. The period between passage and proclamation (the date that the Acts became law) was devoted to planning for implementation. The Acts were the consequence of two comprehensive community consultation processes into child welfare conducted by the Ministry of Social Services in 1991–2. One consultation was devoted to the needs and views on child welfare expressed by the First Nations people of BC, which culminated in the report *Liberating Our Children, Liberating Our Nations* (Report of the Aboriginal Committee, 1992). The opinions of other citizens were expressed in *Making Changes: A Place to Start* (Report of the Community Panel, 1992). Both community panel reports concluded that child welfare in BC required fundamental reform and that the welfare of children should be seen in a societal and community context that recognized that poverty, inadequate housing, and the lack of supports to families adversely affected the ability of parents to care for their children. In addition, the reports criticized the "social cop" approach to practice that restricted the role of child welfare staff to intrusive investigations. The development of new legislation and planning for implementation consumed the time and attention of head-office staff for four years.

If time, conscious attention to planning, and resources could ensure smooth implementation, the experience in BC exemplifies such a process. The painstaking efforts made during the process, as identified by Durie and Armitage (1996) in their study of these implementation activities, are listed below:

- appointment of a head-office steering committee chaired by an assistant deputy minister and staffed by two staff members in the ministry who had extensive experience in child welfare;
- formation of regional committees to gain the input of front-line professionals; the regional committees were staffed by facilitators seconded from other positions in the region;
- attention to the concerns of community organizations, sister ministries, the judicial system, and the BC Employees Union, all of which would be affected by the new legislation;
- establishment of training sessions on a regional basis to acquaint staff with the objectives and provisions of the Child, Family and Community Service Act and the Child, Youth and Family Advocacy Act.

The primary reason for this careful planning was that these Acts were dedicated to changing the culture of the ministry. The plan sought to change, in a very fundamental fashion, the day-to-day practice of staff: from adversarial and intrusive to respectful and courteous approaches; from working with individuals on a one-on-one basis to group and community approaches; and from investigation and referral to purposeful planning for change.

Yet, despite this care and attention, the legislation, as eventually implemented, departed in substantial ways from the vision outlined in *Making Changes: A Place to Start* (Report of the Community Panel, 1992). What happened?

Without doubt, the most important factor was the formation of a judicial inquiry in 1994 and its subsequent report one year later (Report of the Gove Inquiry into Child

Protection, 1995). A child had been killed by his mother in a small northern community and the report by the Superintendent of Child Welfare into the circumstances of the death was deemed to be too defensive of the performance of staff. Although the minister and the Premier at first found the report quite acceptable, it was severely criticized in the legislature and in the media. Bowing to the pressure, the minister sought to deflect attention from the ministry by firing the superintendent and launching an inquiry headed by Judge Thomas Gove.

Had the findings of the inquiry corresponded with those of the community panels, the only effect on the work of the ministry, and in particular on those charged with the responsibility of implementation, would have been the time and energy required to attend hearings and to respond to the many demands from the inquiry for information. But this was not to be. While the new Acts promoted a preventive, family support approach to service provision, Judge Gove favoured a more limited focus on protecting children. Conflicting messages surfaced about the ministry and its objectives—messages that culminated in changes to the legislation and the introduction of a cumbersome and highly intrusive risk assessment process.

In this case the Gove Inquiry is important because it draws attention to the salience of the policy environment as a significant factor in implementation. In an interview, a senior official in the ministry who had been heavily involved in both the development and implementation stages of the legislation identified two revealing criticisms of the process. First, he and other policy-makers did not realize the extent to which the culture of the "social cop" approach to practice was embedded in the ministry. Front-line staff knew how to investigate, how to interview individuals (preferably in their offices), and how to refer families needing counselling or other services to community agencies. Although some had experimented successfully with group and community approaches, the majority remained entrenched in the protection practices with which they were familiar. In spite of this, more staff might have been excited by the approaches called for in the new legislation had not the messages emerging from the Gove Inquiry quickly dashed interest in these approaches. As Smale (1996) has noted, when all about them is changing, when organizational structures are being reconfigured, and when their practice is being scrutinized in the media, practitioners will remain committed to present modes of practice and shy away from ones that are unknown, and therefore, more risky.

The second criticism concerned the turbulent policy environment. In retrospect, the senior official noted that when major changes are involved, when the environment cannot be anticipated or controlled, the most effective strategy may well be to restrict detailed planning in head office, proclaim a new Act or new policy, and deal with difficulties as they arise—in short, to proceed more quickly from implementation planning to a field implementation model that incorporates an adaptive approach to the new policy. Although some planning is required, a lengthy, drawn-out process allows resistance to mount and other events to overtake the new policy.

Example 2: Devolution of Child Welfare Services in Manitoba

A second example is the devolution of child welfare services to new administrative authorities in Manitoba between 2001 and 2005. This case study is described in more detail in Chapter 10, and we focus here on selected aspects pertaining to implementation. The intent of this policy change was to transfer more control over the delivery of child welfare services to Aboriginal people by creating four new administrative authorities. Three of these were Aboriginal: the Northern First Nations Child and Family Services Authority, the Southern First Nations Child and Family Services Authority, and the Métis Child and Family Services Authority. The fourth authority, known as General Child and Family Services Authority, was primarily responsible for the delivery of services to non-Aboriginal people. Each authority was responsible for overseeing agencies involved in service delivery. A collaborative approach to policy development characterized the planning stage, and the structure included provisions for shared policy-making responsibility between government and these semi-autonomous authorities. The transfer of jurisdictional control over child welfare services to Aboriginal people was achieved, and the many accomplishments associated with this collaborative approach to implementation planning, including more Indigenous staff and more community-based resources, are important to recognize. However, flaws in both planning and service delivery became apparent during the implementation stage. Early implementation problems included inadequately trained staff, unanticipated increases in workloads, governance-related issues, and problems in co-ordination at the policy and case management levels. The tragic death of Phoenix Sinclair in 2006 exposed weaknesses in the system. Although her death led to several reviews that resulted in some additional funding and service improvements, a number of shortcomings remain.

In this example, the inability to predict and/or manage the environment following devolution was problematic, as was the case with earlier child welfare reforms in BC. As in the BC case, the death of a child, and related media attention on the faults in the system, was a triggering event that influenced responses to implementation. In the Manitoba case, it is unclear whether some of the changes following field implementation, including new resources, would have occurred without the attention that this tragic event caused. However, as anticipated in advance by Hudson and McKenzie (2003), there were also weaknesses in implementation planning, including ambiguous goals related to service delivery, inadequate attention to accountability and information-sharing protocols, insufficient attention to agency capacity-building needs, and a failure on the part of the government to commit adequate resources up front to ensure implementation success. Some of these shortcomings might have been addressed by central authorities in the implementation planning stage. At the same time, it is probably impossible to anticipate all of the issues that may arise when a major policy change, which quite clearly meets Berman's (1980) criteria for a bottom-up, adaptive approach to implementation, is translated into services by front-line practitioners. If planning had incorporated amore adaptive approach to implementation, with resources for both implementation evaluation and policy adjustments as required, perhaps some of the shortcomings in connecting this policy to practice could have been avoided.

Collectively, these two examples reinforce the importance of some sort of synthesis between top-down and bottom-up or adaptive approaches to implementation. Although the need for leadership from the centre in implementation planning is generally recognized, even in policies requiring an adaptive approach to field application, engagement with front-line practitioners and service users is most often too little and too late. Their involvement at the outset of the policy process would bring their experiences and knowledge to the policy table and make their co-operation during implementation more likely. Their voices are even more important as the policy is rolled out, and these inputs need to be accompanied by commitments to respond to legitimate concerns. This process may be facilitated by inclusion of one or more "fixers" (Bardach, 1977), who help to identify barriers to implementation and assist in finding solutions.

The World of the Front-Line Practitioner

Our discussion now turns to a review of the capacity and commitment of practitioners to the policy process. In theory, one would assume that because policies affect their work and the quality of the services to be provided, practitioners would be keenly committed and actively engaged in the policy process. Although true in some instances, it is not always the case as low staff morale and symptoms of burnout are not uncommon. They feel—in many instances rightly so—underpaid, overworked, and undervalued by their employers. These reactions tend to limit active engagement in policy change.

Lipsky's *Street-Level Bureaucracy* (1980) is the best known of several research studies on the work-life of front-line practitioners. Although Lipsky's research took place in Boston in the late 1970s, his observations remain pertinent today in many public service jurisdictions. Lipsky's **street-level bureaucrats** were welfare workers, police officers, and nurses who dealt with crises on a daily basis:

> Street-level bureaucrats spend their work lives in a corrupted world of service. They believe themselves to be doing the best they can under adverse circumstances and they develop techniques to salvage services within the limits imposed upon them by the structure of their work. At best street-level bureaucrats invent benign modes of mass processing that more or less permit them to deal with the public fairly, appropriately and successfully. At worst they give in to favoritism, stereotyping and routinizing. (Lipsky, 1980: xiii)

Even though policies may be established elsewhere, Lipsky recognized that from the perspective of service users, practitioners make policies: "The decisions of street-level bureaucrats, the routines they establish and the devices they invent to cope with their uncertainties and work pressures effectively become the public policies they carry out"

(Lipsky, 1980: xii). Lipsky found that street-level bureaucrats were generally motivated by a professional commitment to help others at the outset, and the ability to exercise discretion in their jobs gave them both some control over their work and a related ability to provide additional help or support to those in need. Excessive workloads or efforts to remove discretion had counterproductive results by increasing the level of alienation and burnout because discretion could no longer be used in a routine manner to ensure equal benefits to all. In these circumstances street-level bureaucrats resorted to routinizing, stereotyping, or limiting responses to maintain some degree of personal control within an alienating work environment. In these circumstances discretion may be protected for personal use or used more selectively with those service users likely to express appreciation for what may be defined as "special attention."

Discretion is important in the human services because most policies cannot prescribe interventions that will fit the circumstances of all service users. But it is also important to recognize that discretion can be exercised either to enhance or to limit services. For example, a welfare worker dealing with an emergency may decide it is simply easier to invoke a policy guideline in turning down a request than to assess the extent of need, the implications of declining the request, and whether assistance can be provided through the worker's organization or another alternative source of help.

There is a trend across fields of practice to establish cumbersome mechanisms requiring practitioners to comply with standards developed by head offices when service concerns arise, often without input from the local level. Writing more than three decades ago, Elmore pointed out how the connections between implementation and discretion foreshadowed the trend towards standardized approaches to practice:

> The dominant view that discretion is at best a necessary evil and at worst a threat to democratic government pushes implementation analysis toward hierarchically structured models of the process and toward increased reliance on hierarchical control to solve implementation problems. . . . Nowhere in this view is serious thought given to how to capitalize on discretion as a device for improving the reliability and effectiveness of policies at the street level. (Elmore, 1982: 26)

Lipsky's street-level bureaucrats were seen as powerful by service users; however, these same practitioners viewed themselves as oppressed and as having no capacity to contribute to or influence the policy process. In these circumstances, it can be difficult to change the organizational culture to engage front-line practitioners in designing and implementing local policies.

Although Lipsky's conclusions have been regarded by some as overly pessimistic, he did include a number of suggestions to encourage more productive uses of discretion, including efforts to manage workloads and enhance work performance through training and support.

Centralization and Decentralization: The Variable of Distance

A final variable in this discussion of implementation pertains to the centralization of authority. Kernaghan and Siegel (1995) note that a responsive bureaucracy ought to focus on transferring power and authority to the field, yet the common practice is to retain authority close to the centre where it is easier to control what is and is not done in the field. This dilemma persists. At one point, the complaint will be heard that field offices have too little discretion. They cannot adapt programs to meet local needs and cannot take a leadership role in activities such as connecting with community partners. If these complaints are seen as valid, head offices may reduce their control and enhance the autonomy of field offices. However, when different complaints emerge—that programs are too uneven, that programs available in one office are not provided in other locations, that localized staff are unreliable—head offices are quick to pull in the reins and develop centralizing measures, including restrictive regulations and close surveillance of performance.

A further complication occurs in countries such as Canada, where governments are responsible for services to communities differing widely in terms of diversity, history, size, and location. Head offices attempt valiantly to develop policies and programs that will be implemented in a consistent fashion across jurisdictions, but in many ways their efforts are doomed to fail. It is self-evident that the provision of counselling services, daycare, specialized health programs, and other services is heavily affected by issues such as diversity and distance.

Previous research (e.g., Carroll and Siegel, 1999) on the relationships and interactions between head and field offices in the federal bureaucracy has demonstrated a profound distrust of head office by field office staff. This distrust was common across the system, but the degree of autonomy provided to field offices generally increased in direct relationship with the geographical distance between head offices and field offices (i.e., the greater the distance the more autonomy given to field offices). As long as field offices performed their responsibilities in a reasonable fashion without serious complaints or evidence of mismanagement, these offices were left alone to manage their own affairs.

Both positive and negative consequences can accrue from the autonomy afforded by distance. An example of positive consequences comes from the examination of a child welfare office in northern British Columbia in 2002. Like a pendulum, policy directions from head office in Victoria have swung over time from a very residual approach to child welfare to an approach focused on early intervention and supporting families and back to the "social cop" style of work. Regardless of these policy shifts, the Hazelton office had carved out its own mode of practice. In the words of a long-time community resident, "the community makes the office" (Wharf, 2002: 51). Implied in this remark was the fact that the child welfare workers in Hazelton had attuned their practice to the culture and traditions of the communities they served. Staff saw themselves as members of the community; they were open to the community by listing their phone numbers and by responding to after-hours requests. They involved family members, other professionals, and concerned citizens in determining plans for a particular child. This style of work enabled the staff to win the respect of the surrounding communities and to be able to call for help when they required it.

We note, however, that isolation also can lead to **acute localitis** (Montgomery, 1979), whereby standards and practices at variance with those outside the community can occur. Acute localitis allowed the conditions of incest and child abuse to continue over a period of years in an isolated community in Kings County, Nova Scotia (Cruise and Griffiths, 1997). Clearly, the autonomy afforded by distance provides an opportunity for innovative staff to exercise their creativity and to employ an adaptive approach to implementation. Just as clearly, staff who feel overwhelmed by their responsibilities, who are worried about making independent judgments, who, in short, are not well trained or experienced, require more supervision from a central or regional office to ensure adequate and effective services.

Building Capacity for Implementing Innovations

An Implementation Model That Incorporates Organizational Capacity-Building

Efforts to connect implementation research with organizational change factors in evidence-based programs have shown some promise in identifying a more integrated approach to managing implementation in human service innovations. Fixsen, Blase, Naoom, and Wallace (2009) identify seven implementation components, which they argue can support the six stages of implementing human service innovations. The six functional stages of implementation they identify from the literature are exploration, installation, initial implementation, full implementation, innovation, and sustainability. These stages are recursive rather than linear so may occur in a different sequence under different organizational conditions. Based on findings from successful implementation programs, seven core implementation components are identified (see Figure 5.1).

Core implementation components, also identified as "implementation drivers," are interactive processes that support staff behaviour and organizational culture in successfully implementing new innovations. In addition, Fixsen et al. (2009: 533) suggest that these components can also compensate for one another in that a weakness in "one component can be overcome by strengths in other components." These authors offer a cautionary note: good implementation processes do not yield effective outcomes if the program or policy being implemented is flawed; thus, a good implementation strategy must be matched with an effectively designed program model to achieve success. Each of the seven implementation components is briefly highlighted below.

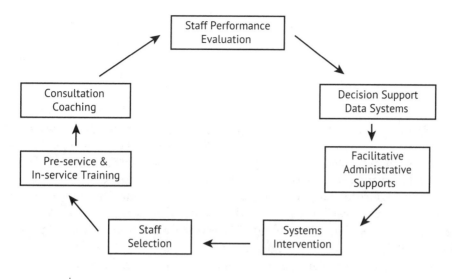

Figure 5.1 | Core Implementation Components

Source: Adapted from Fixsen et al. (2009: 534).

- *Staff Selection*: Staff knowledge, skills, and qualifications should be matched with the demands of the program, and there must be an adequate number of staff to deliver specified services.
- *Pre-service and In-service Training*: New programs may require new skills and approaches, and adequate attention to training is an efficient way to provide information on the values, theory, and skills associated with the innovation.
- *Ongoing Coaching and Consultation*: Learning on the job, particularly in cases where behaviour change is required, is best facilitated through coaching and consultation.
- *Staff Performance Evaluation*: Staff evaluation focused on the application of new skills and knowledge provides a means to support intervention and help assess the effectiveness of components such as training and coaching.
- *Decision Support Data Systems*: Measures to assess service quality and outcomes as well as frequent feedback on results help to support implementation.
- *Facilitative Administrative Supports*: Leadership that focuses on developing supportive policies, procedures, structures, and culture within the working environment assists front-line practitioners in ensuring best practices.
- *Systems Intervention*: Systems intervention strategies with external organizations are important in ensuring the adequate financial, organizational, and human resources required to support practitioners in their work.

Although Fixsen et al. do not include them as a special component, they note the important role of **purveyors**, which are defined as individuals or groups that promote the new practice or program with special attention to program fidelity and principles of best practice. These purveyors play a role that is somewhat like a "fixer" or "advocate" for the new policy.

Building Capacity for Child Welfare Innovations: An Illustration

The following summary, based on information provided by Jay Rodgers, CEO of the General Child and Family Services Authority, and the work of one of the authors with this authority, incorporates a number of the components of the implementation model described above, as well as efforts to use a strategic planning process based on the principles of Appreciative Inquiry (AI). The example on implementation summarized earlier in this chapter involved efforts to devolve the delivery of child welfare services to Aboriginal authorities and agencies throughout Manitoba. But each authority was faced with unique issues in designing and implementing a new approach to service delivery. In the case of the General Child and Family Services (CFS) Authority, it inherited a system that included nine agencies, more than one-quarter of the child welfare cases in the province, and a staff that was quite demoralized by the ongoing series of changes that characterized child welfare in the province between 2000 and 2006. At the same time, there was an opportunity in that recommendations from external reviews conducted in 2006 following the death of five-year-old Phoenix Sinclair led to new provincial funding. There was also a commitment to implement a differential response system for child welfare services where some referrals would be diverted to staff that would provide early intervention and family support services as a first response rather than more traditional child protection services based on an intrusive investigative approach.

From the beginning it was recognized that the detailed design of a new service innovation had to go hand in hand with a capacity-building approach targeted at all organization levels within the General CFS Authority. **Appreciative inquiry**, which emphasizes an inclusive strengths-based approach to planning using a 4-D cycle (discovery, dream, design, and destiny) and is discussed further in Chapter 6, was selected as the preferred approach to planning. The discovery and dream stages were accomplished through a summit (a large gathering) that involved more than 200 staff and foster parents. Building on the identified strengths and positive morale emerging from this summit, follow-up steps included a participatory process to identify values (i.e., strengths-based, inclusiveness, transparency, evidence-based, and respect for staff) for the design stage. In this particular case the authority and its agencies had significant control over designing pilot projects to implement differential response. Implementation components, which were given particular attention in developing pilot projects to provide early intervention and family support services, included staff selection, supportive training, facilitative administrative supports, and data collection protocols. For example, training included in-service workshops for new risk and family assessment procedures; administrative supports included ongoing peer support meetings for supervisors from all pilot projects; and data collection included systems for ongoing monitoring and an external evaluation of the pilot project phase.

However, the General CFS Authority and its agencies also embraced an approach to innovation that included objectives related to broader system change and capacity-building. Values related to inclusiveness and building on strengths were associated with the design and implementation of a Youth Engagement Strategy staffed by youth who had been in care, as well as a Staff Engagement Strategy that included peer support and an inclusive approach to training. New resources for staff positions, although never enough, were particularly important to building capacity. A critical element in this innovation was to support the development of a new practice model, not only in relation to families identified as eligible for early intervention and family support as a first response but also for families requiring a more traditional child protection response beginning with investigation. The new practice model, designed with staff input and training experts, combined a solution-focused approach to child safety that emphasized family engagement with tools to assess both risk and family strengths. Leading practice specialists were appointed for each agency to facilitate training and to act as coaches in applying the new practice model. Three core elements have helped to ensure successful implementation of this new practice model: the selection and use of evidence-based assessment and intervention tools focusing on safety; the development of family engagement skills to enhance the likelihood of building positive relationships with families; and supported learning through continuous access to training, support, and mentoring.

Although the longer-term effects are yet to be evaluated, to date there is evidence of increased organizational capacity among participating agencies, progress on implementing new reforms, including the practice model, and some improvements in service outcomes for children and families. Progress has been aided by the adoption of an adaptive, participatory approach to implementation, with a special emphasis on several of the core implementation components outlined in Figure 5.1:

- systems intervention (to access new resources and external training supports);
- facilitative administrative supports (supportive policies and protocols developed in collaboration with agency managers, supervisors, front-line staff, and service users—e.g., youth);
- training programs (based on staff feedback and co-creation);
- coaching and consultation (input, feedback, and adjustment of both training and practice model guidelines as well as ongoing coaching in applying new training approaches).

Summary and Conclusion

The implementation literature and selected examples on policy implementation included in this chapter support the need for greater attention to a bottom-up, adaptive approach to implementation, particularly in those human services where programs must be flexible enough to respond to the diverse needs of service users. Policies that prescribe benefits requiring very little professional judgment or discretion permit a more structured model of implementation that can be largely controlled from head office; however, these types of policies in the human services are quite limited in number. Although we place considerable emphasis on approaches that incorporate inclusiveness and flexibility, the evidence supports implementation processes that involve some synthesis between top-down and bottom-up approaches. First, there is a general need to ensure a certain level of consistency and accountability across service delivery sites. Second, even when an adaptive approach to implementation that engages more fully with front-line practitioners and service users occurs, it will require supportive responses from head office in responding to locally identified concerns.

In this chapter we also drew attention to a model that connects implementation with internal organizational factors that influence the successful adoption of innovations. Although this model may focus more directly on internal organizational factors, it does direct needed attention to how an emphasis on strengths and capacity-building within organizations can be used in operationalizing an adaptive approach to implementation. Here the role of one or more "fixers" or advocates can help to facilitate the different phases or stages of implementation.

In Chapter 6 additional approaches that incorporate more inclusive responses to the various stages of policy-making, including implementation, are discussed.

Critical Thinking Questions

1. Top-down or programmed and bottom-up or adaptive approaches to implementation were described in this chapter. Identify some policy examples where it might be appropriate to place more emphasis on top-down approaches and some examples where more emphasis on a bottom-up approach is required. Defend your choices.

2. A synthesis of programmed and adaptive approaches to implementation was suggested as having some advantages in implementation. What role should front-line practitioners and supervisors play in such a model?

3. Most literature on implementation neglects the role of service users. How realistic is it for service users to become involved in shaping implementation? How could they be more involved and on what issues might their involvement be most critical? What barriers exist to greater involvement of service users and how might these be overcome?

4. The concept of discretion can be used to enhance or restrict benefits and services to those who require these. Identify examples of each from a field of practice with which you are familiar.
5. How important is the issue of organizational culture and capacity-building to effective implementation of new policies? Review the core implementation components identified in this chapter (Figure 5.1). Do you think all of these factors are important? Should any other factors be added?

Recommended Reading

P. Berman. "Thinking about Programmed and Adaptive Implementation," in H. Ingram and D. Mann, eds. *Why Policies Succeed or Fail*, pp. 205–27. Beverly Hills, Calif.: Sage, 1980. This chapter distinguishes between policies benefiting from top-down and bottom-up approaches to implementation and identifies factors to help in decision-making about which approach to use.

B. Carroll and D. Siegel. *Service in the Field*. Montreal and Kingston: McGill-Queen's University Press, 1999. This Canadian study of the relationship between field and head offices provides a useful critique of the traditional bureaucratic model of operation.

D.L. Fixsen, K.A. Blase, S.F. Naoom, and F. Wallace. "Core Implementation Components," *Research on Social Work Practice* 19 (2009): 531–40. doi: 10.1177/1049731509335549. This article summarizes research leading to the identification of the core implementation components identified in this chapter.

M. Lipsky. *Street-Level Bureaucracy*. New York: Russell Sage Foundation, 1980. This is one of the most influential studies of policy-making and its effects on front-line practitioners.

P. Sabatier. "Top-Down and Bottom-Up Approaches to Implementation Research: A Critical Analysis and Suggested Synthesis," *Journal of Public Policy* 6, 1 (1986): 21–48. Sabatier provides a summary of top-down and bottom-up theories of implementation along with a proposal for a synthesis of these two perspectives.

Chapter

6

Making Policy for Social Change from Inside the System

---• **In this chapter you will learn about:** •---

- some of the efforts being made to engage with communities in policy-making;
- how small-scale planning can be used to connect policy to practice;
- the principles and practices that support inclusive policy-making;
- how the role of backwards mapping, shared decision-making, and policy communities can be used to establish inclusive approaches to policy-making;
- the potential of community-based services and community governance in enhancing a participatory approach to planning.

Introduction

This chapter continues the theme of inclusive policy-making from the last chapter by identifying several specialized models that organizations may use to promote this approach. In the next chapter we consider approaches that can be initiated from outside the system. It is sometimes difficult to make a clear distinction in that a particular strategy may be relevant in promoting policies from both inside and outside the system. For example, promoting citizen participation to support or resist policies can be facilitated by stakeholders from within or outside the organization developing the new policy. In a similar fashion, advocacy approaches are relevant to policy development both inside and outside the system. In practice the distinguishing characteristic in whether a strategy is defined as originating from "inside" or "outside" is the extent to which the policy-making organization is engaged in active promotion of the approach.

We begin this chapter with a discussion of citizen participation and then introduce small-scale planning because of its potential for use in promoting participatory approaches within the organization and in developing policies in collaboration with communities. Following this, more specialized approaches are introduced, including the vertical slice approach, backwards mapping (identified as an approach to implementation in Chapter 5), shared decision-making, policy communities, and community governance. In each case, examples are identified in an effort to critically examine the potential of these to improve the policy-making process.

At the outset, it is useful to acknowledge that more inclusive approaches do not always lead to more progressive policies. Examples of this include citizen movements advocating a "tough on crime" approach and community mobilization aimed at preventing rezoning to permit the development of a community-based group home for intellectually challenged adults. These examples serve to highlight the presence of competing interests that can exist. Inclusive approaches are vulnerable to domination by those with greater privilege, who exercise more control over participatory processes and shape the outcomes of these processes in their interests. Thus, results from inclusive models need to be critically examined to ensure they give voice to all groups and results are not manipulated by those with the most power. If a meaningful participatory process occurs, then the results need to be carefully considered, even if they do not reflect everyone's preferred choice.

The right to participate is anchored in the principle of affected interests, which was discussed in the Introduction. However, Dahl (1970) concedes that the principle gives rise to some practical dilemmas. He suggests that the criteria of *personal choice, competence*, and *economy* can be helpful in applying the principle.

- Personal choice refers to the right of individuals to choose to participate or to opt out.
- Competence suggests that not all individuals can tackle situations requiring advanced skill and knowledge.
- Economy suggests that in issues where a large number of people are affected, some means of representation must be established.

The inclusive models of policy-making presented in this chapter respect the principle of affected interests by including in the policy-making process at least representatives of those who will be affected by policies. However, the adoption of any of these models requires a commitment by senior policy-makers in public-sector or voluntary organizations to relinquish some control and facilitate meaningful participation.

Citizen Participation and Community Collaboration

Citizen participation is associated with benefits to individuals, voluntary organizations, and communities by transferring knowledge and skill development, building community capacity to tackle future social policy issues, and fostering the overall health of the community (Wharf-Higgins, Cossom, and Wharf, 2006). Although citizen participation may reflect goals associated with mutual aid and self-help, we are primarily interested here in how civil society attempts to influence social change, notably in the interactions of citizens with government.

Some will argue that governments are elected to make policies and that, once elected, government members are free to make policies in the public interest. This raises the question about whether representative democracy is all that matters to ensure citizen engagement or whether more participatory forms of democracy are essential to civil society and effective policy-making processes. Although representative democracy is important, it is not enough. Reliance on this form of participation alone reinforces the concentration of power in elites, despite the public having an opportunity at election time to change which elite governs. Even if government initiates processes such as advisory committees, consultations, and consumer surveys, these have done little to overcome voter apathy in elections, a general distrust in government, and citizens' feelings of disempowerment, particularly among those who are marginalized. The opportunities for citizens to participate in public forums, public inquiries, and hearings of bodies like the Truth and Reconciliation Commission, which examined the history and consequences of residential schools, go some distance to enabling meaningful input into key policy issues, but these opportunities tend to be restricted to selected issues.

Government–community partnerships where approaches to collaboration are developed can open up more opportunities for citizen engagement in social change. To be successful these partnerships depend on relationships built on trust and mutual respect, genuine efforts from government to respond to the real needs of the community, some element of local control over local policies and programs, and the development of constructive ways of bridging cultural boundaries. There are risks associated with these opportunities, including a consultative process not directly linked to meaningful policy change or that leaves too much of the decision-making power in the hands of government. However, there are also many examples of successful partnerships in the development of specific programs.

Extending a collaborative approach to neighbourhoods and communities has some similarity to **deliberative democracy**, where efforts are made to exchange views, assess differences based on merit, and develop mutually acceptable solutions in an effort to build **social inclusion** and a vibrant civil society (Wharf-Higgins and Weller, 2012). Community-led development attempts to tackle local problems by building on local strengths, but it also requires government and other organizational support. There are also certain risks, including the possibility that too much decision-making control may be assumed by individuals and groups external to the community or that government-sponsored initiatives may become a way of off-loading responsibilities to the local community (Kelly and Caputo, 2011). However, the greatest risk, as illustrated in Box 6.1, may be the lack of continuity in funding from government.

There are also a number of successful examples of this approach. One example is the Vibrant Communities initiative launched in 2002 with three sponsors—Tamarack, the Caledon Institute, and the J.W. McConnell Family Foundation. The project, which focused on social learning for social change, collaboration across sectors, and building on community assets to reduce poverty in 13 communities across Canada, developed a number of additional funding partners during the 10-year implementation phase. An evaluation of this initiative conducted by Gamble (2012) found positive effects from this model of community engagement, including:

- new ideas for reducing poverty by engaging a variety of organizations and leaders;
- the ability to attract new resources for poverty reduction;
- new policy and practice responses from government and the private sector;
- a reduction in the overall level of poverty within these communities;
- the transfer of learning from these experiences to governments and other organizations engaged in the development of poverty reduction strategies.

As these examples suggest, initiatives for community change can benefit from careful attention to the availability of needed resources to launch and sustain innovations as well as approaches for measuring success (Weaver, Born, and Whaley, 2010).

Box **6.1** | Action for Community Change

An action learning project was launched in 2005 to strengthen neighbourhoods in five cities across Canada (Surrey, Regina, Thunder Bay, Toronto, and Halifax). The focus was on developing each community's capacity to identify barriers to community well-being and to tackle related policy challenges in linking local citizens with government and non-government organizations to create solutions. There were multiple partners, including the federal government (a major funder), United Ways, Tamarack—An Institute for Community Engagement, the Caledon Institute of Social Policy, and the National Film Board. Some success was achieved in overcoming government's tendency to direct neighbourhood activities and in building community structures for addressing community needs. However, the withdrawal of federal funding after the election of the Harper Conservative government left most local neighbourhoods without needed financial support to sustain development goals. Only ongoing support from the United Way of Greater Toronto and the United Way of Halifax Region permitted some aspects of this initiative to continue in those two cities.

Source: Torjman and Makhoul (2012).

It may be difficult to reconcile the notion of power-sharing in successful partnerships and collaboration with the decentralization of power common to community governance discussed later in this chapter. However, the devolution of power to organizations and communities from central authorities, which is then followed by decisions to work together to generate better outcomes to multi-sector problems, is not inconsistent in that agreements to share power are entered into voluntarily. Although not all problems require a large-scale collaborative approach, broad cross-sector co-ordination for collective impact has received more attention recently (Kania and Kramer, 2011). Collaboration among governments, the private sector, and the not-for-profit sector are common to these initiatives. Hanleybrown, Kania, and Kramer (2012) identify a number of successful collective impact projects, including efforts to reduce homelessness in Calgary (Calgary Homeless Foundation), reducing teenage binge drinking in Massachusetts (Communities That Care), and reducing malnutrition internationally (Global Alliance for Improved Nutrition). The multi-sector response to homelessness in Calgary is significant in that a similar model has been adopted in a number of Canadian cities, including Edmonton, Toronto, Vancouver, and Winnipeg.

Strategies from collective impact partnerships need to be sustained over the long term to make a difference, and five conditions have been associated with success. These are:

1. developing a shared vision and agenda for change;
2. collecting data and measuring results consistently across participants;
3. developing mutually reinforcing activities that are well co-ordinated;
4. continuous communication to build trust and maintain relationships;
5. developing "backbone" support from an organization with a small staff dedicated to co-ordinating the initiative.

Despite the difficulties in launching these kinds of initiatives, the results from several projects have been encouraging (Hanleybrown et al., 2012).

Although the neighbourhood development project summarized in Box 6.2 reflects a small-scale community partnership, it illustrates some of the same principles associated with success in larger projects. However, in this disadvantaged neighbourhood, actions were first launched by the local community and partnerships with government and other organizations emerged later in the process.

Partnerships, which begin at the agency level, can also be established to enhance service innovation. Although improved service co-ordination is often the primary goal, increased community engagement is an important element in achieving success. One example of this approach in the criminal justice field is the community mobilization initiative implemented in Prince Albert, Saskatchewan, in response to escalating crime in the West Flat neighbourhood that abuts the downtown area (Turner, 2013). Adopting a model from Glasgow, Scotland, the approach involved the development of the Hub, a cross-section of social service and other professionals who meet twice a week to

Box **6.2** | Rebuilding the Neighbourhood

Point Douglas, located in the north end of Winnipeg, is one of the most impoverished urban neighbourhoods in Canada. It is home to 3,600 children under six, 40 per cent of whom are classified as not ready for school at age five. One in six of these children is taken into care by the child welfare system in this mixed Aboriginal/non-Aboriginal community, and drug use, crime, and public safety are prominent concerns. In June 2007, the children of a local school made national headlines when they appealed to Governor General Michaëlle Jean for help. This appeal became a catalyst for local action that began with the North Point Douglas Women's Centre and an energetic local leader who helped to mobilize community involvement. An initial focus was public safety and the Residents' Committee set up an e-mail account that allowed residents to send tips about criminal activity, which were then referred to police. New relationships were established with police; 30 crack houses were shut down over an eight-month period; the crime rate declined by 70 per cent over a one-year period; and community meetings and events, which once had trouble attracting a dozen members from the community, attracted residents that often exceeded 10 times this number.

   These community-based activities led to a funding partnership with the provincial government that enabled the development of a number of community programs, and the Residents' Committee continues to sponsor a wide range of programs and activities. More children can be seen playing outside in the neighbourhood, residents now feel free to walk the streets any time, day or night, and renovated and restored homes outnumber abandoned ones. In 2013 special funding and development assistance was secured from the J.W. McConnell Family Foundation for the launch of the Boldness Project, which includes new, ongoing investment for early childhood development and other programs for both North and South Point Douglas in collaboration with business leaders, the province, and the city.

Sources: Lett (2008); Roussin, Gill, and Young (2014).

identify and co-ordinate service responses, focusing first on support to high-risk individuals. This service co-ordination strategy is supported by a Centre of Responsibility (COR) that employs analysts to identify and co-ordinate larger systemic issues. Results from this holistic crime prevention strategy, which includes declining crime rates and the diversion of social service intakes, are encouraging, and this innovative model has been adopted in a number of other Saskatchewan communities.

Small-Scale Policy-Making Processes

Addressing the ordinary issues in policy-making can also include small-scale innovations launched by a single staff person, a small team within an organization, or a community group. These types of initiatives can have profound effects on the lives of those who receive services, even if the number of service users is relatively small.

Small-scale policy-making (Schram, 1997) draws on a number of steps associated with some of the policy-making models outlined in Chapter 3 and the stages of policy-making discussed in Chapter 4. An important consideration is the initiation stage of a new small-scale innovation. The individual or group launching the initiative must take the time to establish a consensus about the need for action with those who are responsible for approving the project. The potential for community partnerships may need to be explored, particularly if one is developing a new proposal that will require external funding.

A **strategic planning** approach, which draws on steps outlined in the mixed scanning model of policy-making discussed in Chapter 3, is often used to launch a new initiative. If it is pursued as a participatory exercise that engages key stakeholders in developing the innovation, it can help to resolve any value differences and reach a consensus on central components of the new policy or program. Although the steps followed in strategic planning vary somewhat, the following tasks are usually covered in some form:

- *Understand the historical context of the agency or problem.* This involves an examination of general information on trends, critical events, and any ideals that characterize the agency or sponsoring group.
- *Establish a vision or an idealized image of the service or program three to five years into the future.* This helps to identify any tensions that may need to be resolved and to highlight general goals that are essential in establishing a mission statement for the new initiative.
- *Complete a situational assessment that involves an analysis of both the internal and external environment affecting the agency or sponsoring group.* The strengths and weaknesses of the internal environment are identified along with the opportunities and threats in the external environment.
- *Identify the issues for which there are yet no obvious solutions.* Strategic issues may emerge from tensions that surfaced during the visioning stage or from the situational assessment.
- *Develop strategic options and select the preferred alternative to address each major unresolved issue.* The activities involved here are similar to those involved in the formulation stage of policy-making. Alternatives are first identified and then assessed for their ability to meet the general goals of the new initiative.
- *Assess feasibility, including general implementation challenges that may need to be considered.* One should consider the views of service users as well as the political, financial, and legal implications of proposed changes. Other considerations include an assessment of key stakeholders and the likelihood of obtaining their support for the new initiative. Strategies will need to be designed to deal with those likely to oppose the new initiative if these individuals will be influential in whether the new policy is adopted. One also needs to consider both the material and non-material resources required to implement the new strategy and possible sources of these resources.

Strategic planning has been criticized for its focus on weaknesses and the identification of issues as problems. Other criticisms include its reliance on past trends to predict the future, the reluctance or failure to adapt its five-year plan over this time period, and the tendency to engage primarily with senior decision-makers in formulating a plan (O'Donovan and Rimland Flower, 2013). Although strategic planning continues to have some relevance, an approach that includes more attention to the need for adaptive strategies, increased participation from front-line workers, and inspirational leadership is advocated. Appreciative Inquiry (AI), introduced in Chapter 5, is an alternative approach to planning that focuses more on strengths. AI is similar to strategic planning in that it aims to identify strategies and goals for change; however, the stages of planning are somewhat different, and the approach incorporates a high level of participation by members of the organization as an essential component of the planning process. The four stages of the AI model, as outlined below, are often referred to as a 4-D model.

1. *Discovery.* Participants reflect on and discuss the best of "what is" about the issue or organization (i.e, strengths).
2. *Dream.* This stage involves imagining the group, organization, or community at its best and identifying common goals or aspirations of what could be.
3. *Design.* This stage involves concrete proposals and strategies for change.
4. *Destiny.* This stage involves detailed operational planning and implementation.

The AI process has some parallels to the solution-focused approach common to direct practice. However, in organizational planning the discovery and dream stages are often carried out at a "summit" or large gathering attended by members of the organization. Thus, staff engagement in the process of recognizing and building on strengths to establish new policies or address an organizational change goal is central to the model. The collective approach to laying the groundwork for the design stage, which may be led by smaller committees, can enhance staff morale and their commitment to follow-up action; at the same time, it also creates expectations for transparency and ongoing engagement as the design and destiny stages unfold. Unless these principles guide follow-up action, the AI approach to strategic planning may fail to achieve its general goal of transformative change.

Strategic planning or AI can be useful in resolving differences about general strategies to be adopted and setting the general direction for a new program or initiative; however, results often lack the specificity required for implementing a new program initiative. This stage requires clarity about goals and objectives. In strategic planning this part of the planning process may be defined as operational planning, which occurs following the development of general strategies; in AI it is frequently included as part of the design phase. We define goal statements as general statements of program outcomes or what will be accomplished, whereas outcome objectives are more specific, measurable changes that will be experienced by service users. The criteria for good objectives are identified in Table 6.1. Because goals are more general in nature, each goal

| Table **6.1** | Criteria for Good Program Development Objectives |

Criteria	Explanation
1. Clarity	The meaning of the objectives should be clear to all those who read it.
2. Realistic	An objective should be reasonable given available knowledge, technology, and resources.
3. Time frame	The time frame for achieving results should be specified. If specific dates cannot be identified, the time frame may be indicated in months and/or years after implementation.
4. Targets of change	Outcome objectives should specify the population or elements that are expected to be changed, whereas process objectives will identify the structures or methods to be developed in order to achieve outcome objectives.
5. Products and results	New programs in the human services are designed to lead to changes in behaviour or well-being in service users, and these expected changes can be identified as results. Products can be defined as the outputs, outcomes, or steps to be completed in order to achieve results.
6. Criteria for measurement	Criteria for measurement can include quantitative or qualitative indicators in the case of outcome objectives, although performance targets may vary over time. In the case of process objectives, results may be simply documented (e.g., recruit 25 new foster parents).
7. Responsibility	Responsibility for implementation should either be identified or clearly understood.

may have several outcome objectives. In developing outcome objectives, one may also need to give attention to performance indicators that will help assess whether the new initiative is effective at various stages of the implementation process. While outcome objectives are important in focusing on the anticipated benefits that will emerge from the project, process objectives can be specified to outline things that must be done to build the operating capacity of the project. For example, a new innovation may require the formation of a management structure and a staff training program.

The identification of clear program goals and objectives is essential in defining expected results from a new program or initiative. A relatively common approach in planning a new program or in developing proposals is the development of a **program logic model**. A program logic model is a depiction of a program showing what the program will do and what it is to accomplish. It consists of a series of "if–then" relationships that, if implemented as initiated, lead to desired outcomes. A logic model is like a road map in that it provides a brief summary of where you are going, how you will get there, and what will indicate that you have arrived. In its simplest form it consists of a summary of inputs, outputs, and outcomes (see Figure 6.1). Inputs consist of the investments such as financial resources, staff time, and materials that are mobilized to develop a new program, whereas outputs are the activities carried out in implementing the program and the number and characteristics of service users who will participate in the program. Outcomes are usually broken down as short, medium, and long term. In a program logic model the inputs, outputs, and outcomes specify the elements of the model whereas the arrows in Figure 6.1, which depict the relationship between inputs, outputs, and outcomes, suggest the logic (often outlined as assumptions or program hypotheses that may be supported by theory). Program logic models can be useful tools for both planning and building a framework for program evaluation.

Once objectives are clarified, action plans can be specified for each objective if this is required. Action plans, which on a larger scale may be referred to as implementation or operational planning, are simply sets of activities that may be required to clarify how the changes specified in program goals and objectives will be accomplished. The essential elements of action plans are quite similar to the criteria identified in Table 6.1 for good objectives, although an action plan may focus more concretely on the tasks to be carried out, by whom, and within what time frame. Each action plan may involve a number of action steps or tasks that must be carried out in the implementation stage.

In a new innovation, action plans may need to be established to identify tasks related to the following:

- the governance and management structure for the new initiative;
- an outreach strategy to recruit and select service users or the target population;
- a staff orientation and training strategy;
- the service model or technology to be used;
- the approach to be used in evaluating success and monitoring implementation;
- any special steps to be followed in implementing service activities.

Implementation planning in larger programs may require significant detail. In these circumstances, it is important to establish a timeline where activities are sequenced

Figure 6.1 Format for Creating a Program Logic Model

and integrated within a general policy-making framework. In small programs this can be accomplished by specifying beginning and ending dates for various activities; in larger programs computer modelling can be used to help establish a timeline for program implementation. However, even in small initiatives it is advisable to establish an action-monitoring plan. An action-monitoring plan can be combined with the development of an action plan and might include the following:

- a list of the general set of activities or action plans to be carried out along with information on the resources required, those resources that are available, and what must be done to secure needed resource shortfalls;
- a list of the action steps or tasks for each action plan;
- information on who is responsible for each task and requirements for accountability—in small group initiatives, accountability may be to the group; in larger initiatives a co-ordinator may be identified and written reports may be required;
- a timeline for tasks that specifies the start and completion dates for different tasks.

In small-scale policy-making the development of detailed action plans may follow formal approval of the new initiative, and such plans will guide the implementation process.

Research and development activities can help to facilitate small-scale innovation from either inside or outside the organization. However, central to innovations that see the "light of day" are leadership and commitment from someone willing to take some risks and mobilize support and engagement both from sponsors and potential beneficiaries. The example in Box 6.3 was an outcome of an international development project in Ukraine that was co-ordinated by one of the authors.

Box **6.3** │ Developing Community-Based Innovation in Ukraine

Responding to a request from community service providers, Canadian sponsors of the four-year project to develop a new social work education program established a course called "Innovations in Social Development" that was offered to 13 pairs of participants. Each dyad was admitted to the training based on a project proposal. Training in project planning, implementation, and evaluation was provided. Seed funding, ongoing supervision, and mentoring were provided to those who wanted to implement their project proposals.

One project, developed by an artist, involved creating a small voluntary organization to act as a resource for the homeless. The project was more of a support group in the early stage, functioning with donations and assistance from volunteers. The project leader persisted in seeking support from several sources, and by 2005 she and her supporters had secured a small building in a village bordering

Lviv in Ukraine. Here they opened a residence for approximately eight people. The importance of a home to those who are homeless is a universal need, but additional services, including rehabilitative work, life skills, and art therapy, were introduced to respond to broader needs. Voluntary assistance from a psychiatrist provided needed counselling services. Self-sufficiency activities such as furniture refinishing and community work helped to make some money and reduce the stigma often associated with homeless people with mental health challenges. By 2012 the program had expanded to two buildings, providing housing and a workshop for up to 25 adults. In addition, the program provided a day program for those living in the community. A full-time social worker was employed, and the group published and sold a newspaper. Operating as a type of co-operative based on the European model, the organization has received some external funding; however, it also generates its own revenue through its many local business enterprise activities such as furniture renovations. Most importantly, it has transformed the lives of many who have experienced homelessness, drug addiction, and mental health challenges.

Source: With information from Maureen Flaherty, University of Manitoba.

Enhancing Participation in General Models of Planning and Policy Analysis

The Vertical Slice Approach

A strategy sometimes used as a means to involve those affected by policies within an organization is to create a policy group composed of representatives from different levels of the organization. We refer to this as the **vertical slice approach** because it often includes representatives from front-line service providers, supervisors, program managers, and senior policy-makers. This model may also include service users, and although we advocate the inclusion of service users this does not always occur. Policy groups structured in this way can be assigned responsibility for developing, reviewing, and changing policies within the organization. Such groups can be quite effective in implementation planning, particularly if an adaptive approach to implementation is being used because participants understand the special needs and issues that exist at different levels of the organization.

The vertical slice approach can allow both service users and front-line staff opportunities to learn about budgets and the political aspects of policy-making while providing senior-level policy-makers with much needed information on service delivery issues. Based on our experience, this approach is likely to be most effective in organizations that possess a significant commitment to and experience with a more participatory style of decision-making.

The vertical slice approach is not a panacea for organizational reform or major policy change. In circumstances like these the approval of recommended policies often exists some distance from the policy group; thus, their ability to influence these decisions may be quite limited. There is also a membership accountability issue with the vertical slice approach. Are participants accountable for the views they express to their peers who come from different levels of the organization, or do they exercise their own judgments as individuals once they are selected?

Backwards Mapping

In Chapter 5 we noted the value of backwards mapping to implementing policy. Here we argue that the approach has merit in the development of new policies. This approach, which is quite similar to a bottom-up or adaptive approach to implementation, requires that policy development begin by going back to identify the problems and their characteristics as these are being experienced by service users and front-line practitioners. It must be accompanied by a commitment to incorporate these experiential perspectives wherever feasible in developing a new policy. Ideally, a feedback loop will be incorporated where the draft policy is taken back to front-line staff and/or service users to ensure it addresses identified problems and recommendations. This approach is illustrated by the following two examples.

Example 1: Creating a New Policy for Kinship Care in British Columbia

In British Columbia backwards mapping was used to create a new policy for kinship care. Prior to this policy, children were placed in the care of extended family members through informal arrangements between parents and relatives, in a more formal way by the ministry under the provisions of the Child, Family and Community Service Act, and through the Child in the Home of a Relative (CIHR) program funded through income assistance. Each of these alternative placement arrangements differed in terms of the amount of resources provided to caregivers, the kind of assessment undertaken prior to placement, and the ongoing support provided by the state. These inconsistencies were questioned during a review of the early intervention component of the Ministry for Children and Family Development's (MCFD) action plan, *Strong, Safe and Supported: A Commitment to B.C.'s Children and Youth*. The specific impetus for policy change resulted from an inquiry into the death of a First Nations child who had been placed in kinship care, resulting in a recommendation that a new policy for kinship care be developed that would formalize all aspects of these previously rather haphazard arrangements.

Although the ministry on many occasions has solicited the advice of service users, staff, and community members, consulting front-line staff and service users has by no means been a constant and regular feature of its policy-making approach. In this particular instance the ministry made a formal commitment to an extensive process of consultation. Without explicitly acknowledging the principle of affected interests, it essentially adopted this as the guiding principle for the process. For example, the draft report summarizing the results of the consultations noted that it is important that those who are directly affected by policy, including service providers who use it in their practice, as well as children, family and community members who receive services, have a voice in the development of policy. When practice informs policy we can expect policy to be effective in achieving the expected results. (MCFD, 2008: 17)

Although consultations were restricted to the Vancouver Island region, the number of consultations was extensive. According to the MCFD: "Close to 250 people were involved, including 70 staff members of the Ministry, 30 foster parents, 50 other service providers, and 95 kinship care givers" (MCFD, 2008: 18).

Incorporating an evaluative component to this backwards mapping initiative was made possible through an agreement between the director of the Vancouver Island region of MCFD and one of the authors (i.e., Wharf). The director noted that before proceeding to obtain approval for the draft report from other regions and from head office, he wanted to know if it fairly represented the views of those who had been consulted. Although it was not possible to meet with all who had participated, a day-long meeting was held with 10 staff members of the ministry and a representative from a First Nations child and family services agency.

The participants were unanimous that their views were adequately represented in the draft report and in the recommendations for a new policy on kinship care. Furthermore, they urged that the policy be developed and implemented as soon as possible, and that if other regions in the province expressed reservations about the report, it should be implemented on a pilot basis on Vancouver Island. Nevertheless, several concerns were expressed, and most revolved around one central issue: the need to end the practice whereby new policies prescribe how policies are to be carried out but neglect to provide the resources required. As Greider (1992) notes, policies that fail to include needed resources to support implementation are "hollow." The resources required for kinship care included remuneration for caregivers and medical coverage for children, and these requirements were highlighted in the report recommended for approval.

Example 2: Developing a New Policy for Youth Transitioning from Child Welfare in Manitoba

A second example is the development of a new policy for youth transitioning from child welfare care. This initiative, led by a graduate student completing a practicum in child welfare, incorporated aspects of mixed scanning, the principle of affected interests, and backwards mapping (Fallis, 2013). Approval for the development of a new policy had been provided by the child welfare authority, and initial activities included an extensive literature review, an assessment of policies, legislation, and programs in other jurisdictions, and a review of local policies and standards. Foundational to this process was the engagement process established with staff from agencies within the authority and young people in and from care. The engagement strategy with foster care and youth engagement workers consisted of meetings and interviews. Two fundamental questions guided these discussions:

1. What were the major barriers youth encountered in transitioning from care to emerging adulthood?
2. What can be done to improve outcomes for former youth in care?

Focus group discussions, co-facilitated by a former youth in care and the student, were also held with groups of youth in and from care.

Based on interview results and the literature review, a draft of leading practice guidelines was developed, recommendations were made to the authority, and a proposed action plan was constructed. These results were then taken back to agency staff during a half-day presentation and discussion and to another co-facilitated focus group with youth to ensure that the policy guidelines and recommendations accurately reflected the views expressed during the initial consultation phase.

As in the first example, respondents from both agency staff and youth enthusiastically supported the guidelines, accompanying recommendations, and proposed action plan. These recommendations were then approved by the directors of participating agencies and the authority's board of directors. Guidelines, which included requirements for mentorship, youth participation in developing their own after-care plan, creation of an educational plan, and development of a financial plan, were adopted as policies, and these were supplemented by leading practice tools to facilitate implementation. These tools, constructed as questions and guidelines, are applied when a youth in care is applying for an extension of care. On a somewhat larger scale the results supported development of a Building Futures project, which provides a network of supports to youth leaving care or who have previously been in care.

Shared Decision-Making

Shared decision-making is a form of collaborative planning that combines direct democracy with interest-based negotiation. Typically, government and non-government organizations with a shared interest but divergent positions about how to resolve a policy problem engage in a process of dialogue and negotiation in an effort to reach an agreement that accommodates rather than compromises the interests of all who are involved. Although broad principles or guidelines outlining the scope of activities and the broad goal of discussions may be provided in advance by government, government is only one party at the table and efforts are made to minimize power differentials during meetings. Because different groups value different things, communication, analysis, and building an understanding of each other's interests are central to the process. Typically, information-sharing and negotiation occur through round table meetings that focus on clearly defining problems, narrowing the scope of issues, and identifying a range of possible alternatives for resolution. Although the goal is a consensus-based resolution, this may not be possible on all issues and an outcome that narrows the number of differences through mutual learning and respect may be beneficial. Ensuring each party is prepared to engage in meaningful dialogue and providing skilled facilitators are important to success.

Chapter 10 includes an example of a shared decision-making approach used to try to reach an agreement on a new funding model for the delivery of child welfare services on reserves.

Shared decision-making can also be implemented on a somewhat smaller scale. This is illustrated by a child welfare initiative launched in Winnipeg by the General Child and Family Services (CFS) Authority, one of the four child welfare administrative units for child welfare in Manitoba, in collaboration with new Canadians (see Box 6.4). The initiative, which shares at least some of the features of the shared decision-making model, demonstrates the value of this inclusive approach in small-scale policy-making.

Policy Communities or Networks

Policy networks or communities were defined in Chapter 2 as loosely knit groups composed of individuals from organizations who are interested in and knowledgeable about a particular aspect of public policy. Membership varies depending on the issues, but it is common for government representatives, officials from non-government organizations, and representatives from private-sector organizations, where relevant, to be engaged in the network. Policy communities are not usually registered as voluntary organizations, and activities may be conducted in either a formal or an informal fashion. Meetings do occur, often on an irregular basis, and policy documents may be created and exchanged.

Some policy communities have been extremely influential in shaping public policy, yet they typically receive limited attention in the public policy literature. The only book that has given comprehensive treatment to the contribution of policy communities is *Policy Communities and Public Policy in Canada* (Coleman and Skogstad, 1990).

In Chapter 2 we identified the Canadian Council of Chief Executives (CCCE) as perhaps the most powerful interest group in Canada. Its ability to influence government is a function of shared interests; thus, its special relationship with government officials transcends that of a general advocacy group. When one combines representatives from the CCCE with politicians and senior civil servants from Treasury Board and the Department of Finance, the result is a very powerful federal policy community. In effect, the CCCE is the business partner of this policy network. The influence of the CCCE on federal financial policies, including free trade, reduced corporate taxes, and reduced social spending, has been significant.

Two policy communities relevant to the human services are discussed below. These are the poverty policy community and the disability policy community. We also describe a policy community approach to the development of Aboriginal child welfare in Chapter 10.

Box **6.4** | Child Welfare Collaboration in Newcomer Communities

The delivery of child welfare services in new immigrant and refugee communities is often challenging, given newcomers' past experiences with authorities in their countries of origin and a lack of awareness of normative parenting practices in Canada, including approaches to physical discipline. Aware that their responses to increasingly diverse ethnocultural communities in Winnipeg and the surrounding areas were inadequate, the General CFS Authority recognized the need for outreach and the development of a preventive approach that would focus initially on raising awareness and knowledge among new Canadians about child welfare. Following a feasibility study with newcomer communities that indicated broad support for the initiative, a steering committee consisting of representatives from participating agencies and communities was established in 2010. A focused engagement approach designed to facilitate mutual learning was launched using a technique called "conversation cafés," where people came together in neutral settings to share concerns and identify strategies to build better working relationships. One participant captured the value of this engagement approach in the following way:

> We thank the GA [General Authority] for this first step to value us, to recognize us. . . . We are the key to the transformation of our communities. Their obligation is for care and protection of children. We can be the channels to build trust between the community and CFS. (Biaya as quoted in LeGal, 2011)

One outcome was the formation of a Cultural Community Reference Group composed of over 20 ethnocultural representatives, which met regularly with representatives from the General Authority to design and implement the New Canadian Initiative. A "Creating Possibilities" symposium, held in 2012 and involving more than 110 cultural community members and professionals, identified several strategic directions. Specific initiatives related to these directions are in the process of being implemented. These include:

- a continued collaborative approach to education and awareness;
- training on culturally appropriate positive parenting for new Canadian families;
- increased participation of new Canadians in child welfare governance structures;
- the building of a network of care within ethnocultural communities.

Of significance is the agreement, based on a request from the Reference Group, to broaden its mandate to provide advice on all programs provided by the General CFS Authority and to select two of its members to serve on the Authority's board.

The Poverty Policy Community

The poverty policy community has been through several stages. During its early period, beginning in the 1950s, the network wielded considerable influence. Organized under the auspices of the Public Welfare Division (PWD) of the Canadian Welfare Council (now the Canadian Council on Social Development or CCSD), senior civil servants from the federal and provincial departments of social services and staff of the Council met on a regular basis. The original reason for meetings was to identify and discuss common problems, but under the leadership of several key individuals it became a vehicle to plan major changes in public assistance programs. The work of this policy community culminated in the publication of *Social Security for Canada* in 1958, which laid the groundwork for the Canada Assistance Plan (CAP) enacted by the federal government in 1966.

The CCSD broadened its research and policy-related activities in the 1970s and dissolved the PWD, although cordial and supportive relationships between senior staff of the Department of Health and Welfare and the Council continued until the mid-1970s. In 1976 both the department and the Council issued reports recommending reforms in income security. The Council attacked the departmental report on several occasions, the latter responded in kind, and the long record of support and co-operation between the two collapsed. The Council's collaborative role with government in developing poverty-related policies ended, and its role reverted to that of a think-tank that attempts to influence policy primarily from outside the system.

Although there has not been a collaborative government–non-government policy network at the federal level since the 1970s many examples exist of consultation and policy collaboration between think-tanks and government. One important instance of this was the work of the Caledon Institute in influencing reforms to the Canada Child Tax Benefit (CCTB) in 1998, summarized in Chapter 1 and described in more detail in Wharf and McKenzie (2004: 149–52).

Actions taken at the provincial level pertaining to poverty reduction in recent years have been prompted more by advocacy coalitions external to government. However, evolving relationships between government and non-government organizations in some provinces reflect some of the characteristics of a policy community. For example, there has been a major emphasis on ongoing partnerships and community engagement in the development and adaptation of Newfoundland and Labrador's poverty reduction strategy.

Disability Policy Communities

The story of the efforts of the staff of the provincial government and community agencies coming together to reform guardianship legislation for vulnerable adults in BC provides a textbook example of the workings of a policy community. The story reveals both the advantages and some of the inherent difficulties in policy communities where one partner, usually the state, has access to more financial and human resources than does the community partner.

In addition, this example provides an illustration of the importance of a policy window noted in the garbage can model of policy-making (see Chapter 3). A policy window opens when "a problem is recognized, a solution is developed and available in the policy community, a political change makes it the right time for policy change and potential constraints are not severe" (Kingdon, 1995: 165). With the exception of the policy solution, all the other components were present in this example. A reform-minded government had just been elected. As well, the relevant community organizations and the newly appointed public trustee were keenly aware of the inadequacies of the existing Patients Property Act and were committed to developing new, more progressive legislation.

The initiative for change came from community organizations, and a consortium of five agencies launched a province-wide survey to document problems resulting from the outdated Act. Sometime later, an inter-ministerial committee was formed within the provincial government, and the two groups came together to form a joint working committee. Over a two-year period, 1991 to 1993, this committee worked at a frantic pace: it sought further information from concerned individuals and disability organizations; it prepared a framework document setting out the direction for the new legislation; it provided extensive opportunities for reviews of the document; and it developed new legislation and again sought consultation. In 1993, a new Act passed in the provincial legislature "was heralded by many within both government and the broader community as the best and most innovative legislative framework focusing on the rights of the disabled in vulnerable circumstances in North America. The process of its development and passage—the process of community driven legislative reform—is certainly just as unique" (Rutman, 1998: 104).

Yet all the provisions of the new legislation were not proclaimed until 2000. What happened to delay final approval for seven years? The essential reason was that the policy window began to close. The resources required to implement the new legislation were deemed too expensive and the Attorney General, who had supported the involvement of the disability community and was committed to reforming the legislation, resigned. Political crises, which garnered daily media attention, effectively diverted the government from tending to substantive policy responsibilities. Finally, the disability community simply ran out of funds and energy.

The lessons from the experience of this policy community are instructive. First, the two partners did not have access to equal funds and staff skilled in research and policy analysis; hence, the partnership was an unequal one. Second, the insistence of the community partners that their participation should not be limited to a few advisers, and that wide-ranging consultation with disability organizations was essential in all phases of the process, appeared to government to slow down the pace of reform. Indeed, some government officials simply did not understand why community partners should be part of drafting legislation. After all, legislation is a state responsibility! Only direct intervention from the Attorney General saved the day on this issue.

In spite of these difficulties, assigning at least some policy reform responsibilities to a policy community has considerable advantages. It encourages the collection of comprehensive information, secures the co-operation of community agencies that in the last analysis will be responsible for at least some aspects of implementation, and meets the challenge of transparency on key matters of public interest.

In Chapter 2 there was a brief description of the role of Barrier-Free Manitoba in developing disability rights legislation. These efforts were influential to the passage of the Accessibility for Manitobans Act in its current form in 2013, which includes provisions designed to overcome barriers to accessibility on a cross-disability basis consistent with the International Convention on the Rights of Persons with Disabilities. Although this policy community of disability organizations did not draft the initial legislation, it did submit and lobby for specific amendments, a number of which were incorporated in the final bill. These included an expanded definition of disability, target dates for significant progress with ministerial accountability, and requirements for reports obligated under the Act in accessible formats. Accomplishments summarized by the network were described in this way: "We did not get all that we wanted. The bill is not perfect but it is now truly game-changing landmark legislation of which we can all be proud" (Barrier-Free Manitoba, 2013: 1).

Community-Based Services and Community Governance

Overview

Community-based services and community governance are associated with the trend to decentralize the delivery of certain types of human services over the past three decades, and at least in some cases the motivation has been to improve the level of engagement with those affected by these programs. As we noted earlier, devolving services to communities can be a double-edged sword—it may make it easier for communities to access and engage with those services, but it may also reflect an effort to off-load service responsibility unless this policy change is accompanied by the transfer of adequate resources and local authority. The use of terms such as "community," "decentralization," "community–based," and "community governance" varies, and this further complicates discussion on this topic.

Kelly and Caputo (2011: 5) define **community** "as a distinct group of people who share connections, characteristics, or needs. These may include geographical space, social position, cultural beliefs, religion, occupation or any other common set of values or interests that distinguishes their group from the larger society." Despite this broader frame of reference, the most common definition of community is a geographical one, and in the delivery of many human services this use is most common. However, in a large urban centre, the boundaries of particular communities or neighbourhoods are not always easy to specify.

In general, **decentralization** refers to the devolution of policies or programs to lower levels of authority (e.g., federal to provincial, and provincial to local). We are concerned here with the devolution of policies and services from senior levels of government to local or regional communities.

Community-based services generally refers to the location of organizations providing services within the community. In some cases this type of service model is associated with providing more accessible, family-focused services. For example, transitioning to community-based services in mental health may involve the transfer of residents from an institution to supported living environments in the community. As this example implies, the meaning of "community-based" varies with the service context. The concept is also complicated by the question of who has authority over policies or programs (i.e., local authorities or upper-level government). Thus, an important issue in community-based services is whether or not it is accompanied by **community governance**. Although community-based services are most often linked to some form of community governance, it is possible for services to be located within a community (i.e., community-based) without the community having any significant control or influence over these services. Basic to the concept of community governance, then, is the delegation of authority and responsibility from senior levels of government that traditionally have authority over the delivery of human services. Rein (1972) distinguishes between geographic, administrative, and political decentralization. **Geographic decentralization** consists of the establishment of local offices without any transfer of power. **Administrative decentralization** provides local offices with increased autonomy over service-related decisions, whereas **political decentralization** involves the delegation of a significant level of policy-making authority to the local unit. If political decentralization incorporates mechanisms that permit the community to exercise authority over these decisions, community governance is achieved.

McKenzie's (1994) framework, based on field research on service delivery models in child and family services, has some similarity to Rein's models but also incorporates the preferred model for neo-liberals—the privatization option (see Table 6.2). Although the privatization model is included, this model of service delivery is problematic because the preoccupation with profits and cost savings often trumps service need and quality. Decentralized service teams can provide some benefits in permitting improved co-ordination among service providers but pay little attention to community governance. The community-oriented team and political decentralization options are more likely to connect policy to practice at the community level in ways that engage more fully with the community and service users. The community-oriented team approach reflects a value shift in defining local problems based on community input and developing ways of intervening by working alongside the community and its local resources. This way of working is more likely to respond to local needs and support a more integrated service response. When this service approach is combined with meaningful local participation in decision-making on local needs, policies, programs, and accountability, community governance becomes a reality.

When Is Community Governance Appropriate?

Community governance may not be appropriate for all services in the health and social service sector. For example, a number of income security programs (e.g., pensions, social assistance, EI, and Workers' Compensation) ought to be governed by more centrally developed policies. Here the principle of equity is paramount, and local governance structures are not likely to be helpful in ensuring the rights of citizens to equal benefits. As well, some services within a specific organization should be community-based

Table **6.2**	Models of Decentralized Service Delivery

Model	Characteristics	Strengths and Weaknesses
Privatization option	Attempts to replicate the economic market through contracting and adoption of business-oriented principles and practices.	• Emphasizes efficiency and stresses consumer choice. • Little evidence costs are contained without reducing service quality. • Service users have limited control in many services. • Response to community needs inadequate.
Decentralized service teams	Service teams organized geographically but management structures remain hierarchical and formal opportunities for community input usually limited.	• Some increase in accessibility and outreach possible. • Services remain professionally controlled. • Limited staff participation and focus on broader and community needs often restricted.
Community-oriented teams	Locally organized teams focus on core values, including community input on problems, service co-ordination, and integration. Collaborative working relationships and more participative approach to management common.	• Increased influence of front-line staff. • Improved accessibility and more evidence of preventive and community-oriented services. • Formalized mechanisms for community input as control often not well developed. • Generic role for staff common in this model is sometimes contentious.
Political decentralization	Combines community-oriented teams with formalized mechanisms for community and service user input.	• Meaningful opportunities for community input through representative methods (boards) and more participatory methods (community forums, etc.). • More likely to lead to innovative services. • May decentralize some services that should remain more centralized. • Internal conflict between community groups and local conflict with government can occur.

whereas others, for reasons of efficiency, may be better offered on a more regional or centralized basis. For example, a child welfare agency may adopt a community-based model of service delivery for investigating child maltreatment referrals and providing family counselling and support, but it may be more effective and efficient to co-ordinate foster home recruitment and the development of residential care facilities on a regional basis.

Four principles are associated with community governance in the human services. The *principle of affinity* suggests that people from diverse groups, including those with significantly different faith or cultural traditions, have a right to receive services from agencies and practitioners who are also committed to these values. Examples of the principle of affinity include faith-sponsored, First Nations, and ethnocultural agencies. People coming to these agencies know in advance that they will receive counselling and other services consistent with their values and belief systems.

The *principle of affected interests* was earlier discussed in this chapter. It supports community governance and is a common reason given for the development of specific programs and agencies by groups with a particular interest or cause. Some examples include associations for community living, transition houses, women's centres, ethnocultural agencies, and anti-poverty organizations.

The third principle is *accessibility*. It demands that barriers to access be eliminated. This principle supports decentralization on a geographic basis but it means much more than this. For example, accessibility for people with disabilities means overcoming a wide range of barriers, including physical, attitudinal, and communication. The location of services, of course, is critical to accessibility, but are there meeting places for children, youth, parents, and seniors where necessary? Is daycare available for children when activities for parents are planned? Although the principle of accessibility may be operationalized differently in urban and rural areas, the experience of neighbourhood houses and community schools is that accessibility—in terms of location and a welcoming, user-friendly, responsive approach to service—is a determining factor in the use of services.

Finally, the *principle of a low level of bureaucratization* calls for a more horizontal, rather than hierarchical, structure in organizations. This provides an environment more conducive to collaboration between the executive and front-line staff, and between organizational staff and service users.

These principles are more easily achieved when some form of community governance is present, yet they provide guidance rather than precise direction. Any model of community governance must be suited to the geographic area and the people to be served. Thus, neighbourhood family centres should be governed primarily by residents of the neighbourhood since services are available only to these residents. However, services such as mental health and child welfare, which affect a large number of people, may need to be organized on a regional basis and governed by an elected board that is representative of the citizens in the area. In some cases responsibilities may be delegated to voluntary agencies.

Our rationale for supporting a service delivery model that combines community-oriented practice with political decentralization is based on the benefits associated with a community work approach to practice. In this approach the people being served:

- become partners in developing and managing programs that affect them;
- become partners in identifying and then taking action to change harmful and negative conditions in their neighbourhood;
- have reserved seats at policy-making tables to ensure that not just the professionals and other experienced volunteers participate.

This collaborative approach to service provision may be reflected in an agency's overall service model, and under these circumstances the agency can be considered to have adopted an inclusive approach to policy-making and practice. There are a number of examples of schools as well as health and social service agencies that focus most of their attention on providing effective, high-quality services by building partnerships with the community and developing staff who are committed to this way of working. Much less time is spent on larger systemic issues outside the local community or region that concern central authorities; indeed, a relatively high degree of autonomy from central office is often preferred. Organizations such as these can be thought of as "islands of excellence"; most often they have focused on achieving high-quality programs by building internal organizational capacity, adopting a community-oriented approach to practice, and incorporating models of community governance.

A community-oriented service model is consistent with trends that promote service integration. Since 2000, an emphasis on service integration within the health and social service sector has become more prominent in several provinces, including Alberta, Manitoba, and Ontario, and Quebec has a long-standing commitment to this service principle. Building more effective service partnerships across organizations is one of the potential benefits of community-based organizations, but these do require time to develop, and they must be linked to concrete, measurable results if they are to be sustained. Despite these challenges, research has demonstrated that community-based governance structures can be effective in building community partnerships and supporting the development of innovative services (Hart, Raymond, and Bradshaw, 2010; Mutchler, Mays, and Pollard, 1993; Shragge, 1990). Simply put, community governance provides more space for more people to participate, to develop a constituency for the human services, and to increase the sense of participants' self-worth.

Objections to community governance and the proliferation of multiple service providers sometimes emerge in the devolution of services to community-based organizations. Earlier we referred to one significant disadvantage of community governance—the condition of "acute localitis" (Montgomery, 1979). Acute localitis refers to the potential for communities to become closed and intolerant of people who do not adopt the views of the majority in the community. Although the rural community of old is often romanticized today as a place of mutual support and self-help, we often forget that sometimes these were also places of intolerance and discrimination. In general, differences related to sexual orientation, mental health challenges, or even different religious views have been the subject of ridicule rather than support in some communities.

We have also identified the potential problem that community governance affords an opportunity for neo-liberal governments to off-load service responsibility and costs to local communities. Careful analysis of underlying conditions, including funding, is important in weighing the potential benefits of decentralization and enhanced local control over services. It is noted, however, that sometimes community governance helps to build a constituency willing to advocate for adequate resources to support localized services.

A somewhat related criticism is that much of what passes for participatory democracy wastes time, energy, and money. Community governance, in this view, represents yet another layer of government in our already complicated system, slowing down the policy-making process and adding unnecessary costs. A specific example was the New Directions policy for health care in BC. The intent to establish regional and community health boards to bring health care "closer to home" in the 1990s was initially hailed as innovative and imaginative. Yet, attempts to implement this over a three-year period ended with the conclusion that the approach was too expensive, and too bureaucratic! Modifications to the policy restricted community participation in favour of increased managerial accountability and resulted in fewer benefits to service users (Weaver, 2006).

The mechanisms used to achieve community governance are important to consider. For example, boards may be dominated by those who do not represent the best interests of service users or front-line staff. Methods of giving voice to service users must move beyond merely tokenistic approaches. Although a board of directors with significant authority over policy matters is normally one method of ensuring community governance, it is not the only method. Mechanisms to ensure meaningful input from the community and service users may include such things as ongoing consultative processes, policy development committees with representation from the community, including service users, community forums for input and feedback, direct funding for service user activities leading to policy recommendations, and approaches to evaluation that elicit feedback from key agency constituencies.

Towards a Resolution

This discussion has identified both the benefits and the risks in decentralizing services to communities. Where do we go from here? As the Cheshire Cat explained in responding to this question from Alice in *Alice in Wonderland*, "That depends a good deal on where you want to get to." Some of the failures in community governance can be attributed to weak leadership and inadequate forms of accountability—not only to central authorities but to local communities. With respect to accountability to central authorities it is not unreasonable to expect that the devolution of public services, including funding, to local authorities should be accompanied by appropriate methods of accountability that will help to ensure a co-ordinated approach to information for service provision across jurisdictions, service standards consistent with the rights of service users, and accountability for expenditures. Although community-based agencies do not guarantee an inclusive approach to policy-making, they open up more opportunities for this to occur than the more centralized, heavily bureaucratized option. Brodtrick (1991) suggests that an effective community-based organization must include the following:

- An emphasis on people. People are challenged and given power to act and to use appropriate discretion in providing needed services.
- Participative leadership, which facilitates rather than directs whenever possible.
- Innovative work styles, where staff reflect on performance and seek to solve problems creatively.
- A strong client orientation, where satisfaction is linked to service rather than the bureaucracy.
- Staff who reflect values that encourage them to seek improvement in their organization's performance.

Although forms of community governance can help facilitate these conditions, these criteria also reinforce the importance of a work environment that supports community- and service-oriented practices.

In matching community governance models to this service orientation it is helpful to return to Arnstein's (1969) top three rungs in her ladder of citizen participation (see Chapter 4). The top rung consists of those programs that are purely local, and here, community governance or control should be the rule. The next rung refers to delegated power whereby legislative authority and all or most of the responsibility for funding rests with the federal or provincial level but operating responsibilities are delegated to communities. Education, child welfare, and health services fall on this rung. In a delegated model there is likely to be tension around how policy-making authority and accountability are shared between the local and central governance structures in that both levels may want more authority than they currently hold. It is not unreasonable that the senior governance structure should exercise a certain amount of authority over general policy-making priorities and accountability. After all, the government has a central role in funding such services and is generally responsible for ensuring service adequacy and quality. This requirement is best met through a partnership model that ensures as much local control as possible over those policies, programs, and services that must be adapted to meet local needs and priorities.

The next rung is concerned with programs in which the principle of equity is of fundamental importance. This requires an arrangement between community and a senior level of government whereby government has more control over the policies and programs to be provided, but local citizens have mechanisms that permit local feedback and influence. Examples of these programs include social assistance, employment insurance, and pensions for seniors. Here, community groups and organizations can make an important contribution by evaluating the outcomes of these programs and communicating the results to senior levels of government.

As we note throughout this book, the effectiveness of policy is ultimately determined by the capacity of the local service delivery unit and the relationships that prevail among staff members and those being served. Unfortunately, efforts to reform the human services usually concentrate on changing structures and rarely on redistributing some of the power from politicians and bureaucrats to service providers and users.

In the last analysis, the resolution of the issue depends on whether one favours the centralization or the dispersal of power. Advocates of centralization point to the advantages to be gained from governing structures that enable decisions to be made quickly, and with fewer costs. They view the work of local structures—including meetings that are often long and inconclusive—as a waste of time.

Proponents of a more dispersed model of power base their arguments, in part, on the axiom of Lord Acton: power corrupts and absolute power corrupts absolutely! From this perspective, power-sharing reduces the chances of policy-making by elites alone and contributes to the development of a more informed and more responsible citizenry. Even if more time and energy are required when power is devolved down and out to local organizations and communities, this investment is often cost-effective because it avoids mistakes in implementation that frequently occur when those who must implement a policy have had no part in its development.

Summary and Conclusion

We have made a strong argument for the establishment of more inclusive approaches to policy development. However, we acknowledge that the backwards mapping, vertical slice, and shared decision-making approaches require the support of reform-minded policy-makers and leaders, and that this essential element is not always present.

Policy communities can be effective in some circumstances, but as our discussion demonstrates, policy communities in the human service sectors experience more difficulty in maintaining access to government decision-makers and in sustaining their activities than policy communities in other sectors.

Although most approaches to inclusive policy-making discussed in this chapter are designed to address specific policy issues, community governance is a different proposition because it involves surrendering power to local authorities for long-term policy and program development. To ensure that service users and front-line staff can participate, seats at the policy table need to be reserved for members of these groups; as well, other means to ensure ongoing participation need to be included. Community governance is associated with the decentralization of power, and new relationships between government and these local organizations must be developed to make this arrangement work.

We suggest that the concept of shared learning is one of the most important benefits of inclusive approaches to policy-making. Shared learning breaks down misconceptions that often stand in the way of reaching agreements, it brings in the perspectives of the front-line practitioners and of service users, and in doing so it enriches the information at the policy table.

More inclusive approaches to policy-making require those who hold power to surrender some portion of this power to others. Surrendering power does not come easily, and for many it is an option that they resist or employ in only tokenistic ways. Chapter 7 focuses on some of the options that can be pursued when inclusive approaches from inside the system are resisted.

Critical Thinking Questions

1. Select a social policy problem that could be assessed using the Integrated Model for Policy Analysis discussed in Chapter 4. How could the tasks to be undertaken in analyzing this policy be made more inclusive?
2. Review the strengths and weaknesses identified in this chapter for any one of the following approaches to inclusive policy-making: backwards mapping, shared decision-making, or policy communities. What additional advantages or risks can you think of?
3. Community governance is somewhat different from decentralization and community-based services. Define these concepts and clarify the differences. What type of decentralization is similar to community governance?
4. When we think of services or programs that are subject to community governance, we often think of local boards or committees that have decision-making authority as the primary method of ensuring local governance. However, as noted, citizen participation must go well beyond participation in these structures. Select a community-based program with which you are familiar and identify some ways of encouraging community engagement in this program, in addition to the development of a local board or advisory committee.
5. Think of a small-scale, innovative project you might like to establish. Using the program logic model outline in Figure 6.1 or a more elaborate model by searching online, construct a point-form outline of expected outcomes from your project. Then list some of the inputs and activities that would be required to achieve these results.

Recommended Reading

K. Kelly and T. Caputo. *Community: A Contemporary Analysis of Policies, Programs and Practices.* Toronto: University of Toronto Press, 2011. This book critically examines the role of communities in policy and program development in neo-liberal times. Several case studies are included to illustrate the potential and the pitfalls in pursuing community mobilization for social change.

S. Phillips and M. Orsini. *Mapping the Links: Citizen Involvement in Policy Processes.* Ottawa: Canadian Policy Research Networks, 2002. This review examines the level of citizen participation in policy processes, notably at the federal government level, and includes suggestions for reform.

B. Schram. *Creating Small Scale Social Programs.* Thousand Oaks, Calif.: Sage, 1997. This small book provides a guide to small-scale policy-making.

7

Influencing Policy from Outside the System

────────── • **In this chapter you will learn about:** • ──────────

- the value of combining strategies from both inside and outside the system in promoting participatory approaches to policy and program change;
- the role of unions, professional organizations, individual and group advocacy, and social movements in influencing policies from outside the system;
- the potential of think-tanks and whistle-blowing in affecting policy changes;
- the influence of social media and legal challenges in policy development.

Introduction

This chapter reviews some of the strategies to be considered in attempting to influence social policies from outside the system. There are several reasons for considering these options. One is that actions to promote policy changes that might be taken from inside the system and those pursued from outside the system are often closely connected. This is illustrated in Chapter 9 in the case study on policy resistance. We earlier noted the role of interest groups in helping to open a policy window. Thus, advocacy actions for anti-poverty strategies from outside the system can strengthen the position of those inside the system who might wish to promote a stronger set of anti-poverty approaches by government. Inside strategies can also transition to strategies that occur from outside the system. For example, a front-line worker who has tried and failed to obtain a service or benefit for an individual or a group can provide information on the right to appeal, if this exists, or about community organizations that might assist with advocacy.

A second reason in support of strategies launched from outside is that these actions offer some level of self-protection for staff working in the system if that system is resistant to bottom-up changes initiated from within. For example, a front-line worker who also belongs to an advocacy group on human rights can contribute to the development of policy positions carried forward by the group without having to be personally identified or directly implicated. At the same time, this should not be an excuse for staff inside organizations to avoid taking actions to change seriously flawed policies when these have adverse effects on service users. In these circumstances both individual and group advocacy activities may be undertaken, from such low-risk efforts as identifying the unanticipated consequences of a policy to more assertive objections that carry somewhat greater risks. For example, continuous opposition to existing policies may jeopardize opportunities for promotion, and criticism of important agency policies in a public forum may trigger disciplinary measures or, in some cases, termination. Staff inside an organization may also adopt actions designed to subvert a particular policy. And when all else fails, staff may conclude that they have no option but to disclose issues involving fraud or bad practice to the public by "blowing the whistle." We discuss this option later in the chapter.

Finally, policy-related actions initiated from outside the system inevitably attempt to influence public opinion, often through the media. Such actions are designed to increase public awareness of social issues and, in some cases, to mobilize group or community advocacy for change. They are, by definition, attempting to promote more inclusive citizen engagement in policy-making.

Unions and Professional Organizations

Most human service agencies in the public sector and in larger non-government sectors, such as child and family services and regional health authorities, are unionized, and human service workers in these organizations can rely on unions not only to negotiate collective bargaining agreements but to act on their behalf on issues that affect them personally and have broader implications for service quality and effectiveness. The decline in the rate of unionization in Canada was noted in Chapter 1. Yet, higher rates of unionization in countries are associated with more equality, lower levels of poverty, and better health (Broadbent Institute, 2013; Raphael, 2011). Unions also contribute to progressive social policies in other ways. For example, they advocate for higher minimum-wage laws and have made major contributions to better workplace health and safety regulations, to the extension of programs such as Workers' Compensation, and to improved pensions. For example, the Canadian Labour Congress has been a major advocate of pension reform, specifically in relation to enhanced coverage and benefits in the Canada Pension Plan. Unions have also played important roles in advancing concerns around pay equity and working conditions, including high caseloads that have an impact on the quality of services provided. Each province has unions representing nurses and teachers, and these unions have been prominent in advancing interests that represent the broader policy agenda of health care and education as well as the self-interests of their members.

Advocacy actions on behalf of individuals or groups of workers through the grievance procedures in collective agreements help to protect workers from unfair harassment or discrimination, including the right to Charter protections associated with free speech. At the same time, the accepted doctrine of management rights sets limits to these protections in matters such as public criticism of one's employer or the failure to perform assigned duties and responsibilities.

Unions are often active in electoral politics, and while there is a tendency to provide organizational support to political parties to the left of the political spectrum, the voting pattern among union members is quite diverse. It is relatively easy to engage in union activism by attending meetings of your local union and by becoming a member of one of its many committees, and perhaps a member of the executive or board. Engagement with bodies organized at the city, provincial, and national levels is also possible.

Professional organizations can be a vehicle for change, although most professional organizations are somewhat preoccupied with regulating their profession and acting on allegations of unprofessional practice. Legislation regarding the licensing of social workers has now been enacted in most provinces in Canada, but in most cases membership in professional associations remains voluntary among practitioners. Those professions that require membership in their professional associations as a condition of practice (e.g., teachers, doctors) tend to have somewhat stronger voices. Although critics often assert that professional bodies are more interested in self-protection than in the advancement of progressive reforms, most of the human service professions have supported policies such as public rather than private health care, progressive approaches to taxation, and more adequate income support programs. And the social work profession, despite its limited power, has a record of engaging in progressive advocacy work on social issues (see Canadian Association of Social Workers [CASW] website for an outline of its social policy principles and examples of the policy positions taken by the profession on issues such as the federal budget, a national inquiry to examine the circumstances of missing Aboriginal women, child welfare programs, and amendments to the Criminal Code). Of special interest is the social policy paper released by the CASW (Drover, Moscovitch, and Mulvale, 2014), which contains a series of recommendations intended to achieve greater equity in income security, health services, and social programs.

Individual engagement with unions and professional associations provides opportunities to engage with colleagues in collective action on policies affecting staff and service providers in their workplace settings. Also, personal involvement enables individuals to advance their views on policy reforms within an environment that protects the right to voice these concerns.

Think-Tanks

Think-tanks, as defined in Chapter 2, are organizations established for the purpose of doing research on public policy issues. An advocacy function is often associated with these organizations and they are most often incorporated as non-profit organizations (NGOs). The largest and best known on the international scene are located in the United States and include the Brookings and Hoover Institutes and the Rand Corporation. In Canada there are more than 100 think-tanks, ranging from the Conference Board of Canada, with a staff of more than 200, to the Caledon Institute of Social Policy with only a few staff.

Although all think-tanks are committed to research, some are clearer in locating their research within a particular ideological stance. For example, the Fraser Institute clearly states its frame of reference in its letterhead and publications, noting that it has been committed to "offering market solutions to public policy problems since 1974" (personal communication). Thus the Fraser Institute often seeks to find remedies that will reinforce the contribution of the private market sector and reduce the size and scope of government. By contrast, the research inquiries of the Canadian Centre for Policy Alternatives (CCPA) will most likely lead to solutions in the form of expanded public policies with a focus on social justice. Although these two think-tanks are quite clear in their advocacy orientation, other think-tanks may reflect an underlying ideological stance even if this is not directly stated.

Think-tanks seek to influence government in a number of ways. They bring the results of their research studies—subject to their own interpretations, of course—to the attention of senior officials in government in an effort to convince these officials of the validity of their research and the importance of their proposals. However, they also disseminate results widely through reports and journal articles, as well as in shorter summaries disseminated to the public through the popular media.

The influence of research findings on public policy decision-making is quite difficult to assess, and a similar observation can be made about the research findings of think-tanks. Although good-quality research is essential, there is no guarantee that quality will ensure influence or use. Other factors include the presentation style (i.e., clear and easily accessible), whether results are straightforward, whether guardians or advocates are available to influence utilization, and whether the agency or department has the authority to make use of the information (Davies, 2003). A more important factor may be timing and political factors, including the resonance of findings with the values and priorities of decision-makers. The importance of "what we believe," which is associated with the ideology of the decision-making authority, suggests that conservative governments will favour the research and the findings of more conservative think-tanks and that social democratic governments will look to think-tanks that reflect their commitment to social reform. Given the advocacy stance often apparent in policy positions expressed by think-tanks, it is essential to critically assess their policy positions.

Chapter 9 illustrates this point quite clearly as we see the different stances taken by the Fraser Institute and the CCPA to welfare cutbacks in BC.

At times think-tanks will take on roles similar to policy communities by participating more directly with government representatives, academics, and representatives from the private and non-profit sector in "closed-door meetings" to discuss social and economic policy issues. Abelson (2002: 68) notes that while Judith Maxwell, the founder and former president of the now disbanded Canadian Policy Research Networks (CPRN), saw value in media exposure, she maintained that think-tanks exercised the most influence in working with key stakeholders behind the scene.

It is difficult to know how to classify research policy institutes affiliated with foundations and universities as they are not think-tanks in the way these are usually defined. However, these types of institutes, which may receive financial support from universities, foundations, and national funding agencies or do contracted research, are often important sources of policy information. Such academic institutes are much more common in the US and, in the child and family welfare field, include the Kempe Foundation for the Prevention and Treatment of Child Abuse and Neglect, Chapin Hall at the University of Chicago, and Casey Family Programs. There are also Canadian examples but these operate on a much smaller scale; they include the Centre for Research on Children and Families at McGill University, the Child and Family Welfare Institute at Wilfrid Laurier University, and the Canadian Child Welfare Research Portal, which is sponsored by several organizational partners. Research results from many think-tanks and institutes are available online and can be helpful in preparing policy briefs and position papers.

Advocacy Groups and Social Movements

Advocacy groups and social movements have been a prominent part of the social policy scene in Canada for a long time. For example, first-wave feminism and the social gospel movement were influential in the development of some of Canada's earliest social policies, such as "Mothers' Allowances." Action to protect a specific policy action or promote a response to a social problem often begins with advocacy by a single group; the cause attracts other partners and transitions into a social movement that may be brief in duration or quite enduring. Consider the following examples:

- Occupy Canada, an extension of the Occupy Wall Street and Occupy Together movements, was a collective of peaceful protests and demonstrations in major cities across Canada targeting the global financial system, social and economic inequality, and corporate greed. This grassroots movement based on participatory democracy held a global day of action in 951 cities in 82 different countries around the world in 2011.
- Idle No More is an ongoing protest movement organized by Indigenous people and their supporters in Canada in December 2012. It was inspired by the hunger strike of Attawapiskat Chief Theresa Spence in response to the housing crisis in

her community; however, the larger issue underlying the movement was the abuse of Indigenous treaty rights incorporated in Bill C-45 by the Harper Conservative government. This grassroots movement focuses on the importance of Indigenous ways of knowing, education, and awareness about Indigenous sovereignty and environmental protection. Although the movement has staged a number of protests, including blockades, it places more emphasis on teach-ins and peaceful demonstrations.

- In 2006, the Stephen Lewis Foundation hosted a Grandmothers' Gathering in Toronto where 100 grandmothers and staff from community organizations in Africa met with 200 Canadian grandmothers for three days of dialogue and workshops on the AIDS pandemic in Africa. Following this, the Canadian Grandmothers Movement engaged a host of awareness-raising and fundraising efforts across the country, raising more than $19 million in six years. This has led to the formation of an African Grandmothers Tribunal to focus on broader systemic issues regarding HIV/AIDS, illuminating human rights violations and the need for broader changes to turn the tide of AIDS in Africa (African Grandmothers Tribunal, 2012).
- The We Day movement, which champions youth activism and includes events sponsored in North America and around the world, was launched by Craig and Mark Kielberger of Free the Children in co-operation with organizations from the public, private, and voluntary sectors. The goals are to increase volunteerism and raise funds for a variety of social causes. In 2012–13 alone, 118,000 million students participated in We Day events, and the movement had 3.7 million Facebook followers. Between 2007 and 2012, 7,000 schools had participated in a We Day event, 9.6 million volunteer hours for local and global causes had been provided, and $37 million had been raised for 1,000 causes (We Day website at www.weday.com).

In the following discussion the Independent Living (IL) movement in the disability community is identified as an example of a social movement and Campaign 2000 is described as an example of an advocacy coalition.

The Independent Living Movement

In Chapter 6 we outlined the role of disability organizations in BC and Manitoba as policy communities in promoting legislative changes. But parts of the disability community have also acted as a social movement by significantly influencing the policies of the state with respect to conditions for persons with disabilities. This is particularly evident in the disability community's efforts to promote the **independent living paradigm** as an approach to service delivery. Fagan and Lee (1997: 151–3) identify some of the characteristics of social movements and the extent to which the disability movement can be classified as a social movement:

- *Social movements embrace alternative forms of political action.* Disabled people have done this through self-organization and control by disabled people of the organizations representing their interests.
- *Social movements advance a critical evaluation of the values and structures of dominant society.* The disability movement has done this by highlighting the denial of citizenship rights arising from practices and policies that define disabled people as dependent and in need of care based on a medical model of rehabilitation.
- *Social movements promote collective action to achieve goals in both a national and an international context.* A disability movement based on the independent living philosophy has developed in many countries and has international links through cross-national co-operative endeavours and organizations such as Disabled People's International.

In brief, the disability movement has taken direct action to challenge both the failings of the state and the public view of the disabled. In so doing it has built a sense of solidarity among disabled people for social and economic reform. It is useful to consider the development of the disability movement as a social movement, with a particular focus on Canada, and our analysis pays particular attention to the Independent Living (IL) movement.

Valentine (1994) associates the rise of the Canadian IL movement with the values of consumer control and self-help in the early 1970s. Provincial organizations were formed and a national conference in Toronto in 1973 led to the formation of the Coalition of Provincial Organizations of the Handicapped (COPOH) in 1976 (now known as the Council of Canadians with Disabilities). As a national consumer organization, COPOH focused its energy on human rights legislation, revision of building codes, establishment of public transportation services for persons with disabilities, and efforts to improve employment through job creation and policy change.

Rapid growth of the consumer movement at the local, provincial, and national levels followed, and in June 1980 COPOH held its third national conference in Vancouver. At this conference, Canadians with disabilities were introduced to an alternative view of rehabilitation—the independent living paradigm, a model consistent with the growing grassroots interest in consumer control and self-determination. This paradigm, posed as an alternative to the medical model reflected in rehabilitation programs of the day, identified the problems created by dependency arising out of the medical model and proposed solutions based on peer counselling, advocacy, self-help, consumer control, and the removal of barriers to independent living. This mantra quickly became the guiding philosophy of the emerging Independent Living Movement in Canada.

The expansion of the movement was supported by the development of IL centres across the country, which have helped connect this philosophy to policy and practice within communities. Nyp (2002), who documents the early development of the Independent Living Centre of Waterloo Region, illustrates the growth of this consumer-based self-help organization over 20 years, from a fledgling organization operating out of a Sunday school room in a Mennonite church to a major consumer-based service organization with a budget of nearly $5 million and more than 300 staff. Operating four supportive housing units and a variety of other programs, including peer support and information and referral, the agency has become a model of a consumer-based organization that has successfully combined service with individual advocacy and self-help.

There are more than 25 Independent Living Centres across Canada, as well as a national co-ordinating body known as Independent Living Canada (ILC). Independent Living Centres emphasize consumer control, cross-disability issues, community-based approaches, and the full integration and participation of disabled people in Canadian society. Disabled people make up the majority of staff and board positions in these organizations, and their influence on disability issues with governments at all levels has been significant. Improved accessibility, supportive housing units, new legislation, public transportation for the disabled, and direct support and advocacy services all have been established with government assistance.

What are the reasons for the relative success of the IL movement? First, disability issues are perhaps less partisan in a political sense than many other social policy issues; thus, it has been easier to acquire support from all political parties. Second, the IL movement benefited from growing national and international awareness, led by activists from within the disability movement, of the rights of people with disabilities. Changes in human rights legislation within Canada and approval of the UN Convention on the Rights of Persons with Disabilities in 2006 have helped to support ongoing changes, as did the earlier success of activists to secure inclusion of the rights of "those that are disadvantaged because of . . . mental or physical disability" in section 15 (the equality rights section) of the 1982 Charter of Rights and Freedoms.

Although an early shortcoming of the IL movement was its primary focus on accessibility issues experienced by those who were physically challenged (Lysack and Kaufert, 1994), its commitment to and engagement with cross-disability issues and the multiple nature of barriers experienced by people with disabilities have become much more prominent. A continuing challenge is reaching those in more isolated rural and Aboriginal communities and addressing the multiple barriers faced in these environments. Despite these limitations, the accomplishments of the IL Movement stand as a tribute to the vision of those who have been involved with this consumer-based movement for more than four decades now.

Campaign 2000 and the Anti-Poverty Movement

The impetus for Campaign 2000, which was founded in 1991, came from a resolution in the House of Commons, approved by members of all political parties in 1989, to end child poverty by the year 2000. In an attempt to ensure that the government would live up to this promise, a number of social policy and advocacy organizations, such as the Canadian Council on Social Development, the National Anti-Poverty Organization (now Canada Without Poverty), and the Toronto-based Child Poverty Action Group, developed a national action plan. A cornerstone of this plan was that pressure could best be brought to bear by a network of local and provincial organizations dedicated to the elimination of poverty. The founding organizations sponsored a number of meetings across the country attended by members of anti-poverty groups, academics, and staff of human service organizations. At a national meeting, the following goals for Campaign 2000 were approved:

- To raise and protect the basic living standards of all families in all regions of the country so that no Canadian child would ever live in poverty.
- To improve the life chances of all children so they can fulfill their potential and nurture their talent, and become responsible and contributing members of society.
- To ensure the availability of secure, adequate, affordable, and suitable housing as an inherent right for all children in Canada.
- To create, build, and strengthen family supports and community-based resources in order to empower families so they can provide the best possible care for their children (Campaign 2000 website).

The national office is located in Toronto, but the coalition now includes more than 120 national, community, and provincial partners, such as child welfare organizations, faith organizations, health organizations, school boards, community agencies, and low-income groups.

The principal strategy employed by Campaign 2000 has been to prepare an annual report card for Canada and, in collaboration with provincial partners, a number of provincial report cards identifying the number of children and families living in poverty. These report cards highlight the consequences of child and family poverty and propose strategies to eliminate, or at least reduce, poverty. The report cards, released on or around 24 November, the anniversary of the all-party resolution, have received considerable publicity. Campaign 2000 and its provincial and local partners produce discussion papers, develop proposals for poverty reduction, and lobby all parties in both federal and provincial governments for improved poverty reduction policies.

Over the years two major criticisms have been levelled at Campaign 2000. One is the expected criticism from neo-liberals that the report card overstates the level of poverty because it uses measures such as the Statistics Canada LICOs rather than more conservative measures. A second is the early criticism by some feminist scholars was a child-focused discourse and child-centred strategies played into the hands of business groups that tend to support state intervention only when children are deemed to be at risk (McGrath, 1997). Although the initial choice of child poverty as a focus was strategic in mobilizing broad public support and reflected the 1989 House of Commons resolution, Campaign 2000 has broadened its advocacy focus to include a number of poverty-related issues such as child care, housing, and child and family homelessness

(Campaign 2000 website). Of even more importance are the broad alliances that have been formed at the national and provincial levels.

For example, Make Poverty History Canada is a broad coalition that includes Campaign 2000 as a member. Multi-sector collaborative coalitions, including business, labour, social agencies, and other organizations, are active in lobbying for poverty reduction strategies in some cities, such as Edmonton and Toronto, and in a number of provinces, including Quebec, Ontario, Manitoba, and BC.

It is difficult to assess the effectiveness of the anti-poverty movement in reducing poverty. As discussed in Chapter 1, the measurement of poverty in Canada is contested, and different measures produce somewhat different results. Although modest improvements in poverty using the After-Tax Low-Income Cut-Off, and to a lesser extent the After-Tax Low-Income Measure, were noted in Chapter 1, poverty remains quite persistent, affecting between 8.8 per cent and 12.6 per cent of Canadians according to these measures (Statistics Canada, 2013a). Without the efforts of anti-poverty activists, however, it might have been much worse. Slow economic growth, growing inequality exacerbated by a tax system that provides disproportionate benefits to high-income earners, and the absence of a co-ordinated national poverty reduction strategy are contributing causes to the persistence of poverty in a country that can certainly afford to do more.

Whistle-Blowing

Whistle-blowing is the act of informing or disclosing a perceived wrongdoing to someone in an effort to have it corrected. Generally, the term is usually reserved for those who publicly disclose alleged wrongdoing while still working in the organization. At times the act of blowing the whistle is extended to those who previously worked in the system immediately prior to the public disclosure. Individuals who may disclose issues following retirement or long after leaving their employment are not usually identified as whistle-blowers. Although employees are often required to take an oath of office that forbids them to divulge information learned on the job, those who blow the whistle are so convinced the activities of their organization are harmful that they have no option but to disregard their pledge of confidentiality.

Bok (1984) suggests three components or steps lead to the act of whistle-blowing:

1. The presence of *dissent* follows awareness that the organization is engaged in wrongdoing.
2. A *breach of loyalty* occurs when the individual breaks faith with employer–employee confidentiality provisions and makes a decision to go public with the complaint.
3. Finally, in the *accusation* stage the whistle-blower registers a complaint with the public.

Many people within organizations fail to take action even when faced with questionable organizational practices. Bok suggests that this reflects the predominant pattern of self-preservation and risk-aversion that exists within organizations. Four different types of response by staff are possible. One type of employee does not observe any wrongdoing or negligence and identifies completely with the organization. A second type is the employee who observes acts of wrongdoing but decides to take no action. A third type observes wrongdoing and takes limited action by following established channels, but this person takes no further action even if the matter is not resolved. Because many public and quasi-public organizations have some form of legislation or policy designed to protect those who blow the whistle on wrongdoing to designated authorities inside the system without public disclosure, internal reporting of such matters is sometimes defined as whistle-blowing. Finally, there is the person who takes action up to and including the whistle-blowing stage to bring the matter to the attention of the public.

The person who gave real prominence to whistle-blowing is Daniel Ellsberg. Convinced that the US President and his cabinet colleagues were not receiving accurate information about the war in Vietnam, Ellsberg, a military analyst for the Rand Corporation, released "the Pentagon Papers" to the *New York Times* in 1971. The "papers," a top-secret Pentagon study that outlined the rationale behind government decisions over the course of the Vietnam War, were published in the *New York Times* and other newspapers (see Ellsberg, 2002). Once identified as a source of the information Ellsberg resigned and was charged with breaching confidentiality. Although he was eventually found not guilty, his career as a promising policy analyst with government and the Rand Corporation came to an abrupt end.

Loss of employment is a common consequence of high-profile whistle-blowing. Jeffrey Wigand blew the whistle on the Brown & Williamson Tobacco company on 4 February 1996 because, contrary to its public pronouncements, the company was deliberately increasing the amount of nicotine contained in cigarettes; he was fired. Wigand's story is told in the movie *The Insider*. A recent example is Edward Snowden, who in 2013 blew the whistle on mass surveillance by the US government of its own citizens and its allies, including some senior government officials. Snowden fled the US before the first leaks were disclosed and is now in exile in Russia. To the National Security Agency (NSA) and the US government he is a traitor who will be prosecuted if he returns to the US. To many others, he is a hero who has exposed the violations of privacy and lack of accountability exercised by intelligence agencies in the US and elsewhere. For his part, Snowden faces an uncertain future in exile or likely imprisonment if he returns home.

Two Canadian examples of whistle-blowers are Dr Nancy Oliveri and Bridget Moran. Oliveri is a medical researcher and adjunct member of the Faculty of Medicine at the University of Toronto; her story is discussed in Box 7.1. Bridget Moran was a social worker in the 1950s and 1960s who wrote an open letter to the British Columbia Premier criticizing child welfare services in northern BC. Her disclosure in this case concerned the deplorable lack of social work resources to deal with child and family

Box **7.1** | The Case of Nancy Oliveri

Nancy Oliveri was a medical researcher with the Hospital for Sick Children in Toronto and an adjunct professor of the Faculty of Medicine at the University of Toronto in the early 1990s. Oliveri became concerned about the potentially harmful effects of a drug she had played a pivotal role in developing. Despite the terms of a contract that allowed only the drug company, Apotex, to release results, she published her findings in a medical journal in 1996. The hospital promptly fired her but, because of widespread public indignation, subsequently revoked the firing.

Oliveri's findings were supported by some colleagues and peers but questioned by others. The dispute as to the accuracy of her findings and of her right to break the contract by blowing the whistle continued on both national and international fronts for several years. During this time, Oliveri was maligned both profession- ally and personally. She was accused of having dealt with patients in an unethical fashion and of having stolen from her research grants. In addition, Apotex lashed out by accusing her of rude and intemperate behaviour. In late 2001, the College of Physicians and Surgeons of Ontario fully vindicated Oliveri, indicating that she acted in a manner that was in the best interests of her patients (*CAUT Bulletin*, 2002). A settlement between Oliveri, four colleagues who supported her, and the hospi- tal was reached, and an agreement with Apotex regarding a defamation suit was reached in 2004. However, the battle did not end there and Oliveri was forced to go to court to enforce the agreement. In November 2008, the Ontario Supreme Court ordered Apotex to comply with terms of the 2004 agreement, including payment of $800,000 to Oliveri.

The circumstances facing Dr Oliveri have been extremely difficult. However, she has been somewhat fortunate to have the support of the Canadian Association of University Teachers (CAUT), and their academic freedom fund is enabling her to respond to the legal actions required against the hospital initially and then sub- sequently against Apotex, a pharmaceutical company with deep pockets. In 2009 Oliveri received the American Association for the Advancement of Science Award for Scientific Freedom and Responsibility for her actions to preserve patient safety and research integrity.

issues in this area of the province. Public disclosure led to a promise of new resources that did not occur, and Moran was later suspended from her job. She told her story in the appropriately titled book, *A Little Rebellion*, published in 1992.

Protecting Whistle-Blowers

Some support for whistle-blowers may be available through the courts based on pro- visions in the Canadian Charter of Rights and Freedoms. For example, in 1998 Jason Gibson—a social worker employed by the Alberta Department of Family and Social Services—wrote a letter to a member of the Opposition expressing his concerns about the planned redesign of services to children and families in the province. He sent copies to his own MLA, the minister, and the regional board responsible for social services. As a consequence, Gibson was reprimanded. He filed a grievance that was dismissed and the case was then reviewed by the Alberta Court of Queen's Bench. The court delivered a mixed decision, and both the government and Gibson appealed to the Alberta Court of Appeal. In its judgment, the Appeal Court agreed with Gibson. It cited the Charter in finding that the reprimand of the social worker violated his right to freedom of expression. The Appeal Court also cited the Supreme Court of Canada in concluding that an employee's duty of loyalty needs to be balanced with the right of free expression, including the ability to criticize government, provided it is framed with restraint. In this instance, the concerns expressed related directly to the ability of social workers to effectively protect children from harm, and the social worker's criticism had no adverse effect on his ability to perform his duties (Lancaster House, 2002).

It may well be that most front-line practitioners are unaware of the Charter protections of freedom of expression. While the decision of the Alberta Court of Appeal based on the Charter does offer protection for whistle-blowers, provided that they "frame their concerns with restraint," it can be an expensive and time-consuming process. Specific legislation and policies to protect whistle-blowers are an important consideration, and Box 7.2 outlines one example.

Arguments supporting such legislation stem from recognition that in-house whistle-blowing policies and procedures can be beneficial both to the organization and to service users. However, the Manitoba Act, like similar legislation in other provinces, restricts the complaint process to internal government channels and does not offer protection to those who may go public with their complaints. Although internal protections are of some value there are criticisms that implementation has been flawed. In some cases staff making reports have not been adequately protected from reprisals. Both Saskatchewan and Alberta now have Public Disclosure Commissioners with the power to investigate allegations of reprisal, and this may be helpful in ensuring fair process. A recent review of Manitoba's legislation (Scarth, 2014) found many employees were unaware of the legislation and how to make a report.

The influence of public whistle-blowing is highly dependent on the media. The media's actions in highlighting disclosures of punitive policies and outright wrongdoing are generally sympathetic, at least in the early stage. However, the initial supportive stance extended to whistle-blowers may be fleeting unless other disclosures or additional evidence helps to sustain the matter as a public issue. Blowing the whistle in the public domain is not for the faint of heart—there are often attacks on the individual's motivation as well as job repercussions. Nevertheless, it is a strategy to be considered when other ethically defined actions have been tried and failed. If whistle-blowing is accompanied by supportive actions by unions or advocacy groups who take up the cause, it is more likely to have some impact and, as was the case with Nancy Oliveri and Jason Gibson, sometimes the individual receives some measure of protection.

| Box **7.2** | Whistle-Blowing Protection |

Legislation and policies to protect whistle-blowers have been quite limited histor-ically, but there has been more recent attention to this. Whistle-blowing protection exists in some form at the federal level and several provinces have enacted legis-lation in this area. For example, Manitoba's Public Interest Disclosure Act (PIDA), proclaimed in 2007, which is now called the Whistleblower Protection Act, was the first stand-alone legislation in Canada. The Act applies to all government depart-ments and agencies related to government, including child and family service agencies, regional health boards, and universities. It is designed to facilitate the dis-closure of significant and serious matters related to public service that are unlawful, dangerous to the public, or detrimental to the public interest. The Act also serves to protect persons who make those disclosures, provided these are made in good faith and reported to appropriate authorities within the system. Whistle-blowers are protected in the following ways:

- Employees can make a confidential report about misconduct to a supervisor or union official within the department or agency or to the provincial ombudsman.
- Procedures to enable the confidential investigation of disclosures must be developed within each department or agency.
- When the information is provided to the ombudsman, that person may investigate the matter and make recommendations.
- A whistle-blower who is fired, demoted, or otherwise penalized can file a com-plaint with the Manitoba Labour Board.

Social Media, Individual Advocacy, and Legal Actions

In this section we briefly highlight the role of social media, individual advocacy, and legal actions in influencing policy development from outside the system.

Social Media

The growing use of social media in organizing demonstrations, promoting social movements, and encouraging social action on issues is important to recognize. Online media sites like Facebook, YouTube, and Twitter raise important questions regard-ing privacy and ethical practice, and there are major concerns about abuses, such as cyber-bullying. At the same time, however, social media organization sites like Avaaz, OpenMedia, Leadnow, and All Out are used to mobilize support, often in the form of electronic petitions and letters, against human rights abuses and specific government policies that appear to discriminate against individuals or groups. Two examples of such advocacy organizations are identified below.

- *OpenMedia*, based in Vancouver, has focused on consumer rights to Internet access, but it also advocates for more citizen-centred policies. Steve Anderson, its leader, teaches classes on how to use social media for public engagement.
- *All Out* mobilizes support in opposition to homophobic practices and legislation that discriminate against gays and lesbians both in North America and abroad.

In some cases social media campaigns claim success in influencing companies and governments to do the "right thing" in response to the issue being highlighted. Although the overall success of social media campaigns is difficult to gauge, there can be little doubt that these media have helped to mobilize support for or opposition to certain causes. For example, social media certainly helped promote the issue of education for girls championed by Malala Yousafzai after she was shot by the Taliban on a school bus in Pakistan in 2012. Miraculously, she survived, and with family support she has continued her quest for educational opportunities for the more than 30 million girls worldwide that do not have the opportunity to go to school. In 2014, along with Kailish Satyarthi, a children's rights activist from India, she was awarded the Nobel Peace Prize.

Individual Advocacy

We have emphasized the role of collective advocacy so far, but one can also pursue individual advocacy in trying to influence public opinion or the specific views of policy-makers. Actions such as letters to the editor or opinion articles in the newspaper are examples of actions designed to influence public opinion. One can also write or lobby local politicians and other key decision-makers. Although individual advocacy is quite easy to undertake, advocacy is generally more effective if it is connected to collective advocacy efforts through groups such as Amnesty International, the Institute for International Women's Rights, and others too numerous to mention here.

Legal Actions

Legal actions to challenge existing laws and policies are an often neglected aspect of strategies for policy change. These actions are typically undertaken by a variety of organizations from across the political spectrum. For example, a challenge by a private, for-profit health-care provider against the prohibition on extra billing by medical practitioners could undermine this important provision of Canada's medicare system if it was successful. Legal challenges may also be launched by unions through grievance actions or appeals to judgments in policy-related grievances. Initial challenges may occur first at the provincial level, but alleged violations of Charter rights or the Constitution may be appealed and end up being heard by the Federal Court of Appeal or the Supreme

Court. Initial legal actions regarding federal policy matters are first heard by the Federal Court (Trial Division) but the decisions of this court can be appealed.

We draw particular attention to Charter challenges and alleged violations of human rights legislation here. In the social justice field these types of challenges can be expensive; thus, they are often launched by advocacy organizations such as the Women's Legal Education and Action Fund. As noted in Chapter 2, allegations of a denial of human rights can be made to provincial human rights bodies if it involves a matter under provincial jurisdiction or to the Canadian Human Rights Commission if it is a federal matter (see Chapter 10 for an example pertaining to child welfare funding on reserves). A recent provincial example was an Ontario employer's practice of paying developmentally disabled employees $1.25 per hour for 10 years while paying other employees the minimum wage for substantially the same work. In this case the Ontario Human Rights Tribunal found the practice discriminatory and awarded the employee who filed the complaint over $185,000 for lost wages and damage to self-esteem (Lancaster House, 2014). These decisions, as well as decisions by lower courts, can have significant effects on social policies.

Summary and Conclusion

This chapter reviewed a number of strategies for making policy changes that can be launched from outside the system. Although whistle-blowing and the work of think-tanks are not always associated with the direct organizing work in group advocacy methods, the information disseminated is most often intended to influence and mobilize public action for a cause. And, of course, a legal challenge to an existing decision or policy is also a form of advocacy. All of these strategies are consistent with increasing the level of public participation (i.e., a more inclusive approach) in policy-making. However, an important question is what approach to advocacy makes sense, and what type of information and tactics should be included. Although the answer depends on various factors, the information summarized below may help in determining this.

Stachowiak (2013) examines the central theme of advocacy in her review of 10 theories of policy change. Although there is some overlap between theories, each one postulates a somewhat different set of circumstances that may lead to policy change. Several of these theories are consistent with concepts and models introduced in this book, and we highlight these below along with some comments on the related implications for advocacy.

- The *policy windows* theory is based on Kingdon's (1995) work described in Chapter 3 where importance is attached to agenda-setting, policy streams, and policy windows. If there is evidence that this approach to policy change applies, promising advocacy efforts may include trying to influence the framing of issues through special studies, encouraging public feedback to policy-makers on the issue, developing policy options through research, and building coalitions and media advocacy to promote a particular understanding of the problem and a preferred solution.

- A *power politics* or *power elite* theory of policy change is consistent with the theme of the centralization of power discussed earlier in the book. Although the development of a strong countervailing base of power to challenge elites may be a long-term goal, issue-based advocacy may also require the incorporation of shorter-term strategies. For example, it may be necessary to try to directly influence actions on specific issues through individuals who have or can develop credibility with key decision-makers.

- *Coalition* theory or the *advocacy coalition* framework of change depends on co-ordinated activities among groups that normally target potentially sympathetic decision-makers in an effort to ensure a particular change is adopted. This theory is somewhat consistent with pluralism and draws on approaches to advocacy consistent with the work of policy communities, social movements, and advocacy coalitions.

- *Grassroots* or *community organizing* theory is somewhat more applicable to policy development at the community level. It reflects an emphasis on building civil society and public engagement consistent with our discussion of community governance and decentralization in Chapter 6. In this theory, advocacy efforts will focus on building community capacity so the community can advocate for its own changes. Various methods, such as policy research, action research, protests, whistle-blowing, and media advocacy, may be used at different stages to build a more community-based model of policy-making.

The kinds of advocacy and supporting methods (e.g., research, policy analysis) used will vary with the context and the change theory that appears most applicable to this context. In some cases, of course, a combination of advocacy approaches may be useful. However, in selecting particular approaches it is important to avoid simply adopting a "kitchen sink" approach where one tries a little bit of everything. There is something to be said for focusing one's efforts based on a careful analysis of available resources and a determination of which strategies are likely to be most effective with the targeted decision-makers.

We conclude with two important observations. First, timing is important, and the ability to anticipate "hot topics" or areas likely to become priorities will enhance the possibility of success. Second, as argued at the beginning of this chapter, strategies initiated from outside the system are more likely to be effective if they are supplemented by or resonate with support for these policy changes that may be present inside the system. Building relationships across differences with other groups and organizations as well as with potential supporters inside bureaucracies is important to success. At the same time, the lack of such support does not mean the issue should be abandoned. Some issues are worth pursuing even if short-term success is unlikely; moreover, advocacy, over time, can mobilize action from inside the system even if there is no evidence of initial support.

Critical Thinking Questions

1. Provide an example of where advocacy from inside or outside the organization might be required in an effort to change a flawed policy developed by government or the organization. What strategies might be considered in order to change the policy or mitigate its adverse effects? What are the risks, and how might these be managed?
2. Several think-tanks were mentioned in this chapter. Select two think-tanks and complete a search of their websites. Provide a brief summary of their purposes. Can you identify the ideological orientation of each of these sites? What evidence can you provide to support your conclusions?
3. Review the website of Campaign 2000. What are some of its current activities?
4. Under what circumstances can whistle-blowing involving public disclosure of wrongdoing be justified?
5. Identify an electronically based advocacy organization and investigate its purpose and some of its activities. What are the strengths and weaknesses of electronic forms of advocacy?

Recommended Reading

B. Jansson. *Becoming an Effective Policy Advocate: From Policy Practice to Social Justice*, 7th edn. Belmont, Calif.: Brooks/Cole, 2014. This book discusses skills and strategies for different types of policy practice. Illustrative examples are included.

B. Moran. *A Little Rebellion*. Vancouver: Arsenal Pulp Press, 1992. Moran provides an intriguing account of her experience as a social worker who became a whistle-blower.

S. Stachowiak. *Pathways for Change: 10 Theories to Inform Advocacy and Policy Change Efforts*. Washington: Center for Evaluation Innovation, ORS Impact, 2013. At www.evaluationinnovation.org. This report summarizes 10 theories of policy change and identifies implications for advocacy within each theory.

Chapter

8

Chapter

Chalk and Cheese: Feminist Thinking and Policy-Making

Marilyn Callahan*

In this chapter you will learn about:

- some of the historical contributions of feminism to social policy;
- some of the contemporary challenges in applying feminist thinking to policy and practice in the human services;
- the application of a gender lens framework to policy analysis;
- some of the contributions feminist thinking can make in connecting policy to practice.

Introduction

This chapter reviews the particular contributions of feminist thinking to the central goal of this book: making connections among social policy, human service practice, and the lives of citizens. When this chapter was first published in 2010, I stated that much has changed in the past 20 years, including the vibrancy and currency of the women's movement and that issues of concern to feminists have been swept off the policy table in the rush to clean house of social programs and enhance the role of private interests in what used to be public responsibilities. I noted that there had been a sea change in expectations concerning the role of government in redressing inequalities (Bashevkin, 2002; Cohen Griffin and Pulkingham, 2009a). Even in academia, there was cold comfort. Some scholars claimed that the women's agenda of the past 30 years has been largely accomplished now that women are occupying some of the key roles in academic administration and gaining proportional representation in many disciplines.

* Marilyn Callahan is Professor Emeritus, School of Social Work, Faculty of Human and Social Development, at the University of Victoria.

Some fields, including social work, that were formerly sympathetic turned their attention to other approaches (e.g., anti-oppressive practice) that subsumed feminist perspectives under broader theorizing about oppression and race in particular. Feminism seemed out of fashion in many quarters.

While much of this is still true, some things have changed since then. At least two types of stories have captured considerable media attention and have brought some of the issues back on the table. One is a central attack on feminism: the theme that equality for some women, particularly those in privileged circumstances, has not necessarily made a difference to the organizational cultures where they occupy leadership positions. Women seem as capable of corporate malfeasance as men. This issue has been one that many feminists have tried to highlight for decades. They have argued that it is insufficient to integrate women into organizational cultures and expect them to make necessary modifications to those cultures on their own and while still carrying out many of "women's" duties at work and in their private lives. Instead, women may well become acculturated themselves. And the women who succeed in these environments may not have a particular allegiance to feminist perspectives.

The second story that features in the media is the issue of the degradation of and violence towards women, particularly women at the intersection of race, class, religion, and culture. Many times, these stories focus on the lot of women in other countries, in particular in those areas where culture and religion continue to view women as chattels or secondary citizens. Isabel Allende (2007) captured this sentiment when she said:

> Feminism is dated? Yes, for privileged women like my daughter and all of us here today, but not for most of our sisters in the rest of the world who are still forced into premature marriage, prostitution, forced labor—they have children that they don't want or they cannot feed.

Yet it is apparent that such issues are not merely relegated to other countries. In Canada today we have mounting pressures for a national inquiry into missing and murdered Aboriginal women and have completed a full scale inquiry in BC that illustrated the failure of the police and the justice system to pay attention to a serial killer preying on vulnerable women (Oppal, 2012). This inquiry clearly demonstrated the lack of value placed on such women and how stereotypes about them and their friends impeded the investigation. The laws on prostitution, including prohibiting brothels, were struck down in 2013 by the Supreme Court, which argued that they unfairly discriminated against some already disadvantaged women. Feminist thinking on these issues is clearly required and has been revived through these stories.

In this chapter, I argue that it is crucial to include feminist perspectives in dealing with problems, policy, and practice in the human services and in the ongoing process towards social justice. We are not there yet. Women still occupy most of the front-line positions in human services, and in many fields they make up the majority of the users of these services. While women may occupy significant posts in government and institutions, attend post-secondary institutions in equal or greater numbers than men, and work outside the home as well as within it, their overall economic status in Canada and other Western countries still lags well behind that of their male counterparts (Dobson, 2002; CCPA, 2014). Indeed, Canada consistently ranks lower than many other Western countries in wage equity for women and men (Schwab et al., 2013). Feminist thinking has always focused on the relationships among experiences in everyday life, the practice of professionals, and the policies that shape these practices. It has a rich legacy and pressing agenda to offer to the challenge of making connections.

Feminist Thinking

Several years ago, I was involved in a research project examining policy alternatives to address the issue of women and substance use during pregnancy (Rutman, Callahan, Lundquist, Jackson, and Field, 1999). During the project, a team of Aboriginal researchers met with rural Aboriginal women to discuss whether women should be restrained or incarcerated if they continued to use substances during pregnancy. Initially, the Aboriginal women agreed with the idea, citing their own experiences within their families and voicing concerns about future generations of their people. However, as they considered the question, they thought about how such a policy would actually play out in their lives. Which women would be restrained? Mostly Aboriginal women, they predicted, even though more non-Aboriginal women use substances during pregnancy. Why? Because Aboriginal women are more visible to those in the helping and policing professions, because they have fewer resources to resist and challenge policies, because they frequently live in rural areas where treatment facilities are non-existent, and because they are generally disregarded. The women reflected on the inordinate numbers of Aboriginal people in federal and provincial jails as a similar consequence of applying policies without regard to differing circumstances.

They also suggested that resources used for incarceration would continue to funnel funds away from helpful programs and that the policy would continue the stereotyping of Aboriginal people. They concluded that the policy could promote conflicts within communities already disadvantaged by historical, geographical, and economic realities. They gave examples of hardships that some women and their families would suffer.

Although they resisted an incarceration policy, these women proposed solutions of their own, which included reinstating the practice of traditional home visitors, usually senior women in the community; reforming policies for funding health care so that funds could be distributed to women's organizations concerned with health and social issues; and dismantling the band council structures created under the Indian Act. To them, band councils reflected the colonizing aims of government policies and undermined the hereditary organization of communities, creating artificial elites within the community and disenfranchising many women. The women were also careful to underscore that their suggestions might work for their tribal councils and communities but may not suit others.

Reflecting on the situation in the United States, where several states have enacted policies that result in the incarceration of women who use substances (Guttmacher Institute, 2014), many researchers have raised a central question (e.g., Schroedel and Peretz, 1994; Flavin and Paltrow, 2010): Why has the focus of media and research turned relentlessly on women's behaviour during pregnancy and not on other toxic hazards in the environment or to the effects of alcohol and drug use by men that can damage sperm and lead to violent behaviour towards pregnant women? They argue that there is no overt conspiracy among lawyers, medical professionals, and journalists to define fetal abuse in a manner that blames the woman while ignoring the central role of other factors. Instead, there is simply a predisposition to view the world through analytical lenses that replicate and reinforce the existing gender biases.

This discussion by Aboriginal women and American scholars illustrates several central planks of feminist theorizing. Although it is impossible to provide a thorough review of feminist thinking and its variations and controversies, a few essentials require mention. First, feminist thinking challenges the conventional wisdom that equality can be achieved by treating everyone the same. Clearly, passing legislation to allow the incarceration of women who use substances while pregnant would not play out equally among women. At the turn of the twentieth century when first-wave feminists were fighting for the right to vote, many held the view that once women obtained suffrage they would be able to run for office and make significant strides in addressing inequalities. Yet in 2011 in Canada, fully 93 years after the passage of the federal Women's Franchise Act of 1918, only 28.5 per cent of the candidates in the federal election were female (up 1 per cent from the elections of 2006 and 2008) and women won 21 per cent of the seats, a figure that has changed very little in the past decades (Schwab et al., 2013). Universal franchise has not led to equal opportunities in the political arena. For some, this is a problem for women to address by running for office. Feminist thinking underscores the reality that so-called equal treatment can maintain substantial disadvantages for groups while reducing sympathy for their circumstances. No one would argue that gaining the franchise was not vitally important for improving the status of women. But it alone is insufficient.

Feminist thinking probes how inequality is maintained through everyday practices. Most institutions and policies have been designed and are controlled by middle-aged men, not by any conspiracy but by tradition and by the ongoing advantaging process within the patriarchal structures that maintain this tradition. How that advantaging process works is often unrecognized because it is so familiar, so accepted, and so normalized. One component of this is the creation of knowledge: Whose way of perceiving the world becomes accepted knowledge and whose ways are ignored? For instance, the idea of reforming band structures imposed on Aboriginal nations has not gained the same currency among the general population as incarcerating women who use substances during pregnancy. Feminist thinking seeks to disrupt that sense of normalcy.

Creating space for different ways of knowing is one way to challenge the status quo. From the experiences of women in daily life come the questions: How does this process affect me and how is it perpetuated? Why are things the way they are? This examination frequently reveals the interconnection between dichotomies—the economic and the social, the private and the public, the emotional and the rational—that frame our "usual" thinking. Key to understanding how these dichotomies have disadvantaged women is the unwillingness to recognize women's work in social reproduction as making a central contribution to the economy of any nation. Instead, women's caring has been ignored as part of such calculations, as taking place in the private (non-monetary) rather than the public realm. Neo-liberal thinking has reinforced this dichotomy. For instance, instead of recognizing the need for public child-care expenditures to support women's caring responsibilities, the Conservative government of Canada developed a policy to provide families with taxable grant of $100 monthly (revised somewhat in 2015 budget), an amount far short of the cost of child care, even if spaces were available.

A rallying cry of the second-wave feminist movement of the 1960s and 1970s—"the personal is political"—contains a central plank of feminist thinking. Each individual's experience of disadvantage reveals within it connections to formal and informal workings of power well beyond the individual. Making those connections does not come naturally. We are often inclined to personalize our experience and frequently blame ourselves for our failings. Instead, feminism has traced how what happens on the ground is connected to what happens beyond ourselves. Dorothy Smith, a Canadian sociologist, has made it her life's work to underscore these connections and her book, *The Everyday World as Problematic* (1987), informed by Marxist and feminist thinking, stands as a landmark. The Aboriginal women discussing substance use during pregnancy spoke about being marginalized within their communities, connected this to the behaviour of some men, and, in turn, related this male behaviour to the patriarchal systems imposed on the men by white government policies.

Feminist thinking exposes injustice in many quarters, working from the individual injustices experienced by women. And it benefits from other theories of oppression, such as those developed by Aboriginal peoples and others regarding colonization. It enriches these theories by exposing how gender interacts with other socially constructed disadvantages. Feminism is most misunderstood on this particular issue because there is a common misconception that it reveals the oppression of women only. The strength of feminism lies in its grounding in the everyday experiences of half the population and the movement beyond that to uncover how formal and informal systems work to perpetuate inequities for many.

This process of uncovering injustices reveals clearly that while all women are negatively affected by patriarchal values and systems, some women and some groups of both men and women are more harmed than others. Although those who feel the pain of oppression most severely are those most disadvantaged by race, class, gender, ability, sexual orientation, and other socially constructed categories of privilege, individual identities can change in different circumstances. In one group, for example, individuals can be privileged on some occasions and severely penalized in another. This insight was an important development in feminist thinking as feminism then "lost the moral high ground that comes with the depiction of all women everywhere as victims of patriarchy" (Brodie, 1995: 79).

Perhaps one of the most important advances in feminist thinking is that because of the differences among women it is important to break down such overarching concepts as feminist, oppression, patriarchy, organizing, and the state. Postmodern feminist theorizing has contributed significantly to understanding the many, often conflicting, dimensions of these large, taken-for-granted concepts and how power works well apart from formal structures (Nicholson, 1990).

Embedded in the notion of movement between privilege and disadvantage is another central plank of feminist thinking: Women are not only victims of oppression but also actors within oppressive systems who can both maintain and disrupt them. How these disruptions have and can occur is the subject of the remainder of this chapter.

Feminist Thinking and the Challenge of Connecting Policy and Practice

Earlier in the chapter, I indicated that feminist thinking has a rich legacy to offer to the challenge of connecting policy and practice. The following section highlights some of these contributions. While I illustrate these contributions with broad policy initiatives, it is also true that the same lessons can be applied at smaller group levels and by practitioners in their daily work.

Making Connections between Policy and the Lives of Women

A significant strength of women's groups and feminist research is its focus on the realities of women's lives and then its commitment to making those realities heard in the public forum. This is the first connection: from private to public, personal to political. This has been the work of many women's groups that have successfully and continually kept the spotlight on injustices affecting women. Another process of connecting occurs as feminists analyze existing public policies and professional practices to demonstrate how they affect individual women in different circumstances, testing the impact of public policies on private lives. These two dialectical processes are ongoing. They may occur at broad national and international levels or within much smaller arenas such as an existing program or community. But the aim is the same: illuminating disadvantage and redressing it.

In the process of making these connections, feminist thinking directs policy-makers and practitioners to ask a few central questions:

- How will this particular policy or practice affect people differentially?
- Who will benefit?
- Who loses out?
- How could these inequalities be mitigated?

These are the same questions raised by the Aboriginal women who contemplated the introduction of incarceration of women who use substances during pregnancy. It is first and foremost an analytical stance. "**Gender-based analysis** challenges the assumption that everyone is affected by policies, programs and legislation in the same way regardless of gender, a notion often referred to as '**gender-neutral policy**'" (Status of Women Canada, 1996: 4).

One vehicle for analysis—gender lenses—has promise, although no legislation in Canada requires the inclusion of gender lenses in the policy-making process. Effectively, lenses pose a series of questions and actions designed to assess the differential impact of any one policy or program on the target population. The gender lens developed by the BC Ministry of Women's Equality (1997), the gender-sensitive model for policy analysis developed by Status of Women Canada (1996), and Health Canada's policy on gender-based policy analysis (Health Canada, 2009) are examples of this approach. The lenses are based on some fundamental principles related to feminist thinking and are concerned with both the substance and process of policy and program development and implementation (see Box 8.1).

While not widely embraced by government, gender lens analysis has found traction in quasi-government and not-for-profit organizations, and it is used to scrutinize initiatives both within a particular organization and by outside groups analyzing government policy. For example, the Canadian Centre for Policy Alternatives (CCPA) employs a gender lens perspective in analyzing the effects of federal budgets on women. In the Gender Equality section of the *Alternative Federal Budget 2014*, the CCPA (2014) noted

Box **8.1** | Principles of Gender-Based Analysis

- Every government policy has a human impact.
- Policies affect men and women differently.
- Women are not a homogeneous group.
- Policies must attempt to create equal outcomes for men and women.
- Equal outcomes will not result from treating everyone the same.
- Equal outcomes benefit everyone.
- Policy-makers bring their own biases to the job.
- The best policies are those where consultation has played a considerable role.
- Special measures are required so that those disadvantaged can make their views known.
- Consultation is ongoing and not a one-off business.

Source: Excerpt from BC Ministry of Women's Equality (1997).

that women's economic well-being showed little improvement over the previous five years. Among full-time workers, women still earn 20 per cent less than men, and younger women and visible minority women fare even worse. Women make up two-thirds of the minimum-wage earners and are significantly over-represented among part-time workers. Yet tax breaks benefit higher-income earners, which include a much higher proportion of men. Women are also disproportionately affected by spousal and sexual violence, yet the level of investment in programs and services to address intimate partner violence remain woefully inadequate. Policies more sensitive to women's issues recommended by the CCPA in its 2014 *Alternative Federal Budget* include new investment to better address pay equity, a federal child-care program, and more adequate and accessible income supports for those in the low-wage workforce. This analysis reveals the importance of examining public policies for their differential effects on women and men.

The landmark case of Kimberly Rogers brought national attention to the devastating consequences of failing to evaluate the gender implications of policy. On 25 April 2001, Kimberly Rogers was convicted of defrauding Ontario Works because she was receiving benefits and also had a student loan. She was sentenced to six months of general house arrest and 18 months of probation with no right to receive further benefits for three months. (A lifetime ban has since been implemented for others who commit the same offence.) She lost her drug prescription coverage and, although she had no other income, was required to make restitution of about $14,000. At the time, she was five months' pregnant. A law firm launched a Charter challenge and her benefits were reinstated pending the outcome of the challenge, which was to be decided in September 2001. She committed suicide in August of that year during a heat wave in Sudbury.

The public debate was intense. The policy of a lifetime ban on benefits and house arrest was the focus of the debate. How such a policy affects men and women differently received less attention. As women are most likely to be the ones who care for children, their loss of benefits will affect their children (the regulations cut off the mother but continue payments for her children, reducing family income overall). Further, women with children are more likely to remain longer on income benefits than their male counterparts, making it more likely that they will run afoul of regulations. Even if they find work after being banned from income support, women still earn significantly less than their male counterparts and have to cope with inadequate and expensive child-care provisions. The distinct possibility that the lifetime ban contravenes section 15(1) of the Charter of Rights and Freedoms was considered. This section of the Charter states:

> Every individual is equal before and under the law and has the right to the equal protection and equal benefit of the law without discrimination and, in particular, without discrimination based on race, national or ethnic origin, colour, religion, sex, age or mental or physical disability.

In the end, the Charter challenge was dropped with the death of Kimberly Rogers.

The gender lens approach demands a restructuring of policy-making processes so that these are focused less on the expertise of a few and more on different ways of knowing by many. It requires consultation on a broad and ongoing basis. While seemingly more cumbersome, this consultation also builds alliances that can protect practitioners and policy-makers from egregious errors that erode their own credibility.

Making Connections between Feminists and Those Who May Share Common Cause

The history of women influencing policy and practice to improve their status in Canada is illustrious. Some examples at the national level include the following:

- The work of early feminists who fought for the franchise resulted in federal legislation in 1918. (Aboriginal women and men did not similarly obtain this right until 1960.)
- The Persons case of 1929 finally acknowledged women as persons within the meaning of the British North America Act.
- The Royal Commission on the Status of Women, reporting in 1970, led to a host of policies and programs to redress the status of women.
- The Canadian Human Rights Act, 1977, prohibited sexual discrimination in employment and assured women equal pay for work of equal value.
- The inclusion of equality between the sexes as section 28 of the 1982 Canadian Charter of Rights and Freedoms was won through the lobbying efforts of women's groups.
- Amendments to the Indian Act in 1985 returned status and the right to band membership to Aboriginal women who had lost these rights by marrying non-Aboriginal men.

All of these efforts involved the work of a large number of women identifying specific issues and then joining together on an ad hoc basis and in established groups within and outside government. They strategized, formed alliances, organized protests and demonstrations, and pressured wherever they could. Key to the success of these efforts was the unwillingness to categorize those working for government as the "enemy" of those working on the outside in action groups. Instead, efforts were made to introduce feminist thinking and structures within government and to deploy feminists—sometimes called "femocrats"—in a wide range of state positions where they could, through daily actions within government and connections with community feminist groups, seek to change the culture of policy-making (Rankin and Vickers, 2001). Indeed, it was the partnership between those on the inside and those on the outside that produced results (Rebick, 2005; Cohen Griffin and Pulkingham, 2009b).

Although the state has significantly reduced efforts to address the needs of women, this has not led to increased feminist activism. In fact, the strength of feminist action groups has diminished over the past two decades as neo-liberal thinking has gained prominence. Those protesting the restructured state appear to be out of step with the times, hanging on to the old "nanny state" with no new visions to inform governments. Moreover, the awareness of women's privilege in a country like Canada compared to those living in much poorer and more constraining states has increased markedly.

Not surprisingly, many feminist activists have turned away from a singular focus on opposing state actions at the national level to protest global economies and systems that are wreaking havoc with deeply held beliefs about citizenship, the environment, and social responsibility. Naomi Klein's *No Logo* (2001) is an early and excellent example of feminist analysis about the connections between social and economic well-being at an international level. Feminist groups have many international connections with women's organizations and use these to challenge basic tenets of globalization. Yet it is important to continue to confront inequalities even in a country as prosperous as Canada, where conditions may not seem as bleak but where gains that have been fought for by courageous citizens could be quickly lost.

Making connections between local and global issues affecting women is one very promising area. The Canadian Feminist Alliance for International Action (FAFIA) is a coalition of over 75 Canadian women's groups that aim "to further women's equality in Canada through domestic implementation of its international human rights commitments" (Canadian FAFIA website, 2014). The FAFIA website includes links to women's groups throughout the country. Canada's 1980 commitment to the Convention on the Elimination of All Forms of Discrimination against Women and the Beijing Platform for Action provide leverage to press for change. By holding the Canadian government accountable for its formal international commitments, women's organizations such as FAFIA are challenging the notion that they are merely left-leaning special interest groups who seek to advance exceptional privilege for their members without regard for the whole, a charge that is often used to diminish their efforts. To say that feminist thinking is passé in policy and practice is to ignore the very substantial efforts that have survived and prospered in spite of disappearing state funding. This approach is highlighted by Rankin and Vickers:

> Our research concludes that, particularly in an era marked by globalization and decentralization, "bothering with government" is still pivotal to the achievement of equality and justice for all women. We encourage feminist organizations to engage in an ongoing evaluation of the political opportunity structures they face and call for renewed debate on how feminists can work most effectively with policy-makers. Finally, we argue that women's policy machinery can be an important partner with feminists in public policy debates, but new channels of communication between state feminism and women's movements are required. (Rankin and Vickers, 2001: 36)

Making connections with others who may not share similar aims but who could advance the feminist agenda is a factitious issue. Those within a social movement may share deep suspicions about those on the outside. There can be intense arguments within the movement about who is competent and permitted to speak on particular issues, particularly if they have had little opportunity to speak before. Some argue for a "pure" movement where only those with direct experience of a particular issue can belong. There can be cries of "selling out" when partners who could assist also come with baggage of their own. Others argue for a pragmatic approach, based on fluctuating relationships according to present goals. The indisputable fact remains that both approaches can be very useful in the scrum of political change. Pragmatists can appear reasonable; radicals can keep the issues alive.

Making Connections among Social Workers and between Social Workers and Service Users

Feminist thinking does not begin and end with an analysis of an individual case and the ways in which workers could practise differently. It makes a commitment to connect the individual with the social. This central reality was brought home to me in a study on risk assessment in child welfare conducted by Karen Swift and me and situated in two provinces, Ontario and British Columbia (Swift and Callahan, 2009).

In the study we identified a common phenomenon in human service practice: how workers and their clients consciously *disconnect* policy from practice when policy seems harmful. We interviewed practitioners and mothers involved in risk assessment, a process whereby practitioners investigating a situation of possible child maltreatment are required to complete a checklist of possible risks and assign each one a score based on a common set of descriptors. These scores are then analyzed to determine whether further investigation is required, whether children should be removed from or returned to their parents, and/or whether the family is eligible for supportive services.

While some practitioners felt very positive about the risk assessment process, others chose to go along with it reluctantly, and still others found different ways to subvert it. For instance, these latter workers sometimes raised the risk scores on intake so that people who would not be eligible for service based on their scores could access them nonetheless. In some cases, social workers even ignored the risk assessment altogether by working with the clients as they always had and filling out the forms later to satisfy the demands of the procedures and files. This most often occurred in remote towns and villages where applying the risk assessment instrument dutifully may have resulted in the removal of most children in the local communities. When those social workers who managed to work around the risk assessment process talked to us about their actions, they referred to themselves directly or indirectly as the "good" practitioners, and considered others who complied with risk assessment policy as less professional and more bureaucratic.

Even though these practitioners disagreed with risk assessment policy and practice, they did not appear to make public their concerns in any cohesive fashion. Instead, they reasoned that by subverting it in their practice yet appearing to follow it in their paper work, they were doing what they could to undermine the risk assessment policy while keeping their jobs and reputations. They knew that should the case go badly wrong, it was important to have completed the procedures correctly to protect themselves.

We also noted some of the same behaviour occurring with mothers who were the subject of risk assessments in child welfare. Many of these mothers had been complained about many times and had repeatedly experienced risk assessments. They did not think much of the risk assessment process and disputed many of its claims, at least to us. They told us about the many times they had been required to attend different programs designed to reduce their risks. Like the social workers, they indicated that they were different from other mothers who had complaints made against them. They did not leave their children alone, or keep an untidy house, or use alcohol and drugs, and so forth, all stereotypical behaviours of mothers who maltreat their children. These women kept themselves apart from other mothers under investigation lest they be "tarred with the same brush." They pretended to follow the rules set down by the worker, at least on the surface, in order to get the worker out of their lives. Even though they doubted the efficacy of repeating programs and other activities, they did not usually make their views known to the workers or others. They did not want to appear non-compliant lest they jeopardize further their position as mothers.

This phenomenon of subverting policy by appearing to comply with it in practice and of positioning oneself in the process as "I'm not like the rest of them," in fact, "I'm better than them," has been observed in other studies about workers and clients in the human services (Munro and Rumgay, 2000; Callahan, Rutman, Strega, and Dominelli, 2005). Most of us have done some version of it ourselves. Rather than connect policy and practice, it is a conscious effort to disconnect it without actually challenging it.

Those with postmodern inclinations might argue that everyday rebellions such as this wear away at policy and eventually change it, much like walking diagonally across a stretch of grass may lead to the creation of a formal path in time. But is it the same? The results of walking on the grass can be seen. Individual challenges to policy through subversive practice may create benefits for a few and occasional satisfactions for workers, but do they necessarily lead to policy changes?

Traditional feminist thinking, based on **liberation theory**, would argue somewhat differently (Memmi, 1967; Friere, 1970, Roberts, 1983; Love, DeJong, Hughbanks, Kent-Katz, and Williams, 2008). Public compliance and private rebellion are viewed as a necessary but insufficient component to change: that is, it is only a good starting place. These theorists contend that many people who have overcome oppressions have begun by first learning to rejoice in their own perspectives and debunk the myths about them, sharing their stories of individual rebellions and, from these stories, forging relationships among each other and a common agenda for change.

In the risk study, we did not see social workers and mothers joining together to challenge either the science of risk assessment (doubtful) or its negative effects on their practice, in effect taking the next steps. Although after a decade (1998–2008) the risk assessment process was eventually modified somewhat, primarily because of the rising number of children removed from their parents and the costs of this care, the outcomes of risk assessment were expensive, unexpected, and a high price to pay for a largely failed experiment.

A contrasting example of trying to change policy by collectively challenging it in practice is provided by the schoolteachers in British Columbia (Coutts, 2009). Because they were alarmed by the government policy that focused on mandatory and standardized tests for school-aged children, a few teachers refused to administer such tests. Eventually their individual protests were made public in the media. At the same time, teachers organized within their professional association to put pressure on individual school boards; as a result, some boards withdrew from the testing process. Some school boards also introduced policies permitting individual parents to authorize or reject the testing for their children. While the provincial government was successful in requiring school boards to administer the tests, the opt-out clause for individual parents remained. More recently, the saga continues with the tests still authorized by government but school boards, teachers, and parents continuing to resist (Steffenhagen, 2013).

Although there is substantial difference in the power of public schoolteachers, their professional association, and parents compared to social workers and parents in child welfare, the lessons of making visible the effects of policy in practice remain.

Making Connections between Policy and Program Purposes and Their Outcomes

Feminist thinking emphasizes results because it is tied to a movement with a cause. Therefore, it focuses on how some policies may flounder and others are transformed remarkably from their original intent during implementation.

Pence and Shepard (1999), along with the Praxis International organization in Duluth, Minnesota, have developed an interesting approach that combines monitoring implementation and evaluation. The organization works on addressing violence against women, particularly in the home. The authors observed that although new and progressive policies against violence in the home had been implemented, they often took very different expressions in actual practice and sometimes made matters worse. So, they became interested in evaluating the work of police, the courts, and social workers. In particular, the authors noted that the work of one organization often contradicted the work of another.

An outcome of these observations was the development of the safety audit. Based on the research methods of Dorothy Smith (1987), the safety audit begins with an examination of what happens on the ground: How do police officers decide what should be done when they receive a call involving a domestic dispute? What tools do they use to make that decision? What forms do they fill out? Who do they call, and what happens then? By examining the decision-making processes and the attendant work that accompanies these decisions, the safety auditors trace what happens in the case and whether the outcomes actually led to improved safety. They can identify points in the process where other options could occur and they can raise questions about the data used to make decisions.

The safety audit pays attention to inter-organizational relationships (or their absence), and it is a useful tool for government organizations and community groups to evaluate how policies work in practice (Sadusky, Martinson, Lizdas, and McGee, 2010; Ptacek, 2009). The safety audit is similar (although perhaps a more systematic framework) to the process of tracking individual circumstances and outcomes for service users that should be a primary component of practice in the human services. They are widely used in many areas now, including Canadian university campuses (Tower, 2012).

Summary and Conclusion

Oscar Wilde once said that the trouble with socialism was "that it took up too many Sundays." Some feel that one of the troubles with feminism is similar: it takes too much time and demands too much effort. Throughout the chapter, I have tried to indicate the value of using feminist thinking in policy-making and practice as well as some of the successes associated with such efforts. When I began to participate in feminist groups in the 1960s, the world was a very different place for women. There were few women in any of the well-paid professions such as law and medicine; divorcing women had no claim to the matrimonial property; First Nations women lost their status if they married non-status men; sexual assault was often blamed on women; and most young women did not expect to have a career and children at the same time. Dramatic changes have occurred since then and feminist groups can take credit for many of these, working both outside and within policy-making structures.

What have changed less are these policy-making structures and processes. They still creak along, founded on beliefs about who the experts are and what the proper processes for making decisions are. Some have argued persuasively that the changes to policy-making that have occurred have been primarily negative ones. As managerial thinking about human services as commodities and professionals as suppliers has gained ground, decision-making has become even further removed from the realities of those on the front line and those who are the clients.

Feminist thinking presents a challenge to these processes. It argues for more time, broad consultation, and different expertise. It does not fit well with governments in a hurry and governments under attack: thus the title of this chapter—chalk and cheese—an expression that means "worlds apart" (Schur, 1987). How to open up these processes while recognizing the realities of the hurly-burly of policy-making is the ongoing challenge.

If I were to identify the most important contribution of feminist thinking to policy-making, it would be the feminist practice of building relationships across differences—a process grounded in feminist challenges to dichotomous thinking. For instance, as Pence and Shepard (1999) illustrate, demanding government attention to the issue is only one part of addressing violence against women. Feminist action groups must build relationships with other social movements and with sympathetic professionals, and encourage them to put the issue on their agendas. They must also forge connections with those inside bureaucracies, such as hospitals, police, and governments, who may be able to do something specific about the problem. Relationship-building is essential so that large, sometimes recalcitrant, organizations can move in different directions. It requires the development of tolerance and respect among people with very different views of the world and the relinquishment of a self-righteous stance by groups within and outside the "system." These relationships must be genuine if they are to succeed. All this is well known by human service practitioners and others who have learned the importance and skills of relationship-building as the cornerstone of practice.

Helping to put a problem on the agenda of others is indeed important, but having solutions to those problems is another essential contribution of feminist thinking: women are agents of change as well as victims of oppression. Transition houses are a clear example of the success of this strategy. Women simply opened up safe houses, initially squatting in abandoned buildings and gradually gaining community and government support for their efforts (Pizzey, 1977). By working out solutions, even those that are small and short-lived, groups with little contact can sit down face to face and dispel myths about one another. Relationship-building occurs. Other solutions may be sought. Again, social workers and other human service workers know the value of promoting small steps in the process of change, of celebrating them, and of using them for more relationship-building.

Changing policy-making and practice processes to include the women who are affected by the issues is common sense. And without such changes, the process of addressing inequalities may simply reinforce them, an outcome of no small irony.

Critical Thinking Questions

1. What impact (if any) has feminist thinking and analysis had in your agency and in your practice? If you do not work in an agency, think of an organization where you may have acted as a volunteer or with which you are familiar.

2. In the introduction of this chapter it was noted that in some fields feminist thinking and analysis have been subsumed under broader theorizing about oppression (e.g., anti-oppressive practice). Do you agree with this view? If so, is this a positive development? Why or why not? If you do not agree with this view, explain why?

3. Are we now in a post-feminist era? If so, what are the possible consequences for the human services? What is your perspective on any of these consequences?

Recommended Reading

S. Bear, with the Tobique Women's Group. "You Can't Change the Indian Act," in J.D. Wine and J.L. Ristock, eds. *Women and Social Change: Feminist Activism in Canada*, pp. 185–209. Toronto: James Lorimer and Company, 1991. This chapter provides an excellent example of Aboriginal women organizing to effect change in the Indian Act.

J. Brodie. *Politics on the Margins: Restructuring and the Canadian Women's Movement.* Halifax: Fernwood, 1995. This book provides a thorough examination of the challenges facing the Canadian women's movement in light of globalization.

M. Cohen Griffin and J. Pulkingham, eds. *Public Policy for Women: The State, Income Security and Labour Market Issues.* Toronto: University of Toronto Press, 2009. This book is a collection of chapters by prominent Canadian scholars who address how public policies have failed women on many fronts.

E. Sheehy, ed. *Sexual Assault in Canada: Law, Legal Practice and Women's Activism.* Ottawa: University of Ottawa Press, 2012. This collection of essays on the state of sexual assault policy and practice in Canada is a key reading to unravel the ongoing existence of violence against women in a country such as Canada.

Chapter **9**

Policy Resistance: The Rise and Fall of Welfare Time Limits in BC

Bruce Wallace and Tim Richards*

------● **In this chapter you will learn about:** ●------

- factors that led to civil society resistance to a neo-liberal government policy designed to eliminate welfare benefits to groups of recipients in need;
- the different roles played by two think-tanks that took an active role in this policy debate;
- the different motivations that can lead to coalition-building for policy resistance among partners with different ideological orientations;
- the roles played by "policy insiders" and "policy outsiders" in this example of policy resistance.

Introduction

In Chapter 1 it was noted that civil society involves the mobilization of social capital or the willingness of people to engage in collective civic activities, including advocacy and volunteerism. An active civil society includes citizen engagement in building community, but it also includes citizen actions intended to influence public policies and efforts to hold institutions accountable for policies and programs that should be developed in the public interest. Civil society actions may occur individually or through engagement in voluntary organizations, faith groups, and other organizations. While actions external to government are important, actions from inside government and other major state institutions can also be influential in affecting support for and against a particular policy.

* Bruce Wallace is an Assistant Professor in the School of Social Work at the University of Victoria. Tim Richards is a Senior Instructor in the Faculty of Law, University of Victoria.

In Chapter 7 a number of civil society approaches aimed at influencing policy development from outside the system were identified. However, a dilemma often confronts human service workers and social activists: What do you do when faced with policies designed to reduce benefits to service users that impose punitive procedures or otherwise restrict access to benefits and services? Although individuals may, on occasion, subvert these policies, the benefits that occur are at best restricted to a limited number of individuals. Group advocacy, as a form of resistance, is sometimes possible but such efforts often appear to make little difference to a government with a strong ideological commitment to the policy.

This chapter presents a detailed case study of the successful efforts of individuals and groups in resisting the BC Liberal government's attempt to impose time limits on recipients of income assistance as a requirement for eligibility to receive welfare. **Welfare time limits** were introduced as part of an overall policy of disentitlement, based on the belief that welfare is not a basic support that should be available to anyone in need; rather, it is a temporary benefit accorded only to people who prove that they are worthy of assistance. Neo-liberal policies involving social benefits are often about expanding the definition of what neo-liberals feel are the "undeserving poor," which in turn is used to justify punitive actions against these groups.

In 2002, the BC provincial government enacted legislation under which certain classes of recipients would have their monthly benefits reduced or eliminated if they remained on income assistance for more than 24 months in a 60-month period. This was one among a number of punitive welfare reforms but was noteworthy for being the first such eligibility requirement in Canadian history. This new requirement was notable because of the unprecedented opposition that developed against it, opposition that extended into mainstream civil society and well beyond groups traditionally opposed to punitive changes to the welfare system. Ultimately, the government was unable to salvage the welfare time limits policy, and on 6 February 2004 it capitulated by effectively eliminating time limits through legislative amendment.

This result is significant. Historically, opposition to punitive welfare policies has been limited. In BC since the mid-1990s, when the percentage of people on income assistance approached 10 per cent of the population, successive governments have legislated cuts to welfare benefits and restricted eligibility rules to reduce the numbers of people receiving welfare. Though the impacts have been harsh, none of these previous welfare reforms generated significant public opposition. Time-limited welfare was different, and it is important to understand why.

In analyzing the rise and fall of welfare time limits, this chapter addresses three interrelated questions. First, why was the government unable to impose time limits to income assistance? Second, what can be learned from the process that may have broader implications in resisting the adverse effects of what are essentially "bad policies"? And third, did this short-term victory have any effects on the broader needs of welfare recipients in the province?

In documenting this instance of policy resistance we have drawn on over a thousand pages of internal government material acquired through a Freedom of Information

(FOI) request, and have also examined public documents and media reports. These materials enable an analysis of the complexities underlying the opposition to the policy both within the welfare ministry and within civil society.

The reader is cautioned that the chronology and analysis in this paper have limitations. The dynamics of the process regarding time limits within the ministry and among the public were very complex. Further, we are working with partial information; the Freedom of Information materials we received were heavily censored by the provincial government. The FOI process in this research was an arduous two-year ordeal characterized by the government denying the existence of the records requested, needlessly requiring requests to be reworded in special language, withholding information, and using other tactics to avoid release of information.

The Rise of Welfare Time Limits: 2001–2

In 2001, the BC Liberals were elected, promising a "New Era" for the province. Once elected, they promised to end what they described as the culture of welfare dependency: "We will find them jobs, we will get them training and, for the rest of their lives, they will be self-sufficient," stated the Minister of Human Resources, Murray Coell. As part of this program, in October 2001 the front-page headline of Victoria's daily newspaper announced "Welfare Time Limits Expected in Spring," and quoted the minister as saying, "we are in the early stages of redefining welfare" and that a time limit on welfare payments to people who are capable of being employed would be implemented in the near future (Lavoie, 2001: A1).

In early 2002, the government translated its election slogans into spending priorities with a budget that required significant cuts to social spending. The welfare ministry was directed to achieve a reduction of $581 million—a full 30 per cent cut—over the course of three years. This was the greatest reduction to any ministry. In response, the ministry established caseload reduction targets that corresponded to the drastic reduction in its projected budgets. In the legislature in February 2002, Premier Gordon Campbell assigned the ministry responsibility to "reduce total income assistance caseload" as part of the government's Strategic Plan (BC Ministry of Human Resources, 2004a: 3). The Premier also established performance measures for the ministry's deputy minister along with bonus pay for (1) reducing the number of welfare recipients by 2 per cent and (2) reducing the growth rate in disability assistance by 2 per cent regardless of the need (Francis, 2003: A16).

The specifics of time-limited welfare were delineated in the ministry's "Service Plan Summary":

> Eligible employable singles and couples will receive assistance for a maximum of two years out of every five years. Eligible employable parents with dependent children will receive full income assistance for a maximum of two years out of every five years, after which their rates will be reduced by an average of 11 per cent. (BC Ministry of Human Resources, 2002: 5)

Eight different groups of recipients were exempted from the rule, including those over 65, those receiving certain types of disability benefits, and single parents with a child under three years of age or caring for a disabled child.

In anticipation of public opposition to time limits, an internal briefing note[1] prepared before the introduction of the new welfare legislation discussed the likely opposition and the potential grounds for legal challenges. The note advised that "negative reaction may be expected from advocacy agencies, clients and not-for-profit social agencies who provide emergency shelter, temporary accommodation and food for homeless individuals" and that "new Acts establish a number of provisions that may attract legal challenges"—specifically mentioning the welfare time limits. Of greatest concern to ministry staff was the upcoming Supreme Court of Canada decision in *Gosselin v. Quebec*, which argued the state had a legal obligation to provide adequate assistance under welfare legislation. The briefing note explained how the planned legislation had been purposefully written to impose sanctions such as time limits while avoiding legal challenge, but warned that if the pending Supreme Court of Canada's decision created an obligation on provinces to provide adequate assistance, the ministry would be in a weaker position to defend its time limits sanction.

As anticipated by the provincial government, the proposed welfare time limits were immediately controversial. Policy analysts from across the political spectrum agreed that this initiative was drastically different from other aspects of welfare restructuring, that this was unprecedented in Canada, and that the introduction of time limits in BC could have national implications. The Fraser Institute called welfare time limits "a watershed development in Canadian welfare reform" (Schafer and Clemens, 2002: 16). The Canadian Centre for Policy Alternatives wrote that the time limit rule represented "a fundamental shift in Canadian social policy—the denial of welfare when in need as a basic human right" (Klein and Long, 2003: 4).

Advocates and community groups working with people in need of assistance quickly registered their opposition and their predictions of harm. The planned changes to welfare legislation, and especially the unprecedented time limits, prompted challenging legal and ethical questions from anti-poverty advocates. University of British Columbia professor Graham Riches stated: "Let there be no doubt that [the] welfare reform decisions violate international law and in certain respects the *Charter of Rights and Freedoms*. The Government actions require legal challenges" (Riches, 2002: 1). In February 2002, a coalition of community agencies and poverty law advocates sent their concerns about the new welfare laws to the United Nations Committee on Economic and Social Cultural Rights, which the media reported, noting that "poverty-law experts have claimed that the Campbell government's proposed welfare reforms could violate Canada's Constitution" (Smith, 2002: 10).

The new legislation, identified as the Employment and Income Assistance Act, was debated in the provincial legislature in April and received royal assent on 30 May 2002. However, the welfare time limits were not to come into effect until they were implemented by regulation four months later, on 30 September 2002. This regulation backdated the beginning of time-limited income assistance by six months to 1 April 2002. For an unknown number of individuals in receipt of welfare, their welfare time limit clock had started ticking.

Professor Marge Reitsma-Street from the University of Victoria summed up community concerns about the legislative review process in this way:

> In spite of the significant changes no witnesses were called, no hearings were held, and no research into the legislation's impact was examined. The government permitted only a few hours of debate on the bills before approving them, despite requests of hundreds of people and groups who volunteered to appear before them. (Reitsma-Street, 2002: 5)

The public responses varied from condemnation to acclaim. In June 2002, at the BC Association of Social Workers' annual general meeting, members voted to censure the minister (who identified himself as a former social worker), asserting that the legislation violated the principles espoused in the Social Work Code of Ethics, and suggested the legislation would place social workers in the position of being asked to carry out unethical policies. In contrast, Vancouver's Fraser Institute praised the government's introduction of time limits in its report card on welfare reform, stating that the "Province leaps to the forefront of intelligent welfare reform and sets new standard for Canadian welfare" and that BC's welfare reforms "catapulted it beyond any Canadian jurisdiction and into the realm of reform-minded US states" (Fraser Institute, 2002: 1).

On 20 December 2002, the Supreme Court of Canada announced its decision in *Gosselin v. Quebec*, ruling that the Canadian Charter of Rights and Freedoms guarantee to equal treatment did not encompass a distinct right to social welfare benefits.[2] In this landmark case—the first claim under the Canadian Charter of Rights and Freedoms to a right for welfare—the majority in the 5–4 ruling stated there was no breach of the Constitution. However, the justices also did not rule out the possibility for further challenges that section 7 of the Charter may be interpreted to obligate a government to provide social assistance.

The Erosion of Time Limits from within the Ministry: Spring 2003

Time Limits and the Mandate of the Ministry

In the spring of 2003, senior staff within the Ministry of Human Resources (later renamed the Ministry of Employment and Income Assistance) struggled to implement the politically motivated legislation as ministry practice. Concerns were repeatedly raised by policy analysts that the current wording of the regulations would see time limits imposed in questionable situations, which were "contrary to the policy intent." The FOI documents show that in March 2003 the Social Policy Branch of the ministry provided a list of clients who would face time limits sanctions but who were in fact not "employable" because they may be in job training programs, in hospitals, or caring for a child in the home of a relative (CIHR).[3] A private briefing note[4] to the deputy minister warned of "undue hardship" for some clients under the current welfare time limits legislation; individuals who reached the time limits and lost benefits would continue to be ineligible even if they experienced periods during which they were unemployable. In this briefing note, staff pointed out the potentially negative public reaction to the fact that the legislation had no provision to issue assistance to ineligible applicants who had no other resources. In particular:

> Clients who lose their eligibility for assistance due to time limits, and who subsequently become temporarily unemployable due to medical condition, pregnancy, separating from an abusive spouse, or entering a treatment or rehabilitation program will not be eligible for assistance. In families where all adults are unable to work and who have no other resources, the denial of income support would create undue hardship . . . .

As stated in a "Decision Note to the Deputy Minister," "A reduction [to families] appears to imply a double penalty—one for reaching the time limit, and another for being unable to work or achieve independence through employment."[5] In this document ministry staff also noted that the imposition of time limits could contribute to an individual's inability to be employable and independent, and potentially precipitate health issues such as addictions or depression.

In response, the government began to backtrack on welfare time limits through legislating exemptions. The result was BC Regulation 116/2003, which took effect on 1 April 2003 and exempted certain classes of welfare recipients from the time limits policy. In addition, ministry staff explored policy mechanisms such as hardship grants to ensure that assistance would remain available to welfare recipients who were unable to seek or maintain employment.

Although internal information had already indicated that welfare time limits were inconsistent with the ministry's mission and mandate, the minister maintained its public message supporting welfare time limits. In March 2003 the BC government published an "Opinion Editorial" by the minister stating that in the past "government policies led to a culture of entitlement: there was widespread expectation that welfare could be a lifestyle for employable people . . . . we placed time limits on income assistance for employable people to discourage them from returning to welfare as a way of life" (Coell, 2003: 1).

Time Limits and the Number of Recipients Facing Sanctions

In January 2003, the Ministry of Human Resources established a Time Limits Project Group to advise senior management on issues related to implementation of welfare time limits. In their first internal report[6] in January 2003, the Time Limits Project Group noted that they did not yet know what the impacts of welfare time limits would be: "we require preliminary analysis to determine the potential Time Limits impact to clients, number of clients and their demographics." One week later staff provided the first estimate, stating that preliminary analysis indicated that "19,000 chronic cases may have 24 months accumulated by May 2004."[7] None of this information was made public, and further internal analysis was subsequently scheduled.

In the summer of 2003, internal documents revealed that the Minister of Human Resources was provided with estimates of the number of people facing time limits sanctions. According to an "Information Note" prepared for the minister's briefing, "Time limits will begin to affect clients as of the March 26, 2004 cheque issue. Caseload projections indicate that 7,900 cases are likely to be impacted, either through ineligibility or reduction, in April 2004."[8] In this "Information Note," ministry staff warned the minister that of these 7,900 clients, as many as 60 per cent could be characterized as difficult to employ, and advised that, "It will be important in applying time limits to try to ensure both that they apply to those who reasonably can be expected to work, and that they not unfairly impact children or others who are vulnerable."

The disclosure and leaks of government information began in this time period, with a CBC Vancouver report (2003: 1) on "heavily censored files" obtained under the Freedom of Information Act showing that "senior bureaucrats warned the Minister of Human Resources last year that BC's welfare reforms could create hardship for some people."

By the end of the summer, in a confidential note to cabinet, the minister appeared to request a significant change in the approach to welfare time limits. The minister advised cabinet that "advocates are already beginning to focus on time limits" and that "the decision on the Gosselin Charter challenge on welfare as an entitlement leaves room for further challenge and a challenge is pending in British Columbia in October."[9] In this same note, the minister also presented cabinet with the estimated total number of cases that might be impacted by April 2004: 1,321 families would face reductions to their benefits and 1,882 people would be completely cut off welfare.

A Groundswell of Public Opposition: Summer and Fall 2003

Throughout the fall of 2003, diverse sectors of civil society began questioning the acceptability of welfare time limits. This was prompted in part by the work of anti-poverty individuals and organizations that had opposed time limits on principle prior to their enactment into law. However, the opposition soon spread to "mainstream" portions of society who traditionally had not voiced concerns about poverty or welfare rights. Its failure to be forthcoming with information and its failure to justify the rationale for welfare time limits soon put the government on the defensive and set the stage for the demise of time limits.

By October 2003, concerns about the pending time limits were mounting and critics were becoming more vocal and more diverse. The month began with the Canadian Centre for Policy Alternatives releasing the editorial "The Ticking Time Bomb of BC's Welfare Time Limits" (Klein, 2003), which questioned the assurances from the minister not to worry and repeated the risks outlined by ministry staff, as revealed in information obtained through an FOI request on CBC Radio earlier in the summer.

Numerous groups and individuals launched public campaigns against the welfare time limits, including poverty advocates releasing plans for a legal challenge to the welfare time limits legislation that would build on the *Gosselin* case. Lawyers from the BC Public Interest Advocacy Centre (BCPIAC) explained: "Sections 7 and 15 of our *Charter of Rights and Freedoms* guarantee security of the person and equality . . . cutting people off welfare will leave people without the means to meet basic needs. This is a threat to their physical and psychological security, and a denial of their dignity and equal worth as human beings" (BCPIAC, 2003: 1).

At a major speech to the Union of BC Municipalities, the Minister of Human Resources assured the crowd that "people are better off working than on welfare"[10] however, more and more people were wondering what their municipalities would look like with an unknown number of people neither working nor receiving welfare.

On 8 October 2003, in the provincial legislature, the Opposition quoted an internal report acquired through an FOI request that provided the estimated number of people affected by the welfare time limits, although the numbers were blanked out. The minister's refusal to provide an estimate of the number of recipients facing time limits undermined the government's position that time limits are in the best interests of the public, instead lending support to the perception that the government was withholding information to manage an increasingly sensitive and damaging political issue.

Two days later, a leaked government memo resulted in the front-page newspaper headline "28,000 Could Be Caught in Two-Year Welfare Squeeze" (Lavoie, 2003: A1). The leaked document was dated 9 October, the day after the minister stood in the legislature refusing to provide an estimate of the number of clients affected. In the legislature, the Minister of Human Resources retorted that the Opposition had completely misunderstood the report and that it was not a forecast of people who would be affected by the time limits but rather a simple picture of the entire caseload, including all of those who would be excused from the time limits by the different categories of exemptions. The minister added: "I believe that by the time we get to April [2004], those people who have been on income assistance for two years, who are employable, will have jobs, I am hoping that's the case." In response to the Opposition's earlier press release warning that "Communities across BC should brace for an explosion in the number of homeless British Columbians . . . BC communities need to make preparations in advance of April 1, 2004, when over 27,000 British Columbians will be kicked off income assistance" (BC New Democratic Party [NDP], 2003: 1), Minister Coell shot back, "This is another example of the NDP using numbers that they know are wrong yet persist in putting before the public to cause confusion, fear, anxiety and stress among BC's most vulnerable."[11]

A "Confidential Issues Note" of 17 October 2003, prepared in response to the increasing outcry against welfare time limits, provided the minister with his "key message": "The number of people affected by time limits at any one time is a small percentage of the caseload."[12] Despite the message, the public and a number of key institutions were not buying it.

By November 2003, the efforts of grassroots organizing against the time limits started to yield results in the form of statements by public institutions. On 4 November the Vancouver City Council passed a motion urging the provincial government to rescind the time limits law and resolving to write other municipalities encouraging them to pass similar motions. The meeting included four hours of speakers supporting the motion. Two weeks later the Vancouver School Board passed a resolution condemning the provincial welfare time limits policy, noting that "the provincial government has failed to provide accurate numbers on Vancouver citizens who will be impacted, but it is estimated that it could be in the thousands."[13] The passing of resolutions continued through the month, with Victoria passing a motion on 22 November, Smithers the same week, and Saanich one week later. The BC Association of Social Workers passed a "Resolution to Repeal the Two-year Time Limit on Welfare Assistance in British Columbia" at its annual general meeting, while the deans and directors of the Canadian Association of Schools of Social Work (now the Canadian Association for Social Work Education) passed a similar motion.

In response to the pressure, the ministry implemented a referral of all inquiries directly to the Premier's office. In the legislature the Opposition read an internal ministry memo, which it referred to as a "gag order":

> Please do not provide any information to the public regarding the potential numbers of clients being cut off or the effect of time limits on caseloads. . . .
> The reason for this, likely obvious, is this is a very hot news story, and we can't speculate on how the policy will affect people or the numbers.[14]

In a press release the BC Government Employees Union summarized the situation as gagging their own ministry staff to keep secret the number of people who would be cut off welfare as a result of the time limits.

On 14 November 2003, in a *Vancouver Province* article, the ministry tried to reinforce the message that its policies were working and resulting in far fewer people on welfare, enough to justify a smaller system. The "good news" message was overshadowed by the story's headline, "Welfare Jobs Axed, Offices to Be Closed" (*Vancouver Province*, 2003: A16). The closure of welfare offices and the laying off of ministry staff again prompted media speculation that thousands of people may lose their benefits and raised concerns that the minister had no idea of how many people would be affected by the welfare time limits.

A week later, the *Vancouver Sun* ran a column by Stephen Hume with the headline "What Happens When More Poor Hit the Streets?":

[C]ome April, the province intends to put a lot more impoverished British Columbians on to the streets. That's when people now receiving social assistance will have to rely on their own resources once time limits imposed by the province off-load them from the welfare rolls—a first for Canada. I say off-loading because that is what the province is doing—transferring the social costs to municipalities while pretending it's balancing the books. (Hume, 2003: C7)

Without specific information from the ministry, the public was left to speculate how many people would be living with no incomes and how this would affect their munici-palities. This speculation played into affluent people's fear of living with people in dire poverty, and public opposition to the time limits increasingly became framed as a mat-ter of self-interest. For example, the Vancouver School Board resolution listed impacts not just as "children arriving to school hungry" but also "homeless people sleeping on our school steps"; the Saanich City Council resolution raised the concern of business and the ability of business owners to "do business as a result of the new law." While the affluent public may be willing to support harsh welfare laws, there seems to be less willingness to accept policies and outcomes that could negatively affect their own lives.

Throughout December, public opposition to the time limits continued to mount and diversify. The Social Planning and Research Council of BC released a fact sheet on welfare time limits that became an integral resource for concerned citizens less familiar with welfare rights. The fact sheet capitalized on the fact that the provincial government had "not been forthcoming about the anticipated impact of the time limits policy."

Meanwhile, a vocal Anti-Two Year Time Limit Coalition was organized in Vancouver. Described in its pamphlet as a "coalition of anti-poverty groups, women's groups, faith groups, unions and other concerned organizations and individuals," the group called on people to come together for "leafleting, petitioning, advocating for people's rights, organ-izing days of action, etc." In Victoria, the Anglican diocese of Vancouver Island, repre-senting 70 parishes, passed a resolution to write to every parish in the diocese encouraging people to lobby the minister and Premier to stop the welfare time limits policy.

With no credible response from the provincial government, the Fraser Institute stepped forward to attempt to counter the opposition. In an article titled "Staying the Course on Welfare Time Limits," the authors observed that "social advocacy groups have singled out the time limits policy as their main point of criticism. But the concerns have no foundation" (Gabel, Clemens, LeRoy, and Veldhuis, 2003: 22). They went on to implore the provincial government to disregard public opinion:

Unfortunately, in BC there is an increasingly vocal objection to time limits, and the province's government has thus far shown weak resolve on a number of its initiatives including spending cuts, tax relief, and privatization. It is important that they not cave in on time limits. With enough political will to limit exemptions and enforce this policy effectively, time limits can save a new generation of British Columbians from welfare dependency. (Gabel et al., 2003: 24)

Within the ministry, staff responded not by staying the course on welfare time limits but rather by urgently preparing mitigation strategies, including the possibility of providing "time limit extensions to singles and couples without children, who have been and continue to be, compliant with employment plans."[15] According to this internal document "[t]he first large stream of recipients will be impacted by time limits starting in April 2004. If no changes are made to Time Limits it is estimated that 1378 cases will be impacted (662 single recipients, 55 couples, 143 two-parent families with children, 518 single parent families with children)." In the same memo, ministry staff repeated the warning that the current policy would result in people who are unable to work being ineligible for income assistance, and that, under the current policy, clients cut off welfare due to time limits while deemed "employable" could later face barriers to employment yet still remain ineligible for assistance for three years. Ministry staff also raised the risk of "constitutional challenges" and specifically noted that "legal fees associated with *Charter* challenges on the Ministry's time limits legislation could be very costly. Numerous advocacy groups have stated their intention to launch a charter challenge on time limits." Despite staff concerns about welfare time limits, the document noted that a possible negative consequence of mitigating the time limits would be that "the Ministry may be perceived as reacting to interest groups and media pressure" and that "cost-savings will be significantly reduced."

The year would end with one more challenge as Aboriginal leaders raised unique concerns about the impending time limits. An internal document dated 31 December 2003 noted that:

> Aboriginal leaders have expressed concern that the two-year time limit, which will impact recipients as of April 2004, may lead to an influx of band members returning to reserves. The Sto:lo First Nation in the Upper Fraser Valley estimate that 60 per cent of its members live off-reserve and up to half may receive income assistance. There is growing concern that an influx of natives returning to reservations will place tremendous pressures on resources including housing and existing programs.[16]

The minister's speaking notes—included in the document obtained through the FOI—sought to calm the fears of Aboriginal leaders by stating the "the final number impacted by time limits in April 2004 is expected to be quite small" as a result of "successful employment planning and employment programs." The minister offered assurances that the ministry "wants people to be employed, rather than lose eligibility due to time limits or return to reserves." He attributed the fears of Aboriginal groups not to the welfare policy but rather to "reports by the media and others [who] have greatly over-estimated the number of recipients who may reach their time limit. This may have fuelled fears by native leaders that large numbers of band members may return to reserves."

Government Capitulation: Spring 2004

The period from the start of 2004 until the effective end of time limits on 6 February 2004 was a time of intense activity within both the ministry and civil society. The FOI documents indicate that, by this time, the government had concluded it would have to amend welfare legislation to negate the effects of time limits. It faced the challenge of a very short timeline to achieve this and the public relations problems of backtracking on a central piece of its welfare reform. Within civil society, the opposition to time limits intensified and unified, in part in response to the government's failure to clarify its plans.

Developments within the Ministry

On the first work day of the New Year, the Minister of Human Resources, Murray Coell, made a significant shift in position. In a radio interview he said he was "willing to take another look at sweeping changes to welfare guidelines that are set to start in April,"[17] and stated that if a government committee examining the potential changes reported tens of thousands of people would be suddenly cut he would rethink the changes. However, he added he did not think that would be the case because of the provisions already developed to exempt certain classes of welfare recipients.

The media continued to pressure the Minister of Human Resources to say how many recipients would face time limit sanctions. On 4 January 2004 the ministry's spokesperson promised to release a statistical report that would provide "full disclosure of accurate information that will help people see what the whole picture looks like at the end of the month" (Anderson, 2004: A9). In this interview, Minister Coell insisted that "60 to 70 per cent" of current welfare clients did not fall into the work category and so would be at no risk of being cut off welfare as of April 2004.

Less publicly, government staff scrambled to push back the time limits clock. An internal e-mail emphasized the urgent need to amend the welfare legislation prior to 1 April 2004 when the cut-offs would begin. Ministry staff were told: "The new message is we may be mitigating time limits but our focus is still employment for clients and we will emphasize this by strengthening EP [Employment Plan] sanctions."[18] A subsequent e-mail from the ministry to Attorney General staff explained: "Currently the Ministry is developing an RFL [Request for Legislation] to amend the *Employment and Assistance Act* in order to provide the Ministry with regulation making power to suspend the consequences of time limits in specific circumstances, provided a welfare recipient was compliant with their employment plan."[19]

Ministry staff now faced two looming deadlines: (1) to provide the public with the estimated number of people likely to be impacted by the end of January and (2) to make the necessary legislative changes to mitigate the number of clients affected before the April welfare cheques were released. At the same time, the deputy minister sought a legal opinion from the Attorney General's Legal Services Branch regarding the possible impact of the Charter in relation to the provision for time-limited income assistance.

On 15 January 2004 Human Resources staff submitted their request for an amendment to the Employment and Assistance Act to the Ministry of Attorney General. This application, accessed through an FOI request, was heavily censored but it was noted that the request was a "significant policy change" that has "significant financial implications."[20] The request appears to be more than an appeal to add an additional exemption; the ministry had clearly noted they already had the authority to exempt categories of recipients from the welfare time limits. Instead, the request appeared to seek an amendment to the legislation to allow for the suspending of the consequences of reaching the time limit for some clients in order to allow for case-by-case decisions. At this point, it was the ministry describing the ineffectiveness and inappropriateness of current time limits legislation in accomplishing its policy intent, citing examples such as a client receiving welfare who could be non-compliant with his or her employment plan for 23 months and then complying for one month to be exempt from the welfare time limits; conversely, clients could become unable to work after reaching their time limit (e.g., due to pregnancy). The ministry noted in this memorandum that it did not wish to penalize family units making good-faith efforts to find employment, but it also did want to entirely exempt them from the time limits requirement.

As the mitigation strategies were unfolding, Human Resources staff also appeared to be continually seeking the much-promised statistic of how many people would actually be cut off assistance on 1 April and in the subsequent months. Throughout the correspondence and reports accessed, there were various estimates. Based on our analysis it appeared that ministry staff were continually seeking mitigation strategies and corresponding estimates until the number was brought down to a figure that was felt to be publicly acceptable. The focus was on two estimates: first, the number of clients/cases who could potentially be affected by time limits in the future (i.e., their current months are counting towards time limits); and second, the smaller number of clients/cases who were actually expected to face sanctions (i.e., reduction or total removal of welfare benefits). In January 2004, an internal document[21] calculated that 21,112 adults (45 per cent of all adults on welfare) were on time-limited income assistance in BC—in other words, nearly half of adults on welfare were considered employable and were not protected under any of the existing 24 exemptions. The estimated number of people that had actually reached the 24-month time limit, promised for public release by the end of the month, continued to be reworked throughout January.

In the two weeks leading to the promised announcement on 31 January, staff drafted and redrafted a document titled "Time Limits Management Strategy."[22] According to this document, 1,200 clients would reach their time limit on April 2004, but it was expected that many of these would have significant barriers to employment.

Meanwhile, Premier Gordon Campbell announced a provincial cabinet shuffle on 26 January 2004. Murray Coell, who was responsible for the welfare reforms and time limits, would be shuffled to another ministry (Minister of Community, Aboriginal and

Women's Services) with the new minister, Stan Hagen, inheriting the time limits issue. In the upcoming years the minister's role would continue to change, with five ministers appointed by Premier Campbell; as well the ministry's name was changed three times.

By the end of January, documents[23] obtained indicated that the ministry was more confident of its ability to assess clients affected by time limits, to provide opportunities for employable clients to find work, and to exempt those with barriers to employment. These documents also appeared to reflect a more realistic view that a significant number of recipients had barriers that would prevent employment.

Although the tone of the ministry's internal documents had shifted, on 31 January 2004 the promised release of the number of people facing time limits did not happen. The media reported: "just how many British Columbians will be forced off welfare rolls this spring remains unclear after the provincial government missed a self-imposed deadline Friday to release that information" (Rud, 2004: A4). Although internal records clearly show the minister knew the numbers of people that would be affected, Stan Hagen, the newly appointed minister, told reporters "that a report from Ministry staff isn't complete," that he "hasn't seen it yet," and that "staff are taking their time coming up with a figure in order to ensure that the information is accurate" (Rud, 2004: A4).

Community Opposition

In the face of ministry silence, community opposition to the welfare time limits gained strength and media attention throughout January 2004. Labour activists predicted that "the 'Two-year Time Limit' would be the next significant 'front' on which to base a unified 'Fight Back' against the BC Liberal Government."[24] On 19 January 2004 there was a rally in Vancouver to "Fight the Two-Year Time Limit and the Closure of Welfare Offices." Resolutions were passed by Cranbrook City Council and the Greater Victoria School Board urging the provincial government to rescind the time limits law as well as the laws that reduce welfare benefits. The Canadian Centre for Policy Alternatives initiated a long-term study to analyze the impact of the new welfare time limits.

In the last days of January, a news conference was held in a downtown church in Victoria where school boards, churches, and city councils sat side by side demanding an end to the time limits rule. The event demonstrated the widespread disapproval from mainstream society—not just anti-poverty activists—and portrayed the province as out of step with the shared values of church, school, and local government. The news conference attracted national news coverage, including a Canadian Press article in which Reverend Harold Munn vowed to sleep in the streets to protest the welfare time limits. Robert Arnold of the National Anti-Poverty Group (NAPO) declared that the time limit policy would soon become the focus of a countrywide campaign, stating that "We're picking up the two-year time limit in BC as one of our major campaigns" (Meissner, 2004). A week later a letter was sent to the Prime Minister and BC Premier, signed by over 125 groups, requesting that the time limits be rescinded before 1 April 2004 and that no similar provision be implemented in BC or any other province in the future.

The Twenty-Fifth Exemption: 6 February 2004

On 6 February 2004 the ministry presented a news release estimating "the number of clients to be affected as the government follows through on its commitment to limit income assistance for employable clients as two out of every five" (BC Ministry of Human Resources, 2004b: 1). Just 339 clients would be affected by the time limits over the coming year—"far lower than the tens of thousands that the opposition claimed." Although a number of exemptions to the policy had been included in the policy earlier, the news release contained a less triumphant message: that the government would be implementing a new 25th exemption to the time limits policy to ensure that those clients who were employable and looking for work would be protected. Specifically, this exemption was intended to ensure that time limits would not affect people "who have an employment plan, are complying with their plan, are actively looking for work, but have not been successful in finding employment" (BC Ministry of Human Resources, 2004c: 2).

The media were quick to file stories based on the news release, focusing on the numbers. Many did not immediately notice the significant policy change, and instead repeated the minister's message that the opposition was wrong to claim tens of thousands would be affected. But when reporters called on social policy critics for additional commentary, they were made aware of the significance of the policy shift and the fact that the landmark policy was now essentially made redundant by the government. The next day the front-page story on the *Vancouver Sun* read "Province Backs Off Plan for Dramatic Cuts to Welfare" (Kines, 2004: A1). This headline was more similar to the news release of the Canadian Centre for Policy Alternatives—"Government Backs Down on Welfare Time Limits, But Cutoff Should Be Scrapped All Together"—than to the minister's own release—"Time Limit Policy to Protect People in Need" (BC Ministry of Human Resources, 2004b).

The CCPA was one of several groups to quickly counter the government's message, stating:

> Until today thousands of people were at risk of hitting the two-year time limit. The new exemption makes the whole two-year time limit policy redundant. . . . regardless of whether the number is 15,000, 300 or one, this is a bad law. It remains an awful precedent and should be removed from the books. (CCPA, 2004: 1)

Although community groups, media, and social policy commentators were critical of the government's decision to keep welfare time limits legislation, there was also celebration that the numbers of people who would be affected had been significantly reduced. The BC Coalition of People with Disabilities called the latest exemption "a significant victory for the community" in a letter of congratulations to community groups for their hard work in speaking out against welfare time limits. The leader of the Opposition said she believed the Liberals originally planned to cut off far more people, but bowed to public pressure; this message was echoed by several media outlets.

The following week the initial reactions shifted to deeper reflections. The *Vancouver Sun* editorial noted the following:

> Had the rule been in place at the time it was unveiled, there were, by the human resources minister's reckoning, 30,000 people on welfare who would have been kicked off. After almost two years of speculation, during which the government has refused to divulge its own estimates, we now learn that at most, 37 people will become ineligible on April 1. We say at most because between now and then any or all of those people could fall off the list by virtue of finding a job or meeting the requirements for any of the 25 exemptions that have been created to the rule. So what happened? How could a policy shift of such magnitude have resulted in so little impact? (*Vancouver Sun*, 2004: C7)

The editorial answered its own question: "This extraordinary outcome was achieved partly by the last-minute decision to exempt anyone who is genuinely looking for work." The *Sun* called the released numbers "a mockery of the two-in-five rule" and stated that the provincial government should "scrap this useless rule."

Three days later the *Vancouver Sun* ran two opposing editorials on the announced 25th exemption. Shelagh Day, a lawyer with the Poverty and Human Rights Project in Vancouver, claimed that "What happened last week is that the government retreated in the face of mounting pressure from community organizations, churches, unions, city councils, social policy experts and individuals who let Victoria know that the 24-month rule is both impractical and morally repugnant." She identified the new exemption as "a backhanded admission by the Liberals that applying a time limit to welfare doesn't work," and concluded that "A rule that requires 25 exemptions is a feeble rule. And a rule that, to save the government's face, requires an exemption that guts the rule itself—as the 25th exemption does—needs to be scrapped" (Day, 2004: A9). The Fraser Institute agreed that the government capitulated, characterizing the government action as "backtracking" and calling the addition of the 25th exemption a "policy change that effectively nullifies the time limit rule." It described the exemption as "a disastrous U-turn on welfare reform" that "delegitimized what was one of Canada's most important social welfare reforms to date" (Clemens, Veldhuis, and LeRoy, 2004: A9).

Within the ministry, staff prepared damage-control speaking notes for the minister. One Information Note[25] stated: "the Ministry has been accused of 'gutting' time limits policy. . . . The small number of clients impacted by time limits is primarily due to thousands of clients who have found employment and who no longer require assistance, and not the newest exemption." While this public statement sounded positive, it was false and in fact a direct contradiction of the ministry's own budget fact sheet publicly released at the same time. This fact sheet states: "The Ministry believes the most recent exemption to time limits policy will increase the annual average caseload by about 1,200 cases" (BC Ministry of Human Resources, 2004a).

On 15 April 2004 the government implemented the change of policy through BC Regulation 160/2004. It exempted from time limits any individuals, couples, or families where one person has received welfare for more than 24 months, as long as "each recipient in the family unit who is subject to an employment plan complies with the employment plan." Thus, while still enacted as legislation, welfare time limits were limited to pre-existing provisions regarding ineligibility. Welfare time limits ended, not with a bang, but with a whimper.

Resisting Regressive Welfare Policies: Lessons Learned

The data accessed through the FOI clearly show that thousands of clients were facing time limit sanctions in BC. As a result of events that unfolded to mitigate the policy, early estimates that 10,000 clients would be sanctioned were replaced with a number of less than 50 in the first two years, and even fewer in the third year. Following the introduction of the 25th exemption, time limits for welfare became a redundant policy. That said, approximately 50 people still fell through the cracks and faced severe hardship, driving home the need for action to repeal the time limits legislation in its entirety.

The downfall of welfare time limits is noteworthy because it is one of the few successes in defeating the regressive welfare reforms that have been implemented in Canada over the past decade. A key to this success was the pressure exerted by mainstream society through its representatives, such as municipal councils, based largely on a perception of harm to their communities that might occur from a large increase in the number of homeless people. However, the success of this opposition depended in part on the organizing work of smaller groups involved in the anti-poverty field. And while the opposition from these groups was loosely organized, it was effective in providing accurate and timely information and analysis that resonated with the concerns of mainstream organizations. These smaller groups acted as catalysts to bring together divergent groups, such as city councils, school boards, and faith communities, to voice their shared opposition to time limits to welfare.

The opposition to welfare time limits also demonstrates the potential effectiveness of public interest research. Some of the most vocal criticisms of time limits came from individuals and organizations that would not normally consider themselves activists, such as city councils, school boards, and church groups. They knew that this was an unjust law, but they also knew that the issue was complex and that they did not have enough information to speak to its complexities. Public interest research was available to fill this gap and it provided the necessary evidence for diverse groups to speak out in a convincing fashion. Although activists opposed time limits, they were often not the most visible face of dissent. Rather, activists and advocates were often behind the scenes providing needed analysis and assisting with media releases and press conferences; this enabled mainstream groups and organizations to voice their opposition in an informed and effective fashion. These activists linked concerned citizens to public interest research and facilitated their involvement in the issue.

Public interest lawyers also played a leading role in the opposition to time limits in arguing that the rule violated rights protected in the Canadian Charter of Rights and Freedoms. The threat of legal challenges repeatedly emerged in internal ministry discussions and documents as a significant concern. Legal action, if this option is feasible, may be an important tool for future campaigns regarding welfare eligibility.

As revealed by the FOI materials, within the staff of the ministry there was also opposition to time limits based in part on their beliefs regarding the ministry's purpose or mandate. Time limits were resisted by ministry staff because they were contrary to this purpose and mandate. It appears that this originated from both front-line staff and policy analysts. Both groups expressed concern that the policy would be harmful to the beneficiaries of income assistance and also would defeat the employment-related objectives of the program. They also cautioned the minister that imposing time limits on certain classes of recipients could lead to negative public reactions and become a difficult political issue. The result was an ongoing process of amendments to exempt classes of recipients from the time limits policy. This was an important indication that the policy was fundamentally flawed; in this case it also serves to remind us that simplistic, politically motivated social policy can be ill-conceived, difficult to implement, and disastrous for those it may affect.

The logic of time limits contained the seeds of its own downfall. Its purpose was to cut recipients off welfare, and inherent in the policy was the reality that a potentially large number of recipients would be affected at the same time. This inevitably raised the numbers question. If the policy was to have any useful consequence relative to its purpose, then the number had to be significant. However, the greater the success of the government in cutting recipients off of welfare, the greater would be the harmful consequences for the public. As events unfolded, it became apparent that public acceptance of the policy depended on it having minimal impact. Public concerns over this found expression in the resolutions of city councils, school boards, and other institutions. These concerns were fuelled by the government's secrecy and failure to respond to basic questions concerning the number of recipients who would reach time limits. This secrecy led to the media becoming a force of pressure on government, for regardless of whether the media supported time limits to welfare, their irritation at the government's refusal to answer their questions regarding numbers of recipients facing ineligibility contributed to the government's loss of credibility. In the face of widespread public opposition, the government was left defending its policy to save face while declaring that the number of recipients affected would be insignificant.

By late January 2004 the government decided that the political price to be paid for its deeply unpopular social policy outweighed its ideological commitments, and the time limits policy was essentially gutted by introducing policy changes and exemptions that meant the time limits policy had little or no effect on the welfare caseloads or the eligibility of almost all recipients.

In 2012, 10 years after the introduction of welfare time limits in BC, the Liberal government, which had been elected in 2001 and was now under the leadership of Christy Clark, finally removed the legislation. Since this failed experiment in BC no other government in Canada has so far attempted to introduce welfare time limits. The removal of the welfare time limits from legislation was one part of a larger announcement by Premier Clark of changes to the welfare system. These changes were described by government as "common sense changes" and intended to accomplish the government's "Families First Agenda" by supporting vulnerable families.[26] Although this reflects the lasting success of opposition to welfare time limits, easily overlooked, at the end of the media backgrounder, is the government's stated intent to "Remove time limits (previously 24 months in a five-year period), and replace [it] with intensified work-search requirements to help ensure that those on income assistance are using all available resources to find work."

Advocates welcomed the removal of time limits, but were curious why the "long overdue win" was essentially "buried" in the announcement and questioned if the changes were "common sense" why it took 10 years for the Liberal government to change them.[27] While most of the announced welfare changes were acceptable to advocates, there was opposition to the announced extension of the work search from three weeks to five, which significantly delays income assistance to those deemed employable. Overall, the changes were inadequate in recognizing the needs of families; for example, there was no increase in income assistance rates.[28] As commented in the *Victoria Times-Colonist*,[29] these changes to welfare "fail any fair test of a commitment to helping families . . . [as] the government, as a matter of ideology and policy, condemns the children of people on disability and income assistance to a life of poverty." The NDP Opposition expressed disappointment that the changes were mostly just a restatement of the Liberals' 2001 cuts and not a widespread poverty reduction strategy for BC.[30]

Summary and Conclusion

As described in this chapter, the BC government, in 2002, was the first Canadian jurisdiction to introduce welfare time limits. Although this policy was eventually defeated through civil society opposition, the legislation would not be formally repealed until a decade later, an indication that the government's decision was not based on any enlightened recognition of human and ethical considerations. A question posed at the beginning of this chapter was what effects this policy retreat by government had on the well-being of those on welfare both in the short term and over the longer term.

Research conducted in 2006 demonstrated that the decline in welfare caseloads, which occurred between 2002 and 2006, was largely a result of restricting entry and not increasing "exits" of people who were receiving welfare (Wallace, Klein, and Reitsma-Street, 2006). In hindsight, it is clear that the two-year independence requirement and the three-week wait period imposed in the new legislation led to far greater caseload reductions than time limits to welfare. In fact, before the time limits would have taken effect in BC in April 2004, the cost-cutting and caseload reduction targets were already surpassed as far more people were denied assistance than cut off (Reitsma-Street and Wallace, 2004: 175). Welfare restructuring led to people in need of help being systematically denied, discouraged, and delayed in receiving income assistance (Wallace et al., 2006). However, it is also true that the welfare time limits policy would have caused additional harm to the most vulnerable people in BC, and the risk remains that it could be adopted in other jurisdictions in the future.

The downfall of time-limited welfare in BC prevented thousands of recipients from having their benefits reduced or ended. Many of these individuals would have been those least able to provide for themselves and least able to challenge the government's policies and decisions. Many would have been left homeless and hungry if time limits had taken effect as initially legislated.

In part, the end of time-limited welfare was also the assertion of values basic to a humane society. The policy tied income assistance to arbitrary rules rather than to the needs of individuals. After years of cuts to welfare, the public reacted in limiting the extent to which punitive government policies towards people in need of income assistance would be tolerated. At the same time, it is important to recognize that the opposition to time limits was diverse and included those who opposed time limits in principle and for purely humanitarian reasons, as well as those who believed a dramatic increase in the number of homeless citizens would be harmful to their communities. While the work of groups with a social justice agenda led to broader opposition, the political pressure from more self-interested community groups likely led to the eventual defeat of the time limits policy.

The internal government documents related to time limits indicate that government decision-makers are very sensitive to the prospects of court challenges to legislation. However, it is also significant that the defeat of the time limits policy was achieved through public pressure and opinion rather than legal action. While legal action is a legitimate method of challenging ill-conceived and harmful policies, it is equally important not to leave this work to lawyers and judges alone. Politicians must be reminded that civil society can and will act to curb efforts that will do harm to vulnerable citizens.

Critical Thinking Questions

1. The Fraser Institute and the Canadian Centre for Policy Alternatives took opposing views on the welfare time limits policy. Based on an analysis of their responses, as outlined in this chapter, what underlying values appear to shape their positions? How would you classify the ideologies of these two groups?

2. The authors of this chapter identify a number of factors that appeared to influence policy outcomes in this example of policy resistance. They also suggest a particular role for social activists in pursuing strategies of policy resistance that involve the public. What is this role? Do you agree or disagree? Explain why.

3. Assess how government handled its own policy-making process. What mistakes did the government make? Do you think this had any impact on the outcome? Identify any different actions the government may have taken in dealing with the media or the public in order to gain acceptance for its reforms. Do you think these actions might have made any difference in the way groups and organizations responded?

4. The authors of this case study suggest that both altruism and self-interest played a role in shaping opposition to this policy. Although it is possible that some groups voiced a combination of these concerns, most are depicted as developing positions that reflected more emphasis on one or the other of these two motivations. What were the groups and organizations identified in the chapter that reflected more altruistic motivations? What were the groups and organizations that reflected more self-interested motivations? What conclusions do you draw about using both of these motivations in organizing public opposition to regressive social policies or public support for positive reforms?

5. In this particular case neither front-line staff nor service users figure prominently in resisting this policy, although such involvement may have occurred behind the scenes. What are the possible reasons for this lack of involvement? Is it more difficult to obtain such engagement in policy resistance than it might be if one was developing a new policy designed to benefit service users through a more inclusive policy-making process? How important are other factors, such as the characteristics of these groups, their vulnerability, and the nature and scope of the policy reform? Can any of these factors be mitigated?

Recommended Reading

S. Klein and J. Pulkingham, with S. Parusel, S. Plancke, J. Smith, D. Sookraj, et al. *Living on Welfare in BC: Experiences of Longer-Term "Expected to Work" Recipients.* Vancouver: Canadian Centre for Policy Alternatives, 2008. This report examines the specific experiences of those on welfare who were classified as employable by the Campbell Liberal government in BC.

Notes

1. Internal Briefing Note (undated) prepared for Legislative Review Committee regarding the "Introduction of the Employment and Assistance Act and the *Employment and Assistance for Persons with Disabilities Act* for the Spring 2002 Legislative Session."

2. [2002] 4 S.C.R. 29, 221 D.I.R. (4th) 257, online: CanLII, at: www.canlii.ca/c/sas/scc/2002/2002scc84.html. [*Gosselin* cited to S.C.R.].

3. "Time Limits Scenarios" document attached to e-mails sent 12 Mar. 2003.

4. "Ministry of Human Resources Decision Note," 3 Apr. 2003. (Document heavily censored.)

5. "Ministry of Human Resources Decision Note," 23 May 2003.

6. "Time Limits Phase I Summary Report (Status Report)," 31 Jan. 2003.

7. "Time Limits Phase I Summary Report (Status Report)," 7 Feb. 2003.

8. Ministry of Human Resources Information Note, "Strategies to Refine Specific Elements of Time-limited Assistance," prepared for Minister's Briefing on 18 June 2003.

9. Confidential A & P Note: Advice to Cabinet, "Impact of the Two-Year Time Limit on Income Assistance," 27 Aug. 2003.

10. Confidential Issues Note, "Advice to Minister—Time Limits UBCM," 22 Sept. 2003.

11. Confidential Issues Note, "Advice to Minister—Time Limits—Opposition Numbers," 20 Oct. 2003.

12. Confidential Issues Note, "Advice to Minister—Time Limits (Oct Update)," 17 Oct. 2003.

13. Vancouver Board of School Trustees SD No 39 Board Meeting Minutes of 17 Nov. 2003.

14. Hansard Debates, 6 Nov. 2003 (J. MacPhail).

15. Ministry of Human Resources Decision Note, "Time Limits Mitigation Strategies for Singles and Childless Couples," 3 Dec. 2003.

16. Ministry of Human Resources Information Note, "Background for Minister's Meeting with the Attorney General on the Impact of Time Limits on First Nations Reserves," 31 Dec. 2003.

17. CKNW, "Human Resources Minister Might Re-Think Upcoming Changes to Welfare Guidelines," 2 Jan. 2004.

18. E-mail, Ministry of Human Resources Legislation and Legal Services Branch to Ministry of Attorney General lawyer, 7 Jan. 2004.

19. E-mail from a Ministry of Attorney General lawyer, 13 Jan. 2004.

20. Ministry of Human Resources Memorandum to Ministry of Attorney General RE: *Amendments to the Employment and Assistance Act*, 15 Jan. 2004.

21. One-page document titled "BCEA Clients by Time Limit Status—December, 2003."

22. "Time Limits Management Strategy," internal document attached to e-mail dated 30 Jan. 2003, which states the Strategy document "was just finalized yesterday."

23. "Time Limits Management Strategy," internal document attached to e-mails sent 4 Feb. 2004.

24. "The Two-year Time Limit," message posted 11 Jan. 2004 by Moe: moe@kootenay-cuts.com.

25. Ministry of Human Resources Information Note, "Differences between BC Employment and Assistance and BC Benefits," 12 Feb. 2004.

26. BC Office of the Premier and Ministry of Social Development news release, "Common Sense Changes Encourage Work, Protect Vulnerable Families," 11 June

2012, at: www2.news.gov.bc.ca/news_releases_2009-2013/2012PREM0079-000835.htm. Accessed 8 Oct. 2013.

27. Seth Klein, in "New BC Welfare Rules: Some Positive Steps Forward (and a Couple of Steps Back)," BC Canadian Centre for Policy Alternatives' Policy Note, 12 June 2012, at: www.policynote.ca/new-bc-welfare-rules-some-positive-steps-forward-and-couple-steps-back/. Accessed 8 Oct. 2013.

28. Raise the Rates, "Welfare Changes Help and Hurt BC's Most Vulnerable," 11 June 2012, at: http://raisetherates.org/2012/06/11/welfare-changes-help-and-hurt-bcs-most-vulnerable/#more-71. Accessed 8 Oct. 2013.

29. *Victoria Times-Colonist*, "Welfare Changes Still Fall Short," 13 June 2012, at: www.canada.com/story.html?id=051199a9-88fc-4238-8f0f-93c07607c397. Accessed 8 Oct. 2013.

30. Canadian Press, "BC Welfare Changes Draw Lukewarm Support," 11 June 2012, at: www.cbc.ca/news/canada/british-columbia/b-c-welfare-changes-draw-lukewarm-support-1.1219605. Accessed 8 Oct. 2013.

Chapter **10**

Policy-Making and Indigenous Peoples in Canada

---• **In this chapter you will learn about:** •---

- some of the factors that affect social policy in Indigenous communities;
- the continuing effects of colonization and the importance of anti-colonial and Indigenous approaches to policy and practice;
- the value of collaborative policy-making in an Indigenous context and some experiences in attempting to use this approach in child welfare;
- other strategies that may be used to realize policy objectives associated with equity and social justice.

Introduction

Indigenous people in Canada have been largely subject to policies done *to* rather than *with* them. The continuing history of colonization demands a different approach, and more recently there has been increased attention to policies and programs that are infused with Indigenous knowledge and traditions. Policy development in Indigenous communities draws on other forms of knowledge and experiences as well, but a key underlying principle is the right of Indigenous people to exercise significant control over the process. The process is complex in that creating new policies often requires negotiating new arrangements with federal and provincial policy structures. Thus, more inclusive approaches to policy development, consistent with the main theme of this book, are of special importance. Prior to exploring Indigenous approaches to policy-making and selected examples of collaborative efforts, we identify some of the important factors to be considered in developing these social policies.

Background

Definitions and Diversity

The use of terms to describe the Indigenous population of Canada is somewhat contested. The term "Indian" is used in the Indian Act but has largely been replaced by the term "First Nations" to refer both to those who have "status" under the Indian Act and those who do not. The term "Aboriginal" has largely replaced the term "Native" and is used in Canada to include three broad groups identified in the Constitution: First Nations, Métis, and Inuit. It has become more common recently to use the term "Indigenous," which is commonly used in the international context. This term is referenced in the United Nations Declaration on the Rights of Indigenous Peoples to recognize the sovereignty characteristics that distinguish Indigenous people from other racial or ethnic minority groups, a factor that imposes particular obligations on government. In addition, it connotes the shared oppression caused by colonization. The term "Aboriginal" remains widely used in Canada, and we use "Indigenous" and "Aboriginal" interchangeably in this chapter and throughout the book. However, we note that some (e.g., Alfred and Corntassel, 2005) object to "Aboriginal" because it identifies people solely by their political-legal relationship to the state rather than by cultural or social ties to their community. Another concern is that "Aboriginal" and "Indigenous" are collective terms that do not reflect the diversity among Indigenous peoples. As Sinclair and Hart (2009) note, more selective tribal affiliations such as Cree, Ojibway, and Huron are sometimes used, and self-identifying terms such as Mi'kmaq, Anishinaabe, and Gitksan are increasingly common. Although diversity in Indigenous nations is recognized, it is also argued that a number of common aspects of knowledge and practices across Indigenous populations permit recognition of an Aboriginal or Indigenous world view that is distinctly different from that common to dominant Eurocentric society in Canada (Baikie, 2009; Saulis, 2012).

Diversity among Indigenous peoples also encompasses different types of identification with traditional culture. For example, McKenzie and Morrissette (2003) identify three main groups: traditional, a combination of traditional and mainstream (i.e., non-traditional), and non-traditional, with subtypes within each group. Cultural identity also varies across communities in that one Indigenous community may reflect a stronger identification with traditional Indigenous culture than another.

Selected demographic information in the 2011 National Household Survey (Statistics Canada, 2013b) is noted below:

- Approximately 1.4 million Canadians (4.3 per cent of the population) identified as Aboriginal in 2011.
- About 61 per cent of all Aboriginal people were First Nations, of which 75 per cent were registered Indians.
- Nearly half of all First Nations people with registered status lived on reserves.

- Approximately 452,000 Aboriginal people identified as Métis (1.4 per cent of the population of Canada).
- The number of people identifying as Inuit in 2011 was 59,445.
- Between 2006 and 2011 the Aboriginal population increased by 20.1 per cent compared to 5.2 per cent for the non-Aboriginal population.
- Aboriginal people made up the majority of the population in Nunavut and the Northwest Territories in 2011.
- Aboriginal children aged 14 and under made up 28 per cent of the total Aboriginal population whereas non-Aboriginal children of the same age range made up 16.5 per cent of the non-Aboriginal population.
- About one-third of Aboriginal children aged 14 and under lived in lone-parent families, almost double the rate for non-Aboriginal children in the same age range.

Colonialism and Indigenous Inequality

Poverty rates are normally estimated from census information or the Survey of Labour and Income Dynamics (SLID). However, SLID excludes persons living on reserves so is not a good source in estimating Indigenous poverty for all First Nations people. In addition, changes to data collection procedures for the 2011 census affects the reliability of this information for Indigenous people. Macdonald and Wilson (2013), drawing on data from the 2006 census, found that in 2006 almost 60 per cent of First Nations parents in low-income households (including those on and off reserve) did not have a high school education. Parents in Métis, Inuit, and non-status First Nations low-income households were only slightly better, at 50 per cent; the comparative percentage in non-Indigenous low-income households was 25 per cent.

On average, Indigenous children and families experience much higher rates of poverty than non-Indigenous children and families, and First Nations children are particularly vulnerable. Although there have been modest changes in the rate of poverty since 2006, the rate of child poverty in Canada using the After-Tax Low-Income Measure (AT-LIM) was 17 per cent in 2006, while the average rate for all Indigenous children was 40 per cent. The rate among Métis, Inuit, and non-status First Nations children was 27 per cent, whereas 50 per cent of all status or registered First Nations children lived below the poverty line (Macdonald and Wilson, 2013: 6). Among status First Nations children in Manitoba and Saskatchewan the rates were 62 per cent and 64 per cent, respectively. There are also health-related disparities in that the rate of disabilities among First Nations children was almost double the rate for all Canadian children, diabetes among First Nations people was at least three times the national average, and one-third of First Nations households with children were overcrowded (Assembly of First Nations, 2008). The suicide rate among First Nations youth is five to seven times higher than it is for non-Indigenous youth (Public Health Agency of Canada, 2006).

These structural factors are linked directly to the over-representation of Indigenous children in the child welfare system, because Indigenous children are more likely to be reported and admitted to care for reasons related to neglect than are non-Indigenous children (Sinha et al., 2011). The **disparity rate** for Indigenous children in care (i.e., the likelihood of an Indigenous child being admitted to care when compared with a non-Indigenous child) is extremely high, although it varies somewhat across provinces and territories. Examples of this rate in 2008 were BC at 12.5 and Saskatchewan at 12.3 (Tilbury and Thoburn, 2011). This means that in 2008 an Indigenous child in BC or Saskatchewan was more than 12 times as likely as a non-Indigenous child to be admitted to care in the child welfare system. By 2011, Manitoba's disparity rate had increased to a staggering 19.5 and approximately 85 per cent of children in care in Manitoba were Indigenous (McKenzie, 2012). Once again, First Nations children may fare worse than others. A complicating factor that affects many Indigenous families, but particularly those living in remote communities, is the lack of equitable, accessible, and culturally appropriate services. For example, prior to recent changes in the funding model for on-reserve First Nations agencies, these agencies received much lower rates of funding than agencies providing equivalent services off reserve (Auditor General of Canada, 2008).

Over-representation exists in other systems as well. Incarceration rates for Indigenous people are substantially higher than for non-Indigenous people (Hansen, Booker, and Charlton, 2014). For example, in 2010–11, 27 per cent of all adults in provincial and territorial custody were Indigenous and 20 per cent of all adults in federal custody were Indigenous; this rate was seven to eight times the rate for non-Indigenous adults (Dauvergne, 2012). Violence against women is also higher for Indigenous women. Data from a 2009 study indicate that 13 per cent of all Indigenous women had been violently victimized and were three times more likely than non-Indigenous women to report being a victim of a violent crime (Brennan, 2011).

These circumstances are important to recognize; however, they do not tell the whole story. First, as noted above, these data vary a great deal among groups and communities. Second, descriptive information on social conditions is inadequate without a discussion of causality. As well, such information neglects the strengths and resiliency of Indigenous people, and these are essential to any discussion of policy-making in the Aboriginal context.

The impact of **colonialism** on lower measures of well-being for Indigenous people is well documented (e.g., Adams, 1999; Frideres and Gadacz, 2012; RCAP, 1996), but the nature and scope of these effects are important to highlight. At a fundamental level colonialism is the domination and control by one group of people over another group. However, the methods used to assert control vary, and a distinction has been made between structural and cultural colonialism (Kellough, 1980). **Structural colonialism** involves the appropriation of land and the removal of traditional institutions and decision-making authority from Indigenous people. Treaties, the Indian Act, land taken from both First Nations and Métis people, and the replacement of traditional decision-making structures with governance models from the dominant society are examples of these processes. **Cultural colonialism** involves the devaluation of traditional culture, including the marginalization by the dominant society of Indigenous ways of helping. Instruments of cultural colonization include the residential schools and mainstream health and child welfare services. These institutions removed children from their families, communities, and culture, and they also redefined the world views, beliefs, and values of Indigenous people in ways that forced many to accept their subordinate role in relation to the colonizers. Cultural colonialism is a function of institutional practices that can be described as a form of institutional racism intended to assimilate Indigenous people. Although these processes have been resisted by many Indigenous people, they have also contributed to dependency among many because of the dual loss of economic self-sufficiency and traditional socio-cultural expressions of identity and well-being.

Hart (2009a, 2010) stresses that colonialism is a continuing attribute of the relationship between Indigenous and non-Indigenous peoples in Canada, and its continuing presence is a function of several factors. First, there are the intergenerational effects of experiences related to institutions such as residential schools and the child welfare system, which affected well-being, including the parenting capacity of those exposed to these systems. Second, there are the continuing struggles to establish some level of autonomy through institutions and governance models that can combat racism and provide culturally appropriate responses for Indigenous people. Finally, there are effects of the subordination of Indigenous identity, experiences, knowledge, and ways of knowing that are just beginning to be addressed.

The effects of residential schools have been widely documented, but the Truth and Reconciliation Commission, which wrapped up four years of hearings in April 2014, will provide additional information on this sordid legacy, its continuing effects, and pathways to healing and reconciliation when it releases its final report in 2015.

In one small Manitoba study in 1994, 43 former residents of residential schools were interviewed (Manitoba Joint Committee on Residential Schools, 1994). Respondents related stories of excessive discipline and abuse, ridicule, and demeaning punishment. Almost half the respondents related experiences of sexual abuse. Three additional traumas were identified as having lasting effects on adult adjustment and parenting. One was the lack of love in most relationships with caregivers and teachers. Second was the denial of cultural expression, such as language, and the ridicule heaped on Aboriginal traditions, including spiritual beliefs. Third was the loss of a family experience, including the opportunity for positive bonding with parents; this was identified as having a continuing impact on adjustment and intergenerational parenting practices. As described by one respondent: "[I]t robbed me of my family life because I don't think I learned how to love—my whole childhood was stolen from me." For many, the loss of a family experience was the most traumatic experience of the schools.

While the residential school system was an obvious instrument of colonialism, others (see Fournier and Crey, 1997; Johnston, 1983; McKenzie and Hudson, 1985) have demonstrated how the child welfare system, beginning with the "sixties scoop" that placed thousands of disadvantaged and "neglected" Indigenous children in non-Aboriginal families, acted in similar ways by separating Aboriginal children from their families, communities, and culture.

Although the impact of the residential school system and conventional child welfare practices highlighted here are essential aspects of understanding Aboriginal reality, not all problems can be fully explained by these developments. Other structural causes, such as systemic racism, poverty, and inadequate opportunities, are also important to recognize.

Indigenous Knowledge, Anti-Colonialism, Resistance, and Resilience

Problem analysis and needs assessment, as outlined in Chapter 4, is an essential step in the policy-making process, yet it needs to be matched with an understanding of strengths, resistance, and resilience.

Battiste and Henderson (2000: 35–8) discuss both the validity and complexity involved in defining **Indigenous knowledge**. They note that Indigenous knowledge may be handed down by Elders, that it may include symbols, stories, and ceremonies, but that it is also being constantly revised by each generation. These authors suggest that Indigenous knowledge is a manifestation of human knowledge, heritage, and consciousness as well as an awareness of ecological order. It includes the web of relationships between humans, animals, plants, natural forces, spirits, and land forms in a particular locality. Thus it is part of the lived reality of individuals and communities. Because it is localized and relational in nature, these authors note that it resists Eurocentric efforts at categorization as universal laws. Indigenous people, like people from other cultures with different traditions, make their own decisions about how different forms of knowledge will be used in shaping their world view.

Hart (2009a) discusses how colonization affects Indigenous knowledge and methodology through exclusion, marginalization, or misrepresentation. Even in the human services where Indigenous concepts and practices are becoming more important, they are often viewed as secondary to those from the dominant society. He notes that although Indigenous forms of helping, such as the medicine wheel and healing circle, can lead to **decolonization** and *mino-pimátisiwin* (the good life), there are additional elements to be considered in adopting an **anti-colonial approach**. Anti-colonialism, he argues, recognizes the importance of continuing to struggle against the existing ideology and practice of colonialism. It involves resistance to colonial institutional frameworks at the political, social, and cultural levels; strategies include efforts to recover traditional Indigenous knowledge and cultural revitalization for social transformation, self-determination, and the promotion of the rights of Indigenous peoples.

Indigenous resistance to the assimilative policies of the dominant society has taken a number of forms. First, Indigenous cultural traditions, values, and practices have not only survived but have been more widely adopted. Of particular importance is the assertion of distinct Indigenous world views and identities (Absolon, 2009; Battiste and Henderson, 2000). Second, promotion of the right to self-determination has led to increased jurisdictional control over services to Indigenous people, and in several regions where early treaties had not been signed, new treaty settlements that incorporate new rights have been negotiated. As of January 2014 more than 25 modern treaties had been signed covering areas in the James Bay area, parts of BC and Labrador, and the three territories (Jai, 2014). Although newer treaty settlements pay somewhat more attention to land rights, there are limitations. For example, the Supreme Court of Canada has ruled that while the Tsilhqot'in Nation in BC had Aboriginal title with the right to use and control its land, government could continue to use the land for economic development purposes with the consent of the First Nation or, failing consent, if it could demonstrate a project had compelling and substantial public interest (Hansen and Bear Robe, 2014).

There are somewhat contradictory perspectives on the treaties. On one hand, a narrow contractual interpretation suggests that the treaties have been, and continue to be, instruments of colonization by dispossessing Indigenous people of their land and way of life (Little Bear, 2004; Venne, 2001). Even if this is the case, others, such as Taiaiake Alfred (2005) and Henderson (2002), suggest the treaties can be seen as covenants that can potentially be used to promote understanding of the collective and inherent rights of Indigenous peoples that were intended in these agreements. Thus, they provide a basis for building trust and respect for a new relationship between Indigenous and non-Indigenous peoples. This perspective evokes the adage that "We are all Treaty people" with reciprocal responsibilities to learn about implications flowing from the treaties and to act on this knowledge. Although Métis and non-status First Nations people had been excluded from provisions outlined in treaties and the Indian Act, the 2013 rulings by the Federal Court and the Federal Court of Appeal in *Daniels v. Canada*, which affirmed Métis people as "Indians" under the Indian Act, may lead to changes in the future (Rennie, 2014). Third, challenges to existing policies and practices have involved advocacy, protests, and legal challenges where more collaborative approaches to reconciliation have failed. Legal challenges have taken the form of Charter challenges, claims of discrimination under the Human Rights Act, and representations in the international arena drawing on support from the United Nations Declaration on the Rights of Indigenous Peoples (2008), among other sources. Finally, there are continuing efforts to legitimize Indigenous forms of knowledge, research methodologies, and curriculum content within the public and post-secondary education systems.

There have also been significant changes in services in relation to practice and policy in the past three decades. New agencies have been established to provide a variety of services, often using traditional frameworks such as the **medicine wheel** or circle as methods of organizing interventions. For example, Sterling-Collins (2009) describes the use of the medicine wheel framework in organizing holistic services for her autistic child. **Healing** is a key element in an Indigenous framework and this is closely linked to spirituality, beginning with the individual and building outward to include family, community, and society (Saulis, 2012; Connors and Maidman, 2001). Within an Aboriginal world view, healing and wellness are based on a commitment to **holism**, which can be defined as achieving harmony and balance among the physical, mental, spiritual, and emotional components of one's being. Holism is also connected to the development of a positive Aboriginal identity, and the focus on identity and its relationship to cultural expression has recently received increased attention in the literature on social work practice (Baskin, 2009; Hansen, Booker, and Charlton, 2013; Hart, 2002; McKenzie and Morrissette, 2003).

Without minimizing the important differences in Indigenous and non-Indigenous data on social well-being earlier noted, there have been some increases in educational outcomes. For example, between 1996 and 2006, the number of Indigenous adults living in urban areas who have earned high school diplomas increased by 9 per cent, to 59.9 per cent, and the number with university degrees increased from 4.2 per cent to 6.8 per cent. During this same period the median income for urban Aboriginal people increased by 52 per cent and the unemployment rate dropped from 24.2 per cent to 14 per cent (Rabson, 2009: A9). Despite these gains a significant income gap between Indigenous and non-Indigenous people with similar levels of education remained, with the exception of those with a bachelor's degree, where the gap had almost closed by 2006 (Wilson and Macdonald, 2010).

More recent labour force data from the Centre for the Study of Living Standards (2012) is of concern. The 2008 recession had a significant effect on the economy and unemployment rates for all Canadians. Although economic output as measured by gross domestic product had recovered by the end of 2011, the unemployment rate remained higher than the pre-recessionary rate. More significantly, the rate of unemployment for Indigenous Canadians, excluding reserves where data were unavailable, was much worse than for non-Indigenous Canadians (12.9 per cent vs 7.3 per cent in 2011).

Local governance in the human services has transformed policy-making in many Aboriginal communities, although as noted later, a number of problems remain. In First Nations, local control of many health and education services are common, and the majority of these communities now have locally controlled child and family service agencies providing child welfare services under agreements that require federal funding and compliance with provincial legislation and standards. For example, between 1990 and 2008, the number of First Nations child and family service agencies grew from 34 to 108, and these agencies provided at least partial child welfare services to 442 of the 606 reserve communities in Canada funded by Indian and Northern Affairs Canada (INAC, now called Aboriginal Affairs and Northern Development Canada) in 2008 (Auditor General of Canada, 2008). Aboriginal child and family service agencies have been developed in urban areas such as Toronto, Vancouver, and Winnipeg to provide early childhood education, interventions related to family violence, and a variety of youth and family services. In some urban centres Aboriginal schools that incorporate more extensive treatment of culturally informed curricula have been established, and there are several examples of successful approaches to adult education (Silver, 2013).

Some of the social services that have developed have been quite innovative. On the Kahnawake First Nation near Montreal, a highly successful model of community social services based on the principles of integration and wrap-around services has been developed. An effective model of community-controlled child welfare services has been established by the Cowichan tribes in BC (Brown, Haddock, and Kovach, 2002), and a wide range of community-based prevention services were developed by West Region Child and Family Services in Manitoba using the medicine wheel as an organizing framework. In addition, a well-established range of early services has been established on the Blood First Nation in southern Alberta.   *more info?*

There have also been important developments at the provincial level. Indigenous control of service delivery has been extended to Aboriginal people living off reserve in several provinces, including Manitoba, Alberta, and BC, and in Saskatchewan the Federation of Saskatchewan Indian Nations has developed its own child welfare legislation. Although this legislation does not have legal authority, it is frequently referenced as guidance in decisions affecting First Nations child welfare in Saskatchewan.

Indigenous Approaches to Policy-Making

It is difficult to define a distinct Indigenous approach to policy-making because applied policy-making in Indigenous communities now takes place in a colonized context where structures and processes have been defined from a dominant Eurocentric perspective, and many of these processes have been adopted within existing Indigenous social and political structures. Important to this discussion is recognition of the existence of well-functioning Indigenous societies prior to and during the early contact with Europeans. These systems were based on communal values, such as sharing and respect, recognition of the important role of the Creator and of spirituality, a symbiotic relationship with all living things and the environment, and the important roles ascribed to Elders and medicine people (Morrissette, 2006). Colonialism, as has been described, was designed to replace these with dominant society institutions and values; in so doing it contributed to losses related to economic self-sufficiency and well-being. These losses for many include **internalized oppression**, whereby people not only accept the belief that the social group to which they belong is inferior but also adopt behaviours that are self-destructive and disempowering. Decolonization and an anti-colonial approach is about gaining control over the institutions affecting Indigenous well-being and integrating traditional knowledge, values, and practices within these institutions to establish a positive Indigenous identity and sense of empowerment. It is important to emphasize that self-determination, whether in an urban or rural context, requires work in partnership with other organizations with broad mandates to address common issues, such as homelessness, mental health, poverty reduction, and crime prevention. Indeed, self-determination paves the way for more equal forms of collaboration.

In his analysis of conventional forms of ideological domination in policy-making, Morrissette (2006) proposes certain characteristics of an ideal Indigenous framework for conceptualizing social policy responses. He uses concepts introduced in Chapter 1, such as human nature, values, understanding of society, role of the state, principles of social justice, and response to social problems as an organizing framework. The ideological framework he proposes relies on the relational aspects of traditional values and practices, and some of the key concepts are summarized in Box 10.1. Although the framework is not a specific model for Indigenous policy analysis, it outlines some ideological guidelines that can help in completing this task. Morrissette also qualifies his work by noting these as tentative proposals, subject to further revision.

Morrissette (2006) suggests that this framework shares a number of characteristics with socialism, but that there are important variations. For example, the emphasis on traditional spirituality being essential to an Indigenous perspective, and to the extended symbiotic relationships with the Creator and with all living things in the natural and spirit world, is markedly different from some concepts of socialism, especially the state socialism ascribed to Marx.

Saulis (2012) adopts holism as a core component to an Indigenous world view and as a basis for policy-making. He begins with a medicine wheel framework to illustrate the need for balance among the four directions. These directions, which have implications for well-being and healing, are the physical, the mental (intellectual), the emotional, and the spiritual. The principle of holism also applies to policy and practice in that these domains are interconnected—they must be integrated to be effective. Saulis outlines seven teachings based on knowledge from Elders that must inform social policies. Consistent with some of the principles earlier noted, these teachings reference respect for Creation, the need for harmony and balance, collective responsibilities for community well-being, and the importance of traditional medicines and ceremonies. He proposes a social policy medicine wheel recognizes the different contributions of the mental, spiritual, emotional, and physical dimensions. For example, the mental dimension recognizes the cognitive aspects in social policy development, including the importance of statistical information on need, which must be connected to a holistic world view. On the other hand, the emotional dimension emphasizes the importance of identity and self-concept and the use of Indigenous knowledge in validating an Indigenous world view.

A framework for intersectionality-based policy analysis was briefly introduced in Chapter 4, and this framework pays special attention to the intersecting oppressions often associated with social location (e.g., gender, race, ethnicity, age, sexual orientation) and the inequalities in society that contribute to different policy outcomes for affected groups (Hankivsky et al., 2012). In this framework, two general types of questions guide policy analysis where attention to equity issues is paramount. The first type of question is similar to those identified in the Integrated Model for Policy Analysis in Chapter 4 in that these questions ask about how interpretations of the problem may differ among groups and how these groups may be differentially affected by the problem. The second type focuses on solutions. For example:

Box 10.1 | An Indigenous Ideological Framework for Social Policy Analysis

1. Human Nature

- Human nature is perceived as essentially good, with social and spiritual elements.
- *Mino-pimátisiwin* (the good life) is achieved by recognizing all capacities in individuals.

2. View of Society

- Emphasis is on living in harmony with people and all living and non-living things.
- This view recognizes the role of the Creator; the earth and humans are inextricably connected.
- Society must reflect balance and harmony between the earth and human nature.

3. Fundamental Values

- Basic values are collective in nature, including responsibilities to others and community based on need.
- Differences in individuals are respected as different "gifts" that contribute to collective well-being.
- Individualism is circumscribed by responsibilities to others.
- Spiritual responsibilities are important.
- Commitment to equality is based on equal outcomes and notions of reciprocity, balance, and harmony.
- Freedom means freedom from exploitation.

4. Role of the State

- The responsibility of the state is to exercise the collective will of people, so increased reliance is placed on participatory democracy and collaborative approaches.
- This view rejects the hierarchical model of the conventional system, which has currently been adopted in many Indigenous communities.
- The responsibility of the state is to restore harmony and balance among all things.

5. Economic Development

- Development is based on a strong commitment to self-sufficiency and ecological sustainability.
- Economic development is a means to social development, so collective responsibility and community well-being are stressed.
- Collective ownership is supported.

6. Principles of Social Justice

- There is a need to restore balance and harmony (solidarity) using holism as the guiding principle.

Continued ▶

- Responses should be based on need, including necessities of life and creative expression of gifts.
- Sharing and collective responsibility are important.

7. View of Social Problems

- Social problems result from two general causes: the structural effects of colonialism, racism, and oppression; and individuals who are out of balance with obligations to the Creator, others, and the community.

8. Social Policy Responses

- Social policies must be redistributive as well as integrative (i.e., restore balance and harmony).
- Institutional structures and responses must be harnessed to decolonize the current relationship between the colonizers and colonized (use of cultural traditions and healing is important to these processes).
- Well-being must be supported through responses to individual and collective need.

Source: Adapted from Morrissette (2006) with permission.

- What inequities actually exist in relation to the problem?
- What are feasible short-, medium-, and long-term solutions?
- How will proposed policy responses reduce inequalities?

These questions, with some adaptations, have been used in analyzing policies affecting Indigenous peoples. For example, Clark (2012), in her analysis of violence in the lives of Indigenous girls, added questions to give special attention to colonial violence, family and community history, and resistance to colonial constructions of the problem.

Indigenous research and evaluation for policy-making will make use of a variety of methods, including quantitative and qualitative methods. However, Indigenous methods rooted in Indigenous world views and paradigms are equally valuable (Absolon, 2008). There has been a dramatic growth in applied research using Indigenous research methods, which may also be combined with other research paradigms. For example, Lavalleé (2007) provides an example of integrating qualitative methods with sharing circles and Anishinaabe symbol-based reflection in cultural recreation programming. Although it is not the purpose of this chapter to explore research methodologies in depth, Hart (2009b) and Chilisa (2012) outline some helpful guidelines in pursuing an Indigenous research paradigm.

In any evaluation and research study conducted with Indigenous people it is important to incorporate principles laid out by the Assembly of First Nations (First Nations

Centre, 2007). These are Indigenous ownership, control, access, and possession (OCAP). If these are observed in planning and conducting studies, they help to counter past patterns of appropriating information on Indigenous people and communities without regard to its benefits for these communities, and without the ability of these communities to control the use of this information.

Case Studies in Collaborative Policy-Making

Suggested guidelines for policy-making identified in the previous section are helpful to consider. However, given our focus on inclusive policy-making and the fact that policy-making in an Indigenous context often occurs within structures and processes embedded in the dominant society, this section explores some examples where collaborative approaches have been used. The challenges faced in establishing collaborative approaches have some similarity to those faced by all citizens in that policy-making structures are often quite centralized; however, in an Indigenous context these may also reflect the colonized reality of mainstream dominance and control. Even when participating parties engaged in policy development wish to transform this relationship it is difficult, although efforts can and must be made in building social capital and community capacity from an Indigenous perspective.

The three examples discussed below involve the application of community governance to a child welfare agency, an attempt to implement shared decision-making at the federal level, and the development of a policy community at the provincial level.

Community Governance

Community-based services and community governance models are common to many Indigenous communities as they are consistent with goals associated with self-determination. As discussed in Chapter 6, we interpret community governance broadly in ways that can apply to specific agencies and organizations as well as geographic communities. In this context successful models are those that incorporate local governance structures, build respectful relationships with service users and relevant constituencies in the community, and develop responsive services that make a difference to people's lives. Thus, community governance can incorporate inclusive policy-making in either a rural or urban context. Box 10.2 describes an example of the use of the value criteria model of policy-making to establish a successful model of community governance.

Shared Decision-Making

Shared decision-making was introduced in Chapter 6 as a collaborative approach to policy-making. The following example draws on experiences from the *Joint National Policy Review* (McDonald, Ladd, et al., 2000), an initiative at the federal level affecting the delivery of child and family services on reserves. Two critical issues in Indigenous

Case Study ①

Box 10.2 | Community Governance at an Agency Level

The development of West Region Child and Family Services in Manitoba illustrates how the value criteria model can be used to develop agency policies under a community governance model. Growing awareness of the child welfare system's colonizing effects in First Nations communities in the late 1970s and early 1980s led to a tripartite agreement between Manitoba First Nations, the government of Manitoba, and the government of Canada to transfer administrative control of child welfare services to tribal council authorities in the province in 1982. In 1985, West Region Child and Family Services, serving nine First Nations reserves, became a fully mandated child and family service agency. This agency paid special attention to assessing the impact of the conventional child welfare system on family and community life, an impact represented by the loss of hundreds of children from their families and communities and by the presence of powerlessness within many of these families and communities.

This led to the new agency's adoption of four key philosophical principles used as guidelines for policy development. These principles, which may be expressed as value criteria, are Aboriginal control, cultural relevancy, community-based services, and a comprehensive team-oriented approach to service delivery. These value criteria were incorporated within the medicine wheel framework to establish a service model based on four "circles of care."

- The "Staying at Home Circle of Care" focused on supporting children at home through a continuum of family support and family preservation service.

- The "Alternate Care Circle of Care" supported foster and group care programs with a special emphasis on strengthening kinship care and improving outcomes for children in care.

- The "Family Restoration and Treatment Support Circle of Care" was designed to provide counselling and support services to families where children were in care or at risk of placement.

policy-making are adequate funding and jurisdictional control, and these were directly related to the development of this policy review. Adequate funding is essential to effective policy-making in any context, but this is exacerbated in First Nations communities providing child welfare services because of historical patterns of underfunding and limited access to many of the services routinely available in more urban communities.

Jurisdictional control over human services affecting Aboriginal people reflects the aspirations of Aboriginal people to gain some measure of self-governance over the services affecting their people. Jurisdictional control can be considered from two perspectives: the political perspective, which asserts the inherent right to self-government; and the service perspective, which focuses on decolonization through an emphasis on

- The "Supporting Community Circle of Care" included community-based prevention programs and support to local child and family service committees. In this Circle of Care, authority for planning prevention programs was delegated to community-based staff who worked with local child and family services committees to plan and deliver programs. Thus, a service model was established with community-based staff working alongside local child and family service committees that had considerable responsibility over local services. Specialized service teams were developed and initiatives in training, recreation, and community development were established.

Cultural relevancy shaped policy development through such things as an emphasis on hiring Aboriginal staff, providing culturally relevant staff training, and incorporating the wisdom of Elders. Extensive efforts to promote community participation in policy development were made. For example, operational planning workshops were held every two years in which representatives from each community engaged with agency staff in identifying new service needs and priorities. Implementation of the agency's service vision was facilitated by a flexible funding arrangement with the federal government. This agreement allowed the agency to carry forward surpluses saved from a block grant for child maintenance (i.e., payment for out-of-home care), and to invest these resources in alternative community programs to support families and children. These efforts reduced the number of children requiring care outside their community or culture, and external evaluations demonstrated that the agency provided both high-quality services and a supportive, sustaining work environment for its staff. A cost–benefit analysis of the agency's investment in early intervention services demonstrated annual savings of $1.5 million (Loxley and Deriviere, 2005).

Source: Adapted from McKenzie and Shangreaux (2011).

Indigenous-focused practices as a counterpoint to historical patterns of colonization that were largely based on strategies of subjugation and assimilation.

The *Joint National Policy Review* was a collaborative effort between the Assembly of First Nations (AFN), represented by First Nations child and family services (CFS) agency directors, and the Department of Indian Affairs and Northern Development (DIAND or INAC). Most First Nations CFS agencies located on reserves operate on the basis of a "delegated" model where the province or territory grants agencies the authority to provide child welfare services subject to provincial or territorial legislation and standards, and funding is provided by the federal government. A funding formula, known as Directive 20-1, was initially established in 1991, and was used as the basis for funding on-reserve agencies in all provinces except Ontario. Through a 1965 agreement, on-reserve child welfare services in Ontario are funded directly by the province, which in turn receives a general grant from the federal government to cover most of these costs. Directive 20-1 had not been adjusted for inflation since 1995 and contained a number of other exclusions that contributed to a funding pattern for on-reserve agencies that was well below that provided by provinces for off-reserve child welfare services.

A shared decision-making approach to addressing concerns related to funding and culturally appropriate standards was proposed, and this led to the formation of a national Steering Committee with equal representation from the federal Indian Affairs ministry and First Nations CFS agency directors. As well, a Project Management Team and a Joint Policy Review Group, each adhering to the equal representation principle, were formed.

Policy reviews were completed and combined in a consolidated report with 17 recommendations (McDonald, Ladd, et al., 2000). These included the need to revise funding formulas to provide for a wider range of early intervention services, address inadequate elements in the service operational component of the budget, and develop culturally appropriate service standards. An action plan for implementing recommendations from the report through a continued partnership model was also outlined.

Results from this experience in shared decision-making were quite limited. The process, which used facilitators as required, initially generated goodwill and a shared understanding of issues that helped senior policy-makers in the federal department in their efforts to promote policies consistent with the aspirations of First Nations agencies. For example, submissions for the 2003–4 budget were made for increased funding for early intervention and family support services in First Nations communities. Despite minor adjustments in the funding formula for inflation, new funding for family support services was not approved, and this, along with the failure to address issues of standards and fundamental changes to the funding formula, resulted in considerable frustration on the part of those who were invested in the process. First Nations participants at the policy tables were not invited to meetings beyond the divisional level in INAC. Thus, the development of final proposals, including the presentation of these proposals to central bodies such as cabinet and Treasury Board, were handled by senior departmental staff. Although there was support for both the process and the recommendations within the Social Policy Division of INAC, this was insufficient to overcome resistance at cabinet and Treasury Board. The exclusion of First Nations participants from presentations to senior levels of government indicates the limits set on shared decision-making in this case.

After the initial failure one last effort was made to address funding issues from a more collaborative stance. In 2004 INAC provided funding for a research project to examine in more detail optional funding models for First Nations CFS agencies. The *Wen:De (We Are Coming to the Light of Day)* report was released in 2005 by the First Nations Child and Family Caring Society (FNCFCS) (Blackstock, Prakash, Loxley, and Wien, 2005). It provided further evidence of the gaps in funding between First Nations and provincial child welfare agencies. Although a number of gaps were identified, the failure to incorporate an inflationary factor in the Directive 20-1 funding formula alone accounted for a shortfall of $112 million between 1999 and 2005, a total that amounted to a loss of approximately 14 per cent of operational funding allocated to these agencies over this seven-year period.

Additional funding for inflationary adjustment, infrastructure development, and new family support programs was recommended, and the report demonstrated through cost–benefit calculations how investment in prevention and early intervention would not only improve child and family outcomes but also reduce social expenditures over time. A new funding formula was also recommended.

Shortly after the release of the *Wen:De* report, the Martin Liberal government was replaced by the Harper Conservative government in Ottawa. The new federal government ment refused to accept the recommendations from the *Wen:De* report and commissioned its own review. Although this review was completed, the federal government has never released the results.

Frustrated with the lack of government response to the funding needs documented in the *Wen:De* report, the FNCFCS and the AFN filed a complaint under the Canadian Human Rights Act in February 2007, alleging that chronic underfunding of First Nations CFS agencies amounts to discriminatory treatment of First Nations children. This story is summarized later in this chapter. As well, the Office of the Auditor General of Canada conducted its own examination and reported in 2008 that the funding formula used by INAC was inadequate to meet provincial standards and the needs of First Nations children and families.

Appearing to act somewhat independently of these activities, the federal ministry launched a piecemeal approach to funding adjustments for First Nations agencies on reserves by developing agreements on a region-by-region basis beginning in 2009. Although a number of limitations remain, these agreements have provided funding increases, including some additional money for early intervention and family support services. One is left to speculate about whether evidence from the *Joint National Policy Review* process, the *Wen:De* report, and the still secret policy review conducted by the government influenced these adjustments, or whether the Human Rights complaint and the Auditor General's report were more influential.

Creating a Policy Community at the Provincial Level

This policy-making process, initiated shortly after the NDP government was elected in Manitoba in 1999, was designed to transfer the delivery of child welfare services for Aboriginal people in Manitoba, particularly those living off reserve, to new Aboriginal authorities and agencies. This initiative is known as the Aboriginal Justice Inquiry-Child Welfare Initiative because the recommendation on which the policy was based first appeared in the *Report of the Aboriginal Justice Inquiry* released in 1991 (Hamilton and Sinclair, 1991). In Manitoba, responsibility for the delivery of First Nations child welfare services on reserves occurred in the 1980s, but services for over half of the Aboriginal population, living off reserve and including Métis people, remained in the hands of mainstream agencies. Most staff in these agencies were non-Aboriginal and the service model common to these agencies made only limited efforts to incorporate cultural considerations relevant to the large number of Aboriginal families and children who were being served. The over-representation of Aboriginal children in care, aspirations pertaining to self-determination, and the need to establish more culturally appropriate services were motivating factors for these reforms.

Although the approach to policy-making in this case includes aspects of shared decision-making, we regard the process as a policy community because both Aboriginal and government partners shared a strong commitment to a common policy outcome at the outset, that is, the transfer of jurisdiction to Aboriginal authorities. Participants worked together in developing ways to make this policy goal a reality, and although differences emerged, these were largely related to operational and implementation issues rather than to the essential purposes and intent of the new policy.

The collaborative model of policy-making involved government and three Aboriginal partners:

- the Manitoba Métis Federation (MMF);
- the Assembly of Manitoba Chiefs (AMC) representing Southern First Nations;
- Manitoba Keewatinowi Okimakanak (MKO) representing Northern First Nations.

Memorandums of Understanding (MOUs) were signed between the province and each Aboriginal stakeholder, and a Service Protocol Agreement that identified a framework and principles for the planning process was negotiated. Each stakeholder group (the two First Nations groups were defined as one stakeholder group in determining most committee memberships) had an equal number of representatives on the various policy-making structures, a decision that put government members in the minority. The structure included an Executive Committee, a Joint Management Committee, an Implementation Committee, and working groups.

The Joint Management Committee was generally responsible for the initiative and it reported to the Executive Committee, which included two provincial ministers and representatives from the three Aboriginal partners. An initial conceptual plan and detailed implementation guidelines were established.

Four different child and family service authorities were established under new legislation that entrenches the right of Aboriginal people to receive services from agencies operating under an administrative unit governed by a board approved by each respective Aboriginal political organization. As noted in Chapter 5, the four authorities are Northern First Nations, Southern First Nations, Métis, and General (serving primarily non-Aboriginal children and families). Each authority has a province-wide mandate and can provide services to families and children from its cultural group anywhere in the province. Joint intake procedures have been developed to provide emergency and short-term services in each region and to identify the Authority of Record for the child and family (i.e., the authority from which they would normally receive service based on their cultural affiliation). If an agency representing their Authority of Record exists in the area, they would normally be referred to this agency for any services required after the intake stage. There was an assumption at the beginning that members of First Nations, persons identifying as Métis, and non-Aboriginal persons would want to be served by service providers mandated by their respective authorities. For the most part this has been the case, although the General Authority still provides services to a significant number of Aboriginal children and families.

Implementation Planning

The implementation planning process proceeded reasonably well: there was a significant level of collaboration between government and Aboriginal participants, including a determination to circumvent bureaucratic imperatives that interfered with the general policy intent. For example, the Child and Family Services Authorities Act was drafted in close consultation with the Implementation Committee. This Committee developed detailed specifications of what should be in new legislation and then government personnel drafted the legislation. Draft legislation was then returned to the Committee for comments and suggestions for revision prior to debate in the legislature and final approval. For the most part a problem-solving approach based on respect and goodwill characterized this stage of the policy-making process. New legislation was passed in 2002, and implementation of the service model, including the transfer of staff, cases, and funding to new agencies, occurred between 2003 and 2005.

Despite the collaborative approach taken by government with representatives from Aboriginal stakeholder groups, opportunities for broader community input, including for front-line staff from existing agencies, were quite limited. This failure contributed to feelings of low morale that had implications for policy implementation, particularly in the early stages. Although some of these reactions are normal in any major policy change, much of this might have been avoided by more attention to staff engagement in the process. Indeed, most child welfare staff were supportive of the general policy goal even if they were concerned about implementation issues and processes. As noted in Chapter 5, the involvement of existing staff is essential in ensuring service quality and continuity in the implementation phase.

There were limitations to the implementation planning process. For example, it was largely assumed that agencies might reduce expenditures on high-cost out-of-home care and redirect savings to more community-based services focusing on early intervention and family support. How this service shift would occur without significant increases in funding was not clearly outlined at the outset. As well, no provision was made for evaluating the implementation stage in ways that might have permitted a more adaptive approach to implementation.

In spite of these limitations, the collaborative approach between government and Aboriginal groups during the policy development stage was quite successful and general agreement was achieved on a model for jurisdictional control. As well, a relatively smooth transition process for the transfer of responsibility, staff, and funding for this very complex change was established.

Early Implementation Challenges

Significant case management problems occurred in the early stage of implementation. These were a function of several factors, including inadequately trained staff, unanticipated increases in workloads, governance-related issues, and problems in co-ordination at the service delivery and policy-making levels. It soon became evident that new resources allocated for implementation were quite inadequate. As well, earlier visions of a new focus on early intervention and more culturally relevant services were overtaken by more immediate concerns about child safety, and the growth in caseloads was a particular problem within Aboriginal authorities.

During the early stage of implementation the system was placed under a microscope as a result of the discovery of the body of Phoenix Sinclair in 2006, who was killed by her parents several months earlier, not long after receiving child welfare services. An immediate government response to this crisis involved several reviews of the system, leading to the allocation of new resources and a stronger commitment to early intervention programs. The government also appointed a public inquiry, although it did not commence hearings until 2012. Its report (see Hughes, 2013) recognized a number of positive developments in policies and services since the death of Phoenix Sinclair, confirmed the value of jurisdictional control over child welfare services by Aboriginal people, and made several recommendations for further improvements to the child welfare system.

Policy Outcomes

Although it is too early to assess long-term effects of the devolution of child welfare services to Aboriginal authorities, several observations can be made. The extension of Aboriginal control over services provided to Aboriginal people living off reserve is consistent with the goal of self-determination and has resulted in important service innovations and improvements, including more culturally appropriate practices. However, devolution has not yet resulted in fewer Aboriginal children in care. In fact, there has been a significant growth in the number of children in care, particularly within Aboriginal authorities (McKenzie, 2012). Increased referrals and higher workloads have restricted the ability of Aboriginal agencies, particularly those serving First Nations, to include a full range of early intervention and family support services. Child safety issues have had to take priority, and this has made it difficult for agencies to transition from a **child protection service model** focusing on risk assessment, investigation, and placement to a **community caring model**, which incorporates enhanced family supports and a community-building approach (McKenzie and Shangreaux, 2011).

Provincial funding for family support services is based on a formula applicable to all agencies in the province, regardless of need. This may have the appearance of equity, but this is not the case. First, some of the funding intended for early intervention and family support in agencies with higher rates of referrals for child maltreatment must be redirected to respond to child safety concerns. Second, the province fails to recognize the increased need to invest in capacity development in more marginalized communities and neighbourhoods.

Additional issues involve governance and accountability, and these issues have been more pronounced in First Nations authorities. Conflicts pertaining to the role of chiefs in decision-making within First Nation authorities and agencies have been contentious, and accountability concerns pertain to different views over obligations to share information on children receiving services on reserves. Finally, the concurrent jurisdictional structure, which requires a more centralized approach to intake followed by the referral to several different agencies of families requiring continuing services, complicates service co-ordination.

Lessons Learned in Devolving Jurisdictional Control

The devolution of child welfare services to Aboriginal authorities or agencies is not unique to Manitoba. For example, BC and Alberta have decentralized services to Aboriginal agencies, and Ontario is engaged in a consultative process to further devolve service responsibilities to Aboriginal communities. Both BC and Alberta have opted for models that generally organize services on a geographic basis, unlike the concurrent jurisdiction model in Manitoba. Alberta's service model also includes significant emphasis on service integration. A review of BC's efforts to devolve services to Aboriginal agencies by the Representative for Children and Youth, Mary Ellen Turpel-Lafond, identified several limitations. Her critique, directed at both government and some of the delegated Aboriginal agencies, concluded with the following summary:

> The total spent by MCFD [Ministry of Child and Family Development] on Aboriginal governance endeavours over the past dozen years has been roughly $66 million. That is a conservative estimate, as the provincial government cannot provide a clear record of expenditures. The financial controls were initially dismal and unenforced. The policy context and administrative principles can only be termed chaotic and haphazard, and are prone to undue political influence and lobbying by consultants and others with the ability to convince government to become a funder of programs with questionable policy basis or outcomes. To be blunt, a significant amount of money has gone to people who provide no program or service to directly benefit children. (Representative for Children and Youth, 2013: 4)

Turpel-Lafond noted the lost opportunities associated with these costs: needed development of additional services was sacrificed, and budgets for front-line services elsewhere in the system had experienced budget cuts. Although she was pointed in her criticism, she also drew attention to a number of successful delegated agencies that demonstrated the capacity of communities to care for their own children. What is needed, the report suggested, is a clear plan developed collaboratively between government and agencies that clearly indicates the support to be provided by government, identifies service goals, and outlines accountability mechanisms. She also urged a government-wide strategy to close the gap between Indigenous and non-Indigenous children and youth, especially around education and health.

Governance and accountability remain contentious issues in delegating jurisdictional control. Although MacDonald and Levasseur (2014) focus on the Aboriginal Justice Inquiry–Child Welfare Initiative in Manitoba, their observations have broader implications. While recognizing the value of the collaborative processes that led to the devolution of child welfare services in Manitoba, they argue that government accountability mechanisms related to funding and service standards in the implementation stages have largely reverted to a more centralized "command-and-control" model. At the same time, some chiefs and local agencies have resisted forms of centralized record-keeping and information-sharing that might be required for planning, outcome assessment, and service co-ordination across agency boundaries. MacDonald and Levasseur suggest that more attention to collaborative governance at the implementation stage is required. This requires a more comprehensive approach to accountability where government and Indigenous organizations are mutually accountable to each other, where the importance of community and service user accountability is recognized, and where negotiated agreements identify respective responsibilities. In fact, this requirement applies to all authorities created under the Manitoba initiative in that certain responsibilities for policy-making were delegated to authorities and others were to be shared between government and authorities.

Nonetheless, following the policy change the Manitoba government largely reverted to a more centralized governance model. For example, retroactive cutbacks in funding were announced in 2014 without any consultation with authorities. A new, more collaborative governance model would need to give special attention to increased government transparency for such things as funding relative to demonstrated needs, as well as organizational accountability for expenditures, service quality, and outcomes. In the absence of a more equitable partnership arrangement to address ongoing governance issues, devolution may fail to realize its full potential.

When Collaboration Fails

Various forms of advocacy were identified in Chapter 7, and Indigenous advocacy for policy changes has taken a variety of forms. We earlier highlighted Idle No More as a social movement, and protests and demonstrations have been used at times as strategies in trying to pressure government on important policy issues. Briefs and presentations to international bodies on human rights violations also draw attention to disparities in Indigenous well-being. Legal actions intended to change current policies have also been used. In this regard, the efforts made by the Congress of Aboriginal Peoples in *Daniels v. Canada* achieved recognition of the rights of Métis people under the Constitution Act. The case discussed below, briefly noted earlier in this chapter, involves a complaint of alleged discrimination under the Canadian Human Rights Act.

Human Rights Complaint against the Government of Canada

When efforts to achieve funding equity for First Nations CFS agencies on reserves through the *Joint National Policy Review* largely collapsed in 2006, the FNCFCS and AFN filed a human rights complaint against the government of Canada in February 2007. This complaint alleged racial discrimination against First Nations children on reserves because funding for child welfare services provided on reserves was lower than that provided for equivalent off-reserve services. Leadership on this case has been provided by Cindy Blackstock, the Executive Director of FNCFCS and an Associate Professor at the University of Alberta (see Blackstock, 2010, for details leading up to the complaint).

After determining there was sufficient evidence for a hearing, the Canadian Human Rights Commission referred the matter to the Human Rights Tribunal for a hearing. In direct response to the referral of the complaint to the Human Rights Tribunal, the federal government appointed a new chair to the Tribunal who introduced procedural changes designed to derail the process. In December 2009 the government also introduced a motion to dismiss the case, arguing that the Commission had no jurisdiction to hear it.

In June 2010, the new Tribunal chair began hearing the case but the process soon stalled. The acting head of the Canadian Human Rights Commission also publicly criticized the Tribunal for its unprecedented delay tactics. Faced with the Tribunal's lack of action, the FNCFCS applied to the Federal Court of Canada to force the Tribunal to hold hearings. Less than one month later, the chair of the Tribunal dismissed the case, ruling that federal funding for on-reserve children could not be compared with provincial funding for off-reserve services.

In April 2011, the Canadian Human Rights Commission applied to the Federal Court of Canada for a judicial review of the Tribunal's decision. In April 2012 the Federal Court overturned the decision of the Tribunal and ordered a full hearing on the merits of the case under a new panel. In its ruling the Court also noted that Canadian laws, including the Canadian Human Rights Act, should reflect the principles of international human rights instruments such as the Convention on the Rights of the Child and the Declaration on the Rights of Indigenous Peoples.

On 25 February 2013 the Canadian Human Rights Tribunal began hearing evidence on the case. Access to Information requests made by the FNCFCS revealed that the federal government had spent over $3 million in its efforts to stall and derail a proper hearing and was withholding key documents from the parties to the hearing. The new Tribunal panel, which ordered the records to be provided by August 2013, was critical of the government failure to locate and provide the documents. Final arguments on the case concluded in October 2014, and a ruling is expected in 2015 (see www.fncaringsociety.com and www.fnwitness.ca for details and updates on the case).

The case demonstrates the extraordinary efforts made by the federal government to deny due process on a fundamental social justice issue. The obvious question is why? Is it concerned about potential financial costs for child welfare, and possibly other services on reserves, if it loses? Or is it more concerned about its national and international image if the ruling supports the claim of discrimination? Or is this one more attempt on the part of government to deny the unique status of Canada's Aboriginal peoples and the related need to adequately support more culturally responsive services in their own communities that promote equality and self-determination?

This particular case also illustrates the long delays that can occur in hearing human rights complaints and the need for perseverance and support in pursuing such complaints. Although the federal response in providing enhanced funding for child welfare services on reserves following the initial complaint remains flawed, many view the human rights complaint as an influential factor in the government's decision to provide new funding under this program. Whatever the outcome, the case has exposed the vulnerability of Indigenous children in communities across Canada, and it has raised the level of consciousness about this and other service inequities on reserves, including those related to disability services and education. Based on the precedent set by the FNCFCS, a human rights complaint of unequal disability services on reserves has been launched by Kevin Taylor, an individual with cerebral palsy. The Canadian Human Rights Commission has also referred this matter to the Human Rights Tribunal for a public hearing (Welch, 2014). If this case is successful, it could obligate the federal government to fund some of the services on reserves that are already provided to people with disabilities in other communities, including vocational training, speech therapy, respite services, and independent living options.

Summary and Conclusion

This chapter has explored the circumstances affecting Indigenous peoples in Canada, the importance of recognizing the continuing effects of colonialism in policy-making by and with Indigenous peoples, and the value of self-determination as a key component of decolonization. Some of the seeds of change for self-determination were sown in the 1970s, but the more dramatic changes in social policies advocated by Indigenous people have occurred since the 1980s. The impetus for many of these changes resulted from two parallel processes. On the one hand, Aboriginal organizations evolved to become an effective social movement in making the case for a number of changes consistent with the goal of self-government or sovereignty. As well, a growing number of reports and studies have documented high levels of need and the failures of past government policies. Although these developments have led to important initiatives, funding issues and the inconsistent approach of governments in establishing a policy framework to promote local autonomy, equity, and service quality remain problematic.

As in all organizations, there are problems within some Indigenous organizations and First Nations where politics and hierarchical models of policy-making trump the rights and needs of citizens. Although hierarchical models of power and control may reflect patterns adopted from mainstream organizations as a result of the legacy of colonization, many people involved in the human services (both service providers and service users) are left with unmet needs and feelings of disempowerment. Under these circumstances, local control, as in mainstream society, is an imperfect solution. Although this problem is recognized, it is equally clear that substituting government authority for local control will not resolve these difficulties. First, the state has a poor record of protecting the rights and aspirations of Indigenous people; and second, changes that are likely to be both responsive to community and long-lasting must come from within. This is not to suggest the government has no role. It has a responsibility to collaborate with these efforts, ensure the essential rights of citizens no matter where they live, and facilitate processes consistent with the basic tenets of democracy and community capacity-building. Standards and accountability mechanisms for services delegated to community-based organizations are necessary, and these can enhance the provision of high-quality services. However, these mechanisms must be organized within a governance structure that recognizes the rights of Indigenous people to increased levels of self-determination.

Three examples of policy-making were summarized in this chapter to illustrate some of the inclusive models identified in Chapter 6 within an Indigenous context, and some tentative conclusions can be drawn from these experiences. The shared decision-making approach at the federal level, which focused on funding in First Nations child and family services, was a very time-consuming process. The limited outcomes from this experiment may reflect, in part, the complexity of policy-making processes at the federal level. Without a genuine commitment on the part of government to modify the bureaucratic procedures that often get in the way of collaborative approaches to policy-making, shared decision-making can raise expectations that may not be realized. However, the information generated from the process, coupled with more direct actions including a human rights complaint, appear to have influenced a neo-liberal federal government to respond in some fashion to the funding crisis in child welfare services on reserves.

The policy community approach in the Aboriginal Justice Inquiry–Child Welfare Initiative has been somewhat successful in establishing a framework for policy change that has had significant influences on the provision of child welfare services to Indigenous people in Manitoba. Control over all child welfare services in the province has been transferred to Aboriginal authorities, and new legislation provides a framework for the development of culturally appropriate services. Although the government's commitment to the policy remains strong, problems in implementation have limited outcomes to Indigenous children and families. The importance of community governance was briefly highlighted, and this approach is particularly relevant when establishing community-based services.

At its most fundamental level, making social policy in Indigenous communities must be assessed on what works in improving the social determinants of health for Indigenous children, families, and communities. Some of the strategies adopted will be similar to those adopted in non-Indigenous communities, including targeted programs focusing on the early years, more attention to service co-ordination and integration, long-term sustainable funding, and an approach that builds organizational capacity. However, important issues require special attention in Indigenous communities. These are:

- holistic approaches that take into account the full cultural, social, emotional, and economic context of people's lives, including an awareness of the trauma and loss associated with colonization;
- active involvement of Indigenous communities in every stage of the process in order to build capacity and ensure sustainable partnerships;
- the valuing of Indigenous knowledge and cultural beliefs in promoting positive cultural identity and well-being;
- a commitment to self-determination, which recognizes the inherent rights of Indigenous people and communities within the Canadian context.

Critical Thinking Questions

1. Consider either the framework proposed by Morrissette (Box 10.1) for an Indigenous ideological framework for social policy analysis or the arguments made for an anti-colonial framework in Indigenous policy development. Based on your selected choice, what are some of the implications for social policy development in an Indigenous context? What are some of the strengths and weaknesses in adopting this approach?
2. In June 2008, Prime Minister Stephen Harper presented a formal apology in the House of Commons to Aboriginal people for the harms caused by the Indian residential school system. Locate this speech and critique this apology. How significant was this step in the healing from the effects of residential schools?
3. Select one of the inclusive policy-making approaches described in this chapter or in Chapter 6. Identify some of the factors required to make this approach work.
4. Select an Aboriginal or non-Aboriginal organization with which you are familiar. Critically examine the power structure and approach to decision-making. How inclusive is the organization in developing its policies?

Recommended Reading

Aboriginal Policy Studies. This journal focuses primarily on Canadian Aboriginal policy issues from a broad multidisciplinary perspective. Issues relevant to Aboriginal social policy are included in the journal.

C. Kenny. *A Holistic Framework for Aboriginal Policy Research*. Ottawa: Status of Women Canada, 2004. This publication provides guidelines and a framework for doing policy research with Aboriginal peoples.

M. Saulis. "Indigenous Wholistic Healing Social Policy: Rethinking, Reframing, and Re-presenting Policy Development for Indigenous People," in A. Westhues and B. Wharf, eds. *Canadian Social Policy: Issues and Perspectives*, 5th edn, pp. 79–93. Waterloo, Ont.: Wilfrid Laurier University Press, 2012. Saulis uses a medicine wheel framework to conceptualize policy and program development for Indigenous people.

R. Sinclair, M.A. Hart, and G. Bruyere, eds. *Wíchitowin: Aboriginal Social Work in Canada*. Halifax and Winnipeg: Fernwood, 2009. Although this book focuses somewhat more on Indigenous social work practice, its contents and implications are also very relevant to social policy in Aboriginal contexts.

United Nations Declaration on the Rights of Indigenous Peoples. This declaration, adopted by the United Nations in 2007, outlines the rights of Indigenous peoples as understood by the United Nations.

Conclusion

In this chapter we review:

- the main themes of the book;
- the relationship between inclusive policy-making and critical social work.

Policy and Practice for Progressive Policy-Making

A major obstacle to the development of more inclusive policy-making is the influence of neo-liberal governments and the related social policies they champion. Policy-makers associated with this ideology prefer secrecy over transparency, centralized control over participatory democracy, and the preferences of the elite over the needs of citizens. This is evident in approaches to establish global free trade agreements, but it is also evident in the managerial approach to program development and the centralized bureaucratic structures that support this style of policy-making. The reason is not hard to understand. Those with power recognize that increased public involvement would lead to more progressive policies than they are willing to tolerate. This is reflected in market surveys that consistently show the public ahead of the curve on issues such as medicare and welfare state provision, despite the best efforts of more conservative think-tanks, the media, neo-liberal governments, and the corporate elite to shape public opinion in their own interests. For example, a poll conducted by the Broadbent Institute in 2013 concluded that "Canadian values are progressive values." There was evidence of strong support for such things as publicly funded health care, a willingness to pay to protect social programs, support for crime prevention, and a perception that wealth is increasingly concentrated among the very few at the top.

On a more global scale Avaaz, one of the largest online advocacy organizations in the world, conducted a poll of its members. Although its poll is not necessarily representative of the population in general and is international in scope, the high number of respondents reflects a significant public response to global issues. More than 77 per cent of respondents expressed support for each of the following values: equality, ecology, integrity and compassion, and democratic accountability. The top three priorities for continued advocacy were fighting political corruption, including the corporate culture of government, mobilizing support for policies that benefit the common good over the elite few, and addressing concerns about climate change.

We introduced the notion of *grand* and *ordinary* policy issues in the Introduction. We acknowledge that pursuing more inclusive policy-making approaches on grand issues, such as globalization and monetary and fiscal policy, is exceedingly difficult. Advocacy through engagement with social movements and, in the case of globalization, international alliances with other groups and organizations is much more likely to make a difference on some of these issues. However, with respect to the ordinary issues of health, education, and social service programs, more inclusive approaches can make a difference. Barriers, such as the managerial models in many large organizations, and practical issues, such as the available time and energy of practitioners and service users, must be overcome. Nevertheless, experiences support more collaborative ways of working, such as backwards mapping and the shared decision-making approach described in Chapter 6. The increased focus on working across sectors and engaging with the private sector on issues related to poverty reduction and homelessness are also encouraging developments. In general, it is more difficult to engage service users than staff in some fields of practice, such as child welfare. However, even here it is not impossible, and their participation in the areas of education, health care, and community development initiatives are well known.

A renewed commitment to inclusive policy-making using some of the models outlined in Chapter 3 and the policy analysis model described in Chapter 4 is advocated. The use of special lenses, including the steps outlined in the gender-inclusive model of policy analysis, referred to in Chapters 4 and 8 can help to encourage an inclusive approach.

We draw special attention to three important themes. First, combining participatory approaches to policy-making within the system and advocacy efforts from outside the system is often necessary in promoting progressive policy changes or in resisting neo-liberal cutbacks.

Second, collaborative approaches to policy-making must be extended beyond the policy formulation stage to the field implementation stage. In Chapter 5 we discussed the importance of an adaptive approach to implementation. This model supports the active engagement of front-line practitioners and service users, and we argue that successful implementation of many social policies depends on adopting this model.

This is particularly true in policy-making within Indigenous communities, and we noted in Chapter 10 the tendency of governments and their partners to revert to "command-and-control" models of governance and accountability once new policies reach the service delivery stage.

Finally, we emphasized the importance of community governance and participation, not as a model that should be used as a method of off-loading government responsibilities but as an approach that can facilitate the growth of civil society and improved partnerships with government and other organizations committed to improving the well-being of communities.

Policy, Practice, and Critical Social Work

To a considerable extent progressive or radical human service work based on principles associated with social justice has been rebranded as structural or anti-oppressive practice, and it is important to consider how our arguments for progressive policy-making connect with these models. Bob Mullaly, in *Challenging Oppression and Confronting Privilege* (2010), connects anti-oppressive practice with structural social work and identifies the transformation of society along socialist lines as the goal of structural social work. However, Mullaly (2010: ix) also notes that while the term "anti-oppressive" may be relatively new, the ideas and strategies associated with this approach are not new but reflect experiences and struggles since the 1960s related to a variety of social movements to expand the rights of those less privileged in society. Both Mullaly, who focuses on theory and practice, and Lundy (2011), who outlines a structural approach to practice within a commitment to social justice and human rights, connect personal needs to approaches intended to lead to both personal and political or system change. The intersecting bases of oppression are stressed, including considerations pertaining to race, class, gender, sexual orientation, and (dis)ability. The importance of addressing structural changes, including the development of progressive policies, is recognized, and like us, Lundy begins with a discussion of the challenges posed by neo-liberalism, poverty, and globalization. Similarly, Baines (2011) contrasts anti-oppressive practice with more conventional mainstream approaches in advocating social justice practice that includes participatory approaches.

These models have much in common with the challenges and approaches we have outlined in this book, although we have focused our attention almost exclusively on the policy-making process. In doing so we have emphasized core social justice principles that must guide policy-making, including the need to address inequality and other forms of oppression, the rights of those affected by policies to play a role in the design of policies and programs intended to respond to these purposes, and the need to assess results against social justice imperatives.

Canadian Resources

Social Policy Sites

Broadbent Institute
www.broadbentinstitute.ca
The Broadbent Institute is an independent, non-partisan organization championing progressive change through the promotion of democracy, equality, and the training of a new generation of leaders.

C.D. Howe Institute
www.cdhowe.org
The C.D. Howe Institute, a centre-right think-tank, indicates that it provides policy analysis based on "objectivity, professionalism, and relevance."

Caledon Institute of Social Policy
www.caledoninst.org
The Caledon Institute of Social Policy does rigorous, high-quality research and promotes practical proposals for the reform of social policy in the government and non-government sectors.

Canada's Public Policy Forum
www.ppforum.ca
Canada's Public Policy Forum is an independent, non-governmental organization dedicated to improving the quality of government in Canada through dialogue among leaders from the public, private, and voluntary sectors.

Canadian Centre for Policy Alternatives
www.policyalternatives.ca
The Canadian Centre for Policy Alternatives is a progressive research institute that undertakes and promotes research on a wide range of issues pertaining to social and economic justice. In addition to reports and books on particular issues, it publishes a monthly newsletter, *The Monitor*, which is available free to members.

Canadian Council on Social Development
www.ccsd.ca

The Canadian Council on Social Development (CCSD) is a voluntary, non-profit organization that "aims to develop and promote progressive social policies inspired by social justice, equality and the empowerment of individuals and communities through research, consultation, public education and advocacy." The CCSD is supported by membership fees and contracts with government.

Canadian Feminist Alliance for International Action
www.fafia-afai.org
The Alliance is a coalition of over 75 Canadian women's groups that aim to further women's equality in Canada through domestic implementation of its international rights commitments.

Canadian Institute for Advanced Research
www.cifar.ca
The Canadian Institute for Advanced Research describes its mission as "to lead the world in framing and answering complex questions at the frontiers of understanding. We value knowledge for its own sake. Our research agenda is independent and unbounded by geography or academic discipline."

Canadian Policy Research Networks
www.cprn.ca
Established in 1995, the Canadian Policy Research Networks is a non-profit think-tank that co-ordinates research networks focusing on work, family, and health. These networks involve collaboration by researchers in universities and government agencies across the country. The research is funded by a number of federal, provincial, and private-sector agencies.

Canadian Research Institute for the Advancement of Women
www.criaw-icref.ca
The institute is a non-governmental organization devoted to advancing gender quality through research and action. Online resources include fact sheets about violence against women in Canada, and women and poverty.

Canadian Research Institute for Social Policy
www.unb.ca/research/institutes/crisp
This institute is dedicated to conducting policy research aimed at improving the education and care of Canadian children and youth, contributing to the training of social scientists in quantitative research methods, and supporting low-income countries in their efforts to build research capacity in child development.

Canadian Social Research Links
www.canadiansocialresearch.net

This website is a social research clearinghouse with links to national and international research focused on employment and evaluation.

Centre for Social Justice
www.socialjustice.org
The Centre for Social Justice conducts research, education, and advocacy on issues of equality and democracy in Canada and globally.

Citizens for Public Justice
www.cpj.ca
Citizens for Public Justice is a national organization of members inspired by faith to act for justice in Canadian public policy.

Coalition of National Voluntary Organizations
www.ocl-cal.gc.ca
The Coalition of National Voluntary Organizations (NVO) is a not-for-profit organiz-ation that promotes volunteerism and enhances the profile of Canada's voluntary and charitable sector. This umbrella coalition includes 130 national voluntary charities and not-for-profit organizations whose mandate is information-sharing, awareness-build-ing, consensus-building, and advocacy on behalf of members and for the voluntary/charitable sector in general.

Council of Canadians
www.canadians.org
The Council of Canadians is an independent, non-partisan public interest organization established in 1985. The Council provides a critical voice on key national issues: safe-guarding our social programs, promoting economic justice, renewing our democracy, asserting Canadian sovereignty, promoting alternatives to corporate-style free trade, and preserving our environment. The Council is supported solely by membership dues.

Council of Canadians with Disabilities
www.ccdonline.ca
The Council of Canadians with Disabilities is a national human rights organization of people with disabilities working for an accessible and inclusive Canada.

Fraser Institute
www.fraserinstitute.ca
The Fraser Institute is a think-tank dedicated to "competitive market solutions to public policy problems." It is funded mainly through corporate contributions.

Frontier Centre for Public Policy
www.fcpp.org

The Frontier Centre for Public Policy is a public policy think-tank with offices in Winnipeg, Regina, and Calgary. Its mission is to develop and popularize policy choices that reflect more market-driven solutions to issues.

Imagine Canada
www.imaginecanada.ca
Imagine Canada is a national charitable organization providing support to Canada's charities and non-profits.

Institute for Research on Public Policy
www.irpp.org
The Institute for Research on Public Policy indicates that its mission is to improve public policy in Canada by generating research, providing insight, and sparking debate on current and emerging policy issues facing Canadians and their governments.

Institute on Public Administration of Canada
www.ipac.ca
The Institute on Public Administration of Canada is an association of public servants, academics, and others interested in public administration. The Institute creates knowledge networks and leads public administration research in Canada.

Institute on Governance
www.iog.ca
The Institute on Governance is an independent, non-profit think-tank founded in 1990 to promote better governance for public benefit. It undertakes research and provides consultation services.

Macdonald-Laurier Institute
www.macdonaldlaurier.ca
The Macdonald-Laurier Institute is a national, right-leaning, public policy think-tank with a mission to propose policy alternatives through independent research and commentary.

Mowat Centre
www.mowatcentre.ca
The Mowat Centre is an independent, public policy think-tank focusing on federal policy frameworks and strategies that will affect Ontario's prosperity and quality of life in the next century.

Social Policy in Ontario
spon.ca
The Social Policy in Ontario site is designed as a tool for public reporting about social programs in Ontario.

Status of Women Canada
www.swc-cfc.gc.ca
This website contains resources for gender-based analysis of public policy.

Wellesley Institute
www.wellesleyinstitute.com
The Wellesley Institute is a non-profit and non-partisan research and policy institute that focuses on developing research, policy, and community mobilization to advance population health.

Poverty-Related Sites

Assembly of First Nations
www.afn.ca
This site provides information on current issues affecting First Nations in Canada, including information on poverty in First Nations communities.

Campaign 2000
www.campaign2000.ca
Campaign 2000 was established in 1991 to put pressure on the federal government to implement the all-party resolution of 1989 to eliminate child poverty by the year 2000. Campaign 2000 is now supported by national, provincial, and local partners. Its principal strategy is the annual report card released on the anniversary of the all-party resolution. Campaign 2000 is linked to several provincial sites focusing on poverty at the provincial level.

Canada Without Poverty
www.cwp-csp.ca
Canada Without Poverty is an incorporated, non-partisan, not-for-profit charitable organization dedicated to the elimination of poverty in Canada. It focuses on advocacy on behalf of low-income Canadians.

Centre for the Study of Living Standards
csls.ca
The Centre for the Study of Living Standards is a non-profit, national, independent organization that seeks to contribute to a better understanding of trends and determinants of productivity, living standards, and economic and social well-being through research.

HIV/AIDS and Poverty
www.cdnaids.ca
This site provides information outlining the relationship between HIV/AIDS and poverty in Canada based on the resources available through the Canadian AIDS Society.

Make Poverty History
www.makepovertyhistory.ca
Make Poverty History is a coalition of organizations campaigning for global action against poverty. It is funded by donations from member organizations and individuals.

Ontario Coalition Against Poverty
ocap.ca
The Ontario Coalition Against Poverty is a direct-action anti-poverty organization based in Toronto, focusing on campaigns against regressive government policies as they affect poor and working people.

Ontario Coalition for Social Justice
www.ocsj.ca
The Ontario Coalition for Social Justice is dedicated to expanding the quality, accessibility, and universality of health care, education, and social services. It advocates for economic policies that protect the rights of workers and lead to fair employment at a livable wage; it also promotes the human rights of Ontario residents.

PovNet
www.povnet.org
PovNet is an Internet site for advocates, people on welfare, and community groups and individuals involved in anti-poverty work. Up-to-date information on welfare and related matters in British Columbia is provided, but there are links to current anti-poverty issues elsewhere.

25in5 Network for Poverty Reduction
www.25in5.ca
This multi-sector network, based in Ontario, focuses on eliminating poverty.

Health and Child and Family Welfare Sites

Canadian Association of Family Resource Programs
www.frp.ca
Family Resource Programs Canada is a national, not-for-profit organization representing more than 20,000 family resource programs, centres, and related services across Canada. Its mission is to promote the well-being of families by providing national leadership, consultation, and resources to those who care for children and support families.

Canadian Child Care Federation
www.cccf-fcsge.ca
The mission of the Canadian Child Care Federation is to improve the quality of child-care services for Canadian families. Research results and advocacy positions are provided.

Canadian Child Welfare Research Portal
cwrp.ca
The Canadian Child Welfare Research Portal provides access to research on Canadian child welfare programs and policies. Explore the map to find information on statistics, legislation, research, and researchers, or use the keywords and side menus to access publications and reports.

Canadian Health Coalition
www.healthcoalition.ca
The Canadian Health Coalition is dedicated to preserving and enhancing Canada's public health system. The coalition includes groups representing unions, seniors, women, students, consumers, and health-care professionals.

Centre for Families, Work & Well-being
www.worklifecanada.ca
The Centre for Families, Work & Well-being is an innovative, interdisciplinary research and educational centre responding to dramatic changes in family patterns, paid work, and broader economic and political structures.

Centre for Research on Children and Families
www.mcgill.ca/crcf
This Centre conducts and disseminates research on effective programs and policies for vulnerable children and youth and their families.

Childcare Resource and Research Unit
www.childcarecanada.org
The Childcare Resource and Research Unit is an early childhood education and child-care policy research institute with a mandate to further childhood education and child-care policy and programs in Canada.

Child Welfare League of Canada
www.cwlc.ca
The Child Welfare League of Canada is a national, voluntary organization dedicated to promoting the well-being of at-risk children, youth, and their families. It is governed by a board of directors from child welfare and family-serving agencies across the country.

Evidence Network Canada
evidencenetwork.ca
Evidence Network Canada is a non-partisan project funded by the Canadian Institutes of Health Research and the Manitoba Health Research Council to make the latest evidence on controversial health policy issues available to the media. This site links journalists with health policy experts to provide access to credible, evidence-based information.

First Nations Child & Family Caring Society of Canada
www.fncfcs.com
This website provides reports and information on First Nations children and families in Canada with a particular focus on child and family services issues.

National Alliance for Children and Youth
www.nationalchildrensalliance.com
The purpose of the National Alliance for Children and Youth is to promote the health and well-being of children and youth in Canada in ways that are beneficial to the community.

Prairie Women's Health Centre of Excellence
www.pwhce.ca
The Prairie Women's Health Centre of Excellence is dedicated to improving the health status of Canadian women in Manitoba and Saskatchewan by supporting policy-oriented and community-based research and analysis on the social and other determinants of women's health.

Vanier Institute of the Family
www.vanierinstitute.ca
Established in 1965, the Vanier Institute of the Family provides important information on Canada's 8.4 million families. The Institute advocates for policies that can support the well-being of families.

Youth in Care Canada
www.youthincare.ca
Youth in Care Canada (also known as the National Youth in Care Network) is an organization driven by youth and alumni from care. Youth in Care Canada expresses the opinions and concerns of youth in and from care and promotes the improvement of services for them.

Government Research Sites

Government of Canada
www.gc.ca
This site provides access to all federal departments and agencies and official information about Canada. Links to provincial governments are also provided.

Public Health Agency of Canada
www.phac-aspc.gc.ca
This site contains information as well as links to organizations, including Aboriginal health, minority groups, HIV/AIDS in Canada, environmental health, gender and health, people with disabilities, and violence prevention.

Statistics Canada
www.statcan.gc.ca
This is a general website with links to databases collected by Statistics Canada.

Selected Canadian Journals

Canada's Children
www.cwlc.ca/en/publications/canadas-children
Canada's Children is published by the Child Welfare League of Canada two times a year.
Each issue focuses on one child welfare-related theme or topic and examines and highlights research, practice, and policies affecting Canadian children, youth, and families.

Canadian Journal of Community Mental Health
www.cjcmh.com/journal/cjcmh
This interdisciplinary journal is published twice a year. Areas of priority interest
include program evaluation in the human services, community needs assessment, and
community development with a broad focus on community mental health.

Canadian Public Administration Journal
www.ipac.ca/Research-CPA
Published quarterly, *Canadian Public Administration* examines the structures, processes,
outputs, and outcomes of public management and public policy. It covers executive, legislative, judicial, and quasi-judicial functions at all three levels of Canadian government.

Canadian Public Policy
www.utpjournals.com/Canadian-Public-Policy.html
Canadian Public Policy aims to stimulate research and discussion of public policy problems in Canada. Directed at a wide readership, this quarterly interdisciplinary journal
publishes articles in English or French.

Canadian Review of Social Policy
crsp.info.yorku.ca
The *Canadian Review of Social Policy* is published twice yearly under the direction of an
editorial working group. The articles cover a wide range of social policy issues.

Canadian Social Work
www.casw-acts.ca/en/resources/publications/canaadian-social-work
Canadian Social Work is the journal of the Canadian Association of Social Workers
(CASW). It is an annual publication available to members.

Canadian Social Work Review
caswe-acfts.ca/cswr-journal

Canadian Social Work Review is published twice yearly by the Canadian Association for Social Work Education. Its purpose is to advance scholarly practice and education in Canada.

Journal of Law and Social Policy
digitalcommons.osgoode.yorku.ca/jlsp
The Journal of Law and Social Policy seeks to encourage debate and dialogue on important issues at the intersection of law and society, particularly as they impact low-income individuals and disadvantaged communities. The journal is also interested in a range of questions about legal issues and social change, including the exploration of non-traditional legal strategies such as community organizing.

International Resources

Social Policy Sites

Centre for International Governance Innovation
www.cogionline.org
The Centre for International Governance Innovation (CIGI) is an independent, non-partisan think-tank on international governance. Led by experienced practitioners and distinguished academics, CIGI supports research, forms networks, advances policy debate, and generates ideas for multilateral governance improvements.

European Centre for Social Welfare, Policy and Research
www.euro.centre.org
The European Centre is a UN-affiliated intergovernmental organization concerned with all aspects of social welfare policy and research.

Human Rights Education Associates
www.hrea.org
Human Rights Education Associates (HREA) is an international non-governmental organization that supports human rights learning; the training of activists and professionals; the development of educational materials and programming; and community-building through online technologies. HREA is dedicated to quality education and training to promote understanding, attitudes, and actions to protect human rights and to foster the development of peaceable, free, and just communities.

International Institute for Sustainable Development
www.iisd.org
The International Institute for Sustainable Development is a non-partisan, charitable organization specializing in policy research, analysis, and information exchange. It seeks to champion innovation, enabling societies to live sustainably.

Liu Institute for Global Issues
www.ligi.ubc.ca
The Liu Institute conducts and facilitates research on global issues, mobilizing know-ledge into solutions and policy using an interdisciplinary problem-solving approach to capture innovative thinking for positive social change.

Luxembourg Income Study Database
www.lisdatacenter.org
The Luxembourg Income Study (LIS) Center is a cross-national data archive and a research institute located in Luxembourg. It conducts cross-national comparative research on socio-economic outcomes and on the institutional factors that shape those outcomes.

Metropolis Canada
www.canada.metropolis.net
Metropolis Canada is an international network for comparative research and public policy development on migration, diversity, and immigrant integration in cities in Canada and around the world.

Organisation for Economic Co-operation and Development
www.oecd.org
The Organisation for Economic Co-operation and Development (OECD) website pro-vides comparative information on economic and social issues in OECD countries.

Women and the Economy—UN Platform for Action Committee
www.unpac.ca/economy
Women and the Economy—UN Platform for Action Committee or UNPAC was founded in Manitoba after the United Nations Fourth World Conference on Women that took place in Beijing in 1995. The site contains information on projects related to women's economic inequality, employment, and globalization.

Poverty and Child and Family Welfare Sites

European Data Center for Work and Welfare
www.edac.eu
This site provides information on and direct access to more than 500 data sources on work, care, and welfare and data on a range of related fields.

Innocenti Research Centre
www.unicef-irc.org
The Innocenti Research Centre, which is affiliated with UNICEF, indicates that its prime objectives are to improve international understanding of issues related to children's rights,

to promote economic policies that advance the cause of children, and to help facilitate the full implementation of the United Nations Convention on the Rights of the Child.

Innovations for Poverty Action Network
www.poverty-action.org
Poverty Action Network is Washington State's largest anti-poverty organization and is committed to building grassroots power to end the causes of poverty and create opportunities for everyone to prosper.

International Social Security Association
www.euro.centre.org
The International Social Security Association offers access to a breadth of information on social security through dependable and easy-to-access electronic and printed publications.

National Center for Children in Poverty
www.nccp.org
The National Center for Children in Poverty (NCCP) is a US public policy centre dedicated to promoting the economic security, health, and well-being of the country's low-income families and children.

Save the Children
www.savethechildren.ca
Save the Children is the world's leading independent organization for children. It is committed to ensuring children realize the rights to which they are entitled under the United Nations Convention on the Rights of the Child.

Social Security in Other Countries
www.ssa.gov/international/links.html
The Social Security Administration of the US government links social security agencies and organizations around the world that are publicizing their programs on the Internet. The list is updated regularly.

SocioSite Project: Social Policy, Social Security and Social Work
www.sociosite.net/topics/socpoicy.php
SocioSite, which is located in Amsterdam, Netherlands, provides information and links to resources related to social policy and social work from a global point of view.

Townsend Centre for International Poverty Research
www.bristol.ac.uk/poverty
The Townsend Centre for International Poverty Research was established at the University of Bristol in 1999 and has a goal to eradicate poverty in the world. It provides

high-quality interdisciplinary research on anti-poverty policies in both the industrial and developing countries.

Selected International Journals

Child Welfare
www.cwla.org/child-welfare-journal
Child Welfare is published every other month and links the latest findings in child welfare and related research with the best practice, policy, and program development in the field. *Child Welfare* is international in scope and is published by the Child Welfare League of America.

Community Development Journal
cdj.oxfordjournals.org
This journal is published four times a year and is circulated in more than 80 countries. It adopts a broad definition of community development to include policy, planning, and action as they impact on life in communities.

Critical Social Policy
csp.sagepub.com
Critical Social Policy provides an international forum for advocacy, analysis, and debate on social policy issues. Published quarterly, it aims to develop an understanding of welfare from socialist, feminist, anti-racist, and radical perspectives.

International Indigenous Policy
www.iipj.org
Published in Canada, this journal focuses on a wide range of Indigenous policy issues in a global context.

Journal of Planning, Education, and Research
jpe.sagepub.com
This journal publishes articles on planning theory, planning practice, and planning pedagogy. It also includes articles from fields drawn on by planners, such as urban geography, welfare economics, interest group politics, and policy analysis.

Social Policy
www.socialpolicy.org
Social Policy reports on and analyzes contemporary movements for social change in the workplace, the community, and the world.

Social Policy and Administration
www.psc.isr.umich.edu/dis/infoserv/journal/detail/1160

Social Policy and Administration is international in scope, covering issues in social policy and administration in Europe, the United States, Canada, Australia, and the Asia Pacific. Journal issues often include articles clustered around a specific theme.

Useful Tools for Community-Based Policy and Practice

ACORN Canada
acorncanada.org
ACORN Canada focuses on building a national movement for social and economic justice by organizing low- and moderate-income communities for power and social change.

Canadian Centre for Community Enterprise
ccednet-rcdec.ca
This website includes a resource booklet for community economic development (CED) called *The Community Resilience Manual*. A separate publication called *Tools and Techniques for Community Recovery and Renewal* is also available at this site to provide further assistance to citizens wanting to strengthen or revitalize their local economies. This site lists important CED links and publications.

Community Tool Box
www.ctb.ku.edu/
This site provides resources for all types of community work, including how-to sections on many topics such as community assessment, advocacy, planning, grant applications, and much more. The Tool Box has an international focus and is run by the Work Group for Community Health and Development at the University of Kansas.

Human Resources and Skills Development Canada
www.hrsdc.gc.ca
This website contains several useful tools, including the *Community Development Handbook* and the *Partnership Handbook*.

Human Rights Internet
www.hri.ca
Human Rights Internet (HRI) is an Ottawa-based virtual organization committed to social justice focusing on policy information, knowledge transfer, training, and information distribution. HRI works with governmental, intergovernmental, and non-governmental actors to initiate policy change, to disseminate information, and to empower marginalized groups.

Glossary

Aboriginal Defined in the Constitution Act, 1982 to include three broad groups—Indians (*sic*), Métis, and Inuit. Métis include those with mixed Aboriginal and Euro-Canadian ancestry who self-identify as a separate nation distinct from First Nations and Inuit. Inuit are those whose ancestors were Eskimoan peoples originally inhabiting the far northern regions of Canada.

Acute localitis A condition caused by isolation where standards and practices develop that are at variance, usually in a negative way, with those followed more generally in society.

Accumulation policies The argument advanced under Marxism that government directs most policy attention to subsidizing business development through such things as tax concessions, state expenditures on public works, and bailout loans and guarantees.

Administrative decentralization A form of decentralization that not only establishes offices in local communities but also includes the transfer to those offices of some level of local autonomy over service-related decisions.

Agency-level policies Guidelines and actions taken by an agency or organization that define the nature and scope of programs and services it provides.

Anti-colonial approach Knowledge and practices that oppose continuing expressions of colonialism.

Appreciative inquiry An adaptation of strategic planning that emphasizes an inclusive, strengths-based approach to planning. Appreciative planning is often used in organizational development to facilitate new innovations.

Asset mapping The identification of strengths and resources in analyzing actions for policy and community change.

Backwards mapping approach to implementation An approach to implementation that emphasizes feedback from service providers and service users in developing the implementation plan. It is similar to the bottom-up approach to implementation but typically incorporates a feedback loop to ensure final implementation plans are representative of inputs provided in developing the implementation plan.

Benefit–cost analysis A comparison of the benefits and costs of delivering two or more programs where both the benefits and the costs can be converted to dollar values.

Bottom-up approach to implementation An approach to implementation that recognizes the need to adapt policies and services based on experiences during the service delivery stage; feedback from service providers during implementation and adaptations based on this feedback are central to this approach.

Child protection service model An approach to child welfare focusing on risk assessment, investigation, and placement.

Civil society A concept associated with community capacity-building and the development of local democracy, which includes the ability to hold others, including institutions, accountable for their actions and inactions.

Classical liberalism An economic definition of liberalism that champions the absence of government interference and a belief in the free market as the most efficient method of distributing goods and services for all.

Colonialism The acquisition, exploitation, and expansion of a colony in one territory by people from another territory, leading to the development of unequal relationships between the colonial power and those who originally inhabited the territory.

Community A distinct group of people who share certain characteristics, interests, or needs.

Community-based services The location of organizations providing services within local communities in an effort to ensure greater accessibility and to promote a higher level of community engagement with these services.

Community caring model An approach to child welfare services that incorporates enhanced family supports and community-building.

Community governance In the human services, the delegation of decision-making authority from senior levels of government to local communities.

Content approach to policy analysis In policy analysis, the examination of the actual elements of a policy, such as goals, types of benefits, and results.

Convergence of interest The coming together of a set of factors, such as authority, commitment, and resources, that make it more likely a new policy initiative will be launched.

Cost-effectiveness A comparison of the costs of delivering two or more programs with the outcomes that are achieved by each program where outcomes can be defined in a similar fashion (e.g., employment success) and assessed by policy or program evaluation methods.

Cultural colonialism The processes used to devalue the traditional culture of those who have been colonized. One example in Canada is the use of residential schools to assimilate Indigenous people.

Cultural recognition An orientation in social policy involving efforts made to expand the rights and entitlements of more marginalized minority groups.

Decentralization The devolution or transfer of responsibility for policies or programs to lower levels of authority.

Decolonization The undoing of colonialism and its effects on all those affected by the process, with a particular emphasis on those who have been colonized.

Deliberative democracy An approach to community decision-making where common interests are assumed among citizens, enabling efforts to exchange views, assess differences based on merit, and develop mutually acceptable solutions to local problems.

Disparity rate The likelihood of individuals in one group to experience an adverse outcome when compared to the likelihood of individuals in another group to experience that same outcome (e.g., placement in child welfare care).

Equity The promotion of fairness and justice in trying to understand and provide people what they need to enjoy full and healthy lives.

Evidence-based practice Applying the best available research results (evidence) when making decisions about policy and practice in the human services.

Expressed needs An approach to needs assessment that reflects some attempt to obtain a service (e.g., wait lists or service referrals).

Field implementation The execution or service delivery phase of a policy or program.

First Nations Technically, the over 600 Indian bands across Canada that have a land base. The term has also largely replaced "Indian" even though "Indian" still appears in the Constitution Act and the Indian Act. Thus, "First Nations" also refers to people with First Nations ancestry, and includes both those who are registered as Indians under the Indian Act and those who have First Nations heritage but are not registered.

Formative evaluations Assessments of the components of policy or program, that is, how the program or policy is being implemented and how services are being provided. The general purposes are to determine what is causing certain results and whether the program is being implemented as planned.

Framing the problem Identifying the various dimensions of a problem, including its underlying causes.

Garbage can model An approach to policy-making that recognizes that policy outcomes are shaped by the interaction among identified problems, proposed solutions, and political factors.

Gender-based analysis An approach to policy analysis that examines the differing effects of policies on men and women.

Gender-neutral policy A policy that does not distinguish between effects or services provided to service users of different genders.

Geographic decentralization A form of service decentralization that involves the development of offices in local communities but without any transfer of power to those communities.

Governance The structures and processes used to determine how decision-making and accountability for those decisions occur within organizations.

Healing As used in this text, traditional approaches to health care and well-being practised by Indigenous people. These approaches to health and well-being incorporate spiritual beliefs and supernatural forces in ways that differ from conventional approaches to health practices focusing primarily on physical explanations and related treatment.

Holism A theory that parts of the whole are interconnected and cannot exist independent of the whole; thus, the whole is more than the sum of its parts.

Implementation planning The detailed listing of activities, costs, and schedules required to achieve the objectives of strategic plans.

Incrementalism An approach to policy-making that focuses most attention on making small changes to existing programs based on the ongoing assessment of problems as these are identified.

Independent living paradigm An approach to service delivery for persons with disabilities that defines the problem as dependence on professionals and others;

thus, the proposed solutions combine consumer control with the removal of various types of barriers to achieve equity and access to opportunities that enable full participation in society.

Indigenous Increasingly used in Canada as an alternative to "Aboriginal." Defined in the UN Declaration on the Rights of Indigenous People as including those whose ancestry can be traced to those who originally occupied territory, and who thus have claims to sovereignty and rights that distinguish them from other minority ethnic groups.

Indigenous knowledge Local knowledge, unique to a given culture. Such knowledge, which may include customs, practices, stories, symbols, and ceremonies, may be handed down orally or by example from one generation to another.

Institutional model of welfare The recognition that there are ongoing needs in society that cannot be met through capitalism and the market system and that government must provide ongoing assistance in the form of health and social welfare programs to meet these needs.

Interest or advocacy group Group of individuals who hold similar positions on an issue and attempt to influence how government ought to respond to that issue.

Internalized oppression The process that occurs to some people who are targeted or discriminated against over a period of time whereby they come to accept and live out the inaccurate myths and stereotypes society has communicated to them about themselves.

International Monetary Fund (IMF) International institution established in 1944 to pool funds from several countries to assist in post–World War II reconstruction. It has expanded since then and now works to foster international trade and co-operation, provide financial resources to developing countries, often with strict conditions regarding economic reforms, and reduce poverty.

Invisible hand of the market A metaphor used by Adam Smith to describe the free market as self-regulating because of the belief that competition leads to improved products and/or lower costs for products.

Keynesianism Named after British economist John Maynard Keynes, whose economic theory stressed an activist role for government during periods of high unemployment, including direct investment in stimulating economic growth and job creation. During periods of robust economic growth the government can retreat from its role of directly investing in economic growth and reduce any debts created as a result of directly investing in the economy during recessionary times.

Legitimation policies The Marxist argument that government is sometimes forced to respond to the needs of the working class, even if these responses are somewhat limited. The introduction of such policies provides benefits to the working class that serve to reduce potentially disruptive class conflict and attempt to demonstrate that capitalism can work for everyone.

Liberalism In this text, "reform liberalism," which supports equal opportunity and government intervention or regulation to address problems caused by unregulated capitalism, including extreme poverty and inequality.

Liberation theory A theory supporting efforts to both eliminate and undo the effects of oppression and its causes. Changes include challenges to institutional inequalities, transforming oppressive behavioural patterns, and the "unlearning" of oppressive attitudes and assumptions.

Marxism A political philosophy developed by Marx and Engels that depicts capitalist societies as essentially divided into two major classes: workers and capitalists (the dominant class) whereby the state acts primarily in the interests of the dominant class in oppressing the working class. It is believed that a socialist, classless society can eventually replace capitalism through class struggle.

Medicine wheel A traditional way of depicting four dimensions of health and the circle

of life among some Indigenous tribes in North America; sometimes referred to as a sacred hoop. It takes many forms but movement around the circle occurs in a clockwise or sun-wise direction.

Meta-analysis and synthesis reviews The process of determining the general outcomes or results from a series of research or evaluation studies on the same issue or topic. Such results from a number of quantitative studies are commonly referred to as meta-analysis whereas combined results from a number of qualitative studies are commonly referred to as synthesis reviews.

Mixed scanning An approach to policy-making that combines features of the rational and incremental models; it begins with a more comprehensive scan of an existing policy problem, and then focuses on an incremental approach to implementing solutions.

Monetary policy The use of adjustments in the interest rates by the central bank to control inflation. It is assumed that low interest rates encourage private-sector investment in economic growth, and the benefit of economic growth in the form of new jobs will trickle down to the rest of the population.

Moral underclass discourse The view of poverty as the result of the individual's own personal failures; a more restricted approach to providing benefits is believed to force people to rise out of poverty.

Nanny state A derogatory term used to imply that social welfare programs create dependency among recipients and interfere with personal choice.

Neo-conservatism An ideology consistent with many tenets of neo-liberalism that espouses increased reliance on the free market, reductions in welfare state programs, and the introduction of policies to limit the influence of unions and advocacy groups fighting for equality rights. Neo-conservatives often place a greater emphasis on "traditional" family values and take a conservative approach to social policy issues such as abortion, same-sex marriage, capital punishment, and gun control.

Neo-liberalism The contemporary support for a return to greater reliance on the free market and reduced reliance on government programs and regulation in relation to economic and social matters. Its support for free trade, economic globalization, and reduced government spending provides disproportionate benefits to major corporations.

Normative perspective on need An approach to needs assessment that involves comparison with a commonly accepted standard.

Not-for-profit (NFP) sector Social activity undertaken by organizations outside of government that is not intended to produce profits. Although the label "voluntary sector" is sometimes used to refer to the not-for-profit sector, this text draws a distinction between these two terms. See *voluntary sector*.

Participatory evaluation methods The emphasis on engaging directly with service users in shaping the evaluation, collecting and providing information, assessing results, and, in some cases, taking collective action on these results.

Perceived needs An approach to needs assessment that relies on reporting what people think or feel they need.

Pluralism A theory of public policy based on assumptions that government decision-making is heavily influenced by interest groups that compete with each other in advancing preferred solutions to policy problems. Government, in turn, holds the power to select alternatives that may advance certain preferences or mediate differences between groups.

Policy analysis The process of clarifying a policy problem, analyzing relevant information, including information on the context of the problem, assessing options for action, and making a recommendation for a preferred approach to addressing the problem.

Policy communities or networks Loosely knit groups and/or organizations knowledgeable about a particular issue or topic; policy communities may be used to advocate for new policies or engage more directly in formulating new policies.

Policy evaluation Assessment of the design, implementation, and outcomes of public policies by using social research methods, including qualitative and quantitative techniques.

Policy implementation "The carrying out of a basic policy decision" (Mazmanian and Sabatier, 1983: 20).

Policy window An opportunity in the policy-making process that permits individuals or groups to influence the direction and outcome of a policy response.

Political decentralization A form of decentralization that includes local offices, significant professional autonomy over service decisions, and significant local autonomy over policy decisions. Where policy decision-making includes a significant degree of community control, community governance is achieved.

Principal-agent theory An approach to implementation that places emphasis on the relationships between key actors who define the policy and those who implement the policy. The amount of discretion left to front-line service providers is affected by the complexity of the problem, the policy context, and organizational factors.

Principle of affected interests The right of those affected by a policy decision to participate in its formation and in determining the outcome.

Principle of less eligibility The idea that those who require welfare assistance but who are able to work should receive a lower level of benefits than those unable to work because of such things as illness or a disability.

Problem analysis The process of understanding real-world problems, including service user needs, their contributing causes, and possible solutions to address these problems.

Process approach to policy analysis Examination of how a new policy is developed, including who influences its development, how action occurs, and who makes decisions.

Program logic model A diagram of a program that shows what the program will do and what it will accomplish; inputs (resources), outputs (program activities), and outcomes (results) are depicted.

Programmatic retrenchment Efforts to reduce the size and cost of social programs by reducing benefits, cutting entire programs, or introducing provisions to restrict eligibility.

Progressive Conservatives A Canadian federal political party (1942–2003). The Conservative Party added the "Progressive" to its name when a Progressive, Premier John Bracken of Manitoba, was selected leader in 1942 and insisted on this addition. In 2003, after the joining of forces of the Canadian Alliance (previously the Reform Party) and the Progressive Conservatives, the new federal Conservative Party formally dropped the word "Progressive." Most provincial parties still use the label of "Progressive Conservative" even if many policies adopt a more neo-conservative ideology. Progressive Conservatives have traditionally followed an ideology combining classical liberal beliefs in the benefits of the free market, the role of government in preserving order and stability, and the need for some publicly sponsored health and social programs to address major social problems.

Progressive universalism The notion that social benefits or services in one form or another should be available to all but that there should be higher levels of benefits or services to those who need it most.

Public choice A theory of public policy that assumes individuals make political choices based on their own self-interests as they would do in purchasing goods and services in the private market. Game theory and decision theory are used to explain political behaviours.

Public interest The welfare or well-being of the general public.

Public policies The guidelines and actions taken by government in response to an identified problem or issue.

Purveyors Policy advocates or supporters who promote a new policy and pay special attention to best-practice principles in implementation.

Rational model An approach to policy-making based on identifying goals, examining a wide range of choices to meet these goals by collecting objective data, and basing choices on criteria that include major attention to benefits and costs.

Redistribution discourse A discourse that defines the primary cause of poverty as inadequate economic and social resources; it focuses on redistributing increased benefits to the poor and providing opportunities to realize their rights in achieving greater equality.

Reform liberalism, see *liberalism*.

Relative need An approach to needs assessment that compares needs of one group, community, region, or country with those in another group, community, region or country.

Residual model of welfare The expectation that the individual is primarily responsible for her/his own well-being and if assistance is required this should come first from family, then charitable organizations, and only as a last resort from government, normally on a restricted, short-term, emergency basis.

Selective social programs Those programs that target more narrowly defined segments of the population considered to be at greater risk. Criteria, such as income levels, are used to determine eligibility.

Shared decision-making A form of interest-based negotiation that brings together representatives from key organizations that have a shared interest but divergent positions on how to solve a policy problem. Dialogue and negotiation occur in an effort to reach an agreement.

Social democracy A political ideology that advocates the gradual establishment of socialism through reforms pursued by democratic means. Some forms of social democracy support a mixed economy while eliminating the excesses of capitalism such as poverty, significant inequality, and the oppression of minority groups.

Social determinants of health The economic and social conditions, sometimes referred to as risk factors (e.g., early childhood experiences, education, food security, housing, employment), and their distribution among the population that influence individual and group differences in health.

Social inclusion Realization of full and equal participation in economic, social, cultural, and political institutions. Particular attention is given to valuing diversity and increasing equality among those who are defined as disadvantaged.

Social integrationist discourse The view that the primary cause of poverty is the exclusion of individuals from full membership in society; solutions focus primarily on education and retraining people to enter the workforce.

Social justice A focus on distributing wealth opportunities and privileges to help ensure more equality and to ensure people have access to opportunities to live fulfilling lives.

Social movements Informal networks or coalitions of organizations and/or interest groups that engage in political or social action to bring about policy change in society or government.

Social policy Guidelines, legislation, and actions that address conditions related to human well-being; such policies target problems pertaining to poverty, poor health, inadequate housing, lack of education, and unemployment.

Social protection An orientation to expand social programs and new social investment based on needs.

Social welfare policy A subset of social policies that involves deliberate actions by government or other sectors in society to address human needs through the redistribution of resources. Social welfare programs typically address income security and the provision of social services.

Strategic planning An approach to mid-range planning (i.e., three to five years) where the organization examines information on trends, conducts an analysis of strengths and weaknesses in the internal and external environments, identifies unresolved issues or problems, and develops strategic options to deal with these issues.

Street-level bureaucrats A term popularized by Lipsky (1980) that refers to those who provide front-line public services (e.g., social workers, nurses, and police officers).

Structural colonialism In this book, the appropriation of land and the removal of traditional institutions and decision-making authority from Indigenous people by those who colonized Canada.

Structural model of welfare An ideal model of welfare associated with socialism where health and social welfare benefits are based on need and a commitment to equality of outcome.

Structural theories Theories of public policy based on the assumption that major conflicts exist between a dominant class and a subordinate class and that the state largely acts in the interests of the dominant class. Conflicts result from and are played out by the formal and informal structures or institutions of society (e.g., police, courts, legislatures, education system, social services, patriarchal attitudes). Examples of such theories include Marxism, feminist structural analysis, and anti-colonialism.

Summative evaluations Assessments of policy or program outcomes and efficiency.

Systemic retrenchment Efforts to weaken the ability to improve social policies and programs by such things as restricting the power of labour unions, eliminating funds for interest groups that advocate for improved social policies, and limiting funds for cost-shared programs.

Think-tanks Policy research units that undertake research and use this research to provide information to government and the public or to advocate for specific or general policy changes.

Third Way A variant of social democracy proposed by Anthony Giddens (1998) and first associated with the UK Labour government of Tony Blair (1997–2007), where the emphasis is on modest regulation of the market-led economic policies of neo-liberalism without fundamental changes to capitalism, and equality of opportunity in social policy. It is criticized by some as having more in common with liberalism than social democracy.

Top-down approach to implementation The efforts of senior officials to control implementation processes by setting clear objectives, outlining a clearly defined service model, training service providers how to deliver services, and specifying detailed accountability mechanisms to ensure policies are delivered as intended.

Triangulation Use of one or more of the following approaches in research or evaluation in an effort to increase one's confidence that the findings are valid: collecting data from more than one source; using different data collection methods; using different research methods; and using different investigators.

Universal social programs Those government programs or services available to all, which are defined as rights and are not restricted by income or the ability to pay.

Value criteria model An approach to policy-making that begins with defining the problem and setting goals, but then identifies values or principles to help determine the best solution among a range of alternatives.

Vertical slice approach An approach to obtaining inputs for planning that involves selecting representatives from various levels of the organization for this purpose.

Voluntary sector Organizations located within the not-for-profit sectors that are primarily concerned with social policy and the delivery of health and social services.

Welfare state The circumstance where government takes a major responsibility for the economic and social well-being of its citizens through the provision of policies, programs, and services (e.g., universal health care, social assistance payments to those in need, old age security, guaranteed annual income) that redistribute resources to those in need.

Welfare time limits A term associated with efforts of the government of British Columbia in 2002 to introduce restrictions on how long welfare recipients could receive assistance if they were deemed by the government to be employable.

Westminster model Government based on the parliamentary system established in the United Kingdom whereby the party elected with the most seats normally becomes the governing party and its leader becomes the Prime Minister or Premier. Although there are occasional exceptions, the Prime Minister or Premier appoints members of cabinet from elected members of the governing party.

Whistle-blowing The act of informing or disclosing a perceived wrongdoing to someone higher up in the organization or to the media in an effort to have it corrected. Whistle-blowing is often associated with public disclosure of wrongdoing, although it is also used to describe such disclosures within approved channels and procedures internal to government or an organization.

"Wicked problems" Problems that are difficult to resolve, have no final solution, and for which solutions will be regarded as good or bad depending on one's values and experiences.

World Bank A financial institution established at the 1944 Breton Woods conference and formally called the International Bank for Reconstruction and Development that, as part of the United Nations World Bank Group, provides loans, often under strict conditions of economic and political restructuring, to developing countries for capital programs.

World Trade Organization (WTO) An international organization, formally established in 1995 out of the final Uruguay Round of the General Agreement on Tariffs and Trade, and composed of representatives from countries across the world. The WTO promotes world trade agreements between countries and aims to establish a "level playing field" for international trade.

References

Abelson, D.E. 2002. *Do Think Tanks Matter? Assessing the Impact of Public Policy Institutes.* Montreal and Kingston: McGill-Queen's University Press.

Absolon, K. 2009. "Navigating the Landscape of Practice: Dbaagmowin of a Helper," in Sinclair et al. (2009: 172–99).

Adams, H. 1999. *Tortured People: The Politics of Colonization.* Penticton, BC: Theytus Books.

Alexander, C., and D. Ignjatovic. 2012. *Early Childhood Education Has Widespread and Long Lasting Benefits.* Toronto: TD Economics. At: www.td.com/economics.

Alfred, T. 2005. *Wasáse: Indigenous Pathways of Action and Freedom.* Peterborough, Ont.: Broadview Press.

—— and J. Corntassel. 2005. "Being Indigenous: Resurgences against Contemporary Colonialism: Government and Opposition," *International Journal of Comparative Politics* 40, 4: 597–614.

Allende, I. 2007. "Tales of Passion," speech to Technology and Entertainment Conference, Monterey, Calif., Mar. At: www.isabelallende.com/ia/en/speech/1.

Anderson, C. 2004. "BC Promises Answers on Impact of Welfare Rule," *Vancouver Province*, 4 Jan.: A9.

Armitage, A. 2003. *Social Welfare in Canada*, 4th edn. Toronto: Oxford University Press.

Arnstein, S.R. 1969. "A Ladder of Citizen Participation," *Journal of the American Institute of Planners* 4: 216–24.

Auditor General of Canada. 2008. "First Nations Child and Family Services Program—Indian and Northern Affairs Canada," in *Report of the Auditor General of Canada to the House of Commons.* At: www.oag-bvg.gc.ca.

Baikie, G. 2009. "Indigenous-Centred Social Work: Theorizing a Social Work Way-of-Being," in Sinclair et al. (2009: 42–64).

Baines, D. 2011. "An Overview of Anti-Oppressive Practice," in D. Baines, ed., *Doing Anti-Oppressive Practice: Social Justice Social Work*, 2nd edn. Halifax and Winnipeg: Fernwood, 1–47.

Bardach, E. 1977. *The Implementation Game.* Cambridge, Mass.: MIT Press.

Barrier-Free Manitoba. "What Is a Barrier?" At: www.barrierfreemb.com/whatisabarrier.

Bashevkin, S. 2002. *Welfare Hot Buttons: Women, Work and Social Policy Reform.* Toronto: University of Toronto Press.

Baskin, C. 2009. "Evolution and Revolution: Healing Approaches with Aboriginal Adults," in Sinclair et al. (2009: 133–52).

Battiste, M., and J. Youngblood Henderson. 2000. *Protecting Indigenous Knowledge and Heritage: A Global Challenge.* Saskatoon: Purich.

Bear, S., with the Topique Women's Group. 1991. "You Can't Change the Indian Act," in J.D. Wine and J.L. Ristock, eds, *Women and Social Change: Feminist Activism in Canada.* Toronto: James Lorimer and Company, 185–209.

Benjamin, L.M., and D.C. Campbell. 2014. "Programs Aren't Everything," *Stanford Social Innovation Review* (Spring): 42–7. At: www.ssireview.org.

Berman, P. 1980. "Thinking about Programmed and Adaptive Implementation," in H. Ingram and D. Mann, eds, *Why Policies Succeed or Fail.* Beverly Hills, Calif.: Sage, 205–27.

Blackstock, C. 2010. "The Canadian Human Rights Tribunal on First Nations Child Welfare: Why If Canada Wins, Equality and Justice Lose," *Children and Youth Services Review.* doi: 10.1016/jchildyouth.2010.09.002.

——, T. Prakash, J. Loxley, and F. Wien. 2005. "Summary of Findings," in First Nations Child and Family Caring Society of Canada, ed., *Wen:De (We Are Coming to the Light of Day).* Ottawa: First Nations Child and Family Caring Society of Canada, 7–59.

Bok, S. 1984. *Secrets.* New York: Vintage Books.

Brennan, S. 2011. "Violent Victimization of Aboriginal Women in Canadian Provinces, 2009." Catalogue no. 85-002-x. Ottawa: Statistics Canada. At: www.statcan.gc.ca/pub/85-002-x/2011001/article/11439-eng.htm.

British Columbia Ministry of Community, Aboriginal and Women's Services. 2003. *Guide to Best Practices in Gender Analysis.* At: www.mcaws.gov.bc.ca/womens_services.

British Columbia Ministry of Human Resources. 2002. "Service Plan Summary 2002/03–2004/05." Victoria: Government of British Columbia.

———. 2004a. "Fact Sheet: $80 Million Budget Lift," 17 Feb. Victoria: Government of British Columbia.

———. 2004b. "Time Limit Policy to Protect People in Need," news release, 6 Feb. Victoria: Government of British Columbia.

———. 2004c. "Factsheet: Time Limits Update," 6 Feb. Victoria: Government of British Columbia.

British Columba Ministry of Women's Equality. 1997. *Gender Lens: A Guide to Gender-Inclusive Policy and Program Development.* Victoria: Government of British Columbia.

British Columbia New Democratic Party (NDP). 2003. "BC NDP Newswire: Homeless Explosion Coming with Welfare Changes," 8 Oct.

British Columbia Office of the Premier and Minister of Social Development. 2012. "Common Sense Changes Encourage Work, Protect Vulnerable Families," news release, 11 June. At: www2.news.gov.bc.ca/news_releases_2009-2013/2012PREMOO79-000835.htm.

British Columbia Public Interest Advocacy Centre (BCPIAC). 2003. "Community Groups Prepare for Constitutional Challenge to Welfare Cut-Off," news release, 20 Oct. Vancouver: Author.

Broadbent Institute. 2013. *Union Communities, Healthy Communities.* Ottawa: Broadbent Institute. At: broadbentinstitute.ca.

Brodie, J. 1995. *Politics on the Margins.* Halifax: Fernwood.

Brodtrick, D. 1991. "A Second Look at the Well-Performing Organization," in J. McDavid and B. Marson, eds, *The Well-Performing Organization.* Toronto: Institute of Public Administration of Canada, 16–22.

Brooks, S. 1998. *Public Policy in Canada: An Introduction,* 3rd edn. Toronto: Oxford University Press.

Bronskill, J., and J. Ward. 2014. "Duffy Accused of Fraud, Bribery," *Winnipeg Free Press,* 18 July: A4.

Brown, L., L. Haddock, and M. Kovach. 2002. "Watching over Our Families: Lalum'utul'Smun'een Child and Family Services," in B. Wharf, ed., *Community Work*

Approaches to Child Welfare. Peterborough, Ont.: Broadview Press, 131–51.

Brownell, M.D., N.P. Roos, L. MacWilliam, L. Leclair, O. Ekuma, and R. Fransoo. 2010. "Academic and Social Outcomes for High-Risk Youths in Manitoba," *Canadian Journal of Education* 33, 4: 804–36.

Brownlee, J. 2005. *Ruling Canada: Corporate Cohesion and Democracy.* Halifax: Fernwood.

Callahan, M., D. Rutman, S. Strega, and L. Dominelli. 2005. "Looking Promising: Contradictions and Challenges for Young Mothers in Care," in M. Gustafson, ed., *Unbecoming Mothers: The Social Production of Maternal Absence.* New York: Haworth Clinical Practice Press, 185–209.

Campaign 2000. 2013. *2013 Report Card on Child and Family Poverty in Canada.* Toronto: Family Service Toronto. Website at: www.campaign2000.ca.

Canadian Association of Social Workers (CASW). Website at: www.casw-acts.ca/.

Canada Without Poverty. 2014. *The Cost of Poverty.* At: www.cwp-csp.ca/poverty/the-cost-of-poverty/.

Canadian Centre for Policy Alternatives. 2004. "Government Backs Down on Welfare Time Limits, but Cutoff Rule Should Be Scrapped Altogether," news release. Vancouver: Canadian Centre for Policy Alternatives—BC Office.

———. 2014. *Striking a Better Balance: Alternative Federal Budget 2014.* Ottawa: CCPA.

Canadian Feminist Alliance for International Action (FAFIA). 2014. "About FAFIA," 4 Jan. At: www.fafia-afai.org/en/about.

Canadian Press. 2014. "Truth and Reconciliation: Nearly 4 Years of Hearings Wrap," 30 Mar. At: www.cbc.ca/news/Canada/truth-and-reconciliation-nearly-4-years-of-hearings-wrap.

Carley, M. 1980. *Rational Techniques in Policy Analysis.* London: Heinemann.

Carroll, B., and D. Siegel.1999. *Service in the Field.* Montreal and Kingston: McGill-Queen's University Press.

CBC Vancouver. 2003. "Welfare Reforms Triggered Internal Warnings," 7 July. At: www.vancouver.cbc.ca.

Centre for the Study of Living Standards (CSLS). 2013. *Aboriginal Labour Market Performance in Canada: 2007–2011.* Research Report 2012-04. Ottawa: CSLS.

Chapin, R. 2014. *Social Policy for Effective Practice: A Strengths Approach,* 3rd edn. New York: Routledge.

Chappell, R. 2014. *Social Welfare in Canadian Society*, 5th edn. Toronto: Nelson Education.

Chessie, K. 2004. "Health System Regionalization in Canada's Provincial and Territorial Health Systems: Do Citizen Governance Boards Represent, Change and Empower?" *International Journal of Health Services* 39, 4: 705–24.

Chilisa, B. 2012. *Indigenous Research Methodologies*. Los Angeles: Sage.

Clark, N. 2012. "Perseverance, Determination and Resistance: An Indigenous Intersectional-Based Policy Analysis of Violence in the Lives of Indigenous Girls," in O. Hankivsky, ed., *An Intersectionality-Based Policy Analysis Framework*. Vancouver: Institute for Intersectionality Research and Policy, Simon Fraser University, 133–58. At: www.sfu.ca/iirp/ibpa.html.

Clemens, J., N. Veldhuis, and S. LeRoy. 2004. "Propping Up the Most Vulnerable: BC's U-Turn on Welfare Reform Spells Disaster," *Vancouver Sun*, 16 Feb. At: www.fraseramerica.org/commerce.web/article_details.aspx?pubID=3445.

Clement, W. 1975. *The Canadian Corporate Elite: An Analysis of Economic Power*. Toronto: McClelland and Stewart.

———. 1983. *Class, Power and Property*. Toronto: Methuen.

——— and J. Myles. 1994. *Relations of Ruling: Class and Gender in Postindustrial Societies*. Montreal and Kingston: McGill-Queen's University Press.

Coell, M. 2003. "Opinion Editorial: Income Assistance Changes Support People in Need," Government of British Columbia, Victoria, 5 Mar. At: www.2news.gov.bc.ca/nrm_news_releases/2003MHR0003-000229.htm.

Cohen, M., J. March, and J. Olsen. 1972. "A Garbage Can Model of Institutional Choice," *Administrative Science Quarterly* 17, 1: 1–25.

Cohen Griffin, M., and J. Pulkingham, eds. 2009a. *Public Policy for Women: The State, Income Security and Labour Market Issues*. Toronto: University of Toronto Press.

——— and ———. 2009b. "Introduction: Going Too Far? Feminist Public Policy in Canada," in Cohen Griffin and Pulkingham (2009a).

Coleman, W.D., and G. Skogstad. 1990. *Policy Communities and Public Policy in Canada: A Structural Approach*. Toronto: Copp Clark Pitman.

CAUT Bulletin. 2002. "College Vindicates Oliveri, Rejects HSC's Allegations," 49, 1 (Jan.): 1.

Commission on the Reform of Ontario's Public Services. 2012. *Public Services for Ontarians: A Path to Sustainability and Excellence*. Toronto: Government of Ontario.

Committee Encouraging Corporate Philanthropy (CECP). 2013. *Corporate Giving in Numbers—2013 Edition*. At: www.cecp.ca/research/benchmarking-reports/giving-in-numbers.html.

Community Tool Box. 2013. "Section 6: Participatory Evaluation," Work Group for Community Health and Social Development, University of Kansas. At: www.ctb.ku.edu/en/table-of-contents/evaluate/evaluation/participatory-evaluation.main.

Conference Board of Canada. 2013. *How Canada Performs 2013: A Report Card on Canada*. Ottawa: Conference Board of Canada.

Connors, E., and F. Maidman. 2001. "A Circle of Healing: Family Wellness in Aboriginal Communities," in I. Prilleltensky, G. Nelson, and L. Pierson, eds, *Promoting Family Wellness and Preventing Child Maltreatment*. Toronto: University of Toronto Press, 396–416.

Conteh, C. 2011. "Policy Implementation in Multilevel Environments: Economic Development in Northern Ontario," *Canadian Public Administration* 54, 1: 121–42.

Coutts, M. 2009. "B.C. Teachers Mutiny over Provincial Exam: Union, School Board Tell Parents to Dodge Mandatory Test," *National Post*, 17 Jan. At: www.nationalpost.com/related/links/story.html?id=1187139.

Cruise, D., and A. Griffiths. 1997. *On South Mountain: The Dark Secrets of the Goler Clan*. Toronto: Penguin.

Dahl, R. 1970. *After the Revolution*. New Haven: Yale University Press.

Dauverge, M. 2012. *Adult Correctional Statistics in Canada 2010/2011*. Ottawa: Statistics Canada. At: www.statcan.gc.ca/pub/85-002-x/2012001/article/11715-eng.htm#a7.

Davies, C. 2003. "Policy Development: Making Research Count," in K. Kufeldt and B. McKenzie, eds, *Child Welfare: Connecting Research, Policy and Practice*. Waterloo, Ont.: Wilfrid Laurier University Press, 377–86.

Day, S. 2004. "Time Limits for Welfare Disregard the Humanity of Poor People," *Vancouver Sun*, 16 Feb.: A9.

de Leon, P., and L. de Leon. 2001. "What Ever Happened to Policy Implementation? An Alternative Approach," *Journal of Public Administration Research and Theory* 12, 4: 467–92.

Desimini, N. 2011. "Centralization of Power in Ontario Provincial Cabinets: Its Impact on Ministers," paper presented to Canadian Political Science Association conference, Wilfrid Laurier University, Waterloo, Ont., 18 May.

Doblestein, A.W. 1990. *Social Welfare: Policy and Analysis*. Chicago: Nelson Hall.

Dobson, W. 2002. *Shaping the Future of the North American Economic Space: A Framework for Action*. Toronto: C.D. Howe Institute.

Drover, G., A. Moscovitch, and J. Mulvale. 2014. *Promoting Equity for a Stronger Canada: The Future of Canadian Social Policy*. Ottawa: Canadian Association of Social Workers.

Dunn, P.A. 2012. "Canadians with Disabilities," in Westhues and Wharf (2012: 273–95).

Durie, H., and A. Armitage. 1996. *Planning for Implementation of B.C.'s Child, Family and Community Services Act*. Victoria: School of Social Work, University of Victoria.

Dyck, R. 2004. *Canadian Politics: Critical Approaches*, 4th edn. Scarborough, Ont.: Nelson.

Ellsberg, D. 2002. *Secrets: A Memoir of Vietnam and the Pentagon Papers*. New York: Viking.

Elmore, R. 1982. "Backward Mapping: Implementation Research and Policy Decisions," in W. Williams, ed., *Studying Implementation: Methodological and Administrative Issues*. Chatham, NJ: Chatham House, 18–35.

Etzioni, A. 1967. "Mixed Scanning: A 'Third' Approach to Decision-Making," *Public Administration Review* 27: 385–92.

———. 1976. *Social Problems*. Englewood Cliffs, NJ: Prentice-Hall.

Fagan, T., and P. Lee. 1997. "New Social Movements and Social Policy: A Case Study of the Disability Movement," in M. Lavalette and A. Pitt, eds, *Social Policy: A Conceptual and Theoretical Introduction*. London: Sage, 140–62.

Fallis, J. 2013. "Backwards Mapping and the Principle of Affected Interests: An Approach to Policy Development in Successfully Planning for and Transitioning Youth from the Child Welfare System to Emerging Adulthood," unpublished manuscript, Faculty of Social Work, University of Manitoba, Winnipeg.

Fayant, J., and D. Kerr. 2007. *Living without Food*. Edmonton: Bissell Centre.

Ferman, B. 1990. "When Failure Is Success: Implementation and Madisonian Government," in D.J. Palumbo and D.J. Colista, eds, *Implementation and the Policy Process: Opening Up the Black Box*. New York: Greenwood, 39–50.

Fetterman, D., and A. Wandersman. 2007. "Empowerment Evaluation: Yesterday, Today, and Tomorrow," *American Journal of Evaluation* 28: 179–98.

Fine, S. 2013. "Supreme Court Strikes Down Canada's Prostitution Laws," *Globe and Mail*, 20 Dec.

Finkel, A. 2006. *Social Policy and Practice in Canada: A History*. Waterloo, Ont.: Wilfrid Laurier University Press.

Finlayson, G. 1994. *Citizen, State and Social Welfare in Britain*. Oxford: Clarendon Press.

First Nations Centre. 2007. *OCAP: Ownership, Control, Access and Possession*. Sanctioned by the First Nations Information Governance Committee, Assembly of First Nations. Ottawa: National Aboriginal Health Organization.

First Nations Child and Family Caring Society of Canada (FNCFCS). 2005. *Wen:De (We Are Coming to the Light of Day)*. Ottawa: FNCFCS.

Fixsen, D.L., K.A. Blasé, S.F. Naoom, and F. Wallace. 2009. "Core Implementation Components," *Research on Social Work* 19: 531–40. doi: 10.1177/1049731509335549.

Flavin, J., and L.M. Paltrow. 2010. "Punishing Pregnant Drug-Using Women: Defying Law, Medicine and Common Sense," *Journal of Addictive Diseases* 29, 2: 231–44.

Flynn, J.P. 1992. *Social Agency Policy*, 2nd edn. Chicago: Nelson Hall.

Forsey, E.A. 2005. *How Canadians Govern Themselves*, 6th edn. Ottawa: Her Majesty the Queen in Right of Canada.

Fournier, S., and E. Crey. 1997. *Stolen From Our Embrace: The Abduction of First Nations Children and the Restoration of Aboriginal Communities*. Vancouver: Douglas & McIntyre.

Francis, R. 2003. "Bonus Points for Welfare Cuts," *Vancouver Province*, 24 Feb.: A16.

Frankel, S. 2013. "Poverty Reduction in Manitoba under Neoliberalism: Is the Third Way an Effective Way?" *Manitoba Law Journal* 36, 2: 269–300.

Fraser Institute. 2002. "BC Welfare Reform Receives a 'B'," news release, 21 Oct.

Friere, P. 1970. *The Pedogogy of the Oppressed*. Harmondsworth: Penguin.

Frideres, J., and R. Gadacz. 2012. *Aboriginal People in Canada*, 9th edn. Don Mills, Ont.: Pearson Education Canada.

Gabel, T., J. Clemens, S. LeRoy, and N. Veldhuis. 2003. "Staying the Course on Welfare Time Limits," *Fraser Forum* (Dec.): 22–4.

Gallagher, J., and R. Haskins. 1984. *Policy Analysis*. New York: Ablex.

Gamble, J. 2012. *Inspired Learning: An Evaluation of Vibrant Communities' National Supports, 2002–2012*. Waterloo, Ont.: Tamarack—An Institute for Community Engagement.

George, V., and P. Wilding. 1985. *Ideology and Social Welfare*, 2nd edn. London: Routledge & Kegan Paul.

—— and ——. 1994. *Welfare and Ideology*. London: Harvester Wheatsheaf.

Giddens, A. 1998. *The Third Way: The Renewal of Social Democracy*. Cambridge: Polity.

Gil, D. 1970. "A Systematic Approach to Social Policy Analysis," *Social Service Review* 44, 4: 411–26.

——. 1990. *Unraveling Social Policy*, 4th edn. Rochester, Vermont: Schenkman.

Goggin, M.L. 1990. *Implementing Public Policy: Governance in Theory and Practice*. Thousand Oaks, Calif.: Sage.

Government of British Columbia. n.d. "Information for Persons with Disabilities." Victoria: Ministry of Employment and Income Assistance.

Graham, J., B. Amos, and T. Plumptre. 2003. *Principles for Good Governance in the 21st Century*, Policy Brief No. 15. Ottawa: Institute on Governance. At: www.iog.ca/publications/policy_briefs.

Graham, J.R., K. Swift, and R. Delaney. 2012. *Social Policy: An Introduction*, 4th edn. Don Mills, Ont.: Pearson.

Grassroots. 2013. "African Grandmothers Tribunal Seeking Justice at the Frontlines of the HIV/AIDS Crisis" (Fall): 3–5. At: african-grandmotherstribunal.org.

Greider, W. 1992. *Who Will Tell the People? The Betrayal of American Democracy*. New York: Simon & Schuster.

Guttmacher Institute. 2014. "State Policies in Brief: Substance Abuse during Pregnancy." At: www.guttmacher.org/sections/pregnancy.

Hamilton, A.C., and C.M. Sinclair. 1991. *Report of the Aboriginal Justice Inquiry of Manitoba, Vol. 1: The Justice System and Aboriginal People*. Winnipeg: Queen's Printer.

Hankivsky, O., D. Grace, G. Hunting, O. Ferlatte, N. Clark, A. Fridkin, et al. 2012. "Intersectionality-Based Policy Analysis," in O. Hankivsky, ed., *An Intersectionality-Based Analysis Framework*. Vancouver: Institute for Intersectionality-Based Research and Policy, Simon Fraser University, 33–45. At: www.sfu.ca/iirp/ibpa.html.

Hansen, J.G., T.A. Booker, and J.E. Charlton. 2014. *Walking with Indigenous Philosophy: Justice and Addiction Recovery*. Vernon, BC: J. Charlton Publishing.

Hansen, S., and K.A. Bear Robe. 2014. "SCC Ruling on Aboriginal Title: Tsilhqot'in Nation v. British Columbia, 2014 SCC 44 and Significant Changes in the Legal Landscape," *Miller Thompson Legal Update*, 14 July. At: www.millerthompson.com.

Hanleybrown, F., J. Kania, and M. Kramer. 2012. "Channeling Change: Making Collective Impact Work," *Stanford Social Innovation Review*: 1–8. At: www.ssireview.org.

Hart, B., G. Raymond, and P. Bradshaw. 2010. "Creating Community Governance: A View from the Inside," *Healthcare Quarterly* 13, 2: 29–35.

Hart, M.A. 2009a. "Anti-Colonial Indigenous Social Work: Reflections on an Aboriginal Approach," in Sinclair et al. (2009: 25–41).

——. 2009b. "For Indigenous People, by Indigenous People, with Indigenous People: Toward an Indigenist Research Paradigm," in Sinclair et al. (2009: 153–69).

——. 2010. "Colonization, Social Exclusion, and Indigenous Health," in L. Fernandez, S. MacKinnon, and J. Silver, eds, *The Social Determinants of Health in Manitoba*. Winnipeg: CCPA-Manitoba, 115–25.

Health Canada. 2009. "Health Canada's Gender-based Analysis Policy." At: www.hc-sc.gc.ca.

Henderson, J.Y. 2002. "Sui Generis and Treaty Citizenship," *Citizenship Studies* 6, 4: 415–40. doi: 10.1080/1362102022000041259.

Howlett, M., and M. Ramesh. 2003. *Studying Public Policy: Policy Cycles and Policy Subsystems*. Toronto: Oxford University Press.

Hudson, P. 1998. "Welfare Pluralism in the U.K.: Views from the Nonprofit Sector," *Canadian Review of Social Policy* 41: 1–16.

—— and B. McKenzie. 2003. "Extending Aboriginal Control Over Child Welfare Services: The Manitoba Child Welfare Initiative," *Canadian Review of Social Policy* 51: 49–66.

Hughes, T. 2013. *The Legacy of Phoenix Sinclair: Achieving the Best Fit for All Our Children*, vol. 1. Winnipeg: Government of Manitoba.

Human Resources Council for the Nonprofit Sector. 2012. *Labour Market Information for the Nonprofit Sector: An Investment in the Future*. Ottawa: Human Resources Council for the Nonprofit Sector.

Hume, S. 2003. "What Happens When More Poor Hit the Streets?" *Vancouver Sun*, 22 Nov.: C7.

Imagine Canada. 2013. *Charities and Nonprofit Organizations: Key Findings*. Ottawa: Imagine Canada. At: www.imaginecanada.ca/node/31.

Institute on Governance. 2007. *Citizen Deliberative Decision-Making: Evaluation of the Ontario Citizens' Assembly on Electoral Reform*. Ottawa: Author.

Ivanova, I. 2011. *The Cost of Poverty in BC*. Vancouver: CCPA-BC Office and Social Planning and Research Council of BC.

Ivry, B. 2014. *The Seven Sins of Wall Street: Big Banks, Their Washington Lackeys, and the Next Financial Crisis*. New York: Public Affairs.

Jai, J. 2014. *The Journey of Reconciliation: Understanding Our Treaty Past, Present and Future*. Ottawa: Caledon Institute of Social Policy.

Jansson, B. 2014. *Becoming an Effective Policy Advocate from Policy Practice to Social Justice*. Belmont, Calif.: Brooks/Cole.

Johnston, P. 1983. *Native Children and the Child Welfare System*. Toronto: James Lorimer.

Kania, J., and M. Kramer. 2011. "Collective Impact," *Stanford Social Innovation Review* (Winter): 35–41. At: www.ssireview.org.

Kellough, G. 1980. "From Colonialism to Economic Imperialism: The Experience of the Canadian Indian," in J. Harp and J. Hofley, eds, *Structural Inequality in Canada*. Scarborough, Ont.: Prentice-Hall, 343–77.

Kelly, K., and T. Caputo. 2011. *Community: A Contemporary Analysis of Policies, Programs, and Practices*. Toronto: University of Toronto Press.

Kenny, C. 2004. *A Holistic Framework for Aboriginal Policy Research*. Ottawa: Status of Women Canada.

Kernaghan, K., and D. Siegel. 1995. *Public Administration in Canada: A Text*, 3rd edn. Scarborough, Ont.: Nelson Canada.

Kettner, P.M., R.M. Moroney, and L.L. Martin. 2013. *Designing and Managing Programs: An Effectiveness-Based Approach*, 4th edn. Thousand Oaks, Calif.: Sage.

Kines, L. 2004. "Province Backs Off Plan for Dramatic Cuts to Welfare," *Vancouver Sun*, 7 Feb.: A1.

Kingdon, J.K. 1995. *Agendas, Alternatives, and Public Policies*, 2nd edn. New York: HarperCollins.

Klein, N. 2001. *No Logo*. London: HarperCollins.

———. 2007. *The Shock Doctrine: The Rise of Disaster Capitalism*. Toronto: Random House.

Klein, S. 2003. "Editorial: The Ticking Time Bomb of BC's Welfare Time Limits." Vancouver: Canadian Centre for Policy Alternatives. At: www.policyalternatives. ca/index.cfm?act=news&call=619&do= articles&pA=BB736455.

———. 2012. "New BC Welfare Rules: Some Positive Steps Forward (and a Couple of Steps Back), *Policy Note*, 12 June. Canadian Centre for Policy Alternatives—BC. At: www.policynote. ca/new-bc-welfare-rules-some-positive-steps-forward-and-couple-steps-back/.

——— and A. Long. 2003. *A Bad Time To Be Poor: An Analysis of British Columbia's New Welfare Policies*. Vancouver: Canadian Centre for Policy Alternatives and Social Planning and Research Council of BC. At: www.policyal-ternatives.ca/documents/BC_Office_Pubs/ welfare.pdf.

——— and J. Pulkingham, with S. Parusel, S. Plancke, J. Smith, D. Sookraj, et al. 2008. *Living on Welfare in BC: Experiences of Longer-Term "Expected to Work" Recipients*. Vancouver: Canadian Centre for Policy Alternatives—BC.

Kouzes, J.M., and P.R. Mico. 1979. "Domain Theory: An Introduction to Organizational Behaviour in Human Service Organizations," *Journal of Applied Behavioural Sciences* 15, 4: 449–69.

Krugman, P. 2012. *End This Depression Now*. New York: W.W. Norton.

Kufeldt, K., and M. Nimmo.1987. "Youth on the Streets; Abuse and Neglect in the 80s," *International Journal of Child Abuse and Neglect* 11, 4: 531–43.

Lancaster House. 2002. "Government Muzzling of Social Worker's Criticism Unjustified, Appeal Court Finds", 24 Sept. At: www.lancasterhouse .com/about/headlines_1,asp.

———. 2014. "Human Rights Tribunal Awards over $185,000 to Developmentally Disabled Employee Who Was Paid $1.25 Per Hour for over 10 Years," e-mail, 19 Aug., from: information@lancasterhouse.com.

Lasby, D., and C. Barr. 2013. *Talking About Charities 2013*. Edmonton: Muttart Foundation.

Lavoie, J. 2001. "Welfare Time Limits Expected in Spring," *Victoria Times-Colonist*, 10 Oct.: A1.

———. 2003. "28,000 Could Be Caught in Two-Year Welfare Squeeze," *Victoria Times-Colonist*, 21 Oct.: A1.

LeGal, J. 2011. "Opening Doors through Dialogue." At: www.generalauthotity.ca.

Lett, D. 2008. "Taking Back the Territory," *Winnipeg Free Press*, 4 May: B1–2.

Levitas, R. 2005. *The Inclusive Society? Social Exclusion and New Labour.* Basingstoke, UK: Palgrave Macmillan.

Lindblom, C.E. 1959. "The Science of Muddling Through," *Public Administration Review* 19: 79–88.

———. 1968. *The Policy-Making Process.* Englewood Cliffs, NJ: Prentice-Hall.

———. 1979. "Still Muddling, Not Yet Through," *Public Administration Review* 39, 6: 517–26.

———. 1982. "The Market as Prison," *Journal of Politics* 44, 2: 324–36.

Lipsky, M. 1980. *Street-Level Bureaucracy.* New York: Russell Sage.

Little Bear, L. 2004. "Aboriginal Paradigms: Implications for Relationships to Land and Treaty Making," in K. Wilkins, ed., *Advancing Aboriginal Claims: Visions, Strategies, Directions.* Saskatoon: Purich, 26–38.

Loat, A., and M. MacMillan. 2014. *Tragedy in the Commons: Former Members of Parliament Speak Out about Canada's Failing Democracy.* Toronto: Random House Canada.

Love, A. 1992. "The Evaluation of Implementation: Case Studies," in J. Hudson, J. Mayne, and R. Thomlison, eds, *Action-Oriented Evaluation in Organizations.* Toronto: Wall & Emerson, 135–59.

Love, B., K. DeJong, C. Highbanks, J. Kent-Katz, and T. Williams. 2008. *Critical Liberation Theory.* Amherst, Mass.: University of Massachusetts Press.

Lowi, T. 1979. *The End of Liberalism.* New York: W.W. Norton.

Loxley, J., and L. Deriviere. 2005. "Promoting Community and Family Wellness: Least Disruptive Measures and Prevention," in First Nations Child and Family Caring Society of Canada, *Wen:De (We Are Coming to the Light of Day).* Ottawa: First Nations Child and Family Caring Society of Canada, 113–45.

Lundy, C. 2011. *Social Work, Social Justice, Human Rights: A Structural Approach,* 2nd edn. Toronto: University of Toronto Press.

Lysack, C., and J. Kaufert. 1994. "Comparing the Origins and Ideologies of the Independent Living Movement and Community-Based Rehabilitation," presentation to Progress through Partnerships, National Independent Living Conference, Winnipeg, 24 Aug.

McCain, M., and J.F. Mustard. 1999. *Reversing the Real Brain Drain: Early Years Study Final Report.* Toronto: Government of Canada.

Macdonald, D. 2014. *Outrageous Fortune: Documenting Canada's Wealth Gap.* Ottawa: Canadian Centre for Policy Alternatives.

——— and D. Wilson. 2013. *Poverty or Prosperity: Indigenous Children in Canada.* Ottawa: Canadian Centre for Policy Alternatives and Save the Children. At: www.policyalternatives.ca.

MacDonald, F., and K. Levasseur. 2014. "Accountability Insights from the Devolution of Indigenous Child Welfare in Manitoba," *Canadian Public Administration* 57, 1: 97–114.

McDonald, R.J., P. Ladd, et al. 2000. *First Nations Child and Family Services Joint National Policy Review (Final Report).* Ottawa: Assembly of First Nations and Department of Indian Affairs and Northern Development.

McGrath, S. 1997. "Child Poverty Advocacy and the Politics of Influence," in J. Pulkingham and G. Ternowetsky, eds, *Child and Family Policies: Struggles, Strategies and Options.* Halifax: Fernwood, 248–72.

McKenzie, B. 1994. "Decentralized Social Services: A Critique of Models of Service Delivery," in A.F. Johnson, S. McBride, and P.K. Smith, eds, *Continuities and Discontinuities: The Political Economy of Social Welfare and Labour Market Policy in Canada.* Toronto: University of Toronto Press, 97–109.

———. 2002. *Block Funding Child Maintenance in First Nations Child and Family Services: A Policy Review* (Final Report). Winnipeg: Faculty of Social Work, University of Manitoba.

———. 2012. "Report on Selected Developments in Manitoba's Child and Family Services System with National and International Comparisons for Legal Counsel to Government of Manitoba Pertaining to the Phoenix Sinclair Inquiry," unpublished report. Winnipeg.

——— and P. Hudson. 1985. "Native Children, Child Welfare, and the Colonization of Native People," in K. Levitt and B. Wharf, eds, *The Challenge of Child Welfare.* Vancouver:

University of British Columbia Press, 125–41.

—— and V. Morrissette. 2003. "Social Work Practice with Canadians of Aboriginal Background: Guidelines for Respectful Social Work," in A. Al-Krenawi and J.R. Graham, *Multicultural Social Work in Canada*. Toronto: Oxford University Press, 251–82.

—— and C. Shangreaux. 2011. "From Child Protection to Community Caring in First Nations Child and Family Services," in K. Kufeldt and B. McKenzie, eds, *Child Welfare: Connecting Research, Policy and Practice*. Waterloo, Ont.: Wilfrid Laurier University Press, 323–38.

Mackenzie, H. 2015. *Glory Days: CEO Pay in Canada Soaring to Pre-Recession Highs*. Ottawa: Canadian Centre for Policy Alternatives. At: www.policyalternatives.ca.

McKnight, J.L., and J.P. Kretzman. 1996. *Mapping Community Capacity*. Evanston, Ill.: Institute for Policy Research, Northwestern University.

McQuaig, L. 1987. *Behind Closed Doors*. Toronto: Viking.

——. 1991. *The Quick and the Dead*. Toronto: Viking.

——. 1993. *The Wealthy Banker's Wife*. Toronto: Viking.

——. 1995. *Shooting the Hippo*. Toronto: Viking.

—— and N. Brooks. 2012. *Billionaire's Ball: Gluttony and Hubris in an Age of Epic Inequality*. Boston: Beacon Press.

Marshall, T.H. 1965. *Social Policy*. London: Hutchinson.

Mazmanian, D.A., and P.A. Sabatier. 1983. *Implementation and Public Policy*. Glenville, Ill.: Scott, Foresman.

Manitoba Joint Committee on Residential Schools. 1994. *Proposal for a Manitoba Healing and Resource Centre for First Nations Affected by Residential Schools*. Winnipeg: Assembly of Manitoba Chiefs.

Marris, P. 1986. *Loss and Change*, rev. edn. London: Routledge & Kegan Paul.

—— and M. Rein. 1967. *The Dilemmas of Social Reform*. New York: Russell Sage.

Maslow, A. 1954. *Motivation and Personality*. New York: Harper & Row.

Meili, R. 2014. "Decision on Refugee Health a Victory for Compassion," *Winnipeg Free Press*, 16 July: A9.

Meissner, D. 2004. "Preachers Will Sleep in Streets to Protest BC Government's Welfare Cuts," 28 Jan. Distributed by Canadian Press at: www.canada.com.

Memmi, A. 1967. *The Colonizer and the Colonized*. Boston: Beacon Press.

Miljan, L. 2012. *Public Policy in Canada: An Introduction*, 6th edn. Toronto: Oxford University Press.

Ministry of Children and Family Development (MCFD). 2008. *Kinship Care Review*. Victoria: Government of British Columbia.

Mishra, R. 1977. *Society and Social Policy: Theories and the Practice of Welfare*. Atlantic Heights, NJ: Humanities Press.

——. 1981. *Society and Social Policy: Theories and Practice of Welfare*, 2nd edn. London: Macmillan.

Montbiot, G. 2013. "Billionaires' Rising Wealth Increases Poverty and Inequality Everywhere," *CCPA Monitor* 19, 10: 27.

Montgomery, J. 1979. "The Populist Front in Rural Development. Or Shall We Eliminate Bureaucracies and Get On With the Job," *Public Administration Review* (Jan./Feb.): 58–65.

Montlagh, J. 2014. "The Ghosts of Rana Plaza," *Virginia Quarterly Review* 90, 2. At: www.vgronline.org/reporting-articles/2014/04/ghosts-rana-plaza.

Moran, B. 1992. *A Little Rebellion*. Vancouver: Arsenal Pulp Press.

Moroney, R.M. 1991. *Social Policy and Social Work*. New York: Aldine de Gruyter.

Morrissette, V. 2006. "Towards an Aboriginal Perspective That Addresses Ideological Domination in Social Policy Analysis," Master's thesis, Faculty of Social Work, University of Manitoba.

Mullaly, B. 2007. *The New Structural Social Work*, 3rd edn. Toronto: Oxford University Press.

——. 2010. *Challenging Oppression and Confronting Privilege*, 2nd edn. Toronto: Oxford University Press.

Mullings, D.V. 2012. "Racism in Canadian Social Policy," in Westhues and Wharf (2012: 95–113).

Munro, E., and J. Rumgay. 2000. "Role of Risk Assessment in Reducing Homicides by People with Mental Illness," *British Journal of Psychiatry* 176: 116–20.

Mutchler, S.E., J.L. Mays, and J.S. Pollard. 1993. *Finding Common Ground: Creating Local Governance Structures*. Austin, Texas: Southwest Education Development Laboratory.

National Council of Welfare. 2011. *The Dollars and Sense of Solving Poverty*. Ottawa: National Council of Welfare.

Newman, P. 1975. *The Canadian Establishment.* Toronto: McClelland and Stewart.

———. 1981. *The Canadian Establishment. Vol. 2: The Acquisitors.* Toronto: McClelland and Stewart.

———. 1998. *The Titans: How the New Canadian Establishment Seized Power.* Toronto: Penguin.

Nicolson, L. 1990. *Feminism/Postmodernism.* New York: Routledge.

Nutley, S.M., I. Walter, and H.T.O. Davies. 2007. *Using Evidence: How Research Can Inform Public Services.* Bristol, UK: Policy Press.

Nyp, G. 2002. *Reaching for More: The Evolution of the Independent Living Centre of Waterloo Region.* Waterloo, Ont.: Independent Living Centre of Waterloo Region.

O'Donovan, D., and N. Rimland Flower. 2013. "The Strategic Plan Is Dead, Long Live Strategy," *Stanford Social Innovation Review* 34: 1–4.

Olsen, G. 2008. "Lesson from Sweden," 29 Sept. At: www.policyalternatives.ca.

Olson, M. 1965. *The Logic of Collective Action: Public Goods and the Theory of Groups.* Cambridge, Mass.: Harvard University Press.

O'Neill, B. 2012. "Toward Inclusion of Lesbian, Gay, and Bisexual People: Social Policy Changes in Relation to Sexual Orientation," in Westhues and Wharf (2012: 315–32).

Oppal, W.T. 2012. *Forsaken: The Report of the Missing Women Commission of Inquiry.* At: www.missingwomeninquiry.ca/wp-content/uploads/2010/10/Forsaken-ES-web-RGB.pdf.

Organisation for Economic Co-operation and Development (OECD). 2008. *Growing Unequal? Income Distribution and Poverty in OECD Countries,* 10 Dec. At: www.oecd.org/dataoecd/44/48/41525292.pdf.

———. 2011. *Divided We Stand: Why Inequality Keeps Rising. Country Note: Canada.* At: www.oecd/els/social/inequality.

Osberg, L. 2009. *Canada's Declining Social Safety Net: The Case for EI Reform.* Ottawa: Canadian Centre for Policy Alternatives.

Pal, L.A. 1992. *Public Policy in Canada: An Introduction.* Toronto: McClelland and Stewart.

Panitch, L., ed. 1977. *The Canadian State.* Toronto: University of Toronto Press.

Patton, M.Q. 2008. *Utilization-Focused Evaluation,* 4th edn. Thousand Oaks, Calif.: Sage.

Paul, A. 2013. "Task Force Formed to Fight Homelessness," *Winnipeg Free Press,* 6 July: B2.

Pawson, R. 2006. *Evidence-Based Policy: A Realist Perspective.* Thousand Oaks, Calif.: Sage.

Pelletier, M. 2014. "Wall Street Baits Naïve Retail Investors—Yet Again," *Winnipeg Free Press,* 5 Feb.: B6.

Pence, E., and W. Shephard. 1999. *Coordinating Community Response to Domestic Violence.* Newbury Park, Calif.: Sage.

Phillips, S.D., and M. Orsini. 2002. *Mapping the Links: Citizen Involvement in Policy Processes.* Ottawa: Canadian Policy Research Networks.

Pizzey, E. 1977. *Scream Quietly or the Neighbors Will Hear.* Short Hills, Conn.: Ridley Enslow.

Pressman, J., and A. Wildavsky. 1973. *Implementation.* Berkeley: University of California Press.

Ptacek, J. 2009. "Overview: Restorative Justice and Feminist Activism-Resisting Co-optation: Three Feminist Challenges to Anti-Violence Work," in J. Ptacek, ed., *Restorative Justice and Violence against Women.* Oxford Scholarship Online. At: www.oxfordscholarship.com/view/10.1093/acprof:oso/9780195335484.001/acprof.

Public Health Action Support Team (PHAST). 2011. "Equality, Equity and Policy: Problems of Policy Implementation". At: www.healthknowledge.org.uk.

Public Health Agency of Canada. At: www.hc-sc.gc.ca/fniah-spnia/promotion/suicide/index-eng.php.

Purdy, C. 2014. "Rules on Sex Begin to Vex ID Holders," *Winnipeg Free Press,* 7 Apr.: A10.

Rabson, M. 2009. "Aboriginals Making Strides: Report," *Winnipeg Free Press,* 11 Mar.: A7.

Raise the Rates. 2012. "Welfare Changes Help and Hurt BC's Most Vulnerable," 11 June. At: raisetherates.org/2012/06/11/welfare-changes-help-and-hurt-bcs-most-vulnerable/#more-71.

Rankin, P., and J. Vickers, with the research assistance of A.-M. Field. 2001. *Women's Movements and State Feminism: Integrating Diversity into Public Policy.* Ottawa: Status of Women Canada.

Raphael, D. 2011. *Poverty and Policy in Canada: Implications for Health and Quality of Life,* 2nd edn. Toronto: Canadian Scholars' Press.

Rawls, J. 1971. *A Theory of Justice.* Cambridge, Mass.: Harvard University Press.

Rebick, J. 2005. *Ten Thousand Roses: The Making of a Feminist Revolution*. Toronto: Penguin Canada.

Rein, M. 1970. *Social Policy: Issues of Choice and Change*. New York: Random House.

——. 1972. "Decentralization and Citizen Participation in the Social Services," *Public Administration Review* 32: 687–701.

——. 1974. "Social Policy Analysis and the Interpretation of Beliefs," *American Institute for Planners Journal* 31, 3: 297–310.

——. 1983. *From Policy to Practice*. New York: M.E. Sharpe.

Rennie, S. 2014. "Federal Court of Appeal Upholds Ruling on Rights of Métis," *Toronto Star*, 17 Apr. At: www.thestar.com.

Reitsma-Street, M. 2002. "The New Era of Welfare," *Perspectives* 7: 5.

—— and B. Wallace. 2004. "Resisting Two Year Limits on Welfare in British Columbia," *Canadian Review of Social Policy* 53: 169–77.

Report of the Aboriginal Committee. 1992. *Liberating Our Children: Liberating Our Nation*. Victoria: Ministry of Social Services.

Report of the Community Panel, Family and Children's Services Legislative Review. 1992. *Making Changes: A Place to Start*. Victoria: Ministry of Social Services.

Report of the Gove Inquiry into Child Protection. 1995. *Matthew's Story*. Victoria: Queen's Printer.

Representative for Children and Youth. 2013. *When Talk Trumped Service: A Decade of Lost Opportunity for Aboriginal Children and Youth in BC*. Victoria: Government of British Columbia.

Rice, J., and M. Prince. 2013. *Changing Politics of Canadian Social Policy*, 2nd edn. Toronto: University of Toronto Press.

Riches, G. 2002. "Statement by Graham Riches, Director, University of British Columbia School of Social Work, at BC Association of Social Workers Press Conference," 2 Feb. At: toby.library.ubc.ca/webpage/webpage.cfm?id=105.

Rittel, H.W., and M.W. Webber. 1973. "Dilemmas in a General Theory of Planning," *Policy Sciences* 4: 155–68.

Roberts, S.J. 1983. "Oppressed Group Behaviour: Implications for Nursing," *Advances in Nursing Science* (July): 21–30.

Rodriguez, G. 2013. "A Concept Analysis of Public Participation in Health Care and Health Promotion Governance: Implications for Theory, Policy and Practice," Master's thesis, Faculty of Social Work, University of Manitoba.

Romanow, R. 2002. *Building on Values: The Future of Health Care in Canada (Final Report)*. Ottawa: Commission on the Future of Health Care in Canada. At: www.healthcarecommission.ca.

Rosenblum, S., and S. Frankel. 2011. "Canada's Corporate Tax Policy Sustains Child Poverty," *Toronto Star*, 10 Apr. At: www.thestar.com.

Roussin, D., I. Gill, and R. Young. 2014. "The Boldness Project," *Winnipeg Free Press*, 29 Mar.: D7, D10.

Royal Commission on Aboriginal Peoples (RCAP). 1996. "Report Summary," *Report of the Royal Commission on Aboriginal Peoples*. At: www.ainc-inac.gc.ca.

Rud, J. 2004. "Numbers Remain Vague on April Welfare Cutoff," *Victoria Times-Colonist*, 31 Jan.: A4.

Russell, F. 2012. "Neo-Con Policies Drive Financial Inequality," *Winnipeg Free Press*, 13 June: A10.

Rutman, D. 1998. "A Policy Community: Developing Guardianship Legislation," in B. Wharf and B. McKenzie, *Connecting Policy to Practice in the Human Services*. Toronto: Oxford University Press, 97–113.

——, M. Callahan, A. Lundquist, S. Jackson, and B. Field. 1999. *Substance Use and Pregnancy: Conceiving Women in the Policy Process*. Ottawa: Status of Women Canada.

Sabatier, P.A. 1986. "Top-down and Bottom-up Approaches to Implementation Research: A Critical Analysis and Suggested Synthesis," *Journal of Public Policy* 6, 1: 21–48.

Sadusky, J.M., R. Martinson, K. Lizdas, and C. McGee. 2010. "The Praxis Safety and Accountability Audit: Practicing a Sociology for People," *Violence Against Women* 16, 9: 1031–44. At: www.ncbi.nlm.nih.gov/pubmed/20710003.

Saleebey, D. 1990. "Philosophical Disputes in Social Work: Social Justice Denied," *Journal of Sociology and Social Welfare* 17, 2: 29–40.

Sarlo, C. 2013. "Focus on Real Poverty?" *Winnipeg Free Press*, 30 Nov.: A17.

Saulis, M. 2012. "Indigenous Wholistic Healing Social Policy: Rethinking, Reframing and Re-presenting Policy Development for Indigenous People," in Westhues and Wharf (2012: 79–93).

Saunders, D. 2008. "Trickledown Meltdown," *Globe and Mail*, 27 Dec.: B4–5.

Scarth, D. 2014. *Review of the Public Interest Disclosure (Whistleblower Protection) Act.* Winnipeg: Government of Manitoba.

Schafer, C., and J. Clemens.2002. "Welfare Reform in British Columbia: A Report Card." Vancouver: Fraser Institute. At: www.fraser-institute.org/researchandpublications/2748.aspx.

Schram, B. 1997. *Creating Small Scale Social Programs.* Thousand Oaks, Calif.: Sage.

Schroedel, J., and P. Peretz. 1994. "A Gender Analysis of Policy Formation: The Case of Fetal Abuse," *Journal of Health Politics, Policy and Law* 19, 2: 335–60.

Schur, N. 1987. *A to Zed.* New York: Harper Perennial.

Schwab, K., B. Brende, L. Saadia, Y. Bekhouche, A. Guimault, A. Soo, et al. 2013. *The Global Gender Gap Report, 2013.* Geneva: World Economic Forum. At: www3.weforum.org/WEF_GenderGap_Report_2013.pdf.

Sheehy, E., ed. 2012. *Sexual Assault in Canada: Law, Legal Practice and Women's Activism.* Ottawa: University of Ottawa Press.

Shragge, E. 1990. "Community-Based Practice: Political Alternatives or New State Forms?" in L. Davies and E. Shragge, eds, *Bureaucracy and Community.* Montreal: Black Rose Books, 137–73.

Silver, J., ed. 2013. *Moving Forward, Giving Back: Transformative Aboriginal Education.* Halifax and Winnipeg: Fernwood.

Silver, R. 2002. "Drive to Globalization Creating a Crisis for Nation States," *CCPA Monitor* 9, 2: 30–2.

Sinclair, R., and M.A. Hart. 2009. "Commentary on Terms," in Sinclair et al. (2009: 13–14).

Sinclair, R., M.A. Hart, and G. Bruyere, eds. 2009. *Wíchitowin: Aboriginal Social Work in Canada.* Winnipeg: Fernwood.

Sinha, V., N. Trocmé, B. Fallon, B. MacLaurin, E. Fast, S. Prokop, et al. 2011. *KisisikAwasisak: Remember the Children: Understanding the Overrepresentation of First Nations Children in the Child Welfare System.* Ottawa: Assembly of First Nations.

Smale, G. 1995. "Integrating Community and Individual Practice: A New Paradigm for Practice," in P. Adams and K. Nelson, eds, *Reinventing Human Services.* Hawthorne, NY: Aldine de Gruyter, 59–86.

Smith, C. 2002. "Are Welfare Changes Illegal?" *Georgia Straight,* 14–21 Feb.: 10.

Smith, D. 1987. *The Everyday World as Problematic.* Toronto: University of Toronto Press.

Sower, C., J. Holland, K. Tiedke, and W. Freeman. 1957. *Community Involvement: The Webs of Formal and Informal Ties That Make for Action.* Glencoe, Ill.: Free Press.

Stachowiak, S. 2013. *Pathways for Change: 10 Theories to Inform Advocacy and Policy Change Efforts.* Center for Evaluation Innovation, ORS Impact. At: www.evaluationinnovation.org.

Stanford, J. 2008. *Economics for Everyone: A Short Guide to the Economics of Capitalism.* Halifax: Fernwood and Canadian Centre for Policy Alternatives.

Statistics Canada. 2009. *The Satellite Account of Nonprofit Institutions and Volunteering.* Ottawa: Statistics Canada.

———. 2011. *Aboriginal People in Canada: First Nations People, Métis and Inuit, 2011: National Household Survey.* Ottawa: Statistics Canada. At: www12.statcan.gc.ca/nhs-enm/2011/as-sa/99-011-x2011001-eng.cfm.

———. 2012. *Canada Survey of Giving, Volunteering and Participating, 2004, 2007 and 2010.* Ottawa: Statistics Canada.

———. 2013a. "Persons in Low Income Families: Table 202-0802." Ottawa: Statistics Canada. At: http://www5.statcan.gc.ca/cansim/a26?lang=eng&retr-Lang=eng&id=2020802&paSer=&pattern=&stByVal=1&p1=1&p2=37&tab-Mode=dataTable&csid

———. 2013b. *Immigrant Status and period of Immigration: National Household Survey.* (Catalogue no. 99-010-X2011030). Ottawa: Statistics Canada. At: www12.statcan.gc.ca/nhs-enm/index-eng.cfm

Status of Women Canada. 1996. *Gender-Based Analysis: A Guide for Policy-Making.* Ottawa: Author.

Steffenhagen, J. 2013. "Controversial Standardized Tests to Proceed as Usual in B.C. Schools," *Vancouver Sun,* 8 Jan. At: www.vancouversun.com/news/Controversial+standardized+tests+proceed+usual+schools/7791016/story.html#ixzz3ATiDii8O.

Sterling-Collins, R. 2009. "A Holistic Approach to Supporting Children with Special Needs," in Sinclair et al. (2009: 65–88).

Struthers, M. 2004. "Supporting Financial Vibrancy in the Quest for Sustainability in the Not-For-Profit Sector," *The Philanthropist* 19, 4: 241–60.

———. 2013. *Fair Exchange: Public Funding for Social Impact through the Non-Profit Sector.* Toronto: George Cedric Metcalf Charitable Foundation.

Swift, K., and M. Callahan. 2009. *At Risk: Professional Practice in Child Welfare and Other Human Services*. Toronto: University of Toronto Press.

Tilbury, C., and J. Thoburn. 2011. "Disproportionate Representation of Indigenous Children in Child Welfare Systems: International Comparisons," in K. Kufeldt and B. McKenzie, eds, *Child Welfare: Connecting Research, Policy and Practice*, 2nd edn. Waterloo, Ont.: Wilfrid Laurier University Press, 293–305.

Titmuss, R. 1968. *Commitment to Welfare*. London: George Allen and Unwin.

——. 1974. *Social Policy*. London: George Allen and Unwin.

Torjman, S. 2005. *What Is Policy?* Ottawa: Caledon Institute of Social Policy.

——. 2014. *Paying for Canada*. Ottawa: Caledon Institute of Social Policy.

—— and K. Battle. 2013. *Welfare Re-form: The Future of Social Policy in Canada*. Ottawa: Caledon Institute of Social Policy.

—— and A. Makhoul. 2012. *Community-Led Development*. Ottawa: Caledon Institute of Social Policy.

Toronto Star. 2013. "Canadians Need to Reverse Troubling Trend on Charitable Giving," Editorial, 20 Mar. At: www.thestar.com.

Tower, K. 2012. "Preventing Violence against Women on Campuses Calls for Culture Change," *Sackville Tribune Post*, 21 Nov. At: www.sackvilletribunepost.com/News/2012-11-21/article-3125112/Preventing-violence-against-women-on-campuses-calls-for-%261squo%3Bculture-change%26rsquo%3B/1.

Trebilcock, M.J., D.G. Hartle, J.R.S. Prichard, and D.N. Dewees. 1982. *The Choice of Governing Instrument*. Ottawa: Ministry of Supply and Services.

Trocmé, N., B. Fallon, B. MacLaurin, J. Daciuk, C. Felstiner, T. Black, et al. 2005. *Canadian Incidence Study of Reported Child Abuse and Neglect—2003: Major Findings*. Ottawa: Minister of Public Works and Government Services Canada.

——, B. Fallon, B. MacLaurin, V. Sinha, T. Black, E. Fast, et al. 2010. *Canadian Incidence Study of Reported Child Abuse and Neglect—2008: Major Findings*. Ottawa: Public Health Agency of Canada.

——, B. MacLaurin, B. Fallon, J. Daciuk, D. Billingsley, M. Tourigny, et al. 2001. *Canadian Incidence Study of Reported Child Abuse and Neglect: Final Report*. Ottawa: Minister of Public Works and Government Services Canada.

Turcotte, M. 2012. "Charitable Giving by Canadians," *Canadian Social Trends*: 16–36. Statistics Canada Catalogue no. 11-008-x.

Turner, R. 2013. "The Road to Manitoba Justice Reform Starts in Prince Albert," *Winnipeg Free Press*, 1 June: D8–10.

——. 2014. "An End to Life in the Streets," *Winnipeg Free Press*, 29 Apr.: A3.

Tweedle, A., K. Battle, and S. Torjman. 2013. *Welfare in Canada 2012*. Ottawa: Caledon Institute of Social Policy.

UNICEF. 2012. *Measuring Child Poverty: New League Tables of Child Poverty in the World's Richest Countries*. Florence, Italy: UNICEF Innocenti Research Centre.

UNICEF Canada. n.d. *UNICEF Report Card 10: Measuring Child Poverty: Canadian Comparison*. At: www.unicef.ca/IRC10.

United Nations. 2008. Declaration on the Rights of Indigenous Peoples. At: www.un.org/esa/socdev/unpfii/documents/DRIPS_en.pdf.

United Nations Committee on the Rights of the Child. 2009. At: www2.ohchr.org/English/bodies/crc/index.htm.

United Nations Convention on the Rights of Persons with Disabilities. 2006.

Vancouver Province. 2003. "Welfare Jobs Axed, Offices To Be Closed," 14 Nov.: A16.

Vancouver Sun. 2004. "Victoria Should Dispense with Welfare Time Limits," 13 Feb.: C7.

Valentine, F. 1994. *The Canadian Independent Living Movement: An Historical Overview*. Ottawa: Canadian Association of Independent Living Centres.

Venne, S.H. 2001. "Treaty-Making and Its Potential for Conflict Resolution between Indigenous Nations and the Canadian State," in Aboriginal Rights Coalition, ed., *Blind Spots: An Examination of the Federal Government's Response to the Report of the Royal Commission on Aboriginal Peoples*. Ottawa: Aboriginal Rights Coalition, 81–90.

Victoria Times Colonist. 2012. "Welfare Changes Still Fall Short," 13 June. At: www.canada.com/story.html?id-51199a9-88fc-4238-8f0f-93c07607c397.

We Day. At: www.weday.com.

Weaver, L., P. Born, and D.L. Whaley. 2010. *Approaches to Measuring Community Change Indicators*. Waterloo, Ont.: Tamarack—An Institute for Community Engagement.

Weaver, P.K. 2006. "The Regionalization of Health Care in British Columbia: Does 'Closer to

Home' Really Matter?" Master's thesis, Simon Fraser University.

Welch, M.A. 2014. "Services for Disabled in Focus: Rights Tribunal to Consider How Ottawa Funds On-Reserve Programs," *Winnipeg Free Press*, 4 Jan.: A3.

Westhues, A. 2012. "Approaches to Policy Analysis," in Westhues and Wharf (2012: 43–59).

Westhues, A., and B. Wharf, eds. 2012. *Canadian Social Policy: Issues and Perspectives*, 5th edn. Waterloo, Ont.: Wilfred Laurier University Press.

Wharf, B., ed. 2002. *Community Work Approaches to Child Welfare*. Peterborough, Ont.: Broadview Press.

—— and B. McKenzie. 2004. *Connecting Policy to Practice in the Human Services*, 2nd edn. Toronto: Oxford University Press.

Wharf-Higgins, J., and F. Weller. 2012. "Influencing Policy from the Outside: Are Citizens Game Changers or Sidelined?" in Westhues and Wharf (2012: 61–77).

Wilensky, H.L., and C.N. Lebeaux. 1965. *Industrial Society and Social Welfare*. New York: Russell Sage Foundation.

Williams, W. 1976. "Implementation Analysis and Assessment," in W. Williams and R. Elmore, eds, *Social Program Implementation*. New York: Academic Press, 280–93.

——. 1980. *The Implementation Perspective*. Berkeley: University of California Press.

Winnipeg Free Press. 2013. "Hungry Marooned as Tide Rises," editorial, 6 Nov.: A6.

Witkin, B.R., and J.W. Altschuld. 1995. *Planning and Conducting Needs Assessments: A Practical Guide*. Thousand Oaks, Calif.: Sage.

Witkin, S.L., and S. Gottschalk. 1988. "Alternative Criteria for Theory Evaluation," *Social Service Review*: 211–24.

Yelaja, S., ed. 1987. *Canadian Social Policy*, rev. edn. Waterloo, Ont.: Wilfrid Laurier University Press.

Index